BISMARCK'S RIVAL

DUKE HISTORICAL PUBLICATIONS

Bismarck's Rival

A POLITICAL BIOGRAPHY OF GENERAL AND ADMIRAL

ALBRECHT VON STOSCH

Frederic B. M. Hollyday

DUKE UNIVERSITY PRESS · DURHAM, NORTH CAROLINA · 1960

© 1960, Duke University Press

Cambridge University Press, London, N. W. 1, England

Library of Congress Catalogue Card number 60-7077

Printed in the United States of America
by the Seeman Printery, Durham, N. C.

FOR
MOTHER AND FATHER

PREFACE

The political biography of Albrecht von Stosch (1818-1896), a prominent man of action, opens unique insights into the entire Bismarckian epoch. Stosch became a general, an admiral, and a minister of state. As Chief of the Admiralty he was the founder of the Imperial German Navy. He was also a member of the Prussian Chamber of Peers and of the Bundesrat, and he spoke in the Reichstag. His friendship with members of the royal family, the armed forces, the bureaucracy, and his close ties with journalists, members of the Reichstag and Bundesrat, and other leaders of public opinion gave him unusual opportunities to observe the German military and political system at work. His opportunities for observation, combined with a talent for expression and an objective temper of mind, make his published volume of memoirs one of the chief sources of the history of the German Wars of Unification. Paul Matter and Sir Charles G. Robertson, major biographers of Bismarck, regretted that the volume ends with the year 1871. The present study relies in part on the unpublished manuscripts in which Stosch carried the story into the 1890's.

Though Stosch was trained in the conservative traditions of the military service, he was considered a liberal by his contemporaries. He was one of the most trusted advisers of the German Crown Prince, the focus of German liberal aspirations, whose reign, it has often been assumed, would have inaugurated an era of political reform and freedom. Stosch's comments on the character and ideas of the Prince and his British wife, Victoria, carry singular authority. Stosch's lasting friendships with the liberal publicist, historian, and novelist, Gustav Freytag, and with Franz von Roggenbach, a founder of the Liberal Imperial party, as well as his

close relations with National Liberal leaders, and contacts with
Left Liberals illuminate the whole question of the aims and accomplishments of the German liberal movement.

His acquaintance in other political circles was wide. He
remained in office with the approval of the conservative King-
Emperor, William I, whose confidence he enjoyed. He talked frequently with such diverse political leaders as the Conservative
Moltke and the Centrist Windthorst and survived, for many years,
Bismarck's steady assaults in public and private. Indeed, it is in
the role of the opponent of Bismarck that Stosch appears most
frequently in the histories, memoirs, and correspondence of the
time. Appointed Chief of the Admiralty with the Chancellor's
initial approval, Stosch combined nationalist admiration of Bismarck with an ability to appraise him impartially, to perceive his
failings, and to oppose him when it seemed best. This independence
of mind and action soon brought upon Stosch the unrelenting anger
and hatred of the most powerful figure in Europe. Seen through
Stosch's experience, Bismarck's relations with the sovereign, the
ministry, and leaders of public opinion assume different propor-
tions from those that appear in the customary account.

As Stosch's political influence rested at first on achievements
in army command and in military administration, his life reflects
the great influence of the armed forces in German life. Stosch
was himself an outspoken opponent of the attempt to separate the
Army and Navy from popular influence and a vehement critic of the
stultification of the services which followed. His career also touched
upon such other problems as the position of the Polish minority,
local administration, the power of the Roman Catholics, and the
relationship of the Protestant state church to the monarchy. His
close identification with the era of Bismarck made his relations
with the leaders of the succeeding generation—William II, Waldersee, Caprivi, Tirpitz, Miquel—of especial significance. A biography
of Stosch enables us to view in complication and in detail many
of the leading questions, problems, and personal relationships of
Imperial Germany.

In presenting the political life of Stosch, I have chosen to re-
count the events of his career and the development of his opinions

at some length. It seems to me that truth in modern German history has suffered from the attempts of doctrinaire theorists to cut events and personalities to their own patterns and that what is needed is biographies and monographs which present more elaborate descriptions and more subtle and complex explanations of men and their actions than do books which drive a thesis. Also, it is hoped that to the general historian narrative and descriptive detail in a specialized account will be more useful than a bare statement.

This study originated from hearing of Stosch's conflict with Bismarck in a lecture of Dr. William A. Jenks, Professor of History at Washington and Lee University, and from investigation on a paper for Dr. R. Taylor Cole, James B. Duke Professor of Political Science at Duke University. Its first form was a dissertation written under the experienced and patient guidance of the late Dr. E. Malcolm Carroll, James B. Duke Professor of History.

My debt to others is equally great. Herr Ulrich von Stosch, of Mittelheim, Germany, kindly granted access to his grandfather's unpublished memoirs and permission to publish extracts from them. He has answered many questions and has shown me great cordiality and hospitality. Frau Dr. Rudolf Stadelmann, of Tübingen, M. Constantin de Grunwald, of Paris, Dr. Erich Eyck, of London, and Professor Gordon A. Craig, of Princeton University, courteously replied to my inquiries. Dr. Eyck loaned me his personal copy of Freytag's letters to Stosch and permitted it to be microfilmed. Mr. Clinton R. Beach, of Flint, Michigan, Dr. James H. Glenn, of Washington, D. C., and Mr. John S. Glenn, of Durham, N. C., greatly aided me in the collection of materials. Conversations with Professor M. Jay Luvaas, Jr., of Allegheny College, have improved the military sections. Mr. Ira Gruber, of Pottstown, Pa. has aided me on the naval sections. While the bibliography records my gratitude to those who have labored before me in the field, I must especially acknowledge the stimulus of Erich Eyck's penetrating analysis of Bismarck and of Andreas Dorpalen's perceptive insight into Frederick III's character.

The preparation and publication of this biography was made possible only by the support that I received from all sides at Duke University. The Graduate Council and the University itself have been very generous with financial grants. The officials of the Duke University Library, particularly Miss Gertrude Merritt, Mr. Emerson Ford, and Mr. John Waggoner, have been invariably courteous and helpful. Professor Theodore Ropp has given excellent advice on the naval sections and has permitted me to utilize his unpublished doctoral dissertation, "The Development of a Modern Navy: French Naval Policy, 1871-1904." Professor Harold T. Parker has offered many invaluable suggestions for improvement. Finally, I acknowledge with pleasure the assistance and encouragement of Professors John Alden, Robert F. Durden, William B. Hamilton, John Tate Lanning, and William T. Laprade, and the members of the Duke University Press, especially Mr. Ashbel G. Brice, Editor and Director, Mr. John Menapace, and Mr. William G. Owens. All responsibility for this study is, of course, mine.

Frederic B. M. Hollyday

CONTENTS

BISMARCK'S RIVAL

I

THE SLOW UPWARD CLIMB

1

The German Emperor bent over the kneeling figure before him and invested his General and Admiral with the highest Prussian decoration, the Order of the Black Eagle. William I softly whispered to Albrecht von Stosch: "You have been loyal to me and have proved yourself wherever I have placed you."[1] These words spoken in 1882[2] summed up a good part of Stosch's career.

Albrecht von Stosch was not the first of his name to serve a Prussian king faithfully and well. Of Silesian background, tracing its origins to the medieval nobility, the Stosch family had renounced its noble birth to seek ecclesiastical preferment in Prussia. One member of the family became court preacher to the Great Elector in the seventeenth century and others won renown as theologians. Albrecht's grandfather, in his turn, had been court preacher at Berlin.[3] The name Stosch had also figured in the army lists of

[1] Albrecht von Stosch to Karl von Normann, 9 March 1888, Albrecht von Stosch, *Denkwürdigkeiten,* III, 149. The first volume of Stosch's memoirs, edited by his son, Ulrich von Stosch, was published under the title of *Denkwürdigkeiten des Generals and Admirals Albrecht v. Stosch, ersten Chefs der Admiralität: Briefe und Tagebuchblätter* (2nd ed., Stuttgart & Leipzig, 1908). The Admiral's grandson, Herr Ulrich von Stosch of Mittelheim, possesses the bound typescript of the two final volumes. The first volume of Stosch's *Denkwürdigkeiten* is cited hereinafter as *Memoirs,* I; the final volumes as Memoirs, II and Memoirs, III.

[2] Stosch received the Order of the Black Eagle in the last half of 1881, but the investiture usually took place at the chapter meetings in January.

[3] *Memoirs,* I, 7; B. Schwarze, "Philipp von Stosch," *Allgemeine Deutsche Biographie* (cited hereafter as *A. D. B.*), XXXVI, 464-66; P. Tschackert, "Friedrich Wilhelm Stosch," *ibid.,* XXXVI, 463; P. Tschackert, "Ferdinand Stosch," *ibid.,* XXXVI, 426-63; P. Tschackert, "Eberhard Heinrich Daniel Stosch," *ibid.,* XXXVI, 462.

the eighteenth century.[4] Albrecht's father, Herman Ferdinand Stosch, followed the military tradition.

Influenced by nationalistic feeling, he became a captain in the Landwehr at the age of twenty-nine. In the same year, 1813, he was selected by one of the leaders of the reform movement, Colonel von Gneisenau, as his personal adjutant. Stosch served in this capacity during the Wars of Liberation and, upon the victorious entrance of the allies into Paris, received his majority. After the war he declined Minister Hardenberg's offer of a privy councilorship and accompanied Gneisenau to Coblenz, where he remained after his chief's transfer to the neighboring fortress of Ehrenbreitstein.[5]

The educated and able Ferdinand Stosch had married in 1814 the talented and vivacious daughter of a prosperous Potsdam merchant. Their marriage was a happy one, enriched by six children. Though Ferdinand von[6] Stosch's career was successful, he never held an outstanding post, perhaps because of his association with the reformer Gneisenau. He reached the height of his career when he was named chief of the War Invalid Section of the War Ministry, and made a general in 1840. After his death in 1857, one of his fellow generals praised his "thoroughness and prudence in service duties, his superior scholarly education, the clarity of his reasoning powers, and his nice sense of tact in society."[7]

Albrecht von Stosch, the third son, born at Coblenz on April 20, 1818, was strongly influenced by his ancestry. Reared in a family which had served the Prussian state long and with distinc-

---

[4] Hans F. Helmolt, ed., *Gustav Freytags Briefe an Albrecht von Stosch* (Stuttgart & Berlin, 1913), p. 4.

[5] *Memoirs*, I, 7-8; Ulrich von Hassell, *Tirpitz: Sein Leben und Wirken mit Berücksichtigung seiner Beziehungen zu Albrecht von Stosch* (Stuttgart, 1920), p. 13.

[6] His family was raised again to the nobility upon his brother's marriage to a noblewoman.

[7] *Memoirs*, I, 7-8; Ulrich von Hassell, "Albrecht von Stosch: Ein Staatmännischer Soldat," *Neue Rundschau*, CI (1940), 209. The officer was General von Borstell, one of the opponents of the reforms of 1807-1819. Ambassador Ulrich von Hassell, son of the biographer of Tirpitz, and remembered for his opposition to Hitler, was Albrecht von Stosch's great nephew. Ferdinand Stosch was ennobled on 1 September 1815; L.V. Zedlitz-Neukirch, *Neues Preussisches Adels-Lexicon* (Leipzig, 1836-1839), IV, 245. For Ferdinand's career, see further Kurt von Priesdorff, *Soldatisches Führertum* (Hamburg [1937-1942]), V, 424-25. The picture given is of Albrecht, not Ferdinand, whose first name is erroneously given as Theodor.

tion, he was conscious of a tradition of duty and service, which he never abandoned throughout his career. The religious heritage of his family combined with his environment and education to develop in him a deep and continuing regard for Protestantism. His background, despite his prefix "von," was predominantly middle class, and it was with this class that he was to feel most personal affinity.

The Prussian military heritage was a strong determinant of his political opinions. The Army combined the two traditions of the nobility and the middle class, of conservatism and reform. The noble tradition had been strengthened by Frederick the Great, who organized an army based on honor; the middle-class tradition was the product of the defeats of 1806 and found expression in the establishment of the Landwehr, through which Ferdinand von Stosch, a bourgeois by birth, had entered the Army. The Landwehr system was definitely adopted in a law of 1814. At twenty, a recruit was to enter the regular standing army and serve three years. Following this he was liable first for two years' service in the reserves, and then for seven years in the Landwehr (first levy), which acted with the regular army in time of war. Seven years were afterwards to be spent in the Landwehr (second levy), the potential reserve for the Landwehr (first levy) and for garrison troops during war. After these nineteen years the citizen was placed in the Landsturm, which included every man from seventeen to fifty, capable of bearing arms, who was not in one of the other forces.

Peace brought reaction against these reforms. Now that Napoleon was overcome, the King turned back to his old advisers. The political reformers were dismissed, while the military ones were transferred to the less desirable posts. A Ferdinand von Stosch who had entered the Army in times of tribulation might remain and might even become a general, but was excluded from the King's inner councils. The nobles looked with scorn at the upstarts who had been introduced into "their Army." The career of Albrecht von Stosch was profoundly affected by both traditions of reform and conservatism. He was to consider himself a military reformer in the spirit of his father's chief, Gneisenau, and yet was also to share many of the political and social views of his conservative companions.[8]

Albrecht von Stosch gained the rudiments of education in the Prussian evangelical state schools and in the sixth form of the Coblenz gymnasium. He was then admitted to the Prussian cadet school at Potsdam, automatically becoming a member of the Royal Cadet Corps founded by Frederick the Great. He passed in regular course from the Potsdam Cadet School to the Chief Cadet School in Berlin in 1832.[9] Whatever else his education may have included, it is certain that he gained a writing and reading knowledge of French.[10]

He left the Cadet Corps in 1835 and, at the age of seventeen, was commissioned a second lieutenant in the Twenty-Ninth Infantry Regiment at Coblenz. Here he moved in the society of high officers and officials who frequented his parental home and "remained rather distant from the one-sided life of the officer corps." Since his military duties were usually confined to attending biweekly parades, he had considerable leisure. This he employed

[8] A recent and able treatment of the reform period is Walter M. Simon, *The Failure of the Prussian Reform Movement, 1807-1819* (Ithaca, N. Y., 1955). See also: Alfred Vagts, *A History of Militarism: Romance and Realities of a Profession* (London, 1938), pp. 144-51; Herbert Rosinski, *The German Army* (2nd ed.; Washington, 1944), pp. 22-74; Guy Stanton Ford, "Boyen's Military Law," *American Historical Review*, XX (1914-1915), 528-38; W. O. Shanahan, *Prussian Military Reforms 1786-1813* (New York, 1945), pp. 29, 34, 37, 60, 81-82, 96, 103, 131-32, 138-39, 185-88, 190-97, 200-203, 212-13; Franz Schnabel, *Deutsche Geschichte in neunzehnten Jahrhundert* (Freiburg i. B., 1929-1937), II, 309-42.

[9] *Memoirs*, I, 8-9. On Prussian primary and military education in the nineteenth century, see Henry Vizetelly, *Berlin Under the New Empire: Its Institutions, Inhabitants, Industry, Monuments, Museums, Social Life, Manners, and Amusements* (London, 1879), I, 368-408; Richard J. Nelson, "Notes on the Constitution and System of Education in the Prussian Army," *United Service Journal and Naval and Military Magazine*, 1839, Part III, p. 522; W. B. Hazen, *The School of the Army in Germany and France, with a Diary of Siege Life at Versailles* (New York, 1872), pp. 250-58; Heinrich von Brandt, *Aus dem Leben der Generals der Infanterie z. D. Dr. Heinrich von Brandt* (2nd ed.; Berlin, 1870-1882), II, 3, 7, 8, 12; 'B,' "Albrecht Theodor Emil von Roon," *A. D. B.*, XXIX, 138-43; Albrecht von Roon, *Denkwürdigkeiten aus dem Leben des Generalfeldmarschalls Kriegministers Grafen von Roon* (5th ed.; Berlin, 1905), I, 55, 62-63. While it is probable that Stosch's primary and secondary education proceeded on the lines described in these volumes, this writer has forborne describing it, for want of sources treating the precise period that Stosch served in the Cadet Corps. He himself says little about it.

[10] Stosch to Karl von Normann, Oestrich, 8 June 1888, Memoirs, III, 165.

in diligently studying law and economics, and in reading literary works. In 1839, he passed the examination for the General Military School (later the Royal Military Academy), the Prussian Sandhurst, and was transferred to Berlin.[11] He had been chosen from among his fellows as worthy of further education. Attendance at the General Military School opened the way to accelerated promotion and appointment to the General Staff.

The level of instruction at the General Military School had not impressed Stosch's future friend, General von Brandt, who had taught there a decade before Stosch's entrance. Teachers like Carl von Clausewitz, the military philosopher, had been met with indifference. However, the school seems to have improved during the following ten years. Heinrich Wilhelm Dove, noted in his day as a physicist and meteorologist, gave a course in physical geography. Carl Ritter, the famous geographer, who exerted a strong influence on Moltke and Roon, taught geography and statistics. The first year of study included elementary tactics, field and camp fortifications, universal and general military history, French, and mathematics. The second year courses were history and practice of fortification, tactics based upon past campaigns, military geography, French, history, logic, physics, and some advanced mathematics. The last year offered the student lectures on sieges, the duties of the General Staff, strategy, history of the wars of Frederick and Napoleon, chemistry, belles lettres, and higher mathematics.[12] A friend of Stosch at the General Military School found the instruction in Roman and literary history stimulating, but felt that the other "civilian" courses were dull. Ritter, for example, dictated the same lecture for the nineteenth time. However, the instructors in tactics and those in the history of warfare, which concentrated on the campaigns of Frederick, Napoleon, and the Russians against the Poles in 1831, were knowledgeable and provocative.[13]

[11] *Memoirs*, I, 9.
[12] Brandt, *Aus dem Leben*, II, 18-20; Alfred Dove, "Heinrich Wilhem Dove," *A. D. B.*, XLVIII, 51-69; Rudolf Stadelmann, *Moltke und der Staat* (Krefeld, 1950), pp. 356-57; Roon, *Denkwürdigkeiten*, I, 55-60; Friedrich Ratzel, "Karl R. Ritter," *A. D. B.*, XXVIII, 679-80; Nelson, "Prussian Military Education," *United Service Journal*, 1839, Part III, pp. 501-2.
[13] Julius von Hartmann, *Lebenserinnerungen, Briefe, und Aufsätze* (Berlin, 1882), I, 137-38, 188.

Stosch looked back on these years as a "time rich in spiritual enjoyment," for his outlook was widened by the company of his friends.[14] One of the closest, Julius von Hartmann,[15] combined a love of theology with a taste for fast horses and books. He later had an active military career, liberally seasoned with politics, diplomacy, and military writing, and reached the rank of Lieutenant General. Regimental duties occupied Stosch's summer months. He spent his first summer in Silesia, after touring Saxony and Bohemia and his second in Danzig, where he first noticed the infant Prussian Navy. In the winter months, he attended court and official balls. At a ball in Trier, the Prussian monarch, Frederick William IV, noted his "very expressive face"; this "flattered" Stosch's "conceit." He soon abandoned these social delights for comradely discussions in his room at night, which provoked an interest in Hegel, the most popular philosopher of the day. Stosch went to the extreme of forming all of his ideas on the Hegelian pattern. He reacted violently a year later; when leafing through a volume of Hegel, he suddenly pitched it into the corner of his room. He was disgusted at himself for "ever finding pleasure in this extremely affected philosophy. My mind was directed to practical achievements; I found such abstract meanderings repugnant." Mathematics and works of German, French, and English literature, which he read in the orginal, gave him greater pleasure.[16]

His third year at the General Military School he afterwards felt to have been "one of the richest" of his life. This was the result not only of the joys of learning but also of meeting his future wife, Rosalie Ulrich, daughter of Medical Councilor Dr. Ulrich of Coblenz. They were soon engaged, but secretly because Stosch had no prospects of supporting a wife. Moreover, Dr. Ulrich, "a rabid democrat," objected to having a Prussian lieutenant as a son-in-law.[17] Stosch's years of study ended with a General Staff

[14] *Ibid.*, I, 140-141; *Memoirs*, I, 9.

[15] There were two Generals Julius von Hartmann in the Prussian Army, both of whom fought in the Franco-German war and wrote memoirs. Stosch's friend was the son of the Hanoverian artillery general who fought with Wellington in Spain and at Waterloo and was made a Commander of the Bath.

[16] *Memoirs*, I, 9-11; Heinrich von Sybel, "Julius von Hartmann," *A. D. B.*, X, 691-96.

[17] *Memoirs*, I, 11; Sara von Janson, *Erinnerungen aus dem Hause Holtzendorff* (Gotha, 1925), p. 16.

ride.[18] He then returned to duty with his regiment at Coblenz, finding life rather sterile after the stimulating atmosphere of Berlin.

A portrait of this time[19] suggests the early character of the young officer. The first, fugitive impression is of a broad-shouldered and florid, round-faced Prussian lieutenant, with little to distinguish him from other subalterns. On closer examination his intelligent, compelling gaze gives hints of intuitive common sense, clarity and sureness of judgment, and strength of will, which severe physical, moral, and mental challenges were to develop later to an unusual degree. Penetrating curiosity, which caused Stosch to approach each new friend with the unspoken question: "What can I learn from him?," almost springs from his eyes. Many years were to pass before the robust Prussian lieutenant was to command the other qualities displayed as a Prussian general and German admiral.

After Dr. Ulrich's reluctant consent was obtained, Stosch's engagement was announced in 1843. He was posted to Berlin as an officer of the Guard Artillery for nine months. This appointment in an elite regiment, perhaps obtained through his father's influence, signified that he was looked upon with favor by the high officers of the Army. The duties were not arduous; once he commanded during a firing practice and occasionally he exercised the troops on foot. At the conclusion of this tour of duty, he was ordered to the Topographical Bureau of the General Staff. This was another sign that he was considered a promising young officer. Each year the Staff took approximately ten junior officers into the Bureau. They worked from June through October on the Ordnance Survey and then went to Berlin to report and do military work for the General Staff. On the basis of the report and the performance of duties, at the end of three years two were taken permanently into the staff.[20] Assignment to the General Staff meant

[18] A maneuver in the field to acquaint officers with practical command problems.

[19] This pencil sketch, in the possession of Herr Ulrich von Stosch, is dated "1861," when Stosch was a colonel. Since he is portrayed in a Prussian lieutenant's uniform, it is probable that the date is an error for "1841." Photographs of the sixties showing him in a general's uniform are of a man many years older.

[20] In 1860, when Stosch was finally a member, the regular members of the entire General Staff Corps numbered one hundred. It included many men who later reached the rank of General, including Stosch's brother-in-law, Kritter. See

accelerated promotion and responsible duties, and the competition was keen. Stosch was very ambitious to be one of the chosen few. This new duty also offered him an opportunity to know his country and its people. The first of June 1845 found him in the neighborhood of Cologne on the Ordnance Survey. He was situated in a desolate farm area, amid poor and ignorant peasants, and, as a result, looked forward to a visit from the director of the Survey, Captain von Czettritz. Stosch's task was more in the nature of a sketching tour than an actual survey, for the primitive instruments employed made exactitude impossible, particularly in hilly terrain. When von Czettritz indicated an error to Stosch, the latter replied he was well aware of it. "Now there was an explosion." They returned to the simple quarters which they shared, enraged at each other, not exchanging a word. Suddenly the hot-blooded captain stood up and cried: "I can stand it no longer." He proposed that Stosch admit he had acted in an undisciplined manner and that he, the captain, would admit that he had provoked the argument. Stosch agreed, and they shook hands. He had had a narrow escape, for comrades who later disagreed with the belligerent von Czettritz were punished. The young lieutenant did not emerge from this incident unscathed, for the notation "inclined to indiscipline" was added to his record. This held up promotion for many years. It is indicative of Stosch's character that von Czettritz was later his frequent, and welcome, guest in Berlin.

More significant in Stosch's life was his marriage on 18 October 1845, to the artistic and musically inclined Rosalie Ulrich. In Berlin, their friends included Hartmann, Luck, later a General Staff captain, and Otto von Holtzendorff, husband of Rosalie von Stosch's closest companion and later Attorney-General of the Duchy of Gotha.[21] Holtzendorff and Stosch remained friends for life.[22] Stosch found great pleasure in Holtzendorff's spirited political conversations with Luck and Hartmann.[23] His mood at the time he later described in these words: ". . . I was always industrious, . . . always spiritually stimulated and in an extremely self-

Rang-und Quartier-Liste der Königlich Preussischen Armee und Marine für das Jahr 1860 (Berlin [1860?]), pp. 20-24.

[21] Often confused with the noted South German jurist, Franz von Holtzendorff.
[22] Memoirs, I, 9-14.   [23] Ibid., I, 14.

satisfied frame of mind." His superiors were very much impressed by his abilities. His battalion commander recommended him for General Staff duty, extolling his unblemished and engaging character, his clear intellect and his breadth of knowledge, his good influence on others, and his zeal, punctuality, and devotion in performance of his service duties. His regimental commander praised his "distinction in every respect" and stated that Stosch's accelerated promotion was in the interest of the Army. He had every expectation of being taken into the General Staff, for he and his father had been privately informed he would be chosen. But the notation "inclined to indiscipline" led to his rejection.[24]

This blow struck me in my innermost soul. I knew I had learned and accomplished something. I had considered myself more intelligent and more clever than all my comrades. Now I was shown the opposite. Entrance into the General Staff would have made me a captain within two years and would have aided me financially. I had been a second lieutenant for twelve years already and now had the prospect of remaining one for at least twelve years more. It was a hard lesson in humility, but it has been advantageous all my life.[25]

Frustrated in his ambition, Stosch returned to Coblenz. His father-in-law helped him pull through this period of depression by showing him the difficulty of being the leader of a Protestant congregation in a Roman Catholic city. Temporary attachment to the Ordnance Survey was offered Stosch, but he declined. Frau Ulrich had an interest in a smelting works, and it seemed advisable to enter the business since advancement in the Army was now closed. These plans were shattered by events over which the young lieutenant had no control. The year 1848 "brought new ideas and duties."[26]

2

The separation of Stosch from his friend Otto von Holtzendorff resulted in an extensive correspondence. In political matters Stosch often differed from his friend.

[24] *Ibid.*, I, 14-16; Priesdorff, *Soldatisches Führertum*, VIII, 309.
[25] *Memoirs*, I, 16. Cf. Hartmann's comments on Stosch's dejection. Hartmann, *Lebenserinnerungen*, I, 227-28, 236-37.
[26] *Memoirs*, I, 16.

You look for the cure of everything in political development; I find it in religion. If you give the world freedom today, before strict internal and external devotion has progressed, you create with it the greatest tyranny ever known. Religion within the church—that is the only foundation upon which you can build freedom; otherwise you make vice predominant. . . .I [*sic*] must, above all, create religiously convinced people, then everything else will come right of itself.[27]

His disappointed ambition is visible in many a letter.

. . . one sees everywhere that, when the hour of decision strikes, everything must bow to a capable sword and a strong will. Ah, Holtzendorff, when there is trouble in the world, one is glad to be a soldier, but it is shameful to be almost thirty years old and still be waiting for things to happen.[28]

The year 1848, in which he wrote this letter, brought the action he thirsted for. Revolutionary unrest, given impetus by the dethronement of the Orleans monarchy in France, came to the Rhine province. Stosch, in his thirteenth year as a second lieutenant, was sent as an assistant to the commander of the Eighth Corps to help prepare march routes within the region. He made himself so useful that he came into possession of much greater responsibility and knowledge than were common to his rank. He found the Army enervated by years of peace, and the higher officers old and incapable of firm decisions. The Army was totally unprepared to take a stand against revolutionary unrest and was, indeed, infected by it. Stosch's own unit, the Twenty-Ninth Infantry Regiment, which drew its reserves from the Coblenz area, was no exception. To preserve and improve its discipline, it was transferred to the French border. A citizens' delegation protested to Commanding General von Thile, but he remained adamant. However, he was so disturbed that Stosch was given the order to march the battalions of the regiment to the parade ground and ask the men whether they would march with it. Those who declined to march were to be mustered out immediately. Stosch remonstrated against this order. While this discussion was in progress, the magistrate of Coblenz appeared before von Thile and informed him that the city would revolt unless the march order was re-

[27] Coblenz, 18 Oct. 1847, *ibid.,* I, 29.
[28] Coblenz, 1 Jan. 1848, *ibid.,* I.

scinded. The Commanding General capitulated, but the exasperated Stosch informed the lieutenants of the General's action. As a group, they immediately requested the transfer of the regiment to the French border. General von Thile refused and demanded their obedience.

Nevertheless, the General was so shaken by the lieutenants' protest that he submitted his resignation, which Stosch was ordered to take to Berlin. Thile's Chief of Staff informed the veteran lieutenant that particular weight would be attached to his words and instructed him to use his influence to prevent the acceptance of the General's resignation. Stosch, upon his arrival at the Royal castle, was immediately ushered into the presence of King Frederick William IV, who asked for his opinion. He held his tongue, rightly assuming the King's question to be purely rhetorical. When asked the same question by Acting Minister of War, von Reyher, Stosch replied that the Chief of Staff believed Thile was the only man for the job. Reyher insisted on hearing Stosch's own opinion; he declared Thile should be replaced. As a result, Stosch was directed to carry back the acceptance of his chief's retirement. While in Berlin, he saw a Landwehr and a regular army battalion on the march, a sight he never forgot. In the Landwehr battalion signs of revolution were manifest.[29] "All discipline had vanished. It was a band of robbers, not a Prussian troop. My face was suffused with the blush of shame."[30] The regular army battalion, with its mathematical precision, made a striking contrast. Indeed, the entire mission affected him profoundly:

I had looked deep into the world and was inclined to take a part in events. The direction [of my activity] was preordained both by family tradition and my professional feelings (*Standesbewusstsein*); I would have gone vigorously into the field against all revolutionaries without any pangs of conscience.[31]

He had thus adopted the antirevolutionary views of the conservative officer corps in which he was reared.

[29] *Ibid.*, I, 17-20; Hartmann, *Lebenserinnerungen,* II, 54.
[30] *Memoirs,* I, 20.
[31] *Ibid.*, I. Stosch met Moltke for the first time during this visit. Eberhard Kessel, *Moltke* (Stuttgart, 1957), p. 194.

In September 1848, Stosch was sent to observe conditions
along the French border. He displayed his political perspicuity
by predicting the election of Louis Napoleon as President of France,
despite counteropinions from Paris. He was then employed with
the troops who were restoring order in Baden and Hesse; "we
were able to report that our soldiers were the best Prussian diplomats."[32]

His views of the political situation were increasingly influenced
by his allegiance to Prussia. He hoped for a united Germany led
by Prussia, but had no faith in the protracted deliberations of the
Frankfort Parliament. German political unity, he continued to
feel, would result only from religious unity; the Protestants of
Germany would have to rally to Prussia's banner and fight if
necessary. In "peaceful conquest" he had no faith. "First necessity
must bind us all together, then the bond will be firm."[33]

In November, Stosch, still a second lieutenant, was made adjutant to an active Landwehr brigade in Trier. He was engaged
in reserve and replacement duties for his division for three years.
Here he gained a thorough knowledge of the organization of the
Army. The constant movement of 1848 was replaced by steady
duties, and he was able to take more of an interest in politics by
writing newspaper articles defending the Army against republican
attack. Otherwise, he was bored by "spiritually dead" Trier and
bitterly regretted that he was not in the main stream of events.[34]
He even dreamed of being Prussian Minister-President. Like Holtzendorff, he joined the "Prussian Society for the Constitutional
Kingdom,"[35] a conservative political organization, which, under
the guise of helping victims of revolutions, fought the republicans
and defended the Army.[36] An "iron hand," he felt, was needed
to bring everything into order; German unity could only be brought
about by the Army.[37] News of the new German fleet pleased him

[32] Memoirs, I, 20-21, 34; Janson, Erinnerungen, p. 116. Cf. Rudolf Stadelmann,
Soziale und Politische Geschichte der Revolution von 1848 (Munich, 1948), p.
153.
[33] To Holtzendorff, Trier, 17 Aug. 1848, Memoirs, I, 30.
[34] Ibid., I, 21-22.
[35] To Holtzendorff, Trier, 3 Jan. 1849, ibid., I, 31.
[36] Veit Valentin, Geschichte der deutschen Revolution vom 1848-1849 (Berlin, 1931), II, 229-30, 267, 635.
[37] To Holtzendorff, Trier, 2 Jan. 1849, Memoirs, I, 31.

greatly. At this time, however, he suffered further professional disappointment. A promise to his father that he would be transferred to the General Staff was not fulfilled. His promotion to first lieutenant in June 1849 was poor recompense in comparison.[38]

The threat of conflict with Austria in 1850 brought Prussian mobilization. Stosch was dismayed by the lack of supplies and officers and by the lawlessness of the Landwehr troops. He felt that Prussia had no chance whatsoever against Austria; the "humiliation of Olmütz" was a military necessity. Political inactivity made him fret, for he still hoped to see Germany united by force. He was perturbed that the Minister of War did nothing to bind the Army to the Crown, but he rejoiced at the increasing strength of the Conservative party, whose partisans opposed any loss of the powers of the King and the nobility. Stosch hoped this party would form a Prussian ministry and follow a consistent policy, thus "consolidating the other parties" in opposition and bringing to birth a "real constitutional" system. At the same time, the neo-absolutist actions of the King and his advisers aroused his distaste, not because they were reactionary, but because they were narrowly Prussian, weak, and wavering. Stosch clearly desired the firm implementation of a policy which was both national and conservative.

Stosch was made adjutant with the division in Trier in 1852, but he was the last of the six senior first lieutenants of the infantry regiments of the division to be promoted to Captain Third Class. He continued to feel the pangs of poverty, as he had since his marriage. He needed a horse for his new duties, but even a loan from his father-in-law was insufficient. In the summer of 1853 all but one of the eighteen divisional first adjutants were replaced by majors of the General Staff and transferred to their advantage. Stosch alone returned to his regimental duties, for the General Staff considered him politically unsafe, a sign of the triumph of reaction. His superiors also held him responsible for his aged commander's mistakes during the preceding mobilization; "It was another lesson in humility, but I was not Hegelian enough to enjoy its influence

---

[38] *Ibid.*, I, 21-33; Ernst Schröder, *Albrecht von Stosch, des General-Admiral Kaiser Wilhelm I: Eine Biographie* (Berlin, 1939), p. 112. The German national parliament at Frankfort created a fleet, which was sold after the Revolution failed (see chap. iv below).

upon me." Personally he had given no offense, for he was honored by a farewell dinner given by the generals and most of the staff officers. He returned to his regiment now stationed at Frankfort am Main, where he became a company commander.[39] The regiment returned to Trier in the spring of 1854, and he was soon posted to Coblenz, again as a company commander. Discouraged by slow promotion, that summer he determined to leave the Army. Fate and the friendly influence of two generals intervened, and he joined the staff of the Eighth Army Corps at Coblenz. At last he had achieved his ambition of entering the General Staff Corps.[40]

Coblenz society was amusing, but too lazy and frivolous for his taste. Count Lehndorff, Adjutant to William I, later said to him: "You like to consider yourself a Rhinelander, but you are much too industrious for that." Here he first became acquainted with the Prince of Prussia, the future King William I, then Military Governor of the Rhine Province and Westphalia. The Prince was greatly interested by a lecture Stosch delivered on the importance of the needle gun in combat. Later the King of Prussia and German Emperor often reminded Stosch that he had been the first man to bring this important weapon to the monarch's attention. Captain von Stosch was invited to dine with the Prince and his wife Augusta, whose favor he enjoyed from that day. He found revealing William's exclamations of disgust with the reactionary pro-Austrian policy of his brother, Frederick William IV. Stosch himself did not draw back even from the prospect of a war between Prussia and Austria, as a solution to Germany's problems.

Promotion came in 1856. Stosch received his majority in April and arrived at his new assignment in the staff of the Tenth Division in Posen the following month. His chief, General Heinrich von Brandt, a noted military writer of the time, gave him his complete confidence. They became great friends and, after Brandt's retirement in 1857, carried on an extensive correspondence which broadened the Major's outlook. Stosch characteristically wrote of Brandt: "I can learn much from him." Residence in

[39] Stosch was not acquainted with Bismarck at this time. He wrote later of him in 1853: "We were all proud of him, and every Prussian honored him," *Memoirs*, I, 23.
[40] Stosch had served on temporary duty with the general staff in 1848 and 1850. Priesdorff, *Soldatisches Führertum*, VIII, 308, 310.

Posen brought Stosch into contact with Jews. Unlike Holtzendorff, no Jewish emancipator, Stosch found them "by birth, disposition, and life, in the most complete opposition to the Christian-German element." The latter could control the region only by "exterminating all Philistines." In fact, the social structure in Prussian Poland was difficult for the western-reared Stosch to comprehend. In his other assignments, it had been customary for the officer to care for and look after his men. In Posen, there were only "masters and slaves"; "this is not in my nature."

Still troubled by poverty, he stayed in Posen for five years, except for the mobilization of 1859, which took him to Frankfurt am Main for a few weeks to obtain quarters for his unit. General Vogel von Falckenstein, Chief of Staff of the mobilized army, was extraordinarily pleased, when the Major arranged the entire disposition of the Army and brought the Duke of Nassau, his premier, and twenty-four officials into agreement with it on a single day. The years in Posen were a time of "rich intellectual life" and "quiet creation." Aided by Brandt's advice, he tried to learn all he could about Poland, and he even mastered the language. The opinions formed at this time led him later to oppose the "Prussianization" of German Poland (see Chapter VIII below).

The forty-year-old Major continued to harbor political ambitions. In a half-humorous letter to von Holtzendorff, he remarked that both of them would probably become Ministers-President of Prussia. He considered the political situation in 1858 comparable to that of 1848, with the officials, the clergy, and the propertied classes opposed to the reactionary Government. He placed his hopes in the "simple and true character" of the Prince of Prussia, who had become Regent for his insane brother. Stosch still remained faithful to his battle-cry: "With Prussia for Germany."

Brandt's successor, whom Stosch tactfully does not name in his memoirs, was a less cultivated soldier. He had always been a front-line commander and was an enemy of books. He arrived just before maneuvers, and after the first day, altered Stosch's carefully conceived plans. The Major countered with the observation that the new dispositions would not strike at the enemy. The General flared up, but at the end of the following day, he admitted that his junior was right. Despite this admission of error, or perhaps because of it, he had Stosch transferred to the staff of the Fifth Army Corps, also in Posen. Here Stosch enjoyed the confidence of his general, Count Waldersee, father of the later Chief of the General Staff, and he could act on his own initiative. His handling of the maneuvers of 1858 gained him a decoration and the praise of the Army authorities, including Moltke.[41]

The quiet of Posen bored Stosch, despite his promotion to Lieutenant-Colonel in 1860. His ambitious hopes were again dashed when he was considered "too individualistic" for a post in the War Ministry. He already had the reputation of being a "liberal," probably because of the independence of his views and his frankness in stating them. He greeted with joy his appointment as Chief of Staff of the Fourth Army corps at Magdeburg. First, he was sent to Berlin to the General Staff, which assigned him the task of visiting Hungary and Transylvania on a service trip, where he was able to use his small stock of Hungarian. Upon his return he attended the maneuvers of the Seventh and Eighth Corps. After appraising the performance of one of the generals, he went on a General Staff ride under the supervision of General von Moltke, Chief of the General Staff. Stosch led the Prussian side, and his industry in making his subordinates file reports on the day's activities caused Moltke to complain he was making too much work for him. Although Moltke was little interested in the tactical education of officers, Stosch was delighted to hear him expand on the great strategic problems.[42]

The question of fundamental army reform soon engaged Stosch's attention. The advisers of the Regent William—Albrecht von Roon, Minister of War, Edwin von Manteuffel, Chief of the Military Cabinet, and Helmuth von Moltke—had perceived the

[41] Stosch, in addition to his many Prussian ones, eventually wore decorations of nine German states, and Russia, Austria, Turkey, Italy, and Sweden; *ibid.*, VIII, 307-8; and below p. 300.

[42] Memoirs, I, 22-28, 33-49; Walter von Loë, *Erinnerungen aus meinem Berufsleben 1849 bis 1867* (2nd. ed.; Stuttgart, 1906), p. 46; Theodor von Bernhardi, *Aus dem Leben Theodor von Bernhardis* (Leipzig, 1893-1906), IV, 16. *Rang- und Quartier-Liste 1860*, p. 63, gives Stosch's decoration as the "Order of the Red Eagle, Fourth Class." The plans of the staff ride of 1861 appear in Helmuth von Moltke, *Moltke's Militärische Werke* (Berlin, 1892-1912), Theil III, 148-87. For William's view of the needle gun, see William I, *Militärische Schriften* (Berlin, 1897), II, 80-107. Brandt's successor was Baron von der Goltz.

necessity for reform of the Army. They wished not only to remove the inefficiency of the existing system, but also to extirpate liberal strength within the Army. Under the provisions of a military bill drawn up in 1859, sixty-three thousand recruits were to be conscripted annually to serve three years (instead of two) in newly formed infantry and cavalry regiments. The reserve system was to be reorganized. Landwehrmen of the first levy were to be amalgamated with the regular reserve; those of the second levy were to be relegated to home defense, fortresses, or occupied territory. Landwehrmen were to be mustered out of service at the age of thirty-six. More significant politically was the proposed creation of officers of the reserve, elected by officers of the active regiments, where aristocratic and conservative influence predominated. These officers of the reserve would replace Landwehr officers, hitherto chosen by the predominantly bourgeois and liberal Landwehr officers of their home district. Required for these reforms was an increased tax burden of ten million thalers (about $12,500,000) annually.

The military bill was opposed by the majority of the voters of Prussia, who regarded the reform as an attempt to restore absolutism. They rallied to the standard of the recently organized Progressive party, which soon controlled the Prussian Chamber of Deputies. Every major feature of the bill aroused Progressive distaste. Increased military service meant every youth would be taken from more productive enterprises for an extra year, during which time he would be subject to conservative influences. Indeed, the demand for the two-year term of service was to be the election slogan of the more extreme liberals throughout the nineteenth century. The extra tax burden, which would bear heavily on the middle class, was equally unwelcome. Most objectionable to the Progressive was the alteration of the Landwehr, which was regarded as the means by which the Prussian people achieved victory during the Wars of Liberation and as the stronghold of the liberal middle class. The Chamber of Deputies refused to vote money to carry out the military reforms. William's ministry attempted to compromise by continuing the two-year term of service, but William blocked this.[43]

[43] The literature on the Army reforms is voluminous. See especially, Gerhard

Stosch looked upon the question as a purely military one and seems at first not to have realized its underlying political implications. He wrote to Holtzendorff in 1860:

The augmentation and increase of our cadres is a question of life or death for the Army, because of Louis Napoleon and the German question. A few millions does not matter as much as Prussia's internal unity and its ability to meet the approaching danger with developed military power . . . . The stronger the army is today, the sooner it will be ready to face the enemy. Therefore, I consider the opposition to the bill a misfortune.[44]

He considered war likely within the year and thus held the Army reform to be an immediate necessity.[45]

Opposition to the bill continued from the Progressive party, which refused to vote the budget. William, now King, summoned Otto von Bismarck as his chief minister on 22 September 1862, and carried the reforms into effect without parliamentary sanction and without a parliamentary budget. Stosch wrote six days after Bismarck's appointment:

Rumors of the abdication of the King become stronger and stronger; who knows whether it might not be the right step politically. By the surrender of the King and a victory of the Progressive Party, we would be thrown into the whirlpool of theoretical revolution, of dogmatism, of impractical ambitious democracy. The Crown Prince has used every means to make the old gentleman change his mind.

I feel more and more with each passing year that my own welfare is bound in the closest way with that of the mother country. The pres-

Ritter, *Staatskunst und Kriegshandwerk*: *Das Problem des 'Militarismus' in Deutschland* (Munich, 1954), I, chap. vi.; Vagts, *History of Militarism*, pp. 198-214; Gordon A. Craig, "Portrait of a Political General: Edwin von Manteuffel and the Constitutional Conflict in Prussia," *Political Science Quarterly*, LXVI (1951), 1-36; Gordon A. Craig, *The Politics of the Prussian Army, 1640-1945* (Oxford, 1955), chapter iv; E. R. Huber, *Heer und Staat in der deutschen Geschichte* (Hamburg, 1938), pp. 179-224; Edward M. Earle, ed., *Makers of Modern Strategy: Military Thought from Machiavelli to Hitler* (Princeton, 1948), pp. 173-76; Erich Brandenburg, *Die Reichsgründung* (Leipzig, n. d.), I, 421-24. A recent presentation of the liberal viewpoint in the conflict is Eugene N. Anderson, *The Social and Political Conflict in Prussia, 1858-1864* (Lincoln, Nebraska, 1954).

[44] To Holtzendorff, Posen, 25 Apr. 1860, *Memoirs*, I, 43. In later life, he held that the reserve companies should be organized by local districts from which the officers should be elected; To Karl von Normann, Oestrich, 25 Feb. 1888, Memoirs, III, 146. He also later favored a close bond between the middle class and the Army; *Memoirs*, I, 12.

[45] To Holtzendorff, Posen, 31 Dec. 1860, *ibid.,* I, 43.

ent conditions make me extraordinarily melancholy. Manteuffel must fall. Then Bismarck will persuade the King to accept the two-year term of service for the infantry, and we will have peace. My general [Schack] says nothing can happen in the Army question, because the old people who serve as advisers guard themselves from giving opinions unacceptable on high. And Manteuffel is the man who handles the puppets and puts their lines in their mouths. Below this level, life is pulsing in the Army. . . .[46]

Stosch's opinions in 1863 were quite as trenchant. The first necessity in the military question, he felt, was to obtain a skeleton force ready for war. The goal should be the acquisition of experienced officers and well-trained noncommissioned officers and the increase of battalions to war strength. In addition, "the killing uniformity of garrison life" should be replaced by changing duties. The term of training should vary with the branch of service. "It is nonsense to set an average time for instruction" of the recruit. Infantrymen needed only a year's instruction, while a period of three years was hardly enough time for cavalry training.[47] "The Democrat," who demands the two-year term of service, "only judges by external appearances and does not understand the matter."[48]

Stosch's new chief in Magdeburg was General von Schack, an intermediary between Bismarck and King William I in military matters. Later Governor of Saxony in 1866, he was not as well educated as Brandt, but possessed a great fund of common sense and experience. Schack praised Stosch highly in his first efficiency report, and the following year added the notation: "Fit for every position and every assignment." Moltke's opinion was more qualified. While he was struck by Stosch's "great personal abilities" and his "amiable and promising character," he felt that Stosch lacked operational experience. However, he granted in 1861 that Stosch was a capable chief of staff for an army corps in peacetime and would be very suitable as a brigade commander.[49]

The years of disappointment and depression seemed to be at an end. Through his own efforts, Stosch had gained an excellent education, had reached the rank of colonel in 1861, and had made

[46] To Holtzendorff, Magdeburg, 28 Sept. 1862, *ibid.,* I, 52.
[47] To Holtzendorff, Magdeburg, 28 March 1863, *ibid.,* I, 52-53.
[48] *Ibid.,* I, 53.
[49] *Ibid.,* I, 50; Priesdorff, *Soldatisches Führertum,* VIII, 310.

friends who possessed influence and power. His sixteen years as a lieutenant were long past. There appeared to be no position in the Army to which he could not aspire. On 3 November 1863, the forty-five-year-old colonel mounted his very restive steed for his daily ride. After galloping to bring it under control, he jumped a hurdle, and the animal seemed to calm. At this moment, an officer on an inexperienced horse turned before him. It struck out and shattered the lower half of Stosch's right leg. By Christmas 1863 he had lost consciousness, and his life was in danger.[50]

3

Stosch's leg slowly mended after Christmas 1863, and he was soon engaged in writing articles for the influential Saxon periodical, *Die Grenzboten*. This activity he indirectly owed to his friend, Otto von Holtzendorff, the Attorney-General of Gotha, whom he often visited on vacations. He came to know the intimates of the Holtzendorff circle, including Frau von Holtzendorff's sons-in-law —the British diplomat, art historian and journalist, Sir Joseph Archer Crowe, father of Eyre Crowe; von Janson, later a German general; and Karl Gerhardt, a noted physician. Holtzendorff's son, Henning, was later Chief of the Admiralty Staff under William II. The circle also included the Baden statesmen Karl Samwer, and Franz, Baron von Roggenbach; the budding historian and publicist, Heinrich von Treitschke; the private secretary of Ernst II of Coburg, Edward von Tempeltey; and the novelist, dramatist, historian, and journalist, Gustav Freytag. To this group was soon added, through Stosch's mediation, the gifted Captain Karl von Normann. Stosch found here congenial friends, and delighted in the lively political conversation. One member of the household, Sara von Janson, was impressed by his boldness in expression, his "powerful iron nature," and his blunt manners. She seems to agree with the remark of the Crown Princess of Prussia: "Stosch is the finest man I know, but he likes to contradict too much and too often."[51] Stosch needed money and, encouraged by Freytag, editor

---

[50] *Memoirs*, I, 51.

[51] Janson, *Erinnerungen, passim;* Gustav Freytag, *Karl Mathy: Erinnerungen aus meinem Leben* (Leipzig & Berlin, n. d.), pp. 641-42; Sir Joseph Crowe, *Reminiscences of Thirty-five Years of My Life* (2nd ed.; London, 1895), pp. 410, 429-30. For Freytag's political views, see Paul Ostwald, *Gustav Freytag als Politiker* (Berlin, 1927), and Ottokar Lorenz, *Staatsmänner und Geschicht-*

of *Die Grenzboten,* he wrote articles for that magazine. Since his memoirs contain very casual references to these anonymous articles, their exact number is uncertain. The first series, a study of the American Civil War, appeared in *Die Grenzboten* in 1864 and 1865.[52]

The outbreak of the Danish War in 1864 found Stosch still unfit for active service. He followed its events with close attention, and felt that Prussia's success was to be attributed to the firmness of King William and Bismarck. He found fault with the military leadership and was particularly critical of the King's nephew, Prince Frederick Karl. Stosch was disappointed in his hopes for a great naval victory, but the storming of the Düppel entrenchments brought tears of Prussian patriotism to his eyes. While the war was in progress, he recorded his views of it for his own edification, but was persuaded by Freytag to publish them in *Die Grenzboten.* The anonymous articles entitled "Military Letters on the War in Schleswig" enjoyed considerable popularity.[53] Stosch thought that the war had proved that the Prussian Army rested upon good foundations in doctrine and discipline. Training sought to develop discipline, a bellicose spirit, and the use of weapons. Discipline was the most important of these, but the defeats of 1806 and misfortunes of 1848 had taught that it ought not to be a goal in itself. The great defect of the Prussian military education was the lack of suitable terrain for erecting military training camps—a theme Stosch developed at length in his article "The Importance

---

schreiber des neunzehnten Jahrhunderts (Berlin, 1896), pp. 327-60. It is incorrect to describe Stosch as a friend of Ernst II, as does Rudolf Morsey (*Die oberste Reichsverwaltung unter Bismarck, 1867-1890* [Münster i. w., 1957], p. 132); Stosch's remarks about Ernst are rarely complimentary. See *Memoirs,* I, 51-52, 55, 60, 63, 104.

[52] [Albrecht von Stosch], "Der Krieg in Nordamerika vom militärischen Standpunkt," *Die Grenzboten,* XXIII (1864), vol. IV, 281-90, 325-34, 389-95, 453-58; XXIV (1865), vol. I, 58-69, 227-38, 248-62, vol. II, 352-58. (Each year of *Die Grenzboten,* the liberal-nationalist weekly, made up a numbered volume, which, in turn, was bound into four numbered volumes.)

[53] *Memoirs,* I, 54-57, 66; Helmolt, *Freytag an Stosch,* pp. 1-2; [Albrecht von Stosch], "Militärische Briefe über den Krieg im Schleswig," *Die Grenzboten,* XXIII (1864), vol. I, 513-17, vol. II, 28-36, 66-74, 115-19, 148-53, 191-93, 235-40, 270-76, 312-18, 355-60, 395-98, vol. III, 113-16, 277-80. For a contemporary reaction to this series, see Bernhardi, *Aus dem Leben,* VI, 110.

of the Military Camp, Especially for Prussia."[54] Such camps would relieve the Army of the baneful influence of parade-ground pedants and result in real leadership, which was woefully lacking.

The whole question of the term of military service, wrote Stosch in his series on the Danish War, hinged upon the necessity of inculcating discipline through training. Discipline meant not only mere obedience, but willing and cheerful execution of an order with all one's powers. It took time to accustom the soldier to the change from private freedom to military strictness. He had to realize that his freedom lay in military law. The force of the general will operated with less effect in a small state, so that here the term of service had to be extended. Where the law was strongest, the term of service could be shortened. A state like England or the Southern Confederacy, which gave special privileges to one class, had the advantage of leadership and did not need a lengthy term of service. Prussia was a state in transition, troubled by political conflict, and needed the longer term. Yet Prussia's was the shortest of any large nation.

The opposition to the Landwehr, according to Stosch, had stemmed from its poor discipline and not from political considerations. The necessity of the three-year term had been demonstrated in the Danish War. Necessary as the three-year term was under the existing methods of training, the erection of military training camps would accelerate the education of the recruit and permit the reduction of the term for the infantryman, the engineer, and the artilleryman. The more specialized branches of the cavalryman and the teamster would still need the full three years. The training of the military camp and the retirement of superannuated officers would improve the caliber of the officer corps. Prussia required, on both local and national levels, a form of government which developed a sense of law and discipline in the individual, and military training which put the recruit right to work and prepared him in peacetime for all that war demanded. Stosch concluded that the "weakness of our German fatherland lies not in

---

[54] [Albrecht von Stosch], "Die Bedeutung der militärischen Lager, besonders für Preussen," *Die Grenzboten,* XXIV (1865), vol. III., 425-33. Stosch does not refer to this article in his memoirs, but it is ascribed to him, perhaps on unpublished evidence, by Schroeder, *Stosch,* pp. 21, 107. In any case, internal evidence strongly points to Stosch as the author.

its Northern frontiers, but in its lack of [political] unity and . . . in
the lack of unity in German military administration."

"The Military Importance of the Duchies of Schleswig-Holstein" was the title of an additional article by Stosch.[55] He believed
that the possession of the Duchies was of little military value. The
building of fortresses there was impossible because of the nature of
the terrain and the exposed location of the Duchies. A fortress at
Altona, the suburb of Hamburg, a fleet station at sea, and a naval
base on the island of Rügen would best secure their defense.
Domination of the Baltic Sea would be achieved and the Duchies
would be protected on the East. Of course, a North Sea–Baltic
Canal would require further fortification. However, the North Sea
coast of the Duchies would have to be left unguarded, for the
fortification of all possible landing places was an impossibilty.
In only one way could they be protected on the West; "Helgoland
must be ours. . . ."[56]

Association with Freytag kept Stosch abreast of current literature.[57] Freytag's friendship also brought him into close contact
with Franz, Baron von Roggenbach, who, much to Stosch's grief,
retired from the post of Premier of Baden in 1865. Roggenbach
spent the remainder of his long life on the wings of the political
stage, awaiting the call to office which never came. Prussian-
minded, a founder of the Liberal Imperial party (*Liberal Reich-
spartei*), he was a friend and adviser of the Grand Duke Frederick
of Baden and his consort, of the Prince and Princess of Wied and

[55] [Albrecht von Stosch], "Die Militärische Bedeutung des Herzogtums
Schleswig-Holstein," *Die Grenzboten*, XXIV (1865), vol. III, 192-99. Cf. *Memoirs*, I, 61; Helmolt, *Freytag an Stosch*, p. 5.

[56] Stosch also wrote a review article of Pertz's life of Gneisenau. *Memoirs*,
I, 61, 66-68, 70; [Albrecht von Stosch], "Das Leben des Feldmarschalls von
Gneisenau, von F. Pertz," *Die Grenzboten*, XXIV (1865), vol. I, 353-57 (later
articles on this work appeared in 1866, but there seems to be no evidence of
Stosch's authorship of them). J. v. Pflück-Hartung, "Die Auszeichnung des
Generals Ferdinand v. Stosch über Gneisenau," *Beihefte zum Militärwochenblatt*,
Heft 8, 1911 gives an account of Stosch's father's contributions.

[57] Stosch added to Freytag's knowledge of military affairs. Freytag, *Mathy:
Erinnerungen*, pp. 639-42. Freytag may have been referring to Stosch in his
letter to Treitschke, Siebleben, 14 Sept. 1865, as the editor conjectures, in which
he suggested that the best advisers for Frederick William would be members
of the Prussian Army who had held fast to "Scharnhorst's spirit of reform."
These men should be made responsible Ministers of the crown. Alfred Dove,
ed., *Gustav Freytag und Heinrich von Treitschke im Briefwechsel* (Leipzig, 1900),
p. 61.

their relative the monarch of Rumania, as well as of Queen Augusta of Prussia and the Crown Prince and Crown Princess of Prussia. The model of an elder statesman, Roggenbach was a German Cassandra, who was only too acute in his observations on Germany's future. Next to von Normann, Roggenbach was probably Stosch's closest friend in his last years.[58]

The most trusted friend of Stosch came to be Captain Karl von Normann. The two officers formed with the Baden statesman an informal personal alliance that was known as the "Normann—Stosch—Roggenbach circle."[59] Through Stosch's relations with the Holtzendorff group the trio were brought into close contact with Crown Prince Frederick William of Prussia. The Holtzendorffs had an entry into the councils of the Crown Prince through Ernst von Stockmar, secretary to the Crown Princess. His illness in 1864 necessitated a replacement, and Stockmar turned to Holtzendorff for advice. He, in his turn, asked Stosch's opinion. Stosch recommended Captain Karl von Normann, both for his knowledge and his character. Normann received the approval of the heir to the throne and his wife. He served them for almost twenty years and kept them in continual contact with Stosch. The royal pair enjoyed Stosch's articles in *Die Grenzboten* and expressed a desire to meet him. His first meeting with the Crown Prince, a very cordial one, took place at the Magdeburg Railway Station on 14 May 1865. They met again in September, when the Crown Princess in particular charmed him. Death alone was to sever these new friendships.[60]

In the tradition of Prussian royal heirs, the Crown Prince had come into political conflict with his father, William I. Frederick William, seconded by his gifted and intellectually superior wife, opposed the policy of Bismarck in governing in opposition to the

[58] *Memoirs,* I, 62, 66; Karl Samwer, *Zur Erinnerung an Franz von Roggenbach* (Wiesbaden, 1909); Willy Andreas, *Kämpfe um Volk und Reich* (Stuttgart & Berlin, 1934), pp. 125-49; Julius Heyderhoff, ed., *Im Ring der Gegner Bismarcks: Denkschriften und Politischen Briefwechsel Franz v. Roggenbachs mit Kaiserin Augusta und Albrecht v. Stosch, 1865-1896* (2nd ed.; Leipzig, 1943), pp. 7-43.

[59] See, for example, the casual reference in *Memoirs of Prince von Bülow* (Boston, 1931-1932), I, 87. Roggenbach is here rendered as "Roggenberg" and the three men are grouped together as one person in the index.

[60] *Memoirs,* I, 51, 55-57, 61-62.

Progressive majority in the Chamber of Deputies. He spoke out publicly against some repressive press decrees in 1863 and attempted to disassociate himself from government policy by remaining silent in Prussian State Council sessions, from which he later withdrew entirely. His wife, Victoria, daughter of Queen Victoria and the favorite child of Prince Albert, a woman of very decided opinions, with advanced views in politics, religion, and social questions, was the mainstay of her rather vacillating husband. This royal couple was the focal point of liberal aspirations and progressive hopes.[61] In these early years Stosch feared that Victoria's political ideas were too radical for a future Queen of Prussia, while he felt that Frederick William should take a greater interest in public affairs, particularly those concerning the Army. He was disturbed by Normann's reports of the Crown Prince's pessimism and stated that he himself would be happy if he had prospects so brilliant.[62]

Bismarck's policy in 1864 and 1865 greatly pleased Stosch. He wrote of the Prussian Minister-President: ". . . the fellow is active and untiring, that always brings success. This personal intervention in the right spot is the sign of a great statesman."[63] He thoroughly supported Bismarck's opposition to the erection of a throne for Frederick of Augustenburg, pretended heir to Holstein and friend of the Crown Prince, but he criticized the Minister for disregarding the opposition his policies provoked.

Stosch's continuing illness was lightened not only by the intellectual stimulation of the articles for Freytag, and by his interest in the political scene, but also by the society of fellow officers, among whom were Meydem, later General and Director of the Telegraphs, and Julius v. Verdy du Vernois, later a noted military

[61] A realistic biography of the Crown Prince is badly needed. He is treated in a very favorable light in Margarethe von Poschinger, *Kaiser Friedrich* (Berlin, 1899-1900); J. W. Otto Richter, *Kaiser Friedrich III* (Berlin, 1901); and Werner Richter, *Kaiser Friedrich III* (Zürich, 1938). A critical reappraisal of his political actions is found in Andreas Dorpalen, "Emperor Frederick III and the German Liberal Movement," *American Historical Review,* LIV (Oct. 1948), 1-31. A sympathetic defense of Victoria, which summarizes the conclusions of his other works, is Erich Eyck, "The Empress Frederick," *Quarterly Review,* no. 589 (July, 1951), pp. 355-366.

[62] *Memoirs,* I, 58, 61-65; Helmolt, *Freytag an Stosch,* p. 17.

[63] To Holtzendorff, Magdeburg, 31 Aug. 1864, *Memoirs,* I, 57.

writer and War Minister. Stosch was forced to go about on crutches for a time, but he refused to let his body master his will and check his career. He stood high in the favor of William I, who received daily reports of his progress and even telegraphed to him. The King told Stosch's doctor: "I particularly recommend the Colonel to you; the Army still expects much of him." Stosch, spurred by Moltke's promise of a brigade if his leg improved,[64] went on maneuvers to show that he was physically able to carry out his duties. In his usual terse style, Moltke wrote of Stosch's abilities: "A promising personality; a firm, benevolent, and amiable character. Conscientious, trustworthy, frank, and true, of valiant disposition, Colonel von Stosch will, in my opinion, accomplish even more as a troop commander than in . . . the General Staff."[65]

By 1865 he had recovered sufficiently to take a military tour of France for the General Staff. There he received the news that he had been rejected as a candidate for chief of staff of the Crown Prince's Second Army Corps.[66] Frederick William was very upset by this,[67] but attempted to secure Stosch's services as his adjutant. These negotiations fell through, according to General von Schack, because the Military Cabinet, which advised the King on appointments, considered Stosch politically unreliable from the mere fact that the Crown Prince had asked for him. The Military Cabinet gathered all reports on Stosch, but could find nothing politically objectionable. The Crown Princess was approached indirectly and was asked why she liked Stosch, who was, after all, the firm friend of Schack, the conservative adviser of the King. Could Stosch and the Crown Princess co-operate? Victoria innocently replied with her usual frankness: "Stosch is already indispensable to me," and his fate was sealed.[68] The Crown Prince wrote indignantly in his diary:

Colonel von Stosch . . . is now being persecuted by the Military Cabinet, because I wanted him with me. Things have already reached these lengths!! Furthermore certain circles are furious that "the Crown Prince

[64] *Ibid.,* I, 51, 53-54, 58, 60, 62-64.
[65] Priesdorff, *Soldatisches Führertum,* VIII, 311.
[66] *Memoirs,* I, 65.
[67] Heinrich Otto Meisner, ed., *Kaiser Friedrich III: Tagebücher von 1848-1866* (Leipzig, 1929), p. 405; entries of 12 and 13 Sept. 1865.
[68] *Memoirs,* I, 65-66.

dared to select his adjutant behind the back of the Military Cabinet."
Signatura temporis.[69]

On 1 February 1866, he wrote of Stosch: "He pleases me greatly, inspires trust, and can become instructive and stimulating after the first self-consciousness is overcome."[70] He avoided political matters at a meeting with Stosch a short time later.[71]

Professional growth, an enlarging circle of acquaintances, and frustration were thus the keynotes of Albrecht von Stosch's career up to his forty-eighth birthday. Scarcely had he begun to surmount the bars to promotion and win the approbation of his superiors when he was seriously injured. By 1866, after two years of semi-invalidism, he had barely conquered his infirmity by exercise of great strength of will. It seemed as if fate had singled him out for misfortune. There was little indication that he stood on the threshold of professional success after years of a slow upward climb.

His promotion had been persistently retarded and checked because of an alleged liberalism; it is thus important to examine his opinions and the reasons for his liberal reputation. Prior to 1848 Stosch believed in a simple Christian and moral solution to the problems of the day. Let the population be truly religious, he seems to say, and all political difficulties will be resolved. The disorderly mobs of 1848 caused him to champion the suppression of rebellion by force, to back the neoabsolutist conservative party, and to publish articles defending the Army. More significantly, perhaps, his nascent German nationalism found clearer expression. Unlike the ultrareactionaries, who at this time numbered Bismarck in their ranks, Stosch favored the *Kleindeutsch* solution of the German question; unification was to be wrought by Prussia's excluding Austria from German affairs. However, unlike the nationalist liberals, he favored use of the Prussian Army to bring the new state into being. This opinion continued to divide him from the liberal Progressive party, which gained a majority in Prussia in the sixties. He supported the reorganization of the Army, which the Progressives vehemently opposed. They felt that the military reforms of Roon and Bismarck were directed at their basic prin-

---

[69] Entry of 10 Jan. 1866, Meisner, *Friedrichs Tagebücher, 1848-1866*, p. 407.
[70] *Ibid.*, p. 409. [71] *Memoirs*, I, 69.

ciples; Stosch held that a stronger army was necessary to achieve unification. At the same time, he was critical of the ultrareactionaries who were grouped around General von Manteuffel, Chief of the Military Cabinet. He considered their uncompromising and sycophantic influence on the King detrimental to the Army. His opinions, maintained with startling consistency, were predominantly nationalist and conservative and were based on practical considerations rather than on theoretical principles. Only under an extremely reactionary regime could he have been thought a liberal at all; it is significant that even the Military Cabinet was unable to find anything politically objectionable about him.

Why then was his career checked by a liberal reputation? In part, great independence of mind, boldness in expressing his beliefs, and an evident ambition aroused the suspicions of his superiors. Moreover, people of pronounced liberal views were his intimate friends. He was associated with the liberal writer and publicist Gustav Freytag and the liberal Premier of Baden, Baron Franz von Roggenbach. He was coming into increasing contact with the court of the Crown Prince and the Crown Princess, who were open enemies of governmental policies. These ties of friendship were not the result of liberal principles, but of a common interest in politics and devotion to *Kleindeutsch* unity. Nor can the appeal of Stosch's character—his integrity, common sense, practicality, and outspokenness—be discounted. These friendships coupled with bold independence were quite enough to scotch the career of a man whom the liberal majority in Prussia would have considered an arch-conservative. This duality between his political reputation and his actual beliefs was to dog Stosch throughout his life.

II

MILITARY SUCCESS AND
POLITICAL ACTIVITY

1

In April 1866, while Stosch was consoling himself for the professional disappointments of the previous year with the reflection that his leg would now have more time to heal, his chances of advancement were brightening. He had maintained close relations with the Crown Prince, whose pro-English proclivities in foreign policy and reliance on the anti-Prussian counsels of Stockmar the younger disturbed him. The Crown Prince turned to Stosch as the Austro-Prussian conflict drew nearer. Like most of his contemporaries, Stosch did not foresee the outbreak of war; William's love of peace, he believed, would triumph over "Bismarck's inclination to play *va banque.*" Nevertheless, military preparations were being made. Frederick William approached him through von Normann to ask whether he would accept the post of Quartermaster General (*Oberquartiermeister*), equivalent to assistant Chief of Staff, if the Crown Prince received the command of an Army. Stosch agreed, although he did not believe that anything would come of the proposal. When mobilization was ordered, he was greatly concerned lest he be ignored. However, the Military Cabinet wired his superior, General von Schack, inquiring whether the ambitious Colonel was physically fit for duty. Schack replied in the affirmative, and Stosch's appointment as Quartermaster General of the Prussian Second Army, under the command of the Crown Prince, followed on 18 May 1866.[1] His immediate su-

[1] *Memoirs,* I, 71-72. Schröder, *Stosch,* p. 112, erroneously gives the date of his appointment as May 8. It is of interest that Schack attempted to keep Stosch as chief of staff to the Fourth Corps. Moltke, *Militärische Werke,* I, Theil II, 163 n.

perior was General Leonhard von Blumenthal, Chief of Staff designate, a commander of definite military talent, but hampered by little
understanding of men and an overbold and egotistical manner.

Colonel von Stosch immediately left Magdeburg for Berlin.
The Chief of the General Staff, Count von Moltke, said that he had
no immediate duties, for war was not imminent. His main object should be "to put the first Chief's [Blumenthal's] gifted ideas
into effect." The King cordially received him and declared that
he and Blumenthal had been chosen as veteran councilors for the
"still young and inexperienced" Frederick William, a man of thirty-
four. Stosch attended an indecisive "council of war" on 25 May,
at which the King; Bismarck; Roon, the War Minister; Moltke;
Tresckow, Chief of the Military Cabinet; the Crown Prince and
his cousin, Prince Frederick Karl, commander of the First Army,
and their staffs were present.[2] Stosch wrote of the three-hour
meeting: "Bismarck was decidedly the clearest and keenest. I
had the conviction that he directed the whole state proceedings
with the sole purpose of influencing the King for war." As they
emerged, Frederick William remarked with disgust: "We know
just as much as we did before—the King does not want to [go to
war], but Bismarck does."[3] Stosch still believed that Bismarck
would not be able to shake William's desire for peace, which seemed
more certain with the passage of each day. Nevertheless, he
drafted a letter to the King from the Crown Prince stressing the
necessity for Frederick William's presence in Silesia to gain acquaintance with his troops and the terrain. The request received
William's consent, and the first week of June found Stosch engaged
in his duties.[4] A subordinate and friend, Verdy, describes him
at this time:

General von Stosch had a tall, imposing figure and always carried
himself rigidly erect, even though he limped slightly. . . . Only his very
healthy and powerful nature enabled him to overcome . . . [the operation
on his leg]. He was also the picture of virile strength, which was expressed in indefatigable activity. His powerful frame was surmounted
by an expressive head, out of which two shrewd eyes looked sharply

[2] Memoirs, I, 73-74. On Moltke's relations with Stosch at this period, see
Moltke, Militärische Werke, I, Theil II, 150-51, 163, 165-67, 265.
[3] Stosch to his wife, 26 May 1866, Memoirs, I, 75.
[4] Ibid., I, 75-78.

into the world, and his candid features gave the impression that he grew more joyful the more difficult a situation became. The back of his dark head showed . . . a wide white swathe, which had turned this color in the night following his accident.

An unusual energy, which could attack details industriously, but which, in all emergencies, proved to be of the greatest profit for the whole, emanated from his entire being, his speech, and the mode and manner of his behavior. Proof of this was later shown in his speedy familiarization with partially and completely foreign spheres, as Commissary General of the Army in the War of 1870-1871 and next as Chief of the Admiralty. . . . Quick and energetic in his decisions, brief and precise in all that he said, blunt in all his methods of expression, he was generally considered a gruff character. However, the person who came into contact with him for a long time and to whom his trust afforded the opportunity to penetrate his inner nature soon recognized that under this exterior was hidden a warm and loyal heart. . . .

The Crown Prince . . . was attached to him to a high degree. During the war, the Prince once said: "As soon as I see Stosch, if only from afar, I get an extraordinary feeling of wellbeing; it is always a pleasure to me when I see his splendid countenance." The Crown Prince loved the frankness with which the General always spoke to him and knew that he could depend upon his clear judgment as well as his personal devotion. The relations between them were strengthened more and more during the course of the war. . . . .[5]

The actual operation of the General Staff system depended upon the personalities involved. While officially the Chief of Staff and his assistant, the Quartermaster General, could only advise the Commander to issue orders, in practice the Chief of Staff was often the dominant figure. During the campaign of 1866 against Austria, the Chief of Staff of the Prussian Second Army, von Blumenthal, was the real field commander; he initiated and drafted almost all orders which were issued in the name of the Crown Prince. Stosch had the opportunity to dictate orders only in the absence of his Chief, and documents from his hand are few.[6] It is significant, nonetheless, that the Crown Prince unfailingly linked Stosch's name with Blumenthal's as responsible for

[5] Julius von Verdy du Vernois, "Im Hauptquartier der II (schlesischen) Armee 1866," *Deutsche Rundschau,* CI (Oct.-Dec. 1899), 71-72.

[6] Oscar von Lettow-Vorbeck, *Geschichte des Krieges von 1866 in Deutschland* (Berlin, 1899), II, 130.

his military success.[7]   Stosch's influence on the campaign emerged gradually as the Prussian Armies advanced.

As the Second Army moved forward,[8] its headquarters became less comfortable, and Stosch's leg caused him much suffering.   He ignored his pain and kept hard at his duties.   In his official capacity he sucessfully worked for the appointment of the Crown Prince as Civil Governor of Silesia in order that complete advantage might be taken of the resources of the province.   He was impressed by Frederick William's ability to make himself popular with the troops, but hoped that he would know how to be "harsh and strict at the proper time," for these characteristics were the "healthiest foundation for amiability" in a commander.   Stosch wished him to devote more attention to the details of daily routine, a continual plaint until 1888.   As his principal assistants the Quartermaster General had Verdy du Vernois, "who is developing the unusual talents of asking the right questions, giving the right instructions, forming correct opinions of people and synthesizing reports correctly," and Hahnke, "a very gifted and excellent staff officer."   The staff waited impatiently at Neisse for the war to begin.   Blumenthal, with his arrogant and tactless nature, was not an easy chief to work with, particularly for so independent a man as Stosch, who early felt that the Chief of Staff was dissatisfied with his views.   He had Verdy put his ideas before Blumenthal.   This method succeeded, and good relations were maintained throughout the campaign.[9]

On 15 June 1866, Stosch was promoted to Brigadier General (*General-major*).   The orders for the advance of the Army into Austrian territory followed soon thereafter.   By 26 June the Sec-

[7] *Memoirs,* I, 99, 114; Meisner, *Friedrichs Tagebücher, 1848-1866,* p. 451; Frederick William to Prince Carl of Hohenzollern, 27 January 1867, in Carol I, King of Rumania, *Aus dem Leben König Karls von Rumanien* (Stuttgart, 1894), I, 175.

[8] The role of the Crown Prince's Army in Moltke's plan of campaign was to form the left wing of the German forces which were extended on a front of over two hundred miles.   Moltke, governed by the slow progress of Prince Frederick Karl's First Army, which contrasted unfavorably with the rapid advance of the Second Army, altered his original plan of having the Armies concentrate at Gitschin and decided to have them meet on the battlefield.   See the brief discussion in Earle, *Makers of Modern Strategy,* pp. 182-85.

[9] *Memoirs,* I, 78-81.   It is interesting to note that the Crown Prince had served in a similar intercessionary role in 1864.   Anneliese Klein-Wuttig, *Politik und Kriegführung in den deutschen Einigungskriegen 1864, 1866 und 1870/71* (Berlin-Grünewald, 1934), p. 13.

ond Army had made its quarters at Braunau in Bohemia, although
Stosch's place at the Crown Prince's side kept him from seeing
anything of the enemy.   On the same day, much to the surprise
of Second Army Headquarters, the advance guard of the subordinate Fifth Corps occupied the small town of Nachod, after meeting
only token resistance.[10]   On 27 June Stosch, who was riding with
the Crown Prince and Blumenthal toward Nachod, heard the roar
of cannon.   They passed through the deserted streets of the village
and soon found themselves in the midst of lively small arms fire.
The Crown Prince, oblivious to danger, rode steadily forward.
His adjutant requested Stosch to ask him to withdraw.   The General replied: "Yes, you are quite right; but I am under fire for
the first time in my life.   Ask General Blumenthal who has already
had much combat experience."   Blumenthal consented, and they
changed direction.[11]   Leaving the Crown Prince, Stosch rode forward and encountered Verdy, who told him of reinforcements coming up.   This news made the "General smile with pleasure and he
said: 'Up to now things have been rather slow, but now we will see
some action.' "   He soon observed a retreating Prussian battery and
turned it back into battle.   Supported by Verdy, he ordered the
road freed for advancing infantry, thus clearing the way for their
direct intervention.   Then he turned to Verdy and remarked:
"Now everything will take care of itself.   Let us find out where
the Crown Prince is."   Frederick William was greatly impressed
by Stosch's decisive action.[12]   If he had not taken this "entirely
instinctive" measure to secure prompt reinforcements, the advance
guard of the Fifth Corps, with its commander, General von Steinmetz, would have been cut off, with incalculable results on the tide

[10] *Memoirs,* I, 81-85.   The battle of Nachod of 27 June 1866 was one of
the "classic" battles studied in the military academies of the world.   Approximately 30,000 Austrians were defeated by the same number of Prussians.
Austrian casualties amounted to 5,719 and Prussian, 112.
[11] *Ibid.,* I, 85; Verdy, "Im Hauptquartier," *Deutsche Rundschau,* CI, 68,
249-50, CII, 57-58. Stosch, whose account of his baptism of fire is based on his
diaries of the time, places it during the battle of Nachod. Verdy, who bases his
account on memory, places it during the battle of Koniggrätz. It is probable
that Verdy was told this incident by the Crown Prince's Adjutant Mischke and
in his memory confused the two battles.
[12] *Memoirs,* I, 85-86; Meisner, *Friedrichs Tagebücher, 1848-1866,* p. 433;
Verdy "Im Hauptquartier," *Deutsche Rundschau,* CI, 250-52. Stosch's account
of his action is thus supported by both Verdy and the Crown Prince. Cf. Priesdorff, *Soldatiches Führertum,* VIII, 311-12.

of battle. This fact was unknown to Stosch at the time. His first reaction, after the victory, was horror at the sight of the casualties and pride at the Prussian success. The arrival of a report that the retreating Austrians had received reinforcements caused Stosch immediately to order troops to Steinmetz's support, an action afterwards sanctioned by the Second Army Commander. Disgusted with the laughing and joking between unwounded Austrian prisoners and the victorious Prussian officers, Stosch halted the fraternization with the uncompromising rebuke that an "unwounded captured officer was a vile contemptible fellow [*Hundesfott*], until a more complete investigation" proved otherwise. He was extremely pleased with the actions of the common soldiers during the battle. The respect they showed him made him proud "to be a Prussian" like them. This confidence in the Prussian soldiers was to increase as a result of their actions at Koniggrätz.[13]

Stosch's influence on this decisive battle of 3 July 1866 was of the greatest importance. He persuaded the Crown Prince to issue an order on 2 July to take effect early on the morrow, which directed the advance of reinforced Prussian troops toward the enemy.[14] This action was one of the main factors which contributed to Prussian success. He wrote later of his decision:

. . . before the battle of Koniggrätz, when I had to give orders in the absence of Blumenthal, I, entirely unobserved, left Moltke's advice out of consideration and acted simply under the impression of the momentary situation, so successfully that we intervened earlier and more decisively than was expected by higher headquarters.[15]

[13] *Memoirs*, I, 85-92.　　　　[14] *Ibid.*, I, 91.

[15] Stosch to Freytag, Oestrich, 28 July 1891, Memoirs, III, 256. It may seem questionable that at two of the most important battles of the campaign, Stosch intervened decisively. Support for his action at Nachod is corroborated by other accounts (see n. 12). However, the Crown Prince's diary does not mention Stosch's part in the issuance of the order of 2 July (Meisner, *Friedrichs Tagebücher, 1848-1866,* p. 443) nor does Blumenthal (Count Albrecht von Blumenthal, ed., *Journals of Field Marshal Count von Blumenthal for 1866 and 1870-1871* [London, 1903], pp. 37-39) nor Verdy ("Im Hauptquartier," *Deutsche Rundschau,* CI, 415-16, 425). However, neither Blumenthal nor Verdy were present at the time the order was issued, as their accounts supported by Lettow-Vorbeck (*Geschichte des Krieges von 1866,* II, 413) show. Stosch's account is based not only upon his memory twenty-five years later (the letter of 1891 cited above), but on his diary at the time (*Memoirs,* I, 91). There is nothing implausible in this account. The Crown Prince rarely took the initiative in issuing orders and depended on his chief of staff Blumenthal for advice (see, for example, Prince Frederick Karl, *Denkwürdigkeiten* [4th ed.; Stuttgart and

He was little more than an observer during the battle itself. He had no doubts of Prussian triumph, after his first glance at the battlefield. This assurance of victory was felt by the "students" on the Crown Prince's staff, who before the battle ended compared his march to the support of Prince Frederick Karl's First Army with Blücher's arrival on the battlefield of Waterloo. In fact, the Second Army's advance decided the issue. Royal Headquarters was also busy with historical comparisons. The King saw the battle as a second Auerstädt, the catastrophic defeat of the Prussians in 1806. After the battle, William greeted the first news of success from the Crown Prince with the remark that it was not one at all, because the enemy had withdrawn in full order. He was immediately reminded that orders had been received to stop pursuit, a decision which he would not alter. In his diary Stosch bemoaned the fact that fatigue from the old leg wound prevented him from personally requesting that the direction of the pursuit be entrusted to him. He ended this "best and greatest day in Prussian history" by making his soldier's bed on the ground.[16]

The next morning, 4 July 1866, the news arrived that the King was ready to conclude an armistice, and Stosch accompanied the Crown Prince to Royal Headquarters to protest. He advised Frederick William to suggest stiff conditions which would have to be met before an acceptable armistice was agreed upon.[17] William was temporarily absent, so the Crown Prince explained his demands to Bismarck, Roon, and Moltke. The Chief of the General Staff immediately objected that the Prussians needed an armistice, their

---

Leipzig, 1910], II, 75). In his chief of staff's absence, it was natural that he would turn to his "assistant Chief of Staff," Quartermaster General von Stosch, whose opinion he unquestionably valued. Moreover, Stosch's accounts are substantiated by an independent and even hostile (see chapter III below) source. Prince Frederick Karl (*Denkwürdigkeiten*, II, 76) declares that the order was issued by Stosch, i.e., at his suggestion. In the absence of any positive statement by the Crown Prince, this evidence seems practically conclusive.

[16] *Memoirs*, I, 91-94.

[17] It is quite possible that Stosch had a hand in originating these conditions. His diary is not clear on this point (*Memoirs*, I, 94). It reads: "It had been agreed among us [Stosch, the Crown Prince, and probably Blumenthal] to accept a three-day armistice only under the condition that the Austrians evacuate the three fortresses Josefstadt, Königgrätz, and Theresienstadt. Then we would admit the Elbe as the line of demarcation." Blumenthal (*Journals*, pp. 43-44) and the Crown Prince (Meisner, *Friedrichs Tagebücher, 1848-1866*, pp. 453-54) shed no light on the person who originated these conditions.

troops were exhausted, and Königgrätz "was not important." The
Crown Prince countered with the enumeration of the more than
one hundred cannon and approximately twenty thousand prisoners
captured and suggested that instant pursuit was required and an
armistice was totally inadmissible. Finally agreement was reached
on an armistice, incorporating the Crown Prince's requirements.
He took the responsibility for securing the King's consent. Then
he turned to Bismarck and asked what he wanted from the war.
The Minister-President of Prussia listed his proposals, and the
Crown Prince stressed the necessity of bringing to a close the internal constitutional conflict in Prussia over the reorganization of the
Army and the voting of the budget. The Minister-President agreed,
and the antagonism between him and Frederick William was temporarily at an end. The first result of the understanding was an
invitation from Bismarck to dinner.[18] Stosch wrote:

> It was the first time that I encountered Bismarck personally, and I
> am glad to acknowledge that I was actually overpowered by the im-
> pression I received of him. The clarity and grandeur of his views gave
> me the greatest pleasure. He was assured and original in every direc-
> tion, and each thought included a whole world. The fact that we ate
> and drank quite excellently besides did not injure the happy operation
> of Bismarck's powers of enchantment.[19]

Upon the return of the King, the Crown Prince secured his approval of the condition for an armistice. In the meantime Royal
Headquarters had received Blumenthal's protest against Moltke's
recent troop dispositions, which would have confused the operational areas of the First and Second Armies. Stosch supported Blumenthal's objections, and Moltke reluctantly consented to the new
disposition which placed the greater burden of pursuit upon the
Crown Prince's Army. Stosch took advantage of his presence at
Royal Headquarters to consult a doctor about his old leg wound,
which was troubling him. ". . . He wished to put me in bed,
send me home, amputate, and perform other similar amenities."
Nothing daunted, Stosch returned to work and rode forward with
the Army into Bohemia and Moravia. The overpowering effect of
Königgrätz became clearer each day the Army advanced, taking

[18] *Memoirs*, I, 94-95, 97-98.   [19] *Ibid.*, I, 95.

prisoners. Fortunately for Stosch's health, the Army's rate of advance slowed after July 11.[20]

However, Moltke's "orders" soon brought Stosch into the saddle once more. On 15 July the Crown Prince received highly confused instructions, together with unofficial reports of Moltke's complaints at the slow rate of march of the Second Army. Blumenthal was incensed, and Frederick William threatened to resign. Stosch was sent to Royal Headquarters to point out the distance Frederick William's troops had covered and to emphasize that if the Second Army was not proceeding in the right direction, it had acted only at Moltke's "orders." He conferred with the King, Moltke Tresckow, Roon and Bismarck, and he obtained approval of the Crown Prince's dispositions and plans.[21]

On 16 July General von Stosch, at the request of the Crown Prince, had a long conversation with Bismarck at Royal Headquarters in Brunn. He arrived late in the morning, found that the Minister was still in bed, and was amused to see that the "gentlemen of the Foreign Office speak of their chief with as holy a respect as the believers of the Prophet . . . ." After an hour, he was admitted and cordially received by Bismarck, as soon as he heard from whom Stosch came. The Minister developed the idea that Austria should be excluded from Germany, but suffer no territorial losses, for Prussia would need Austrian support later. Napoleon's intervention for peace, he predicted, would gain nothing for France. He remarked that "dazzling military success was the best prop of the arts of diplomacy." Turning to the domestic scene, he noted that the Crown Prince's backing was necessary for him to "steer a liberal course."[22]

The peace negotiations with Austria were conducted from the Castle of Nikolsburg on the Austro-Moravia border. The main difficulty that Bismarck encountered in the negotiations came from his own sovereign, William I, who did not want to dethrone any

[20] *Ibid.*, I, 95-100.

[21] *Ibid.*, I, 101-2; Blumenthal, *Journals*, pp. 49-51; Meisner, *Friedrichs Tagebücher, 1848-1866*, pp. 463-65. All orders came officially on the authority of the King, not Moltke. Stosch, when he wrote of "Moltke's orders," was, of course, referring to their real originator. On Moltke's increasing independence in issuing orders, see Craig, *Politics of the Prussian Army*, pp. 194-95.

[22] Stosch to Karl v. Normann, Prodlitz, 17 July 1866, *Memoirs*, I, 102-3.

German monarch, but desired to gain territory from Austria. Here the Prussian Premier made use of his new alliance with the Crown Prince. He secured Frederick William's wholehearted support for a peace which excluded Austria from Germany while maintaining its territorial integrity and which dethroned several German Princes, whose lands were annexed to Prussia. Stosch took no direct part in the discussions, but he accompanied his royal chief to Nikolsburg and talked over everything with him. Frederick William, who had an exaggerated regard for princely prerogative, regarded the dethronement of the German monarchs with some misgiving. While riding with his Quartermaster General, he suggested that they be "mediatized"—that is, given small estates of which they would be absolute sovereigns. Stosch remarked, "somewhat incautiously," that "then they will have no power, and a prince without power is a comical figure." Frederick William, taking this as a description of his own position, put the spurs to his horse and galloped forward. However, in a few minutes he relented and his blunt General was readmitted to favor.

The opinion that Frederick William formed of Stosch in 1866 was to change little throughout his life. No doubt the General's interventions at Nachod and before Königgrätz had much to do with this good opinion, as did his general military conduct. Stosch himself considered his greatest service in the war to have been the maintenance of good relations between the Crown Prince and Blumenthal, a task which was eased when the Chief of Staff saw that his second-in-command was content to stay in the background. Stosch worked to secure unanimity, because he felt that the Royal Commander would remain firm, if his advisers were agreed among themselves. Moreover, he considered Blumenthal to be an excellent field commander, but not an exceptional Chief of Staff, since he always needed someone "to put his ideas into effect," as Moltke had said.[23]

Stosch's views on the conduct of the war found expression[24] in an anonymous brief history,[25] which he wrote at Freytag's re-

[23] *Ibid.*, I, 103-14.

[24] Cf. Stosch to Holtzendorff, 20 Aug. 1866, *ibid.*, I, 113-14, which presents some of his views on the war.

[25] [Albrecht von Stosch], "Der Deutsche Krieg im Jahre 1866," *Die Grenzboten*, 1866, XXV, vol. IV, 201-10, 241-47, 295-303, 337-48, 385-92, 449-53.

quest.[26] The six articles in this series, the best organized that he wrote for *Die Grenzboten,* discussed the strength of the opposing armies, the campaigns, and the military consequences of the war. Stosch was very much amused when Verdy praised them, and he was forced to pretend total ignorance of their authorship.[27]

Although military operations were now at an end, the Second Army remained in Bohemia for about six weeks. Stosch continued to enjoy the marked favor of the Crown Prince. This was not without its annoyances, both great and small; in one letter he wryly remarked: "Despite all the honor, hunger often bothers me . . . at the Crown Princely table." His friendship with the heir to the throne attracted the attention of all round him. He wrote on 27 July 1866: "The world begins to believe in my power, entirely forgetting that the young Prince himself has none yet. . . ." He attributed at least a portion of his "quite extraordinary favor" to the Crown Princess; Frederick William, he observed, "is, above all things, his wife's husband; she determines the course of his ideas, even when far from him, and it is touching to see how he depends on her." When the Crown Prince made a farewell speech to all his assembled staff officers on 8 August, he told Stosch that "the bond between us is tied for all time." However, the independent and ambitious General had had enough "court air" to last him for life. "It would be a great sacrifice if I were placed in the same relation to the Prince," he wrote. The Chief of the Military Cabinet, von Tresckow, said that he would probably receive a brigade, which he preferred.

The friendship with the heir to the throne had already begun to play a large part in his life. He strongly disapproved of the Crown Princess' extreme activity in hospital work and her great generosity toward benevolent causes, both qualities which he held to be more English than German. At the same time, he did not doubt her knowledge, keenness, or self-confidence. Politically, he believed, the Crown Prince should be firmly allied with the King and Bismarck against particularistic and dynastic interests. As the guest of the royal couple, Stosch stayed for a week at Erd-

[26] Helmolt, *Freytag an Stosch,* pp. 10, 12.
[27] *Memoirs,* I, 106. See also pp. 110, 122, 124.

mannsdorf in September 1866. The question of the Crown Prince's becoming Governor-General of Hanover was first raised here. The royal pair was inclined to attach conditions and to stress the difficulties of the position. Stosch strongly urged them to accept, believing that the Crown Prince should beware of falling into a negative attitude toward governmental affairs. A prince who was content with private life alone "could not expect to be considered a great man." These remarks were well received. He also attempted to combat the "radical" views of Victoria, who enchanted him with her conversational powers. She was "very much surprised" to be informed bluntly that her "stormy struggles for reform" were the result of her extreme youth. He explained to her that lasting innovation could be produced only slowly, "doubly slowly" if one wished not to destroy, but to reform. This doctrine of conservative development visibly impressed her.

At the end of the Austrian occupation, Stosch was relieved of his duties and transferred temporarily to the retired list with the rights of a brigade commander and the option of choosing his own dwelling place. High praise and the most coveted Prussian military decoration, the order *Pour le mérite,* were conferred upon him.[28] On 27 September 1866 he was named temporary Director of the Military Economic Department of the War Ministry, an appointment which became permanent on 18 December. His chief reason for accepting the position was his friendship with the Crown Prince, who still wanted him to enter his entourage. This Stosch declined, but, as a compromise, accepted the Berlin post, in order to be available for consultation.[29]

The Military Economic Department,[30] which was one of the two main sections of the War Ministry and included supervision of all Army administrative and supply matters, had shown serious defects

[28] *Ibid.,* I, 103-17. The decoration was granted on the warm recommendation of the Crown Prince to the King. Priesdorff, *Soldatisches Führertum,* VIII, 308.

[29] *Memoirs,* I, 118; Schröder, *Stosch,* p. 112.

[30] For technical details of his administration, see *Memoirs,* I, 118-20, 124, 125, 134-35, 146-47, 180, 187; Curt Jany, *Geschichte der Königliche Preussische Armee* (Berlin, 1934), IV, 122-24, 260-61, 291; Edwin A. Pratt, *The Rise of Rail-Power in War and Conquest, 1833-1914* (Philadelphia, 1916), pp. 106-10.

during the Seven Weeks' War with Austria,[31] and Stosch was appointed to reorganize it. Here he had the opportunity to put into practice the reforming ideas he had expressed in his *Die Grenzboten* articles. The post had the additional advantage of keeping him well-informed on Prussia's military strength and war plans. Moreover, his position in the Ministry was an "extremely independent" one. War Minister Albrecht von Roon, who was in poor health and worn out, was nearly as opposed as William I to change in the Army. (William opposed even the introduction of drawers for the common soldier, until Stosch overcame his reluctance.) However, Roon took little interest in Stosch's activity and rarely corrected his written projects of reform. The War Minister spoke with his subordinate only twice on business in all Stosch's four years at the Ministry. Stosch attempted to gain his backing for new plans and projects, such as the reformation of field and fortress artillery according to the lessons of 1866; "Roon acknowledged the correctness of my views in everything, but nothing happened." Stosch maintains that had his views on the reform of the artillery been adopted, there would have been much greater economy of lives and material during the Franco-German War. Within his own sphere of supply, he had a comparatively free hand to reorganize the Army. Spurred on by ambition, love for hard work, and the belief that war with France was soon to be expected, he channeled his energies into the daily tasks of military administration. As a member of commissions to improve the War Ministry and by annual tours of inspection, he was able to exert considerable influence toward improvement of the Army in accordance with the experiences of 1866.[32]

2

The Prussian triumph in the Seven Weeks' War was followed by complex negotiations between Bismarck and the North German states over their entrance into one confederation. Many of these

---

[31] Wilhelm Engelhardt, "Rückblicke auf die Verpflegungsverhältnisse im Kriege 1870-1871," *Beihefte zum Militärwochenblatt,* 1901, p. 483.

[32] *Memoirs,* I, 118-19, 123, 126, 128-30, 134, 137. Cf. Memoirs, III, 242, Stosch to Roggenbach, Oestrich, 6 Dec. 1890: "I have read the Roon matter [memoirs?] with the greatest interest. Roon has risen tremendously in my estimation. When I entered the War Ministry, he was decidedly worn-out and ruined."

arrangements concluded in 1866-1867 continued in force until the fall of the German Empire in 1918. Stosch played at this time, as well as later in the sixties, a major role in the discussions with the Saxons concerning their relation to the Prussian Army. In these military talks something of his underlying political motivation emerges clearly and the nature of his dealings with Bismarck is also illuminated.

Austria's defeat in 1866 meant the defeat also of its ally, the Kingdom of Saxony. By the Treaty of Nickolsburg, the territorial integrity of Saxony was guaranteed. However, Prussia reserved the right to treat separately with Saxony on the war indemnity and the future Saxon position in the North German Confederation. It was even conceivable that Prussia would dethrone the Saxon dynasty.[33] The negotiations were conducted in an atmosphere of mutual suspicion. Bismarck desired, in general, the voluntary entrance of Saxony into the North German Confederation, with a common parliament and central control of foreign affairs and the Army. The Saxons wanted to maintain as much autonomy as possible, and King Johann particularly wished to protect his military prerogatives. Therefore, it was in military matters that the greatest difficulty was encountered. Negotiations began in September 1866 at Berlin, with General von Fabrice representing the Saxons, and General von Podbielski, Director of the General War Department of the War Ministry, representing the Prussians. They drew up a convention which yielded to practically all the Saxon demands. Such an agreement was possible only because Bismarck was absent from the capital.

[33] Fritz Dickmann, *Militärpolitischen Beziehungen zwischen Preussen und Sachsen 1866-1870: Ein Beitrag zur Entstehungsgeschichte des Norddeutsche Bundes* (Munich, 1929), p. 13. For brief accounts, see Helmut Klocke, "Die Sächsische Politik und der Norddeutsche Bund," *Neue Archiv fur Sächsische Geschichte und Altertumskunde,* XLVIII (1928), 97-163, and Otto Becker, *Bismarcks Ringen um Deutschlands Gestaltung* (Heidelburg, [1958]), pp. 208-10, 338-46. Cf. Richard Dietrich, "Der Preussisch-sächsische Friedensschluss von 21. Oktober 1866," *Jahrbuch fur die Geschichte Mittel-und Ostdeutschlands,* IV (1955), 109-56. The chronology and details of the Prussian-Saxon military negotiations were totally confused until Dickmann's excellent monograph appeared. Based upon the documents of the Saxon and Prussian archives, liberally supplemented by published works, Dickmann makes clear the errors of both Stosch (*Memoirs,* I, 121, 274), and Bismarck (Otto, Prince von Bismarck, *Die Gesammelten Werke* [Berlin, 1924-1932], XV, 299)—to mention only two irreconcilable accounts.

The text of the convention reached William after reports of its conclusion had been published in the newspapers. The press "leak" greatly angered him. Previously sympathetic to the pro-Saxon court faction led by his wife, Augusta, a Saxon princess, he was now more inclined to lend an ear to the counsels of the anti-Saxon faction captained by his son, Frederick William. The Crown Prince was influenced by Stosch's anti-Saxon advice, given under the urging of Gustav Freytag, who wished the complete annexation of the Saxon Kingdom to Prussia. William desired nothing less than the incorporation of the Saxon Army into the Prussian, leaving to King Johann the sole right of employing Saxon troops to quell internal disorder. Governed by these views, and supported by the Crown Prince, William refused to sanction the Podbielski-Fabrice Convention. The Prussian-Saxon peace treaty of 21 October 1866 postponed any consideration of the military question until the commencement of negotiations over the establishment of the North German Confederation.[34]

By January 1867 Prussia was more willing to compromise. Bismarck had returned to Berlin with the realization that the support of Saxony, the second largest North German state, would greatly facilitate the establishment of the Confederation. Under William's urging he held firm to the principle that the King of Prussia should be *Bundesfeldherr* (Commander in Chief of the Confederation) in fact as well as in name, but he was now more inclined to yield on points of detail. The actual negotiation of a new draft military convention was intrusted to Brigadier General von Stosch, Podbielski having proved himself incapable of arriving at an agreement acceptable to William. Dickmann, the historian of the discussions, considers Stosch a poor choice, for, despite his administrative talents, he was too blunt and outspoken to be a successful diplomat. The General's instructions[35] from the War

---

[34] *Memoirs*, I, 121-33; Dickmann, *Militärpolitischen Beziehungen*, chap. i, and pp. 105-6, 111.

[35] Stosch's memory betrays him in *Memoirs*, I, 120, when he states that he received no instructions. This portion of his recollections written on detailed negotiations under the stress of public controversy in 1890 (?) (*Memoirs*, I, 274) must be differentiated from those written in a calm and reflective mood. His letters written at the time have been used to supplement Dickmann's account, as have his recollections of his interview with Bismarck, which naturally made a strong impress upon his memory.

Ministry warned him that the Saxons would attempt to achieve a privileged position in the Confederation. At the same time, he was instructed to proceed circumspectly in order to forestall Saxon leadership of the opposition to Prussia within the Confederation. More specifically, he was told to assent to the Saxons' desire for a separate military administration, if they assumed the financial burden of it. Saxony's military contribution was to be set at a fixed annual sum per soldier with any excess over expenses (as well as any deficit) becoming the responsibility of the Confederation treasury. The soldier's oath of allegiance was to be taken to William as *Bundesfeldherr,* not as King of Prussia. The question of military appointments was left open, but the King of Saxony was to be consulted about them. The *Bundesfeldherr* was to have complete control over the stationing of troops. The instructions skirted the question whether Prussian military legislation was to be introduced into the Saxon Army formally by an act of the Saxon Chambers or merely considered an implicit concession when Saxony ratified the North German Constitution. These instructions from the War Ministry were in general accord with Bismarck's views that the *Bundesfeldherr* should have complete control over the garrisoning of troops and that the oath of allegiance should be required of all ranks, while the King of Saxony could be allowed to appoint all officers and to maintain a separate military administration.

The Prussian Minister-President believed that the concessions he offered were sufficient to secure Saxony's approval of a military convention. As a result, his anger was great when he learned that Saxon General von Fabrice was raising difficulties over the terms. At this juncture his mistrust of Saxony overcame his desire for its support. Stosch, oblivious of this temporary shift in the Minister-President's views, submitted a draft convention to the Foreign Office, which was in strict accord with neither the instructions of the War Ministry nor Bismarck's opinions. By this draft convention, the Saxons were granted a separate War Ministry and were left in direct command of their officers. The King of Saxony named all low-ranking officers. He appointed generals in conjunction with the *Bundesfeldherr,* while fortress commanders were chosen by the *Bundesfeldherr* alone. The generals and fortress commanders were to swear to carry out their duties "only in the interest of the North German Confederation and of the orders of the *Bundesfeldherr*." The latter received the right to station troops as he pleased in wartime, but in peace he had to consult the Saxons. The questions of the common soldier's oath of allegiance and the disposal of surpluses from the Saxon military contributions were unresolved. Stosch, modifying his extreme anti-Saxon views either under the pressure of actual experience, the conciliatory attitude of Moltke and Roon, or under the influence of his instructions, felt that he had extracted all possible concessions. He was pleased by the congratulations of Bismarck's Foreign Office representative, who promised to inform the General of his chief's reactions.[36] Bismarck's reception of the draft convention stands out most clearly in Stosch's own account:

> After a few days Bismarck summoned me. He had previously seen in me a man who openly honored his high spirit and his restless energy, and, as long as I possessed a certain importance for him in his efforts to reach an understanding with the Crown Prince, I could always boast of his great courtesy. Now I was to him just another temporary assistant and I had to be made to feel that.
>
> He permitted me to sit down and went over my work with me like a schoolmaster does with the opus of a stupid and refractory pupil. There was not one good thing in it. From the inaccessible heights of his superiority, he overwhelmed me with the full abundance of his anger and the pointed arrows of his scorn. He demonstrated that I had seriously wronged King and Fatherland, Emperor [*sic*] and future Empire.
>
> Every objection was cut off short. I could do nothing but remain silent and leave.[37]

This scene was significant as a foreshadowing of the future relations between these two strong-willed, ambitious men. The final break between them did not come until ten years later. It was only after the "Chancellor Crisis" of 1877 that Bismarck reached the viewpoint given in his memoirs. Here he confused the Fabrice-Stosch Convention of 1867 with the Fabrice-Podbielski draft of 1866 and accused Stosch of trying to maintain the inde-

[36] Dickmann, *Militärpolitischen Beziehungen,* pp. 9-85; *Memoirs,* I, 120-21. Bismarck approved Stosch as a negotiator, in an attempt to win the Crown Prince's support.

[37] *Ibid.,* I, 120.

pendence of Saxony.[38] The immediate effect of this scene on Stosch
was to make him resolve never to find himself in such an uncomfortable position again.   In retrospect he saw the attack as characteristic of Bismarck's assumption of credit for his subordinates' successes and disavowal of their failures.[39]

Bismarck entered into direct negotiations with Fabrice[40] and
secured the extension of the oath of allegiance to all Saxon soldiers.
The Prussian Minister-President accepted a vague formula which
declared that the *Bundesfeldherr* would make use of his complete
power to assign stations to Saxon troops only in exceptional circumstances.   Bismarck was now satisfied.   However, the military
advisers of the King were still suspicious of the Saxon attitude
toward the Confederation.   General von Tresckow, Chief of the
Military Cabinet, consulted Stosch, who had resumed conduct of
the discussions, and laid a report before His Majesty demanding
more stringent conditions.   At this time, reports were reaching
William about strong anti-Prussian feeling in Saxony, and he
agreed that the terms should be stiffened.   When the Saxons were
informed, they became greatly embittered.   The Saxon Government felt, not without reason, that their effort to meet Prussia half-
way had only caused that state to increase its demands.   Therefore,
they decided to disavow all compromises and assume a purely
negative attitude.[41]

However, under the pressure of the negotiations for the entrance
of Saxony into the North German Confederation, concessions soon
came from both sides.   Prussia dropped the demand that Saxon
troops be uniformed by the Prussians and agreed to evacuate Dresden by 1 July.   Saxony acquiesced in the right of the *Bundesfeldherr* to appoint its contingent commander, with the understanding
that he would always accept a Saxon general proposed by the Saxon
government, and also agreed to drop the question of the disposal
of profits from the military contribution.   On 5 February, Fabrice

---

[38] Bismarck, *Gesammelte Werke,* XV, 299.
[39] *Memoirs,* I, 121.
[40] Stosch is mistaken in declaring (*ibid.*) that Bismarck changed only the
punctuation of the draft. It is true that the main articles remained unaltered.
[41] Dickmann, *Militärpolitischen Beziehungen,* pp. 85-93.

and Stosch reached final agreement.[42] King William, influenced by Bismarck's attitude and the necessity of showing the Prussian chambers that some progress had been made toward the formation of the North German Confederation, approved the convention the following day. King Johann gave his reluctant consent on 7 February 1867, and Stosch and Fabrice signed the agreement that day. Thus the Saxon Army entered the North German Confederation as a separate Saxon Corps with special rights and privileges. All other North German states were bound by the military provisions of the North German Constitution, but Saxony was exempt. To be sure, effective control over the Saxon troops was given to William, as *Bundesfeldherr*.[43]

Stosch criticized the convention for its many pretentious oaths of allegiance, not foreseeing the reliance German officers of the future would place upon such forms. He himself had desired to amalgamate the Saxon and Prussian officer corps, but here he had met the "greatest resistance" from the Saxon negotiators and received the "least support" from his own government. He did concede that the many new officers, resulting from the introduction of other North German contingents and new Prussian formations into the Army, would be difficult enough to assimilate without the addition of the entire officer corps of the Saxon Army.[44] However, he did not abandon his desire to standardize the Saxon system on the Prussian model, and he used his position in the War Ministry to further a policy of eliminating the special Saxon military privileges.

3

The special rights of the Saxon Army under the Military Convention of 7 February 1867 aroused Stosch's hostility.[45] His

[42] See Stosch to Frau von Rosenstiel, Berlin, 2 Feb. 1867, *Memoirs*, I, 125. For Stosch's view of his success, see Stosch to Savigny, 5 Feb. 1867, in Becker, *Bismarcks Ringen*, p. 508.

[43] Dickmann, *Militärpolitischen Beziehungen*, pp. 93-101. This study contains the text of the Convention (pp. 128-33). The constitutional position of the Saxon Army puzzled even the most supple intellects studying German political theory (see B. E. Howard, *The German Empire* [New York, 1906], pp. 399-401, for Laband's view, and Georg Meyer, *Lehrbuch des deutschen Staatsrechtes* [2nd. ed.; Leipzig, 1885], p. 590). The Saxon War Ministry owed its separate existence only to the Prussian-Saxon Military Convention of February 7, 1867, which, unlike the military agreements with other German states, was not mentioned in the Constitution itself.

[44] To Freytag, Berlin, 18 Feb. 1867, *Memoirs*, I, 125-126.

[45] My principal source for the discussion of Stosch's policy toward Saxony

criticism of the Saxon Army was perhaps most strikingly shown in a short report he laid before Roon, after a trip to Dresden in 1868. Nothing gained his approval. The soldiers' uniforms, their salutes, and their public bearing gave no indication that they belonged to the North German Army. The officer corps evinced the greatest defects; they were only "commanding machines" and needed Prussian instructors.[46]

Strongly nationalistic, influenced by the anti-Saxon feelings of his friend Freytag,[47] and loving order and efficiency, Stosch viewed the special rights of Saxony under the Military Convention as a constitutional excrescence which ought to be removed. As Director of the Military Economic Department of the War Ministry, he had the duty of preparing the military estimates of the Confederation. He employed his power in an attempt to force Saxony to abandon her peculiar position in the Confederation.

The Military Convention of 7 February 1867 was very unclear on Saxony's right to have a separate military budget. Article Three declared only that the "Royal Saxon Army enters the budget and estimates of the Army of the Confederation on 1 January 1868." Stosch's first move was to assume as self-evident the combination of the Saxon with the Confederation military budget from 1 January 1868. He asked the Saxon War Ministry in June 1867 to furnish details about its military establishment, in order that the Confederation military estimates might be drafted. This note was received in Dresden with the greatest astonishment. The Saxon Government believed that the Military Convention had secured, in practice, the complete independence of its military administration and its budget. At first the Saxons thought that there had been an error in the War Ministry and the able Saxon military

---

in 1866-1869 is Fritz Dickmann's penetrating article "Bismarck und Sachsen zur Zeit des Norddeutschen Bundes," *Neue Archiv fur Sächsische Geschichte und Altertumskundes,* XLIX (1929), 255-88. This excellent study is based primarily upon research in the Prussian Secret State Archives and the Berlin and Dresden branches of the Imperial Archives. Cf. Richard Dietrich, "Preussen als Besatzungsmacht im Königreich Sachsen, 1866-1868," *Jahrbuch fur die Geschichte Mittel-und Ostdeutschlands,* V (1956), 273-93, and Becker, *Bismarcks Ringen,* pp. 494-97.

[46] Stosch to Roon, 30 July 1868, Prussian Secret State Archives, summarized in Dickmann, "Bismarck und Sachsen," *Neue Archiv,* XLIX, 260. Cf. *Memoirs,* I, 147.

[47] *E.g.,* Helmolt, *Freytag an Stosch,* pp. 12-13, 23-24.

plenipotentiary in Berlin, Colonel von Brandenstein, was directed to initiate inquiries. He found that no mistake had been made. He reproached Stosch with breaking the Convention, but made no impression. The Saxon Government was uncertain what course to take. Brandenstein was of the opinion that Stosch stood alone in his interpretation of the Convention and that a strong attitude of opposition would cause the Prussian War Ministry to modify its attitude. The Saxon War Ministry decided on the provocative course of addressing a letter to its Prussian counterpart, in which the separate Saxon military budget was treated as a matter of course and merely informed the Prussians that work had already begun on it. However, the Saxons opened the way for compromise by surrendering on another point at issue. The Convention did not clearly establish whether Saxony was to contribute to the support of the Confederation military administration. The Saxon War Ministry conceded this point by inquiring how much of the total military contribution of two hundred twenty-five thalers per man annually was to be obligated to the support of the general Confederation military establishment. This communication was designed to secure either an immediate agreement or a clear definition of Prussia's aims. Stosch's letter and his conversation with Brandenstein were completely ignored.

The Saxon note precipitated the question in the Prussian War Ministry. Stosch's own branch, the Military Economic Department, by supporting the Saxon interpretation, established the fact that its chief had acted without the approval of his subordinates and entirely upon his own. The other departments and sections also opposed his stand.[48] The historian of the negotiations, Dickmann, notes:

> Stosch was the only one in Berlin who decidedly used his influence for the establishment of the budget in Berlin. He wished to concede only the "freedom of administration under the control of the Bundesrat" to Saxony; this act would be "politically of great significance."[49]

Nevertheless, it appeared that his view would prevail. Both Roon, who was on leave, and Podbielski, the Acting War Minister, appear to have supported Stosch's interpretation at this time. But the War

[48] Dickmann, "Bismarck und Sachsen," *Neue Archiv*, XLIX, 255-66.
[49] *Ibid.*, XLIX, 266.

Ministry had one chink in its armor, of which the Saxons were fully aware. Saxony had supported Prussia in the Bundesrat against the particularist opposition of the smaller states, and Bismarck was accordingly grateful. The possibility that the dispute with Saxony would arouse Bismarck's ire by coming before the Bundesrat was a threat the Prussian War Ministry could not ignore in the long run.[50] Too, at this time Roon was attempting, against the Chancellor's wishes, to convert the Prussian into a Confederation War Ministry.

At the beginning of September 1867 the Confederation military budget was ready for presentation to the Bundesrat and Reichstag. In it the Saxon Army Corps was treated like the Prussian Corps, and there was no mention of a separate Saxon military establishment. The question immediately arose whether this budget was binding on Saxony or whether it merely "figured in it by appearance only." The North German Constitution of 1867 had taken the control of the military budget out of the hands of the two houses of the Confederation Parliament until 1871, as long as the total annual sum allotted in it was not exceeded. Thus its submission was for information only. Brandenstein, by threatening that Saxony would combat the budget in the Bundesrat, tried to force Stosch and Podbielski to surrender to the Saxon viewpoint. Neither man gave way.

King Johann of Saxony disapproved of any open opposition in the Bundesrat, and Brandenstein, who also functioned as a Saxon representative to the Bundesrat, was instructed to attempt quietly to modify the budget, but not to press the matter. If possible, he was to establish that Saxony was to allot to the general costs of the Confederation military administration only the balance left after providing for its own troops. However, opposition to this was foreseen, and Brandenstein was authorized to offer to pay eight to ten thalers a year per member of the Saxon contingent for a period of ten years. On the other hand, he was to secure from Prussia a completely free hand in administration.

---

[50] Stosch had attributed Saxony's desire to "make Bismarck comfortable," as he put it, to a wish to discourage the Chancellor from making concessions to liberalism, Saxony's "most dangerous enemy." To Freytag, Berlin, 18 Aug. 1867, *Memoirs,* I, 133.

Meanwhile, Brandenstein's threat of an appeal to the Bundes-rat began to have an effect on Stosch. After lengthy and dis-putative conferences, Stosch, early in September 1867, gave the verbal assurance that he would present Saxony with an exact esti-mate of its contribution to the Confederation military administra-tion, while permitting Saxony to have its own budget. He hesitated to commit himself on the question of an addition to the Convention affirming his verbal stand, for the consent of Bismarck, the newly appointed North German Chancellor, who was very much at odds with the War Ministry, was necessary for any alter-ation of a state treaty. However, he finally promised to do his best to bring about this result. If this annex were not added, Branden-stein was instructed to record the results of his conferences with Stosch and obtain the General's signature.

Colonel von Brandenstein listed three conclusions which had resulted from his discussion with Stosch. Saxony was to pay annually 11 thalers of the military obligation of 225 thalers per man for the expenses of the Confederation Army. The rest of the contribution was to be the basis for Saxony's military budget, which had to be laid before the *Bundesfeldherr* for approval. Lastly, any balance remaining from the military contribution was to be paid into the Confederation's war chest, while the Confed-eration assumed responsibility for any extraordinary military ex-penses that Saxony might incur. The Saxon War Minister, von Fabrice, approved these results, with the exception of the right of the *Bundesfeldherr* to scrutinize Saxony's military estimates. This, he felt, would render its separate budget an illusion. Despite this reservation, Brandenstein felt that these points of agreement would be accepted. Stosch and Podbielski approved the terms. Thus Saxony had apparently achieved its aims, if only at the cost of surrendering some points at issue; the threat to turn to Bismarck had had its effect. Brandenstein believed that there was nothing more to fear from the Prussian War Ministry. He reported that Podbielski had supported the Saxon stand, and Stosch, "who loved crooked, underhanded ways and would like to destroy all inde-pendence in the Confederation, but the Prussian," was without power. Brandenstein hoped, and Fabrice expected, after confer-ences with Stosch and Podbielski in June 1868, that the separate

Saxon budget would be acknowledged in the Confederation budget of 1870.

Saxon hopes were disappointed. Roon returned to duty in June 1868, and Stosch's anti-Saxon influence was felt once more. Fabrice had expected difficulties to arise, but the attack when it came was such an inclusive one on Saxon independence that he was caught completely off guard.[51] Stosch, finding he was unable to deprive Saxony of its own budget, resorted to different tactics to eliminate the Saxon military administration. In an official intra-ministerial letter of 20 October 1868 he proposed to strike from the Saxon budget *all* items whose cost exceeded the corresponding expenditures of the Prussian corps. In fact, he planned to make the separate Saxon military administration impossible simply by removing its War Ministry, Auditor General, Finance Office, and other departments from the budget.[52] Podbielski felt that this action was a breach of the Military Convention, but Stosch expected support from Roon, who, as events demonstrated, desired such anomalies as the Saxon War Ministry as little as did his ambitious subordinate. The departure of Stosch on a service trip at this time stimulated the hope in the Saxons that the War Ministry could be brought to change its attitude in his absence, but nothing was done before his return. Roon accepted Stosch's viewpoint entirely and was only willing to let the Saxon Corps have a few more staff officers than other contingents. Saxony's desire to retain its own War Ministry found no sympathy whatsoever with him. He held that it should be replaced by a corps commissary on the Prussian model. Did not the Convention state that the organization of the Saxon Army should be based on the Prussian?

However closely Roon's proposals, based on Stosch's suggesttions, might adhere to the letter of the Military Convention of 1867, they were in direct opposition to its spirit. The economies effected by the elimination of the separate Saxon military establishment were comparatively small; politically they shook the foundations of the North German Confederation. Brandenstein, who knew that the source of all these demands was Stosch, pursued him

[51] Dickmann, "Bismarck und Sachsen," *Neue Archiv,* XLIX, 266-73.
[52] Military Economic Department to the General War Department, 20 Oct. 1868, *ibid.,* XLIX, 273.

relentlessly in an effort to alter his mind. Brandensein did not trust him and, indeed, considered him "completely incalculable in his perfidious insolence." He received the distinct impression that Stosch was willing to guarantee the independence of the Saxon military administration by an annex to the Convention, but it is extremely doubtful that Stosch conceded so much. In any case, the decision now rested with Roon. Brandenstein felt that the only course was to appeal to Bismarck.

The Saxon reply to the Prussian demands, a detailed defense of the independence of its military establishment, was presented to Roon with a request for verbal discussion. He was not inclined to admit the validity of any of the Saxon claims, but he did not refuse the invitation to further negotiations. The War Minister excluded all political implications from consideration and valued the Convention only as a means of extracting military concessions from Saxony. However, Roon was well aware that Bismarck would have to be approached eventually, and it would be well to avoid any open conflict with the Saxons. To achieve this end, he was prepared to offer a minor financial concession to the Saxons if they would recognize the freedom of decision of the *Bundesfeldherr* in military-financial matters. He took this suggested compromise to Bismarck, who, laying great weight on the necessity of friendly relations with Saxony and knowing nothing of the War Ministry's recent actions, approved the proposal as a basis for opening discussions with the Saxons. Stosch was designated to represent the Prussians in these conferences.

As representative of the War Ministry, Stosch was reluctant to make concessions. Only the knowledge of Bismarck's attitude forced him to retreat step by step. Influenced probably by the recent conflict over the budget in Prussia, he nevertheless held firm to one principle—the Saxon military budget must be computed according to the effective, not the constitutional, strength of its corps. The Constitution had established the effective strength of the Army at 1 per cent of the population, and the Saxons wanted their contribution to the military expense of the Confederation to be 225 thalers per head of 1 per cent of the Saxon population. This would be enough to enable them to support the burden of a separate War Ministry. But the *Bundesfeldherr* had the constitutional right to determine the number of effectives in each contingent. Stosch insisted that the Saxon budget be based on this number, which was lower than the constitutional effective strength. He pointed out that the Prussian budget was determined on this basis. This, of course, touched upon the real question at issue. The Saxons wholeheartedly objected to any linking of themselves with Prussian examples. Negotiations between Stosch and Fabrice began on 18 December 1868. Stosch was willing temporarily to grant all the concessions the Saxons demanded, as long as the principle of a separate War Ministry was not established.[53] To put his position in his own words: "I have been generous with money, but have saved the principles."[54]

Curiously, the Prussian War Ministry placed its hopes of eventual success upon the Reichstag. In 1872 the military budget would have to be approved by that body, and it was hoped that the expenses for the separate Saxon War Ministry would then be disapproved. Therefore, the Prussian War Ministry was quite willing to accept these expenses for the next fiscal year, but it was very loath to commit itself for the future. Fabrice immediately detected what the Prussians wished to attain. He turned to Bismarck, explained the difficulty, and asked for help. The events of the preceding years had shown the wisdom of Bismarck's conciliatory policy toward Saxony, for he had won the support and trust of her ruler. The Chancellor was aroused by the reports. He was not indeed willing to bind the Bundesrat and Reichstag to support Saxony's separate military establishment in the future, but he did insist that the Prussian War Ministry surrender to all other principal demands of Saxony and perpetuate the special Saxon privileges. Moreover, he decided that the Saxon military budget should be based upon the constitutional strength, and any surplus remaining from the Saxon military contribution should go into the Confederation treasury only if the Saxon Army had no use for it. At first Roon made only a few concessions to the Saxons, hoping they would weaken. They again turned to Bismarck, and Roon gave in completely. Fabrice came to Berlin in February, and the

[53] Ibid., XLIX, 273-81.
[54] Stosch to Freytag, Berlin, 2 Jan. 1869, Memoirs, I, 151; Stosch held essentially the same view in the 1867 negotiations, Stosch to Savigny, 5 Feb. 1867, in Becker, Bismarcks Ringen, p. 508.

results were embodied in a note from Bismarck to the Saxon Foreign Ministry of 12 February 1869. The Saxons received practically all they demanded, and Prussia was committed to maintain Saxony's special military position in the Confederation.[55]

Actuated by a strong Prussian-German nationalism and a desire for military reform and administrative unity, Albrecht von Stosch had used great skill in attempting to destroy the military administration of Saxony. Misled perhaps by the strong anti-Saxon sentiments of Gustav Freytag, he failed to perceive or had disregarded the political implications of his actions. He showed himself to be less wise than Bismarck, who clearly recognized the need for Saxony's support to crush particularist feeling in the North German Confederation and to pave the way for German unification. The success of Bismarck's Saxon policy was shown time and time again when he came into conflict with the other North German states. Without the support of Saxony, no opposition in the Confederation could make any headway. Strangely, despite friction with Bismarck and disagreements over Prussian policy toward Saxony, Stosch was, at this time, using all his influence to secure the support of the Crown Prince for the Chancellor's general policy.

4

Berlin began its great expansion in 1866, and Stosch's social contacts widened accordingly.[56] The friendship of Stosch and Freytag was particularly close at this time. Freytag's journalistic activities raised momentary scruples in Stosch's mind about confiding freely in him, but he overcame them by trust in his friend. *Die Grenzboten's* editor continued to urge him to write for his journal. Apparently Stosch found time to write only two articles: one was concerned with the defense of German coasts against the French; the other was a sketch of the Crown Prince's Near Eastern tour.[57]

[55] Dickmann, "Bismarck und Sachsen," *Neue Archiv,* XLIX, 281-88.
[56] *Memoirs,* I, 128.
[57] Helmolt, *Freytag an Stosch,* pp. 48, 55; *Memoirs,* I, 124, 126, 127, 134-35; [Albrecht von Stosch], "Unsere Küsten in einem Kriege mit Frankreich," *Die Grenzboten,* XXIV (1867), vol. I, 246-48; [Albrecht von Stosch], "Die Reise des Kronprinzen von Preussen," *Die Grenzboten,* XXIX (1869), vol. I, 81-88.

Ambition continued to characterize Stosch. A close friend even told him that his "entire ambition is 'power.' " He acknowledged that this remark might be correct, but did not find his ambition satisfied in the War Ministry. His brief diplomatic activity with the Saxons afforded him great pleasure as offering a wider scope for his talents than military administration.[58]

His future military career in the event of war remained uncertain. The Crown Prince desired him to become his Quartermaster General once more, but Stosch was determined not to accept the second place again. Nonetheless, Moltke's War Plans of 1868 envisaged Stosch in this post. The possibility of becoming Commissary-General of all German armies was first suggested to him in 1867. He was told that a "powerful and adroit general" who was familiar with provisioning, was needed for the job, and he had been tentatively chosen. Personally he found the idea "monstrous," for he desired an active field command, not an administrative post. His first thought was to have the Crown Prince exert pressure to have him appointed his Chief of Staff. The question of his employment in wartime was finally settled only after the outbreak of war in 1870.[59]

Administrative burdens were not so great that he ignored politics. In August 1868, when Roon proposed him as a Prussian representative to the Bundesrat, it seemed likely that he would achieve his aim of observing at first hand Bismarck's efforts to consolidate the North German Confederation. He was struck off the list, but consoled himself with the thought that it "was good" to "keep away from active politics." In fact, he maintained a rather reserved attitude in political matters to protect his military career. However, his private letters of the years 1866 to 1870 contain decided views on a variety of political questions. He was a strong supporter of Roon's attempt to replace the Prussian War Ministry with a Confederation one and he requested Freytag to back this endeavor by writing articles for the newspapers. He also favored the creation of Confederation Trade and Finance Ministries. In foreign affairs he believed in the exclusion of Russia from German politics by diplomatic action alone, holding that Eastern entangle-

[58] *Memoirs*, I, 124-25.
[59] *Ibid.*, I, 126-28, 135; Moltke, *Militärische Werke*, I, Theil III, 93.

ments and the Poles would keep her occupied internally. Most of his attention in foreign policy was focused on France. He wrote Holtzendorff in April 1867 that the "French are fools enough to want war, and the Emperor plays for high stakes because he sees that he can do no other." Prussia could not start a war at this time, because it needed "public opinion" on its side for internal development.[60] The future relations between France and Prussia seemed clearer to Stosch in November 1867:

> . . . Napoleon has become the slave of his bigoted wife and speeds toward the abyss. Since the beginning I have expected a great crisis and cannot beleive that I delude myself. For this reason I work like a horse in order to prepare the Army, improving it by all the experiences of the last war.[61]

Bismarck was viewed by Stosch through unclouded lenses, in marked contrast to his friend Freytag's complete distrust and hatred of the Prussian statesman.[62] By May 1867 Stosch declared it was a mistake "to speak of Bismarck's desire for war." The North German Chancellor certainly did not shrink from an unavoidable conflict, but he would gladly bypass it, if he could maintain Prussia's position of power by peaceful means.[63] Bismarck's personality greatly interested Stosch. He wrote in August 1867:

> The more Bismarck increases [in power], the more uncomfortable persons who think as individuals and act independently become to him; the more nervous he becomes, the more he fears sharp personal conflicts. I know from my own experience that there are days of spiritual overexertion when I can indeed give order, but when business with able, independent officials is more than burdensome.[64]

He observed a month later that Bismarck's power was continually increasing, but he questioned whether the statesman possessed self-control, "the first basic characteristic of all moral greatness."[65] Nevertheless, in a letter of October, 1868, he described with admiration Bismarck and his policy.

---

[60] *Memoirs*, I, 126-27, 131, 133, 135-38.

[61] To Freytag, Berlin, 3 Nov. 1867, *ibid.*, I, 134.

[62] *E.g.*, Helmolt, *Freytag an Stosch*, pp. 27-30; Edward Tempeltey, ed., *Gustav Freytag und Herzog Ernst von Coburg im Briefwechsel* (Leipzig, 1904), p. 237.

[63] *Memoirs*, I, 127.

[64] To Freytag, Berlin, 18 Aug. 1867, *ibid.*, I, 132-33.

[65] *Ibid.*, I, 136.

. . . He is vigorous and bold in thought and clear in what he wants; he will never set a goal beyond his reach. He will ruthlessly destroy men and stituations that stand in his way. But here his thoroughly monarchial conviction, which is innate in him, comes into consideration. Bismarck only uses liberalism and the Constitution in order to lead and sway the King and the Conservatives, but never as an assured element of power. Bismarck wants a united monarchial Germany. . . .[66]

Stosch's aim in these years was not to strengthen liberalism, but to induce the Crown Prince to give wholehearted support to Bismarck's diplomacy.

Frederick William met Stosch frequently during these years. When Stosch was not summoned to the palace of the Crown Prince, he encountered him on tours of inspection and at the sessions of the military commission of which they were both members. This association was not without its drawbacks. Envious courtiers watched Stosch's every visit and noted his every word. Although he frequently came into contact with William I on business and with Queen Augusta on hospital affairs, he was excluded from the King's table. William's favor had not lessened, but the courtiers wished to drive home the lesson that Stosch could not serve two masters. He used every opportunity to prepare the Crown Prince for his prospective reign. In September 1866 he urged Frederick William to abandon his negative stands toward Bismarck and activity in public affairs, attitudes which Stosch felt came from Victoria. His interviews with her were often stormy, but they retained a high regard for one another.[67] In the summer of 1867 he spent a few days at Frederick William's summer home on the Baltic. Here the question arose: What policy should the Crown Prince pursue toward conquered Hanover, where anti-Prussian feeling was strong and loyalty to the old Guelf dynasty endured? Stosch acted as an intermediary between the heir to the throne and the Hanoverian leaders, Rudolf von Bennigsen and Johannes von Miquel. Freytag, at his friend's request, got in touch with these two prominent National Liberal leaders, and they entered into correspondence with Frederick William. He had the pleasure of startling Bismarck with his knowledge of Hanoverian conditions,

[66] Stosch to Freytag, 4 Oct. 1868, *ibid.*, I, 150.
[67] *Ibid.*, I, 122, 124, 128, 130-31, 136.

gained from the reports of the two statesmen.[68]   One of the Crown Prince's occasional advisers provoked Stosch's contempt.   Heinrich Geffcken, the "great diplomat with the limited field of vision," seemed to him insane.   "What," Stosch disgustedly queried, "can one make of a man who has not once slept soundly?"[69]

His royal friend had Stosch appointed the highest ranking member of his entourage during a state visit to Italy in April and May 1868 and again had him included in his suite during a trip to the opening of the Suez Canal lasting from October to Christmas 1869.   Stosch's duties included writing reports to the King and the Chancellor, conversing with leading statesmen, drafting reports for the Crown Prince, and representing him in meetings with prominent people.   Stosch's pride in the presence of Prussian warships in Near Eastern waters presaged his future satisfaction as Chief of the Admiralty.   The fleet was to him important not only as the official representative of German power, but also as a "protection against the arbitrary will of foreign officials and the conflicting interests of other Western nations."   He remarked with particular patriotism that the Prussian corvette *Hertha* was the first large warship to traverse the Suez Canal.[70]

His activities in Italy caused great alarm to the Prussian military attaché, Theodor von Bernhardi, whom Stosch described in his travel diary as "embittered," liked by neither the Italian officers nor the diplomatic corps.[71]   Bernhardi's gossipy diaries, not the most unimpeachable source of information,[72] contain several strik-

[68] *Ibid.,* I, 132; Helmolt, *Freytag an Stosch,* pp. 20, 22-23, 296-97; Hermann Oncken, *Rudolf von Bennigsen: Ein deutscher Liberaler Politiker* (Stuttgart and Berlin, 1910), II, 91-97; Hans Herzfeld, *Johannes von Miquel* (Detmold, 1938), II, 140.

[69] *Memoirs,* I, 127-28, 134.

[70] For details of these trips, see *ibid.,* I, 138-45, 156-79: [Albrecht von Stosch], "Die Reise der Kronprinzen von Preussen," *Die Grenzboten,* XXIX (1870), vol. I, 81-88.   Freytag attempted to gain a wide circulation for this article; see his letter to Heinrich Geffcken, Leipzig, 17 Jan. 1870, in Carl Hinrichs, "Unveröffentliche Briefe Gustav Freytags an Heinrich Geffcken aus der Zeit der Reichsgründung," *Jahrbuch für die Geschichte Mittel-und Ostdeutschland,* III, (1954), 110.

[71] *Memoirs,* I, 142-43.

[72] Cf. Stosch to Freytag, Oestrich, 4 Nov. 1893, Memoirs, III, 299-300: "Bernhardi's new volume has stimulated and entertained me in many ways. The book has the advantage that one can read in it for five minutes and can put it aside again. One meets with a throng of noted people who are more or less slandered. Wise alone . . . is Bernhardi. People who have done nothing in life like

ing comments on Stosch. Rumors of his friendship with the Crown Prince had already crossed the Alps when the news of Stosch's inclusion in the entourage first reached Bernhardi on 8 April 1868. "General Stosch! The future War Minister of a Progressive Party Ministry! That does not please me at all!" Bernhardi saw the General also as a member of the "Augustenburg coterie," supporters of the claims of Frederick of Augustenburg to the crown of Holstein.[73] In another entry Bernhardi again repeated the rumor of Stosch's being the future Progressive Party War Minister, linked him correctly with Freytag and *Die Grenzboten,* and then attributed to him anonymous articles *against* the King's reorganization of the Army and the three-year obligation to serve (!). He gives a highly colored account of an interview with Stosch, when he tried to persuade him that the Crown Prince should receive the pro-French general Lamarmora's foe, General Cucchiari, in Stosch's view, "a bad fellow" (*ein schlechter Kerl*). Bernardi inquired: " 'Who says that?' 'The entire Army. . . .' 'Well then, what wrong has he committed?' 'He is in thick with the deputies, he creates opposition in the Army. He who does that is a bad fellow.'"[74] Despite Bernhardi's comments, Count Karl von Usedom, the Prussian Minister at Florence, in an official dispatch to Bismarck, made special mention of the "very significant impression" Stosch's military views had made upon Italian officers.[75]

The Minister did not find equal favor with Stosch. He was out of the sympathy with Usedom's open opposition to the Lamarmora, who, if he came to power, would not be able to co-operate with the Prussian Minister.[76] These opinions influenced the Crown Prince, who, in a report to the King, doubtless drafted by his ambitious adviser, defended Lamarmora and demanded the recall of the entire German delegation including Usedom and Bernhardi. William was astounded. Neither he nor Bismarck had any illu-

---

Etzel, Gewin, etc. are praised; a man like Moltke is represented as limited. — I was often forced to think of Varnhagen and also of Geffcken, who certainly will leave such a diary behind." Stosch died before Bernhardi's diary of 1868 was published.

[73] This charge, later also made by Bismarck, is false.

[74] Bernhardi, *Aus dem Leben,* VIII, 200, 220, 230-31.

[75] Florence, 12 June 1868, *Die Auswärtige Politik Preussens, 1858-1871: Diplomatisches Aktenstücke* (Oldenburg, 1932 ff.), X, 79.

[76] *Memoirs,* I, 142.

sions that such an idea had originated with the Crown Prince, but they did not link Stosch with it.[77]   Yet when Bismarck angrily dismissed Usedom for not following his policy and neglected to inform the King, the Crown Prince took a more favorable view of the Prussian diplomat.   Stosch, at Frederick William's behest and probably wishing to smooth over matters for William, asked Freytag to write articles in Usedom's defense and persuade him to accept the King's offer of a new assignment.[78]   When, at the beginning of the Near Eastern tour, the Crown Prince, pleased by Usedom's guidance through the art galleries of Venice, proposed to include him in his suite, Stosch was quick to point out that a "public scandal in Berlin" would result.   All his tact was needed to induce the Crown Prince and Usedom to abandon the plan.[79]

All Stosch's tact was also needed to combat Frederick William's indifference to public affairs, which was in strong contrast to his father's diligence.[80]   Characteristic of the General's advice to the future monarch is a letter dated 5 February 1869, which is also a significant statement of Stosch's attitude toward Bismarck.

At the moment a considerable opposition to Count Bismarck is asserting itself in the Prussion State Ministry. It is using as a means the introduction of a Confederation Ministry of Foreign Affairs. Prussian particularism is especially noticeable. . . . Since it is of the greatest importance for our progress that Count Bismarck remains the victor in this battle, I would like to ask Your Royal Highness to support him vigorously, and, by no means to take steps against him because of his "tactlessness" in Your Royal Highness's house, about which Your Royal Highness writes so ill-humoredly. Count Bismarck is only one who helps us forward.[81]

It was such advice as this that caused Frederick William to tell Stosch repeatedly that he "was the only person who really instructed him."[82]   Association with the Crown Prince only made Stosch value his own independence all the more.   He wrote:

The more my life is directed into political spheres, the more intensive becomes my desire to possess enough wealth to be able to pass off

[77] Bismarck, *Gesammelte Werke*, VIa, 351, 406.
[78] *Memoirs*, I, 146, 152-54; Bernhardi, *Aus dem Leben*, VIII, 366.
[79] *Memoirs*, I, 160-61.   [80] *Ibid.*, I, 147.
[81] *Ibid.*, I, 149. The present writer has found no other reference to the "tactlessness" mentioned.
[82] *Ibid.*, I, 151.

the scene at any time without having to struggle for a living. *I want to be a free man, so I can maintain my independence in higher posi-tions.*[83]

Financial independence and economic security came in 1871 when he received a grant for his outstanding services in the Franco-German War.

The year 1870 opened with Stosch at his desk at the War Ministry. The Crown Prince, who had come to depend upon him during the Near Eastern trip, gave him chores to do which often extended his work far into the night, but his gratitude for the journey enabled him to bear these extra tasks with good will. He continued to be amused at the popular "delusion that I am in an uninterrupted and most intimate relation with him." In fact, Stosch saw him seldom and never alone. The delights of the journey led him to suggest a North American tour for 1871, but the home-loving Crown Prince was cold to the suggestion. Stosch was critical of the Prince's adviser, Heinrich Friedberg,[84] a rising official in the Prussian Ministry of Justice; he objected to his "general political orations" in the Crown Prince's presence. Friedberg, he thought, saw in the Prince a "hero of the future"; Stosch perceived, on the contrary, only a "good will" and a confused intellect. He believed that clear, detailed reports would best erect a foundation "which would secure the future of the state" in the royal mind. All in all, he felt that Friedberg's counsels would not be followed, "for all this intercourse with the Liberals only pleases the Prince because they pay court to him, and, as a result, he feels that he is some sort of a power."[85]

In his own relations with the Crown Prince, Stosch practiced what he preached. He presented Frederick William with a memorandum of the military budget, which he had abbreviated, for "too long an opus would not be read through."[86] When a struggle developed in the North German Parliament over the abolition of the

---

[83] Italics mine. To his wife, Königsburg, 12 Sept. 1869, *ibid.*, I, 155.

[84] Heinrich Friedberg (1813-1895) served as Undersecretary of the Prussian Ministry of Justice, 1873-1879, Secretary of the Imperial Ministry of Justice, 1876-1889, and Prussian Ministry of Justice, 1879-1889. He fathered German criminal law legislation and was an intimate of Frederick William until the latter's death. For a brief sketch of his life, see Poschinger, *Bismarcks Bundesrat*, II, 130-33.

[85] *Memoirs*, I, 179-80, 183-85.

[86] *Ibid.*, I, 181-82.

death penalty in criminal cases, Stosch tried to mediate between the Crown Prince and his father. Frederick William supported the abrogation, the Ministry was inclined to yield, and the King would have surrendered but for Roon's influence. Stosch, ever desirous of improving relations between William and his heir, urged the Crown Prince to support his father's decision. Although his advice was not taken, he continued to enjoy Frederick William's confidence.[87]

Meanwhile Bismarck's efforts to achieve German unity excited Stosch's admiration. The Chancellor's endeavors to make William Emperor, a move which increased Frederick William's distrust of him, would fail, Stosch maintained, because of Prussian particularist feeling and the opposition of the South German states, who would offer the Imperial Crown to William only "under extreme pressure." Here events were to prove him correct. He had no sympathy with Bismarck's efforts to protect the prerogatives of the various German princes and feared that concessions would be made to them in the military budget of 1872. "Bismarck," Stosch approvingly observed in April 1870, "unconditionally follows his great goal, the unity of Germany, and may achieve it without war." He foresaw that the Chancellor would be forced to seek strong liberal support to attain his ends.[88] The General looked hopefully to the future:

> . . . when I compare our situation with that in Austria or France, I cannot stop thinking that we are called to be a Great Power! The House of Hohenzollern is the representative of godly order in Europe, and we must hope that our young Prince has the pride and the will for such a position.[89]

Difficulties between the Reichstag and the Government over the Army caused the General to ask Bismarck whether a new conflict was in sight. The Chancellor declared that such a disagreement was impossible under the Constitution. Nevertheless, Stosch feared that particularistic feeling in the newly conquered Prussian provinces and among the separate sovereigns would direct itself at

[87] *Ibid.*, I, 181; Poschinger, *Kaiser Friedrich*, II, 391; Heinrich von Poschinger, *Fürst von Bismarck und der Bundesrat* (Stuttgart and Leipzig, 1897-1901), I, 305-7.
[88] *Memoirs*, I, 180-82
[89] To Freytag, 5 April 1870, *ibid.*, I, 181.

limiting the King's control of the Army. "The person who reopens the military conflict," Stosch roundly declared, "is betraying both Crown and Fatherland." He noted that although the question of the existence of the Army under royal control was a matter of life or death for the state, the great burden it placed on the individual aroused strong opposition. A conflict could thus be prevented only by agreement among the leading statesmen.[90] Stosch's concern with the burden on the individual showed a significant broadening of his outlook on military questions when it is compared with his narrow views earlier in the decade. The outbreak of the Franco-German War was to place these questions in the background.

The years 1866 to 1870 were of importance in Stosch's development, for they presaged the future. Militarily, he won his spurs in combat and began his career as an active and forceful administrator, eagerly accepting responsibility. He developed an interest in the Navy, which was to emerge with increasing strength in the following years. Politically, these years were of equal significance. He became acquainted with Heinrich Geffcken, who was to play an unusual role in his life, despite Stosch's detestation of him. Of greater moment was the inseparable linking of Stosch's name with that of the Crown Prince, who was bound to him by ties of comradeship and by respect of his outspoken integrity and for his talents as a mediator with the King. The effect on Stosch's career was twofold. On the one hand, he sacrificed opportunites of becoming an active field commander and entered military administration in order to be near the Prince. On the other, his powerful ambition to influence state policy found an outlet in advice to Frederick William. Stosch began his attempts to rouse the heir to the throne from his lethargy and to stimulate his interest in the day-by-day details of military and political affairs. Holding a modest opinion of the Prince's abilities, Stosch considered the flirtation with the liberals an indication of political impotence, not agreement on common principles. Far from encouraging liberal tendencies, Stosch sought to bring the Crown Prince into an alliance with his father and the Chancellor.

This aim of co-operation with Bismarck reflects Stosch's own underlying conservatism, nationalism, and monarchial devotion.

[90] *Ibid.,* I, 182.

He continued to favor a "godly order" and the unification of Germany by the Prussian Army, as he had in his earlier years. Conflict with France he considered inevitable, and used his administrative abilities to prepare the Army for it. Stosch's deep admiration for Bismarck's policies and appreciation of the charm of his personality persisted despite the clash of their headstrong natures. He felt the full weight of the Chancellor's displeasure when his own strong nationalism led him to seek the total incorporation of the Saxon military establishment into the Prussian, with no regard for the political consequences. His refusal in later years to bend his independent character to the Chancellor's will stems from their stormy interview over the Saxon Army. Obviously, by July 1870 the fifty-two year old General was well launched on the stormy seas of his political career.

III

THE FRANCO-GERMAN WAR

1

The years of the Franco-German War of 1870-71 were the most active of Stosch's life. The high esteem in which his military abilities were held was amply justified, and it was upon this foundation of military success that his political influence was based. He showed himself to be a man confident of his own powers, willing, even eager, to accept new responsibilities, and outspoken in his opinions. It would be a grave error,[1] however, to see in him the very model of the rude, opinionated, gruff, old infantryman. When bluff outspokenness was needed to obtain practical results, as it was, for example, in his relations with the Grand Duke of Mecklenburg-Schwerin in December 1870, he was heartily, even impolitely frank. When minor concessions and tactful phrasing could smooth over difficulties, he conceded willingly and spoke with great care. He was a gentleman and a staff officer and resorted to rudeness only when other measures failed. He understood and usually respected the thoughts and emotions of others, even when he disagreed, as his comments on William I, Frederick William, and Bismarck amply demonstrate. Blunt, direct, and forceful he often was, but stupidly obstinate, strongly opinionated, or unfeelingly tactless never.

[1] Schröder in his study of Stosch presents him throughout as a bluff and hearty individual, a man of talent, but lacking all tact. This interpretation, which Schröder may have derived from Admiral von Tirpitz (*My Memoirs* [London, n. d.], I, chap. ii), is not supported by the evidence. The high esteem in which William I and Frederick William, not to mention Moltke, continued to hold him rested not only on his outspokenness, but also on the careful choice and timing with which he presented his views. This emerges clearly from his own memoirs and the accounts of him by others. There was little of the professional courtier in him, but he was too sensible to attempt to alter what would, or could, not be changed.

When the diplomatic situation began to show signs of storm in July 1870, Stosch, like his leading contemporaries, was on vacation. Even Bismarck was at his home in Varzin, for, as he remarked to Stosch later in the year, he had not expected the "French to bite so quickly."[2] On July 15, a dispatch[3] summoned Stosch to Berlin.[4] Looking back upon these days of war he wrote: "It is a joy to live in such times and immeasurable good fortune to participate actively in them. How many good and virtuous men must waste their powers in a petty age for petty goals without ever seeing one great moment!"[5] His position at the beginning of the war was uncertain. The Crown Prince strongly desired to make him his chief of staff, but Moltke insisted that Blumenthal was the right man for the job. War Minister von Roon decided the issue by the "long-feared" decision that "I was the only General who could direct the provisioning of the Army in war." Stosch was immediately named Commissary General of the German armies.[6]

This appointment was a great disappointment. Since 1866 Stosch had been accustomed to make military decisions of the highest importance, based on intimate knowledge of the most secret military information. Now in wartime he had, at first, access only to information concerned with provisioning and no direct influence on the course of events. He was a purely administrative official. Moreover, he, and his friend Freytag, had always envisioned him as a field commander in direct contact with the enemy. "My consolation," he later wrote, "lay in the great labor and immense responsibility of my task."[7]

The provisioning of armies in the nineteenth century presented new and unexpected difficulties to military administrators. The great numbers of men engaged in warfare naturally resulted in an increase of the provisions needed to feed and equip them. This factor was further complicated by extended lines of supply. The

[2] Stosch interpreted this to mean that Bismarck had incited the French to war. *Memoirs,* I, 186. Cf. Stosch to Freytag, Oestrich, 31 Dec. 1894, *Memoirs,* III, 322.

[3] Doubtless sent by the War Ministry.

[4] *Memoirs,* I, 186.   [5] *Ibid.*

[6] *Ibid.;* H. O. Meisner, ed., *Friedrich III: Tagebuch 1870-1871* (Berlin and Leipzig, 1926), p. 6.

[7] *Memoirs,* I, 186-87; Freytag to Salomon Hirzel, Siebleben, 22 July 1870, *Freytag an Hirzel,* p. 184.

eighteenth-century system of gathering supplies at central points in magazines and depots proved to be totally inadequate. However, the issuance of the "iron" ration, consisting of biscuit, bacon, coffee, rice and salt, the precursor of the American alphabetical rations, and the requisition of supplies in occupied territory alleviated the problem somewhat. The German Army arrived at its system of provisioning not by any preconceived plan, but by trial and error. During the Danish War of 1864, the numbers of men and distances involved were comparatively slight, and the Prussian Army was largely provisioned by magazines already in existence or hastily improvised. When, during the Austro-Prussian War, large bodies of troops were engaged on extended lines of supply, this system collapsed. The troops suffered frequently from hunger. One corps of Prince Frederick Karl's Army and the Crown Prince's entire force fought the battle of Königgrätz on empty stomachs. After the battle it was necessary to disperse the Prussian forces to avoid putting too great a strain upon one line of supply. Provisioning, which had been intrusted to each separate unit, was combined under Moltke. He, by use of extraordinary measures and the capture of enemy provisions and storage depots, was able to remedy, but not completely overcome, the difficulties encountered.[8]

Moltke's experience led him to the sensible conclusion that no general plan to cover all contingencies could be evolved, but officials who combined a "high degree of prudence with swift power of decision and will power" could resolve all difficulties.[9] He found these qualities in the Brigadier General, soon promoted to Major General, Albrecht von Stosch. As head of the Military Economic Department in the War Ministry, Stosch had evolved a plan of centralized procurement of provisions by taking provisioning from the corps commissaries and placing it in the hands of the commissaries on the lines of supply (*Etappenintendanten*). Opposition from ministerial officials and lack of support from Roon had made the plan inoperative, but in 1870, as Commissary General, Stosch used his authority to put it into force. Although he had informed his subordinates of this plan previously, only one of the higher

[8] Moltke, *Militärische Werke*, IV, Theil I, 273-86; Engelhard, "Rückblicke," *Beiheft zum Militärwochenblatt*, 1901, pp. 483, 491.
[9] Moltke, *Militärische Werke*, IV, Theil I, 274-75, 287.

personnel actually became a field commissary during the war; the others were physically disqualified for field service and had to be replaced. Stosch cut through much red tape by avoiding the clogged channels of regular military communication. Instead of sending orders to the commissaries of each corps and army, he found that he got speedier results by communicating directly with the army corps commanders, who trusted him. He was able to overcome the difficulties of royal interference, blocked railways, opposition of subordinates, rapidly changing lines of supply, the provisioning not only of mass armies, but of prisoners of war and the French civilian population as well, and the cattle plague.[10]

The provisioning of the German Army in 1870-71 was almost universally conceded to have been well performed by Stosch, under the most trying circumstances. The historical painter, Anton von Werner, records that the French continually remarked of the German soldiers: *"Ils sont tous d'une santé insultante."* Werner attributed their health primarily to Stosch. More significant are Moltke's opinions that the German Army in 1870-1871 was the best provisioned in the history of great wars and that "provisioning difficulties were overcome without endangering the health of man or beast." William I impressed an old friend at Ems in 1871 with the praise he lavished on Stosch. The Emperor declared that "his provisioning of the Army exceeded anything previously heard of." Stosch had, in fact, proved himself to be a superior and resourceful administrator. The high opinion held of his abilities and the weight attached to his political views were in no small measure the result of his activities as German Commissary General.[11] This recognition of his talents was reinforced by his actions in the field.

[10] *Memoirs,* I, 118-19, 184, 187-203; Jany, *Preussische Armee,* IV, 281; Englehardt, "Rückblicke," *Beihefte zum Militärwochenblatt,* 1901, pp. 484, 487-502; Moltke, *Militärische Werke,* IV, Theil I, 288-95, 302; Pratt, *Rise of Rail Power,* pp. 110-14; Blumenthal, *Journals,* p. 171.

[11] *Memoirs,* I, 187; Anton von Werner, *Erlebnisse und Eindrücke, 1870-1890* (Berlin, 1913), p. 43; Moltke, *Militärische Werke,* IV, Theil I, 287, 301; Heinrich von Ham, "Erinnerungen an den preussischen Hof im Koblenz: nach Aufzeichnungen der Frau v. Breuning (1850-1871)," *Deutsche Rundschau,* CCLII (1937), 105; Julius Verdy du Vernois, *Im grossen Hauptquartier, 1870-1871: Persönliche Erinnerungen* (Berlin, 1895), p. 32.

2

The defeat of Sedan on 1 September 1870 toppled the Second French Empire, which was replaced by the republican "Government of National Defense." The French ministers were divided between besieged Paris and Tours. Léon Gambetta injected a new spirit into the French defense and sought to rally the whole populace into mass armies based upon the model of 1792 to relieve the beleaguered capital. The French could draw upon a large stock of undamaged war material and a total of nearly one million men.

The Germans were confronted with a totally different problem from that which they had previously faced in the wars of unification. The campaigns of William I had been based upon the Clausewitzian thesis of the annihilation of the enemy's forces at one blow by the concentration of masses of troops on the battlefield. The War of 1864 and Koniggrätz had shown the effectiveness of this theory and the battles of Gravelotte and Sedan seemed to demonstrate its further validity. However, the French republican armies, gathered along the Loire River near Orléans, offered a new problem, for here the principle of annihilation met with no success. The Germans were fighting not a smaller professional army, but a superior popular force and an aroused population, whose *franctireurs* caused great losses in their ranks. Further difficulties were soon encountered. Lines of operation and communication were extended to dangerous lengths. German intelligence, which had been familiar with the organization of the Imperial Army, was at a loss when faced with the "People's Army of the Loire." The heavily wooded terrain around Orléans offered an additional obstacle to the Germans. They were slow to recognize that they were, in fact, fighting a new kind of war; Imperial France had been defeated, but republican France might prove a more dangerous adversary. They underestimated the enemy after the capture of Orléans on 11 October but exaggerated his powers after a defeat on 9 November forced a retreat from Orléans.[12]

[12] Fritz Hönig, *Der Volkskrieg an der Loire* (Berlin, 1893-1897), I, 1-18, 52. I have been unable to secure the account of the Loire campaign in *Der Antheil unter dem Kommando der Grossherzogs von Mecklenburg-Schwerin vereinigt gewesen Truppen am Kriege 1870-1871* (1875), which is said to have been written under Stosch's direction. General v. Wittich, *Aus meinen Tagebuch, 1870-1871* (Cassell, 1872), and General Chanzy, *La Deuxième Armée de la Loire* (4th ed.; Paris, 1872), are detailed accounts of troop movements. Both contain some of Stosch's dispatches.

The Second Army, led by the King's nephew, Field-Marshal Prince Frederick Karl, and a so-called "Army Section" (*Armeeabteilung*), commanded by Lieutenant General Frederick Francis II, Grand Duke of Mecklenburg-Schwerin, were dispatched to the Loire to defeat the French. Frederick Karl was a very cautious commander, who preferred to develop operations slowly, while weighing every factor. On the other hand, Frederick Francis exhausted his troops in a ceaseless activity which brought no results. Neither commander bothered to keep Royal Headquarters at Versailles fully informed of his movements. The Grand Duke's Command[13] brought the greatest dissatisfaction. Its movements were erratic and, despite hurried marching, it was incredibly slow at reaching a goal. In an effort to concentrate the German forces on the Loire, Royal Headquarters placed the Grand Duke under Frederick Karl's orders on 22 November 1870. This decision had little immediate effect, for the two were widely separated. Meanwhile, the French were increasing the army of the Loire, and the German operations against Paris were threatened. William and Moltke grew more dissatisfied as each day passed. General concern over the Grand Duke's procrastination in joining forces with Frederick Karl and his failure to report regularly raised the question whether it would not be the wisest policy to replace his chief of staff, Colonel von Krenski.[14]

At a conference of the King and his chief military advisers at Versailles on 25 November it was agreed that Krenski should be superseded. The names most frequently mentioned as suitable replacements were those of the German Quartermaster General von Podbielski and Commissary General von Stosch. At the end of the meeting, Lieutenant Colonel von Verdy, who was chief of one of the sections in the General staff, accompanied Stosch back to his quarters. Stosch expressed his deep concern at the course of the Loire compaign, adding: "I would be ready to assume this difficult post, and, if the conversation returns to it, you can mention

---

[13] It is thus (at the suggestion of Professor Jay Luvaas) that I hereafter refer to the *Armeeabteilung* under Frederick Francis' command.

[14] Hönig, *Volkskrieg*, I, 48, 265-66, 295-300, 312-14, 334-44, 350-53; *Memoirs*, I, 206-9; Blumenthal, *Journals*, p. 202; Verdy, *Im grossen Hauptquartier*, p. 242; Meisner, *Friedrichs Tagebuch 1870-1871*, p. 211; Ernst Feder, ed., *Bismarcks grosses Spiel: Die geheimen Tagebucher von Ludwig Bambergers* (Frankfurt a. M., 1933), p. 233.

me as a candidate." Verdy informed Moltke of the General's statement the following morning. After asking Stosch whether he was
willing to leave immediately, Moltke gladly accepted this solution
of the problem. War Minister Roon was willing to take the duties
of the Commissary General for the moment, but insisted that
Stosch could not be spared for any extended period of time. Moltke
replied that, of course, the future progress of the campaign could
not be predicted with certainty, but it was hoped that the French
Army of the Loire would soon receive an "annihilating defeat," and
Stosch could then be released for duty at Royal Headquarters. As
a result of this five-minute conversation, Roon consented. Moltke
then went to William and received his immediate approval. Stosch
departed for the Loire the same day, November 26.[15] Though
Stosch had never previously held an active command in the field,[16]
Hönig, the authority on the Loire campaign, regarded his appointment as excellent. He wrote:

The naming of General v. Stosch as Chief of Staff of the Army
Section was a real event, for, without a doubt, the General was one of
the most outstanding men of that great time and had the reputation of
a distinguished officer of the General Staff. Assured in his bearing,
he combined a high degree of common sense [Lebensweisheit] with
good judgment and a wide and inclusive point of view [Blick]. The
General, as a result of his high rank, could expect that more attention
would be paid to his advice than that of Colonel v. Krenski, and, moreover, he was in such close contact with Count v. Moltke that professional relations between them were expected to be advantageous. He
was completely informed of Moltke's ideas through his participation in
the conversations which preceded the Chief of the General Staff's daily
reports. Colonel v. Krenski had previously served under Stosch, and
could be expected to serve willingly under him again. They did not foresee in Versailles on 26 November that such important demands would
later be made upon the Chief of Staff of the Army Section. Under the
circumstances it was certainly good fortune that they decided to change
the Chief of Staff at once, for without the penetrating clarity and

[15] Hönig, Volkskrieg, I, 353-54; Paul Bronsart von Schellendorf, Geheimes
Tagebuch, 1870-1871 (Bonn, 1954), pp. 193-94.
[16] The Grand Duke of Mecklenburg was, of course, officially in command.
However, Stosch's influence was paramount and the orders issued in the Grand
Duke's name were his. This emerges clearly both from Hönig's and Waldersee's
accounts, as well as Stosch's memoirs.

energy of General v. Stosch . . . the conduct of the war would not have taken its favorable course.[17]

On 27 November 1870 Stosch arrived at the headquarters of the Grand Duke, handed him his letter of authorization from Moltke, and added that he "would remain until a military decision took place." Frederick Francis received him with extreme formality and few words. It was the custom in the German Army for the individual commander to approve, if not indeed to suggest, the selection of his chief of staff, and this custom was even more rigidly applied when the commander was a reigning prince. Frederick Francis was thus touched to the quick in his pride both as a commander and as a sovereign, when Royal Headquarters suddenly sent him a new second-in-command. To soothe the Grand Duke's wounded feelings, which were already injured by the consciousness of being outgeneraled by the French and of being placed under Frederick Karl's command, required all Stosch's tact and arts of conciliation. He managed to gain the Grand Duke's support and co-operation by the confidence of his bearing, his assurances that victory would soon fall to the Germans, and his apparent willingness to remain in the background.[18] Subordinate officers did not ease this task. Stosch remarked to his wife in December: "It is not easy at all to work with the Grand Duke. Naturally everyone turns to me with their questions and he takes offense."[19] On 13 December, during during a conference with Lieutenant General v. Voigts-Rhetz, the very able commander of the Tenth Corps, and his staff, the Grand Duke suddenly interrupted Stosch in a loud voice: "What are you doing there? That goes against the first rules of tactics."[20] Voigts-Rhetz countered with such disdainful remarks that Stosch was forced to pour oil on the trouble waters by altering the operations in the sense Frederick Francis desired. "But from that hour on I have had a master who makes my task very difficult," he wrote. Prince Albrecht of Prussia, brother of William I and commander of the Fourth Cavalry Division, looked upon the Grand Duke's pretensions as a general with a humorous eye. The day following the incident with Voigts-Rhetz, he entered the room where Frederick Francis and Stosch were discussing the

[17] Hönig, *Volkskrieg*, I, 354.
[9] 16 Dec. 1870, *Memoirs*, I, 216.
[18] *Ibid.*, I, 355, 386-87.
[20] *Ibid.*

course of operations and asked: "Well then Stosch, what shall I do today?' " Then the Grand Duke said curtly: " 'I command here.' " The Prince replied: " 'We all know what the score is [*Wir sind hier unter uns Mädchens*] and don't need to inconvenience ourselves; . . . Stosch, what shall I do?' "[21]

The continual obstacles which faced Stosch in beating the French would have daunted a lesser man. First of all, he remedied the total disorder prevailing in his own staff. Next he attempted to persuade Frederick Karl through messages that he should move to the offensive. Only a telegram from Moltke made the reluctant Prince advance. Throughout the operation, Frederick Karl remained obstinately convinced, in the face of all intelligence reports, that his own Army confronted the preponderance of French forces. As a result of Frederick Karl's delays, Stosch, fully realizing the true strength of the enemy, met a French Army two and one-half times greater than his own on the battle field of Loigny-Poupry on 2 December.[22] In command of field troops in battle for the first time in his fifty-two years,[23] Stosch won a "dazzling victory."[24] The Grand Duke was officially the commander, but it was Stosch who had conceived the action and who saw it through. At Loigny-Poupry the French Republic suffered its bloodiest and most decisive defeat in the war in the provinces. It blocked the French effort to liberate Paris and rendered ineffectual any further attempts. This "moral, political, and material" defeat made further defense of Orléans impossible. This the French and Stosch immediately perceived, but it was not clear to Prince Frederick Karl, who held the responsibility for the German advance.[25]

Prince Frederick Karl prevented the full fruits of victory from falling to the Germans. Governed by the Clausewitzian principle of annihilating the enemy, the Grand Duke and Stosch wanted to pursue the defeated French on 3 December. There is little doubt

[21] *Ibid.*

[22] On the course of operations, 27 November through 2 December, see Hönig, *Volkskrieg,* I, 172-74, 386-89, 392; III, 17-18, 20-23, 40-41, 65-67, 112-17, 193-202, 211, 255-56; IV, 3, 28-31, 33-36, 61, 191-93; *Memoirs,* I, 209-13; *Memoirs,* II, 167; Moltke, *Militärische Werke,* I, Theil III, 421-22; Fritz Hönig, *Loigny-Poupry* (Berlin, 1896).

[23] See n. 16 above.

[24] "I consider the battle a dazzling victory," Count von Waldersee to Prince Frederick Karl, 6:00 P.M., Janville, 2 Dec. 1870, Hönig, *Volkskrieg,* IV, 196.

[25] Hönig, *ibid.,* IV, 98-102, 171, 201, 216-17; *Memoirs,* I, 213.

that the enemy would have been destroyed had the pursuit been allowed on that day. However, Frederick Karl still labored under the misapprehension that the forces fighting the troops immediately under his eye were in greater number than those opposing the Grand Duke. He underestimated the totality of the victory of Loigny-Poupry and felt that Stosch, through ignorance, exaggerated the hostile forces facing him. Though prodded into the offensive by Moltke's directives, Frederick Karl made the decision not to follow the fleeing French, but to concentrate against Orléans. The Grand Duke could only acquiesce in these orders from superior head-quarters.[26] Stosch used all his persuasive powers to alter the Prince's decision, but to no avail. As a result, the Grand Duke's Command advanced alone toward Orléans and made a triumphant entry on December 5. Frederick Karl, who had planned to capture the city himself, was outraged. He still maintained that he faced overwhelming French superiority in numbers and dispatched the weary and decimated troops of the Grand Duke in pursuit of the French. Stosch encountered a force five times his own and, unable to bring the seriousness of the situation home to Frederick Karl, called on Moltke to order Frederick Karl to send reinforcements. Their arrival managed to save the day for the Germans at the end of the three-day battle of Beaugency-Cravant. The French threat thereupon vanished and Stosch was recalled to Versailles on 19 December.[27] Hönig attributes German success on the days follow-ing the capture of Orléans solely to "General von Stosch's strong will and iron firmness. Up to this point, he had only proved him-self to be an excellent chief of staff; from then on he showed himself a hero in his bearing, thoughts, and actions."[28]

The Orléans campaign established the reputation of Stosch as a field commander of genius. His greatest obstacles seem to have

[26] Hönig, *Volkskrieg,* IV, 202-10; V, 164-67.

[27] On the course of the campaign from 2 December to 19 December, see *ibid.,* V, 164-67, 216, 221, 237-38, 244-46; VI, 20-23, 25, 58-69, 147-51, 157-59, 164, 176, 197-98, 205-8, 210, 213, 221-28; *Memoirs,* I, 213-16; Alfred, Count v. Waldersee, *Denkwürdigkeiten des General-Feldmarshchalls Grafen Alfred von Waldersee* (Stuttgart & Berlin, 1923-1925), I, 111-12; Schröder, *Stosch,* pp. 51-59; Moltke, *Militärische Werke,* I, Theil III, 426-27, 437-38, 462-63. Sir J. F. Maurice, ed., *The Franco-German War 1870-1871* (London, 1900), contains an interesting account of the whole Loire campaign. It is a translation of J. v. Pflügk-Hartung, ed., *Krieg und Sieg 1870-1871: Ein Gedenkbuch* (Berlin, n. d.).

[28] Hönig, *Volkskrieg,* VI, 274.

been not the French, but his superiors. In later years he bemoaned his patriotic duty of paying public tribute to the Grand Duke's military talents.[29] With a rare combination of firmness, tact, and military genius, he had achieved great military success. He wrote on his return to Royal Headquarters: "I emerge from the campaign as a soldier and not without recognition. I thank God for that."[30] Honors were conferred upon him. On 12 December the King sent him the Iron Cross First Class. Upon his return, William warmly praised him: "You have fulfilled all my expectations and have done exactly what I wished."[31] The undemonstrative Moltke exclaimed: "We have felt your energetic hand."[32] The Crown Prince was also impressed by Stosch's military skill.[33]

Stosch's generalship gained him no popularity with the German people. Patriotic histories of the war glossed over errors, and monarchical prestige was maintained by praising the German princes for their decisions and omitting the role of their official advisers. Hönig might consider Stosch's generalship at the battle of Beaugency-Cravant "perhaps the greatest performance with insufficient resources in the entire history of modern warfare,"[34] and a sharpsighted historian might make a chance reference to his activities,[35] but his military accomplishments remained generally unknown. Frederick Karl and Frederick Francis received the fulsome praise of German patriotic writers for their part in the Loire victory. However, it is significant that the standard bearers of the

[29] To his wife, Berlin, 17 May 1878, Memoirs, II, 149-50.

[30] Memoirs, I, 217.

[31] Ibid. Stosch also received in the course of the war the Iron Cross Second Class and the "Star of a Commander of the Order of the Royal House of Hohenzollern with Swords"; Hassell, Tirpitz, p. 19. Cf. Fred Graf Frankenburg, Kriegstagebücher von 1866 und 1870-71, ed., Heinrich von Poschinger, (Stuttgart, 1896), p. 286. In addition, Stosch received the Oldenbourg "Great Cross with Swords" and the Saxon Military Service Order. Memoirs, I, 220, 228.

[32] "Wir haben Ihre energische Hand gesperrt," Stosch to his wife, Versailles, 21 Dec. 1870, Memoirs, I, 217. Verdy, apparently an eyewitness, gives Moltke's words as: "Wir haben Ihre Starke Hand stets durchgefühlt"; entry of 21 December 1870, Im grossen Hauptquartier, p. 255. These words have, of course, much the same sense as those recorded by Stosch at the time. I have preferred Stosch's account since he would be more likely to remember Moltke's exact words.

[33] Meisner, Friedrichs Tagebuch 1870-1871, pp. 251, 260, 262-63, 286.

[34] Quoted from Hönig's obituary of Stosch in the Kölnische Zeitung by Vice Admiral Batsch, "General v. Stosch über die Marine und die Kolonisation," Deutsche Revue, XXII (1897), 53.

[35] Alfred Stern, Geschichte Europas seit dem Verträgen von 1815 bis zum, Frankfurter Friede vom 1871 (Stuttgart & Berlin, 1913-1924), X, 452.

patriotic military legend, Moltke and Verdy, did not subscribe to these views of the generalship of the Prince and the Grand Duke. Moltke refused permission to Frederick Karl's intimate, Colmar von der Goltz, to publish the laudatory second volume of his work on the Loire campaign.[36] Verdy's published memoirs differed from the official history in its criticism of the Grand Duke and praise of Stosch.[37] Thus, though he gained no public renown, William I, Frederick William, and Count von Moltke, as well as other informed persons, entertained a high appreciation of his abilities.[38] His service on the Loire was a major factor in his relations with William I. The Prussian King, with his deep sense of loyalty, never forgot that Stosch had served him well in a difficult situation; Stosch could count upon his personal support for his lifetime.

3

Throughout the war Stosch, despite his work in the Commissariat and his three weeks on the Loire, took an active interest in the progress of events about him. As a high official at Royal Headquarters, he had daily contact with William I, Count von Moltke, Bismarck, and War Minister von Roon, to mention only the most outstanding figures of the time.

His early letters to his wife during the war are filled with expressions of patriotism and complaints of thwarted ambition. In early August he was received so cordially by the King that he felt "everything would be all right, were I not Commissary General." He was torn between the desire for an assignment in the field and the patriotic hope that the war would be too short to make this possible. His joy at the continuing triumph of German arms was tempered by the loss of his youngest brother, Colonel Max von Stosch, who was mortally wounded at the battle of Wörth, and the death of other relatives in October 1870. Stosch had already encountered the Crown Prince, who was en route to assume the

---

[36] Schröder, *Stosch,* p. 59.

[37] This is pointed out by Captain Walter H. James in his introduction to the English version of *Im grossen Hauptquartier,* entitled *With the Royal Headquarters in 1870-1871* (London, 1897). Cf. Waldersee's favorable comment in Hans Mohs, ed., *General-Feldmarschall Alfred Graf von Waldersee in seinem Militärischen Wirken* (Berlin, 1929), I, 336-38.

[38] See, for example, the favorable opinions in Bronsart, *Geheimes Tagebuch,* pp. 203, 211, 237-38, 241, 246-47, 265.

command of the Third Army. "He was extremely cordial, kissed me, told me that he had missed me and spoke an entire hour with me," Stosch recorded. He told Frederick William how he had been able to restore order among the troops at St. Privat, which he witnessed as a member of the King's entourage.[39]

Stosch observed the battle of Sedan first in the company of his friends, the Crown Prince and Gustav Freytag, who was visiting Headquarters, and, in its final stages, was with the King on a height overlooking the battlefield.[40] This battle was the culmination of the German campaign against the French Empire, for it led to the surrender of Napoleon III and his besieged troops. Stosch, never willing to be a passive spectator of events, helped hasten the French surrender. After the French had been herded into the fortress of Sedan, he went to the King and suggested that all German cannon be ordered to fire into it. William turned a deaf ear to the suggestion. The Commissary General then went to Moltke and secured his intercession. The King remained adamant. Finally, Bismarck threw his weight in support of the proposal, and William gave in. All German batteries concentrated their fire on Sedan, and the French soon put out a white flag.[41]

The Crown Prince continued to depend heavily upon Stosch for advice and counsel.[42] Indicative of his attitude is his praise of his Quartermaster General for acting in the same pattern as Stosch in 1866.[43] Stosch was continually surprised that "world events assumed the character of family politics in princely eyes," and he

[39] *Memoirs*, I, 188-92, 202; Meisner, *Friedrichs Tagebuch 1870-1871*, pp. 34, 67, 179.
[40] *Memoirs*, I, 194; Freytag, *Mathy: Erinnerungen*, p. 666; Meisner, *Friedrichs Tagebuch 1870-1871*, p. 92. The picture of the scene painted by George Bleibtreu is reproduced in Hermann Müller-Bohn, *Kaiser Friedrich der Gütige: Vaterländisches Ehrenbuch* (Berlin, n.d.), pp. 360-61.
[41] Hönig, *Volkskrieg*, III, 90 n. Hönig's source is perhaps Stosch himself. He mentions the incident as an aside, indicating Bismarck's ability to overcome the King's obstinacy. Stosch makes no reference to the incident in his memoirs. Cf. Kessel, *Moltke*, p. 566.
[42] Friedrich Thimme in a note in Bismarck, *Gesammelte Werke*, VIb, 473, maintains that Stosch and Freytag were supporting an attempt by the Crown Prince in September 1870 to reconcile Duke Frederick of Augustenburg with Bismarck. I have found no evidence to support this assertion. Stosch had previously opposed Duke Frederick, and the only reference in the Freytag-Stosch correspondence of the period is definitely anti-Augustenburg (Helmolt, *Freytag an Stosch*, p. 69).
[43] Meisner, *Friedrichs Tagebuch, 1870-1871*, p. 111.

attempted to orient the Prince in the views of his future subjects.[44] Stosch used his ameliorating influence with Frederick William to avoid a direct clash between him and his father. On 6 September 1870 the Crown Prince had established, as an independent charitable organization, the Victoria National Invalid Foundation to care for war wounded. Queen Augusta was outraged, for she insisted that all institutions of this sort were in her province, and the King spoke "very ungraciously" to his son, greeting him with marked coldness whenever they met. Stosch was called in by Frederick William for advice and perceived immediately that the "Prince's barometer registered stormy weather." After finally calming him, Stosch had his task to do over again when a letter from Normann threw "oil on the flames." No time and no issue, he felt, could have been worse chosen for a quarrel between the Prince and his father. The General sought busily to remove the cause of disagreement by tactful letters and counsel. "There is no pleasure in being the confidant in such matters," he wrote his wife. Normann continued to write him angry letters. He contented himself with conciliatory replies and the private aside that "people are always very shrewd far from the firing line." Finally, after a month of wrangling, the Crown Prince approached Stosch and announced his willingness to accept the General's advice. As a result, the Victoria National Invalid Foundation was united with other charitable organizations under the direction of Queen Augusta.[45] This incident illustrates the controlled and tactful way in which Stosch exercised his influence.

The principal political issue which aroused the Crown Prince's interest was the establishment of a united Germany under the King of Prussia as Emperor. William I was extremely hostile to this idea, feeling himself to be the guardian of the Prussian royal tradition, which, in his view, would be imperiled if the Prussian and German crowns were united. During the autumn of 1870, negotiations were in progress between Bismarck and the South German states to establish a united Germany. The Crown Prince, imbued with lofty dreams of the medieval Empire, was extremely dis-

[44] *Ibid.,* p. 165; *Memoirs,* I, 197-99.
[45] *Ibid.,* I, 201-6; Meisner, *Friedrichs Tagebuch, 1870-1871,* p. 216; Poschinger, *Kaiser Frederich,* III, 67-69.

tressed, he told Stosch, that no mention was made during these meetings of the proclamation of an Emperor. Stosch set no value upon this symbol of unity. Morover, he had one strong objection to the proposed united state: the Chancellor would be in an even stronger position than he was in the North German Confederation. He wrote prophetically that the "first and most important question in all politics of the future will be: 'How is Bismarck feeling?' "[46]

As the German armies approached and, on 19 September, surrounded Paris, a bitter conflict broke out in Royal Headquarters over the means by which the war was to be brought to a close. Bismarck, supported by Roon, felt that French resistance could be broken quickly if Paris were bombarded and taken by storm. The Chancellor was guided principally by fears of foreign intervention and the uncertain fortunes of war. His party of "Shooters" was opposed by the "Anti-Bombardiers," who felt that their method of investment and blockade would produce the desired result just as quickly and more safely. The Crown Prince, perhaps influenced by the humanitarian views of his wife, Victoria, and his mother, Queen Augusta, belonged to the latter party, as did most of the military specialists, who saw the difficulties of transporting siege guns over destroyed railways and of placing them once they arrived. The "Anti-Bombardiers" were captained by Moltke. Impressed by the bloody historical examples of the storming of fortresses, particularly that of Sevastapol in the Crimean War, he wished to avoid heavy loss of German lives and declared for the policy of starving the Parisians into capitulation. With the passage of each day, the conflict grew more bitter.[47] Bismarck was intolerant of opposition, and the military seem to have been mo-

---

[46] *Memoirs*, I, 206, 209.

[47] Hönig, *Volkskrieg*, III, 65-112 (his account is based upon the published accounts of Roon and Moltke and private information furnished by Bismarck and Stosch); Stadelmann, *Moltke*, pp. 212-64; v. Häften, "Bismarck und Moltke," *Preussische Jahrbücher*, CLXXVII (1919), 85-105. Two recent studies of the relations of Bismarck to Moltke are chap. viii, Ritter, *Staatskunst und Kriegshandwerk*, I; chap. v, Craig, *Politics of the Prussian Army*. For an amusing comment by Moltke on Bismarck made to Stosch, see Eberhard Kessel, *Moltke Gespräche* (2nd ed.; Hamburg, 1940), pp. 148-49. For the opening of the conflict between Moltke and Bismarck, see Helmuth von Moltke, *Gesammelte Schriften und Denkwürdigkeiten* (Berlin, 1892), V. 281-82. On Moltke's changing position, see Eberhard Kessel, "Bismarck und die 'Halbgötter,' " *Historische Zeitschrift*, CLXXI (1956), 264.

tivated by the desire to force home the lesson that their technical advice was sounder than that of the civilian minister.[48]

Stosch was identified completely with neither the "Shooters" nor the "Anti-Bombardiers," who were to continue their arguments to the end of the year. Like Bismarck, Stosch favored the storming of Paris at this time. However, on the basis of inspection of the forts of the French capital during his trip in 1865, he thought the St. Denis front, north of the city, afforded greater opportunity for success than the official plan to mount the assault from the south front, with support from the northwest. Difficulties arose and this plan was dropped.[49] But like Moltke, Stosch opposed bombardment. Waldersee, later Chief of the General Staff, who was much in Bismarck's company at this juncture, wrote in his diary on 23 October that Commissary General von Stosch was blocking German transport with food provisions to prevent the sending of cannon and munitions to Paris.[50] This charge was repeated in the Chancellor's memoirs with the embellishment that the food material was meant for the provisioning of Paris and later, after it was spoiled, was issued to the German soldiers.[51] The last charge appears to be true.[52] Stosch expected the immediate fall of Paris[53] and did have provisions sent in preparation for that event. There is no evidence to prove wilful obstruction of the shipment of munitions and siege guns, though it is possible that Moltke's order of 26 October halting the shipment of guns and munitions to relieve the overburdened railways, appeared at Stosch's behest.[54] The issue of spoiled provisions to the troops certainly shows some slackness in the Commissariat, but it was probably unavoidable in the confusion of war. Bismarck in early November blamed the failure to reach any clear decision on the capture of Paris to the influence of three people: Stosch, Tresckow, Chief of the Military Cabinet, and Podbielski, the Quartermaster General.[55] Generally Stosch

[48] Stadelmann, *Moltke*, p. 236.   [49] Hönig, *Volkskrieg*, III, 79-81.
[50] Waldersee, *Denkwürdigkeiten*, I, 102-3. See also Mohs, *Waldersee*, I, 327-28.
[51] Bismarck, *Gesammelte Werke*, XV, 322.
[52] Hönig, *Volkskrieg*, III, 87 n.
[53] *Ibid.*, III, 78; *Memoirs*, I, 198, 203, 207-209.
[54] Hönig, *Volkskrieg*, III, 82-83. On this question see also Klein-Wüttig, *Politik und Kriegsführung*, p. 129.
[55] Busch, *Bismarck*, I, 315.

appears to have tried to hold aloof from the dispute raging about him.[56]

Nerves were frayed, as Paris, which seemingly had less faith in Clausewitz than the German General Staff, continued to hold out during November. Roon argued with Blumenthal, and Bismarck and Moltke had stormy interviews. Everyone was dissatisfied. The "Shooters" complained because their views had not been adopted; the "Anti-Bombardiers" despaired because Paris showed little signs of famine. William wavered between the two camps and reached no decision.[57] It was at this time that the Loire operations threatened the German position in Northern France and Stosch was sent to bring victory to German arms.

General Albrecht von Stosch returned to Versailles with his ambition allayed, but not quenched. He had "acquired a taste for blood" and hoped to be sent to the field again.[58] This was not to be. Roon's ill-health led to persistent rumors that Stosch would become Minister of War.[59] Waldersee wrote under the date of 26 December[60] that Bismarck had been trying to establish contacts with officers on the General Staff but certain generals had not "fallen entirely into his net." He continued: "It is different with Stosch. For a long time he has been the secret adviser of Bismarck. It is calculated that Roon will soon die or resign. Then Stosch will become his successor through Bismarck's friendship."[61] These rumors proliferated throughout January and February. However, Stosch told his wife not to believe a word of them. Nor did his ambition permit him to thing of becoming Roon's second in the Ministry.[62]

The disagreement between the "Shooters" and the "Anti-Bombardiers" was at its height when Stosch returned from the Loire. He recorded on 22 December that he, as a man whose con-

---

[56] Cf. Stosch to his wife, 22 December 1870, *Memoirs*, I, 217.

[57] Hönig, *Volkskrieg*, III, 84-94.

[58] *Memoirs*, I, 218-19.

[59] *Ibid.*, I, 208-9; Feder, *Bismarcks Grosses Spiel*, p. 223; Bronsart, *Geheimes Tagebuch*, p. 80.

[60] This entry was actually added in Berlin in April 1871 from notes made at the time.

[61] Waldersee, *Denkwürdigkeiten*, I, 117-18. Cf. Bronsart, *Geheimes Tagebuch*, p. 304.

[62] *Memoirs*, I, 224-29.

victions were fixed on neither side, was much in demand for his opinion. This he found as "flattering as it is difficult." He saw that William "had more than enough of conflicts," was inclined to pessimism, and feared Bismarck's violence. Moltke had subsided into angry silence. The Crown Prince was disturbed, because his "Anti-Bombardier" stand was attributed to his wife and "English influences." On 23 December the "Shooters" finally won out with the approval of active preparations for the bombardment, but bitterness still rankled in Bismarck's and Moltike's breasts.[63]

Stosch persuaded the Prince to intercede between Bismarck and Moltke. The Chief of the General Staff held that the Chancellor had no right to interfere in strategic decisions and, more specifically, that the negotiations for the capitulation of Paris were purely a military matter. Their opposing stands were concisely depicted by the Crown Prince in his diary: "Both unite least on what shall follow an armistice, because Count Bismarck wants peace, but General Count Moltke desires a war of extermination."[64] Stosch's view of the matter was presented in a letter to the Crown Prince of 14 January 1871:

I have just returned from General von Moltke's, where I learned that yesterday's meeting with Count Bismarck ended with an explosion of suppressed rancor on both sides. Following this meeting, the General laid his proposals on the terms of the capitulation of Paris before His Majesty the King, and Minister Bismarck will do the same. I entreated the General to try one more time to reach an agreement with the Minister, in order that the King should not be faced with opposing opinions from his two most important advisers. The General believes that this is not the case at all, for he reports on the purely military point of view, while the Minister is only concerned with the political. But this separation is fundamentally false, for, in war, the two matters cannot be separated. Both sides will submit detailed proposals on negotiations for the capitulation of Paris to His Majesty the King. These differ from each other on very material points, and His Majesty must decide. This is admittedly very difficult for him without a mediator

[63] *Ibid.*, I, 217-23; Hönig, *Volkskrieg*, III, 94-112. Waldersee attributed the deferment of the bombardment to Stosch's influence against the will of the King, Bismarck, and Moltke. Mohs, *Waldersee*, I, 325 (entry of 25 Dec. 1870).

[64] For the Bismarck-Moltke controversy on this matter, see Stadelmann, *Moltke*, pp. 206-7, 239-64; Meisner *Friedrichs Tagebuch 1870-1871*, pp. 325-26; Bismarck, *Gesammelte Werke*, VIc, 665-69; Ritter, *Staatskunst*, I, chap. viii; Kessel, "Bismarck und die 'Halbgötter,'" *Historische Zeitschrift*, CLXXI, 266, 269.

[*Vorträgender*], and the latter is lacking. Minister von Roon is very sick, and, even if he were heard, is completely uninformed, and in very decisive opposition to Count Moltke. — General von Tresck[ow] is absent. The King will listen to no one else. It is thus of the greatest importance that an arbitrator intervene in this matter. I, therefore, would like to request Your Royal Highness to undertake this difficult role.

I believe that it is a duty to support the views of the General, but I do not know the views and proposals of Count Bismarck and can give no positive opinion. If Your Highness is also not informed of the two standpoints, the first step must be to speak with His Majesty on the matter and to obtain possession of the memoranda. Such great interests of state lie at stake in the eventual decision that Your Highness can surely bear gladly the unpleasantness of the matter.[65]

Although the intervention of the Crown Prince, assisted by his uncle, the Grand Duke of Baden, failed to prevent the sharpening of the conflict between Moltke and Bismarck,[66] Stosch's letter is a significant document in evaluting his political role at the time. It shows his frank and impartial appraisal of the events and personalities of the situation, and his freedom in offering advice to the Crown Prince. The letter, with its lucid statement of the problem at issue and the practical suggestions for its solution, is an example of the method he used to exert his influence upon, and educate, the heir to the throne. It demonstrates his constant endeavors to increase Frederick William's participation in daily politics and his desire to save his King from embarrassment. Most striking, perhaps, is his impartiality. Although he strongly supported Moltke's "war of extermination," he realized that no final judgment could be reached until Bismarck's views were known, an attitude which may have stemmed from his recent relations with the Chancellor. Moreover, he saw that the principle of the separation of the conduct of war from politics, upon which Moltke based his arguments, was a false distinction.[67] He was less concerned with the immediate issue at stake than with the future of Germany.

[65] Meisner, *Friedrichs Tagebuch 1870-1871*, pp. 483-84. See also Hermann Oncken, ed., *Grossherzog Friedrich I von Baden und die Deutsche Politik von 1854-1871: Briefwechsel, Denkschriften, Tagebücher* (Berlin & Leipzig, 1927), II, 317-18; *Memoirs*, I, 224. Cf. Kessel, "Bismarck und die 'Halbgötter,' " *Historische Zeitschrift*, CLXXXI, 270-71.

[66] Klein-Wüttig, *Politik und Kriegsführung*, pp. 145-46.

[67] See *ibid.*, p. 146.

He felt it more important for the King to work in harmony with his two chief advisers than for the French to be defeated totally.

On 22 January Stosch related that the Crown Prince was still acting as a mediator in the question of peace negotiations, and that he, as Frederick William's adviser, was a much sought after personage, who even ate at Bismarck's.[68]   Indeed, Stosch used his influence with Moltke to prevent another clash.[69]   "It is often not pleasant at all," he remarked two days later, "to look behind the scenes; the great men vanish."   "For me, Moltke and Bismarck alone remain above reproach in their specific greatness."   The dispute between the two was decided in Bismarck's favor, and he was given complete charge of the negotiations of peace.[70]

As the fall of Paris became more certain, Stosch was called in as a technical adviser to Bismarck on armistice negotiations with the French.   He was chosen probably because of difficulty in provisioning the city and the Chancellor's awareness of his connection with the Crown Prince and his disassociation with Moltke's "die-hards," who bitterly resented his contact with Bismarck.[71] At first Bismarck, in a long memorandum to the King, opposed Stosch's plans for provisioning Paris. Stosch attributed the Chancellors's attribute to his "nervous mood," but was forced to give William a detailed explanation.   The difficulty of supplying Paris appears in the fact that half of Parisian daily requirements for gas lighting necessitated six train loads of coal [Kohlenzüge], which represented one-fourth of the total coal supplies at the Commissariat's immediate disposal.   Another clash with the Chancellor developed when he complained to the King that Stosch would need state funds to provision the city.   The Commissary General informed His Majesty that this was false; the French would have to pay the Germans.   But William ordered him not to supply Paris in any circumstances.   In the last weeks of January 1871 Bismarck changed his mind and requested Stosch to use all his

[68] *Memoirs*, I, 226.

[69] Bronsart, *Geheimes Tagebuch*, pp. 303-4.

[70] *Memoirs*, I, 225-27; Bismarck, *Gesammelte Werke*, VIc, 660; Stadelmann, *Moltke*, pp. 245-64; v. Häften, "Bismarck und Moltke," *Preussische Jahrbucher*, CLXXVII, 98-103.

[71] Cf. Bronsart, *Geheimes Tagebuch*, pp. 348, 353, 359-60.

energies to provision the city upon its fall. Bismarck, who desired to pose before the neutral powers as the "protector" of the French and who was at odds with most of the German generals, was now particularly gracious to Stosch. The latter began negotiations with the enemy. French police prefect Cresson[72] had an interview with him on the provisioning question on 30 January. Stosch, who was in civilian dress, impressed Cresson with his "very gracious manners" and his diplomatic attitude of "listening to everything and saying nothing." Stosch, who had the sole authority to issue passes into the defeated city, used his powers to discourage the hordes of food jobbers and speculators who descended upon it. His efforts were directed toward the reopening of the city markets and the revival of local trade. To pay for the provisions he furnished, the French handed over to him millions of francs.[73]

During the preliminary peace negotiations, Stosch was also the general adviser of Bismarck, or, in his own words, the Chancellor's "military dictionary." Here he enjoyed observing Bismarck in discussions with the French. Julius Jolly, the Baden Minister-President, who was in Versailles to sign the preliminary peace, found Stosch to be an "extremely prudent and firm man."[74]

The preliminary treaty of peace contained a clause[75] stating that the French would negotiate with the German Commissary General on the provisioning of the occupation troops. By order of the Emperor, Stosch was given complete authority to treat with the French. Assisted by Wilhelm Engelhardt, an able subordinate in the Commissariat, he took the opportunity to determine the whole question of the relations of the occupation army to the

[72] Cresson habitually refers to Stosch as "Stock."

[73] *Memoirs*, I, 222-23; Moritz Busch, *Bismarck: Some Secret Pages of His History* (London, 1898), I, 516-51; Robert von Keudell, *Fürst und Fürstin Bismarck: Erinnerungen aus den Jahren 1846 bis 1872* (Berlin & Stuttgart, 1901), p. 473; Cresson, "Les premiers jours de l'Armistice en 1871; trois jours à Versailles," *Revue des Deux Mondes*, XI (1881), 515-35; Heinrich von Poschinger, *Fürst Bismarck: Neue Tischgespräche und Interviews* (Stuttgart, Leipzig, Berlin, & Vienna, 1895-1899), I, 66-68.

[74] *Memoirs*, I, 237; Poschinger, *Bismarcks Neue Tischgespräche*, II, 61.

[75] Article IV, "Préliminaires de Paix entre la France et l'Émpire Germanique," *Archives Diplomatiques*, 1873, I, 9-14.

French. Bismarck had left at the beginning of negotiations, but had instructed his representative, Saxon War Minister von Fabrice, to lay the completed agreement before him for approval. The Chancellor let it be known that the French were to provide rations and forage for the actual strength of the Army at any given time. Stosch, on the other hand, wanted the French to pay a fixed sum based on the expected average strength of the occupation force, which would have the dual advantages of the concealing from the French the real size of the Army and of preventing delays in payments resulting from disputes over the actual number of troops in France. His attitude was chiefly determined by experiences following the Austro-Prussian War. Prussian occupation troops in Moravia had been paid on the basis of the number of troops in occupation. The Austrians had disputed the correctness of the figure furnished them, had deferred payment until an agreement could be reached, and, in fact, never fully met their obligations. On the other hand, occupation troops in Bohemia were provisioned on the basis of a previously determined average strength, and the Prussians here returned home with a sizable balance. Governed by these considerations of prudence and experience, Stosch disregarded Bismarck's instructions, fixed upon an average strength with Moltke's aid, and concluded an agreement with the French. As finally approved, the Convention provided that the French would furnish rations for 500,000 men and 150,000 horses until the conclusion of the definitive peace. After that date, they would pay for a steadily decreasing number as each instalment of the war indemnity was handed over. The Germans were to evacuate certain French departments as each instalment was received; as soon as the full amount was paid, the Germans would evacuate France completely. Stosch, making full use of his powers, signed the Convention with the French Foreign Minister at Ferrières on 11 March 1871 and dispatched the document to Fabrice and the Emperor. William signed the implementary decree prepared by Stosch, and Bismarck was faced with a *fait accompli.* This incident did not seem to arouse Bismarck's ire at the time, but in his memoirs and in private conversation, he later reverted

to it time and time again.[76] For example, he remarked sourly to
Busch in 1880:

He [Stosch] concluded that mischievous agreement with Saxony. I
knew nothing whatever about it until the Saxons appealed to its provisions, and then it was too late. He did us harm also in France in
1871, when we were negotiating respecting compensation for troops that
remained behind, making us lose at least sixty millions. I do not want
to bring any charge against him, but one cannot help wondering what
he got from the Saxons and Thiers.[77]

These views were distinct afterthoughts. As a matter of fact, the
Chancellor did attempt to institute treason proceedings against
Stosch in 1876 on the basis of the Convention of Ferrières. However, his subordinates were quick to point out to Bismarck that he
had made himself responsible for its provisions when he signed
the definitive Treaty of Frankfort of 10 May 1871, which had
incorporated Stosch's decisions. Needless to say, the idea of ini-
tiating legal proceedings was hastily abandoned. Nor did the
Convention cause hardship to the German soldiers and treasury.
The troops were well fed, and the treasury received a surplus of
forty million marks at the end of the occupation. It is true, however, that Bismarck's freedom of action in bringing pressure on the
French in the immediate postwar period was somewhat hampered
by the Convention, for he might otherwise have threatened the
French with an increased army of occupation and forced them
to pay for its actual strength.[78]

    Although busy with his Commissary duties, his assistance to
Bismarck on the conclusion of the armistice and the preliminary
peace, and counsel to Frederick William, Stosch continued to evince
a strong interest in the other events around him. He was present

    [76] Memoirs, I, 239-42; Moltke, Militärische Werke, IV, Theil I, 301; Engelhard,
"Rückblicke," Beihefte zum Militärwochenblatt, 1901, pp. 529-31; Archives
Diplomatique, 1873, I, 58-69; Bismarck, Gesammelte Werke, XV, 322; Ernst
Bethcke, Politische Generale! Kreise und Krisen um Bismarck (Berlin, 1930),
pp. 101-2; Hans Herzfeld, Deutschland und das geschlagene Frankreich 1871-
1873 (Berlin, 1924), pp. 20-21. Cf. "Die Beschiessungen von Paris," Ham-
burger Nachrichten, 19 Aug. 1895, in Horst Kohl, ed., Bismarck-Jahrbuch
(Berlin & Leipzig, 1894-1899), II, 698-99, and the corrosive comments in Bronsart,
Geheimes Tagebuch, pp. 376-78.
    [77] Interview of 9 March 1880, Busch, Bismarck, II, 414.
    [78] Memoirs, I, 242; Moltke, Militärische Werke, IV, Theil I, 301; Archives
Diplomatiques, 1873, I, 132-43; Herzfeld, Deutschland und das geschlagene
Frankreich, p. 21.

at the proclamation of William as German Emperor at Versailles on 18 January 1871.[79] He was deeply moved by the ceremony and was particularly impressed by the "true Prussian" spirit shown by the new Emperor, who spoke with noncommissioned officers and common soldiers after receiving the congratulations of his fellow princes and high German officers. As a soldier, Stosch thought, like Moltke, that the peace was too easy on the French. Neverthless, and despite his nationalistic hatred of the enemy, he realized that to encourage the conservative element in France and prevent the unpredictable "red Republic coming to power," some consideration had to be shown for French wishes. In a short time, however, he came to accept Bismarck's view that a republic was better than a monarchical restoration, because it could not be strong. He resolutely opposed the entry of German troops into Paris on the sensible grounds that it was only an empty formality, which recklessly exposed the soldiers to the epidemics raging in the city; an additional hundred million francs of war indemnity would be a more tangible sign of defeat. However, he was in the vanguard of the German Army on 1 March 1871 when it made its triumphal march into the city.[80]

The approach of peace brought Stosch's ambitions once more to the fore. He speculated on what post he would be given. He was privately informed that, like most of the prominent German leaders, he would receive a grant of money from the Emperor to be paid from the French indemnity and he was later given such a "donation." During February he had hopes of becoming Governor-General of Alsace.[81] However, Bismarck said he was "able enough, but I cannot use him here."[82] Tresckow, Chief of the Military Cabinet, which controlled military assignments, was plagued by numerous demands. Stosch thought it probable that the Military Cabinet would take the easiest way out of its difficulties, and every man would be returned to his peacetime post. At the end of February he had his eye upon the post of Military Governor of Paris, an active military command. At the same time Frederick

---

[79] He is portrayed in Werner's familiar painting of the event.

[80] *Memoirs*, I, 225-27, 234, 236, 238-39.

[81] *Ibid.*, I, 225, 231, 234. His donation amounted to 100,000 thalers; Priesdorff, *Soldatisches Führertum*, VIII, 308.

[82] To Freytag, 26 June 1883, Memoirs, III, 25.

William put the strongest personal pressure upon him to join his entourage. "My disinclination to court service is and remains the same," Stosch wrote in early March, "but it does not help me." He tried to convince the Crown Prince that he would be of more service, if he were in an "influential post *au courant* with events," and he asked Frederick William to use his influence to the end. Stosch also kept after Tresckow to assign him to a high post. He was divided between the idea of remaining in the Commissariat to reform it in the light of wartime experience, and the fear that he would end his days as Commissary General. Service in the General Staff held no appeal. When he returned to Berlin in the middle of March, his future was still undecided. As long as the main body of the Army remained in France, he continued to serve as Commissary General.[83]

4

Commissary General Albrecht von Stosch accompanied the Emperor home to Berlin. The pleasure he took in the enthusiasm of the patriotic crowds was tempered by the many signs of mourning for the dead. His letter describing the homecoming so impressed Freytag that he published it in his new periodical, *Im Neuem Reich*.[84]

Stosch's relations with the Crown Prince and the Emperor remained cordial; William saw him on the streets of Berlin in early May and asked him to call at the palace. At their interview the Emperor said that he was aware that Stosch was his son's adviser. William, feeling his life was approaching its end, wished to bring his son into agreement with the Ministry and prepare him for his future duties. His Majesty recalled that, as Prince of Prussia, he had participated in the meetings and work of the State Ministry and asked Stosch to persuade the Crown Prince to follow a similar course. The General consented and wrote to the Crown Prince setting forth the Emperor's proposals. Frederick William replied on 10 May 1871 that he fully realized the necessity of keeping informed of current affairs and the views of leading statesmen. Therefore, he requested that he be sent regularly all records of the actions of the Ministry and the Bundesrat together with the

[83] *Memoirs*, I, 239-40.

[84] *Ibid.*, I, 242-43; Helmolt, *Freytag an Stosch*, p. 74.

votes of the Ministers. He would also consent to receive oral reports from the Ministry, when he desired fuller information. "For many reasons, which I forebear to mention," he concluded, "I consider this method the only one that is suitable, without resulting in certain inconveniences." These guarded words indicated his unwillingness to sit under the Chancellor's tutelage in the State Ministry, where he would not have been able to express his own views. Stosch saw the sense in this refusal. He reported to William and succeeded in having the documents sent regularly to the Crown Prince. Friedberg, later Minister of Justice, had a weekly interview with Frederick William on these matters, and the heir to the throne came into some contact with public affairs. He did not actually undertake any serious business of state, but Stosch's mediation resulted in a definite improvement in the relations of William with his son.[85]

On his return to Berlin, after an inspection tour in France in May and June 1871, Stosch rode in the vanguard of the German Army in its victory parade. He received a decoration from the Emperor as a sign of his "grateful recognition for your glorious share in the success of the campaign." In the middle of June he was appointed temporary Chief of Staff to the German Occupation Army in France, in order to represent its commander, Edwin von Manteuffel, when the latter went on leave. During his tour of inspection he had already met Manteuffel, who told him, with other compliments, that he was the only man fit to be made War Minister. Stosch was well pleased with the new post, which entailed temporary command of 150,000 men and political discussions with the French. Before his departure for German Army Headquarters in France at Compiègne, Stosch was summoned to attend the Emperor at Ems on 17 and 18 July. He found William in very poor health, and the end seemed near. The thought of William's death disturbed him, for the Crown Prince needed many years of "calm work before he ascended the throne." While at Ems, Stosch was repeatedly assured that his stay in France would be short. This pleased him, since he had no desire to be permanently subordinate to Manteuffel.[86]

[85] *Memoirs,* I, 250-51. There was a brief flareup between William and his son in June (*ibid.,* I, 253).

[86] *Ibid.,* I, 248, 251-54.

The middle of July found Stosch ensconced in the former French Imperial palace at Compiègne. Manteuffel was extremely agitated, for he had just received a letter from the Emperor instructing him not to be "cheated by Thiers," the French President. Stosch managed to calm Manteuffel and prevented him writing an excited reply to William. After a week Stosch was impatiently awaiting his chief's departure, so that he could assume command, On 31 July he mused on the reasons for the hatred of Manteuffel, even by his fellow ultra-reactionaries. To be sure, the German Commander was an egotist, but he seemed basically honest, "although completely the diplomat." By 8 August he was beginning to understand the reasons for his chief's unpopularity; ". . . he reduces the whole world to himself and scorns mankind." Stosch noted that he would have "to stay on his toes" in order not to be taken in by Manteuffel's powers of persuasion. Strong attacks on Manteuffel were appearing in the German press. Through Stosch's mediation, Freytag published articles in *Im Neuem Reich* defending him.[87]

The definitive Treaty of Frankfort of 10 May 1871,[88] which had officially concluded the Franco-German War, had left certain loopholes concerning the speed with which designated French forts and territory would be evacuated on the payment of successive instalments of the war indemnity. Bismarck instructed German representatives to observe extreme caution in dealing with the French and to avoid any concessions. Negotiations with the French were carried on simultaneously by the German plenipotentiary von Arnim in Frankfort, the German representative at Paris, Count von Waldersee, and the German Commander of the Occupation Army, von Manteuffel. The French naturally tried to play the German negotiators against each other and secure alleviation of the terms.[89]

As part of the French attempt to secure concessions, Finance Minister Pouyer-Quertier and his relative by marriage, the Marquise

---

[87] *Ibid.*, I, 255-58; Helmolt, *Freytag an Stosch,* pp. 81-83; Manteuffel to Leopold von Ranke, 2 and 11 Aug. 1871, in Alfred Dove, *Ausgewählte Schriften vornehmlich historische Inhalts* (Leipzig, 1898), pp. 237-41. See also p. 245.

[88] For the text, see Hans Goldschmidt, *Bismarck und die Friedensunterhändler 1871* (Berlin & Leipzig, 1929), pp. 129-40.

[89] *Ibid.*, pp. 141-45.

de Valon, appeared at Compiègne. Stosch was charmed by the Finance Minister, and wrote his wife that the Marquise was "an old hag full of sense and possessing skill at intrigue." Pouyer-Quertier, after protracted discussions with Stosch and Manteuffel, concluded an agreement with the German Commander whereby the evacuation of German troops was somewhat expedited. The French idea seems to have been to force Bismarck's hand by facing him with the dilemma of accepting a treaty he did not desire or disavowing his representative. They little understood their antagonist. It is interesting to note Stosch's reaction to this action of Manteuffel, in view of his own independent action at Ferrières. Stosch told Waldersee that he attempted to dissuade Manteuffel from concluding the agreement without consulting the German representative in Paris, who felt that he alone was responsible for such negotiations. Meanwhile, on 7 August, both Manteuffel and Stosch had dispatched letters in an effort to secure approval of the agreement. Manteuffel's letter to the King betrays misgivings at having acted on his own, while Stosch's letter to Tresckow was a diplomatic attempt to win acceptance of his chief's action. He even toned down the Marquise's character, characterizing her as "very shrewd and well-informed." On the face of the evidence, Stosch's action in disavowing the agreement to Waldersee and supporting it with Tresckow would seem to prove his duplicity. However, the observation of Goldschmidt, the historian of the negotiations, that Stosch was merely loyally supporting his chief against his own convictions is probably correct. Stosch, it seems, was in favor of withdrawing German troops from the forts around Paris, for he felt their position there was indefensible militarily, and wished Germany to receive quickly as much of the French indemnity as possible, but he believed that Manteuffel's independent action was the improper way to achieve these ends. His letter to Tresckow was passed to the Foreign Office[90] and probably accounts for Bismarck's temporary suspicion of Stosch's stand in the matter, which was expressed in a dispatch of 27 August. When Bismarck learned of Manteuffel's efforts to secure approval of the agreement behind his back, he threatened him with dismissal and

[90] This is inferred. Its time of arrival was noted by Keudell (*ibid.*, p. 209), an official of the Foreign Office.

the French with a German attack. The French promptly backed down, disavowed Pouyer-Quertier's action, and threw the blame on Manteuffel. William stood by his Chancellor.[91]

Stosch was an eyewitness of the raging battle between Bismarck and Manteuffel. Remembering the bitter struggle between the Chancellor and Moltke, he was of the opinion that Manteuffel "had taken off his gloves" too willingly. A significant clue to his own feelings is the fact that he asked Tresckow to speed Manteuffel's departure on vacation. He thought the Crown Prince's absence in England unfortunate, for he might have been able to intervene in the interest of harmony. The flood of telegrams, dispatches, and newspaper articles which the dispute engendered, Stosch considered "very instructive for the political future and the judgment of man." His own position was "highly uncomfortable," for Manteuffel preferred to conduct the fight from his own head-quarters, instead of departing for his cure. Stosch's wife and Freytag were afraid that his chances for future employment might be endangered by his official connection with Manteuffel. Stosch felt that he had kept himself clear of the dispute, and, even if he were dismissed, he "would not die of hunger." At this time his concern for William's welfare was less marked. He trenchantly remarked of the disturbance of the Emperor's vacation by the controversy: "He who reigns has no right to repose."

Manteuffel's departure in September was welcomed by Stosch. He was all the more astonished to receive letters from Normann, Holtzendorff, and Freytag in rapid succession, which tried "to save the miserable wretch from reaction's sink of corruption," only because he had managed to remain on good terms with Manteuffel. "Do you therefore think me so weak," he chided Freytag, "that you are filled with horror when I associate with men who perform in different keys?" Schach, he recalled, was a much more dangerous reactionary than Manteuffel, for he had more real influence. The whole dispute increased Stosch's admiration for

---

[91] *Ibid.*, pp. 145-49; *Memoirs*, I, 257-58, 261; *Die grosse Politik der europäischer Kabinette, 1871-1914* (Berlin, 1922-1927), I, 60-75; *Documents Diplomatiques Français (1871-1914)* (Paris, 1929 ff.), I, 56-70; Waldersee, *Denkwürdigkeiten*, I, 148-54; Mohs, *Waldersee*, I, 404, 406; Herzfeld, *Deutschland und das geschlagene Frankreich*, pp. 67-85; *Occupation et Liberation du Territoire, 1871-1875* (Paris, 1903), I, 19-101.

Bismarck's political skill, but reinforced his belief that no man should remain in the highest post too long.[92]

Stosch now settled down to a relatively quiet life. As acting Commander-in-Chief in France, he had many political reports to read and prepare and much public entertaining. He wanted to leave the post as soon as Manteuffel returned, and this was granted him. His future was still uncertain. He heard that a new division was being formed at Strassburg and thought it would be pleasant to be in the company of his old friends, von Möller, the Governor-General of Alsace-Lorraine, and Roggenbach, who was engaged in establishing the university there. In a letter to Freytag in October, he mentioned that Manteuffel had advised him to be very friendly to the French. He had acted in direct opposition to this advice and found them more courteous as a result. Home politics are rarely referred to in his letters from France. He did remark that he thought the Government's withdrawal of a military bill, which permanently fixed the military budget and the number of men to be conscripted, in exchange for a measure to run for three years, was unfortunate. Every year, he correctly predicted, the struggle over the military bill would become more severe. His attitude here was directly contrary to that of the parliamentary liberals. In November Stosch was back in Berlin, his brief, but tempestuous, service with the Occupation Army concluded.[93] Indeed, his active army career was ended. He had been chosen first Chief of the German Admiralty.

The years of the Franco-German War marked the recognition of Albrecht von Stosch as a forceful administrator and exceptional field commander. His military reputation bolstered his position with the King and the Crown Prince. Stosch's eagerness to accept responsibility, his independence in action, and his meeting of the day-by-day problems of administration and command with practical solutions had been crowned with success.

Politically, Stosch's aims and ideas underwent no change. Just as before the war, he continued to act as a mediator between Frederick William and his father, and attempted to bring the Prince

[92] Goldschmidt, *Bismarck,* p. 209; *Memoirs,* I, 258-66; Helmolt, *Freytag an Stosch,* p. 81; Hassell, *Tirpitz,* pp. 19-20.
[93] *Memoirs,* I, 256, 258-61, 266-71.

to the fore in political matters as arbiter between Bismarck and Moltke. While not in total agreement with the Chancellor, Stosch supported him generally and was willing to co-operate with him, when most members of the German High Command were deeply distrustful of Bismarck. Nonetheless, while serving as negotiator at Ferrières, Stosch acted independently of his instructions, when common sense and practical experience conflicted with them. Designated temporary Chief of Staff to General von Manteuffel in occupied France, he loyally supported his superior against Bismarck, despite his personal views and the danger to his career. In sum, the years 1870-1871 showed no deviation from Stosch's devotion to the monarchy, to conservative ideas, and to national unity.

IV

CHIEF OF THE IMPERIAL GERMAN ADMIRALTY AND ADVISER TO THE CROWN PRINCE

1

The appointment of Stosch as Chief of the Imperial Admiralty[1] was decided only after months of negotiations. Crown Prince Frederick William intervened to secure him the post. He wrote to Bismarck suggesting the General and making clear his view that the Admiralty Chief should have as much independent authority as possible. The Chancellor replied on 3 June 1871 that he was in complete agreement with the idea of an independent naval administration, adding: "I shall gladly, and with complete agreement, suggest to His Majesty the person named by Your Imperial Highness."[2] This letter is conclusive evidence that Bismarck did not seriously object at this time to Stosch's independent actions in his negotiations with the Saxons and the French. In early June Tresckow, Chief of the Military Cabinet, informed Stosch that both Bismarck[3] and the Crown Prince were backing him as a candidate for the naval post, and Roon had added his weight to the proposal. The Emperor received Stosch with "extraordinary favor" on 7

---

[1] Stosch's interest in the Navy, though sporadic, dated from 1840. Cf. Freytag's remark, in a letter of 20 July 1870, that Stosch had once expressed a wish to direct Prussian naval defense. Helmolt, *Freytag an Stosch*, p. 62.

[2] Bismarck, *Gesammelte Werke*, VIc, 7. Schröder, *Stosch*, pp. 65-66, traces (giving no citation) the Crown Prince's intervention to Normann. Morsey, *Die Oberste Reichsverwaltung*, p. 131, sees in the Chancellor's letter to the Crown Prince evidence of Bismarck's antipathy to Stosch!

[3] Presumably Bismarck reached this decision because of Stosch's ability as an organizer and with the aim of pleasing the Crown Prince.

July, saying to him: "Why are you fit for everything? How are you able to give star performances everywhere?" Stosch commented joyously: "Thus the future laughs."[4]

He survived the stigma of his association with Manteuffel and was informed by Normann in the middle of October that his appointment as head of the Navy was assured. The question of how far his competence would extend was still undecided. There were at that time no imperial ministers, except the Imperial Chancellor. In any case, Stosch did not want to be in a position of responsibility to Bismarck, where he would be forced to "dance to his tune," and, in fact, have no individual responsibility at all. He still had doubts whether it would not be better to continue his army career. The Navy, he wrote Freytag on October 24, did not interest him especially, but the "individuality and difficulty of the task there" did. He declared that "it is a fine thing to be able to create from the ground up and with the goal in mind." The current plan was to make him a Minister of State, which would make him the responsible head of a governmental department. On 3 December Stosch reported to Freytag that his appointment as Chief of the Admiralty[5] would follow in the new year.[6] His position was to be a unique one constitutionally:

> The business is so regulated that I become a Minister of State with a seat, but no voice in the State Ministry. I direct the supreme command of the Navy under the orders of the Emperor, but in administration with responsibility to the Imperial Chancellor. According to the Imperial Constitution, it cannot be otherwise, and I am satisfied in the hope that Bismarck will not be able to collide with me in the political sphere and, if possible, will leave me in peace in my own province.[7]

While the constitutional aspects of Stosch's position are more conveniently discussed below (see Chapters V and VI), it is well to point out here that his position was a constitutional anomaly. The German Imperial Government was in its infancy, and it had its

---

[4] Memoirs, I, 254.

[5] Stosch bore the titles of "Chief of the Imperial Admiralty," "Minister of State," and "Prussian Representative to the Bundesrat." He was also referred to in official publications as "Minister of Marine" and "Naval Minister." He will be designated "Chief of the Admiralty," "Naval Chief," "General," and "Admiral" throughout the remainder of this study. The constitutional significance of his titles will be considered in later chapters.

[6] Memoirs, I, 269-71.   [7] Ibid., I, 271.

only real predecessor in the North German Confederation of 1867. Constitutional lines were loosely drawn, precedents were lacking, and no one could be certain of the exact delimitations of his authority. Personalities counted for more than institutions. The German Empire, moreover, was a federal state of a rather special type. The twenty-five separate states, some of which retained special privileges, were mostly monarchies, which shared in German sovereignty. Prussia maintained a dominant position. No change in the Constitution, in the Army and Navy, and in the customs and excise could be made without Prussian approval. The German Emperor was the Prussian King; the Chancellor, responsible to the Emperor alone, not to the Parliament, was usually also Prussian Minister President. The Emperor was the living embodiment of German unity, controlling foreign affairs, domestic policy, the armed forces, and the imperial administration. In the seventies there were, in name, few imperial organizations, except the Navy, and no imperial ministers, except Bismarck. Yet, for all practical purposes, there was an imperial administration under the Chancellor, to whom as Prussian Minister President, the Ministers were responsible. The Prussian Ministry, in practice, often functioned as an imperial one.

Legislative power rested in the Reichstag and Bundesrat, which had other powers as well. The Bundesrat was composed of representatives of the several states who met in secret, voted only on instruction from the home governments, and had the right to defend their decisions before the Reichstag. More in the public eye, the Reichstag, whose members were elected by universal suffrage, came to be the representative of the nation. The two houses voted the budget, but this power was curtailed by existing legal limitations, including the practice of voting the Army, not the Navy, budget for extended periods of time.[8]

No other Minister had the same or similar powers or stood in the same relation to the Emperor and the Chancellor as did Stosch. His position had been created to give him as much independence as the Constitution allowed and Bismarck would permit. Stosch combined in his person the power to give the

[8] For an excellent general discussion, see Fritz Hartung, *Deutsche Verfassungsgeschichte* (7th ed.; Stuttgart, [1954]), pp. 273-97.

Emperor's commands, to make naval appointments with the Emperor's approval, to determine plans and strategy, and to issue administrative regulations. In the Army the corresponding functions were divided among three men: the Chief of the Military Cabinet, the War Minister, and the Chief of the General Staff. For problems of command he was responsible to the Emperor; for problems of administration to Bismarck. But no one knew where "command" ended, and "administration" began. Stosch's conflicts with Bismarck developed, in large part, from the simple fact that neither could be sure how far his governmental responsibility extended until experience had set limits.

The first concern of Stosch, however, was not constitutional difficulties, but technical matters. He busied himself in gaining knowledge of the Navy. He studied naval documents "until my head swims," visited the Kiel and Wilhelmshaven naval bases, and sought every means possible to master his new post. He intended to "fight as long as I have an office, but I will go when my powers are exhausted, and my subordinates [*die Leute*] have nothing more to fear from me."[9] On 31 December 1871 Emperor William relieved Minister of War von Roon of his duties as Naval Minister;[10] the way now lay open for Stosch to asume his duties as Chief of the Admiralty. His outstanding service with the Army ended in 1871. His future activity lay in the unknown waters on which the German fleet floated.

2

The Navy of which Major General Albrecht von Stosch assumed command on 1 January 1872 was of recent origin. Prussian naval tradition had a tenuous link with the time of the Great Elector, but the German fleet was created by the Frankfort Parliament in 1848 to answer the Danish threat against the German coast. Scarcely had the fleet come into existence when the Frankfort Government collapsed and the ships were sold. A small Prussian Navy, headed by Prince Adalbert,[11] William I's first cousin, was the only remaining German fleet of any size. During the wars of unification, the Prussian Navy played a role so minor

---

[9] *Ibid.*, pp. 271-72.   [10] Roon, *Denkwürdigkeiten*, III, 312.
[11] See Vice Admiral Batsch, *Admiral Prinz Adalbert von Preussen* (Berlin, 1890).

and insignificant that the Naval Ministry was combined with the War Ministry under Roon. Its ships were few, and its officer personnel, drawn from the merchant marine, was undistinguished.

The Prussian Navy's inactivity in the Franco-German War had aroused universal dissatisfaction through no fault of its own. The French fleet of 1870-1871 had six times the strength of the Prussian Navy, but failed to gain its objectives of annihilating its opponent, destroying Prussian naval bases and the German merchant marine, effectively blockading the coast, and landing an army in the rear of German armies in France. Prussian ironclads abroad escaped unharmed: the French blockade of the German coast was the "most useless demonstration in French naval history." The French failure resulted from the lack of organization and material and the disbandment of the fleet to provide fighting forces after Sedan, rather than from any German activity.[12] German public and official opinion was outraged that the Prussian Navy had not rivaled the successes of the Army. The spectacle of a French fleet in the Baltic and North Seas, harmless though it was, galled the pride of the new nation. The lack of competent high officers led the King to turn to the Army for a talented organizer, and thus, through the King's favor and the influence of the Crown Prince on Bismarck, Albrecht von Stosch had been appointed Chief of the Admiralty.

Prince Adalbert, who had fought as a general in the wars of unification, became "Inspector General of the Navy," with the right to report directly to the Emperor. This post was largely a "position of honor," for the Prince restricted his duties to supervising the execution of the Naval Chief's decisions. The Prince's death in 1873 removed an adviser who might have assisted Stosch, from that time the sole naval functionary directly responsible to the Emperor. The only senior naval officer of note, Vice Admiral Jachmann, resigned when he was passed over for the highest naval post. The guarded words of the writers of this period, who took great care not to offend princely and official sensibilities, give the impression that the aid Stosch might have received from Prince

---

[12] On French naval action in 1870, see Theodore Ropp, "The Development of a Modern Navy: French Naval Policy, 1871-1904" (unpublished Ph.D. dissertation, Harvard, 1937), pp. 38-43.

Adalbert's and Jachmann's knowledge and experience would have been more than offset by their opposition to his projects.

While the Navy awaited with understandable misgivings the appointment of an infantry general as their chief, one of the highest officers, Reinhold Werner, assured Stosch in September 1871 that the Navy could not but benefit from the administration of a "reasonable and energetic general who introduces military discipline." He promised the new chief his support and that of his fellow officers. One of Stosch's first acts as Admiralty Chief was to secure the Emperor's approval of the redesignation of the Royal Prussian Navy as the "Imperial German Navy." Practically every other governmental department including the Army remained Prussian at this time. This move was in accord with Stosch's nationalism and was probably an attempt to regain the popularity the German Navy had enjoyed in 1848, by appealing to the patriotism of the liberal nationalists who viewed Prussian particularism with great mistrust. The measure was also in agreement with the Imperial Constitution. Albrecht von Stosch was thus the first head, and founder, of the Imperial German Navy.[13]

In the opening years of his administration, he faced serious difficulties. The fleet was too small to perform the tasks intrusted to it. There was no settled policy on its mission. German facilities for ship and armor-plate construction were almost nonexistent. Naval personnel were mediocre, lazy, and undisciplined. After an early inspection, Stosch, whose personality impressed a subordinate as sharp as "jagged iron," began a "fierce reprimand" with the disturbing words: "Sheer slop—from the commander to the lowest cabin boy!"[14] The Navy was not ready for combat. In January 1872 Stosch reported that a German squadron had been ordered to proceed to Rio de Janeiro two months before, but such

[13] Stosch's speech of 4 March 1880, mentioning the Inspector General, *Verhandlungen des Reichstags*, 4 Leg. Per., III Sess., 1880, 12 Sitz, LVIII, 248; Paul Koch, *Albrecht von Stosch als Chef der Admiralität: Skizzen aus dem Akten* (Berlin, 1903), pp. 1-6; Eckhardt Kehr, *Schlachtflottenbau und Parteipolitik 1894-1901* (Berlin, 1930), pp. 3-6; Hassell, *Tirpitz*, pp. 3-13; Hans Hallmann, *Der Weg zum deutschen Schlachtflottenbau* (Stuttgart, 1933), pp. 1-9; Tirpitz, *Memoirs*, chap. i; Vice Admiral von Mantey, *Histoire de la Marine Allemand* (Paris, 1930), pp. 29-111; Howard, *German Empire*, p. 424; Morsey, *Die Oberste Reichsverwaltung*, p. 130.

[14] Tirpitz, *Memoirs*, I, 20, 25. "Ships' boy (*Schiffjunger*)" altered to read "cabin boy."

was the condition of the fleet it would not be ready until March.[15] He commented: "So I am going to direct my efforts to introduce an element of combat readiness in order to be able to act immediately next time."[16]   Naval bases and dockyards were inadequate.   The naval administration needed complete reorganization.   These technical problems were compounded by political duties.   The Emperor's approval had to be sought for all Stosch's projects.   He had also to prepare the naval budget, justify it to the Chancellor and his financial subordinates, and defend it and the whole Navy before the Bundesrat and Reichstag.[17]   There were no real precedents to guide the Admiralty Chief.   He met his tasks as they arose in the regular, day-by-day, course of business.

Fortunately Stosch possessed outstanding qualifications for his post.   He had varied experience as a military administrator and demonstrated great resourcefulness and a considerable talent for improvisation.   He showed himself eager to assume responsibilities and was frank in making his opinions known.   With these characteristics, he combined an abundant reserve of energy and a great capacity for work.   He wrote in 1877:

I have not had one quiet moment in Berlin.   Saturday I attended the launching at Stettin, where I made three speeches and had to let persistent rain ruin my new hat.   At 6:00 I returned here [Kiel] in the evening.   Today I must inspect Hollmann's gunnery and maneuvers on the Medusa.[18]

Less than a week later, he went on an inspection tour of Kiel and Wilhelmshaven.[19]

He did not gain mastery over naval problems until 1873, if one may take at face value his expressions of ignorance in the Reichstag in 1872, and the National Liberal Eduard Lasker's congratulations on his competence in 1873.   Yet his knowledge of naval affairs astonished his subordinates from the first.   He bore the responsibility for the Navy upon his own shoulders, for he would not simply acquiesce in others' suggestions or sign what he did not read.   His approval was necessary even for a change

---

[15] To Freytag, Berlin, 31 Jan. 1872, Memoirs, II, 3.
[16] Ibid.   [17] Koch, Stosch, pp. 5-6.
[18] To his wife, Kiel, 24 July 1877, Memoirs, II, 142.
[19] To his wife, Berlin, 29 July 1877, ibid., II, 143.

of insignia in the seaman's hat. The archives of the German Admiralty contained a mountain of documents from his hand on the more significant business of his office, while penetrating minutes, which praised, damned, or sarcastically probed, witnessed his attention to detail.[20] The mood in which he entered upon his manifold duties found expression in his memoirs:

I had . . . a rich sphere of activity before me and approached with great joy the weighty task I was given. Everywhere in the Navy I met frank co-operation. They [sic] soon recognized my good will and saw that I strove mightily to help them forward. My past told me Germany's Navy must only resolve defensive tasks, but a look at the future gave me the aim of preparing it for more extensive duties. It was not in my nature to remain content with half-measures. Much would be accomplished, if I could count on a few years of activity.[21]

Time-consuming ceremony complicated his daily round. His was the responsibility for the smooth operation of visits by delegations from the Reichstag to the fleet, of reviews by the Emperor, the Crown Prince, and foreign dignitaries, and of official entertainments. An eyewitness has left an account of his appearance at a ball he gave at his residence on Leipziger Platz in the winter of 1876-1877.

I saw a tall man in Naval uniform, who . . . limped a little, a peculiarity not often encountered in generals. On his broad shoulders and strong neck was a head that one could not easily forget, with a powerful forehead, a sharp Roman nose, clear-sighted eyes, rather thin graying hair and mustache—a real man and a picture of inner and external strength. There was in his gait and the set of his shoulders no sign of his almost sixty years.[22]

The Chief of the Admiralty had only a small group of assistants to aid him. It included five staff officers, five lieutenants, five privy councilors for technical, judicial, and administrative business, four construction engineers, the chief medical officer, and nineteen

[20] Koch, Stosch, pp. 1, 5-6; Hassell, Tirpitz, pp. 23-24; Stosch's speech of 27 May 1872, Verhandlungen des Reichstags, 1 Leg. Per., III Sess., 1872, 29 Sitz., XXIV, 559; Lasker's speech of 26 May 1873, ibid., IV Sess., 1873, 39 Sitz., XXVIII, 856-57; Paul Koch, Beiträge zur Geschichte unserer Marine, Neue Folge (Berlin, 1900), p. 47.

[21] Memoirs, II, 1-2.

[22] Hassell, Tirpitz, p. 14. Cf. the impressions of a child, Adalbert von Wilke, Alt-Berliner Erinnerungen (Berlin, 1930), p. 26.

civil servants to manage correspondence and records.[23] Many of Stosch's projects had direct political implications and consequences, and in that connection they are considered later (see below and Chapters V and VI). Here his naval duties, which engaged a great part of his energies, may be briefly mentioned.

The German Navy changed greatly during Stosch's eleven years of office. He set clear and definite strategic goals before it. They were defense of the coast, protection of trade, and avoidance of provocative action at sea against France and particularly against Britain, the great maritime power. They harmonized with Moltke's view that the fleet should delay or prevent landings, while troops were being concentrated by rail.[24] In accordance with these conceptions, Stosch drafted a ten-year plan for shipbuilding, which was approved by the Reichstag, and carried through during a period of technological change in construction of ships, harbors, and dockyards. The German fleet, which had forty-six ships in 1873, numbered eighty-one in 1882, with five additional ships under construction. Stosch pressed for the building of German ships in German yards, backed much experimentation including extensive torpedo research, and favored such projects as a North Sea—Baltic Canal.[25] His most significant contribution to the

[23] Koch, *Stosch,* p. 6.

[24] *Verhandlungen des Reichstags,* I Leg. Per., III Sess., 1872, 29 Sitz., XXIV, 559; Moltke to Stosch, Berlin, 22 Feb. 1873, in v. Schmerfeld, *Graf Moltke: Die Deutschen Aufmarschpläne 1871-1900* (Berlin, 1929), pp. 31-34; Stadelmann, *Moltke,* pp. 345-49; Batsch, "Stosch," *Deutsche Revue,* XXI, 35; Mantey, *La Marine Allemande,* pp. 117-18; Tirpitz, *Memoirs,* I, 24, 28, 240, and II, 372; Ropp, "Development of a Modern Navy," p. 46 n. 14; Theodore Ropp, "Continental Doctrines of Sea Power," chap. xviii in Earle, *Makers of Modern Strategy:,* and bibliographical note, p. 545.

[25] For Stosch and construction matters, see *Verhandlungen des Reichstags,* 1 Leg. Per., II Sess., 1872, 29 Sitz., XXIV, 559, 30 Sitz., Vol. XXIV, p. 573, 44 Sitz., XXV, 1053; IV Sess., 1873, 59 Sitz., XXVIII, 1373, 1375; 2 Leg. Per., II Sess., 1874-1875, 22 Sitz., XXXIV, 415; 3 Leg. Per., II Sess., 1878, 19 Sitz., XLVII, 377; Batsch, "Stosch," *Deutsche Revue,* XXI, 35, 212, and XXII, 361-62; Mantey, *La Marine Allemand,* pp. 117-18; Tirpitz, *Memoirs,* I, 24, 26, 28, 35-37, 41, 49, 240, and II, 372; Koch, *Stosch,* pp. 2, 7-16, 37-42; S. Eardley-Wilmot, *The Development of Navies during the Last Half Century* (London, 1872), *passim;* Memoirs, II, 18-19, 35-36, 59, 209, and III, 240; Ropp, "Development of a Modern Navy," pp. 19-21, 26-28, 45-49, 62, 126, 178, 243-46; Kehr, *Schlachtflottenbau,* p. 220; Hassell, *Tirpitz,* pp. 27-28; Hallmann, *Der Weg zur Schlachtflottenbau,* pp. 20-23; Poschinger, *Bismarcks Bundesrat,* III, 157-58. For Stosch's correspondence with Krupp, see Wilhelm Berdrow, *Alfred Krupp* (2nd. ed.; Berlin, 1928), II, 235, 242, 251, 274-75, 281, 297.

German Navy was probably the increase in the number, and the improvement in the caliber, of naval personnel. The budgetary strength of naval officers and engineers rose from 294 in 1871 to 573 in 1883, while the lower ranks grew in numbers from 6,525 to 11,314 in the same period. He founded the Naval Academy, made German naval training better than that of any other nation, instituted a naval staff course, raised the status of technical personnel and seamen, and reorganized the commissariat and paymaster corps.[26] He taught the Navy to work. Discipline became so severe and duties so arduous that old sea officers complained that the "one spot left in Prussia where one could live," the fleet, was now gone; English observers commented of German crews: "They are soldiers."[27] Even Stosch himself once complained that "there is too much of the infantry spirit in the war ports."[28] He did all in his power to ready the fleet for combat and ships were constantly in service. Indeed, in 1876, of all the ships available, only two were in port.[29]

The accomplishments of establishing a strategic doctrine, building new ships, docks, and harbors, raising the number and caliber of personnel, and improving combat readiness were not achieved without censure. Bismarck even pretended in his memoirs that Stosch left his post because of "certain injuries" he had caused the Navy.[30] The critics of the Admiralty Chief believed that drill and

[26] For details of these matters, see Hallmann, *Der Weg zur Schlachtflottenbau,* p. 24; Koch, *Stosch,* pp. 17-23, 31-37; Memoirs, II, 77, 176-77, and III, 241; Mantey, *La Marine Allemand,* p. 12; Tirpitz, *Memoirs,* I, 20-24; Lothar Persius, *Menschen und Schiffen in der Kaiserlichen Flotte* (Berlin, 1925), pp. 6-7; Ropp, "Development of a Modern Navy," pp. 86, 99 n. 32; Koch, *Beiträge, Neue Folge,* pp. 63-64, 67-68; *Verhandlungen des Reichstags,* 2 Leg. Per., II Sess., 1874-1875, 30 Sitz., XXXIV, 679; 3 Leg. Per., II Sess., 1878, 19 Sitz., XLVII, 472-73.

[27] Tirpitz, *Memoirs,* I, 18-20.

[28] Batsch, "Stosch," *Deutsche Revue,* XXII, 353.

[29] Mantey, *La Marine Allemande,* pp. 122-31; Stosch's speech of 27 April 1881, *Verhandlungen des Reichstags,* 4 Leg. Per., IV Sess., 1881, 34 Sitz., LXII, 834. For an example of Stosch's concern over his ships overseas, see the letter to his wife, Berlin, 21 Oct. 1882, Memoirs, II, 234. For his other naval activities, see especially *ibid.,* II, 3, 64, 214-15, 229-30, 234; *Verhandlungen des Reichstags,* 2 Leg. Per., II Sess., 1874-1875, 22 Sitz., XXIV, 415; 3 Leg. Per., II Sess., 1878, 19 Sitz., XLVII, 473; 4 Leg. Per., IV Sess., 1881, 34 Sitz., LXII, 834; Tirpitz, *Memoirs,* I, 14-16, 24-26; Hassell, *Tirpitz,* pp. 24-25; Koch, *Stosch,* pp. 23-31; Koch, *Beiträge, Neue Folge,* pp. 82-83.

[30] Bismarck, *Gesammelte Werke,* XV, 534.

training were carried too far and created a personnel problem, since the fleet offered less attraction to German youth.[31]   In any case, increase in personnel did not keep pace with ship construction,[32] while the demands of Bismarck's Foreign Office for displays of naval force kept too many ships in commission and aggravated the overburdening of the crews.   On the other hand Stosch believed that the increase in sea duty had very beneficial results in making the fleet ready for combat.[33]   In the view of Admiral von Tirpitz, he did not always succeed in translating his army ideas into naval terms and did not realize that personnel needed to accustom themselves to their ships; he expected a ship to be mobilized in three days like a regiment.[34]   Too much work, too much drill, and too much speed were the cardinal points of the attack on Stosch's "infantry system" of naval administration and command, which developed when Bismarck's opposition to him was publicly known, and increased in intensity after the sinking of the German battleship *Great Elector* in 1878.

3

The pressure of work during his first months in office left Stosch with little time for indulgence in political speculation and activity.[35] When he did relax from official business, his thoughts immediately turned to politics.[36]   His friend, Gustav Freytag, saw the Navy as a step toward greater power, offering "participation in politics" and a convenient post for "this time of expectancy."[37]   In short, Stosch should prepare himself for the high post which would await

[31] Tirpitz, *Memoirs,* I, 18-20.

[32] Stosch's speech of 1 Dec. 1874, *Verhandlungen des Reichstags,* 2 Leg. Per., II Sess., 1874-1875, 22 Sitz., XXXIV, 415.

[33] Stosch's remarks before the 1878 Reichstag Budget Committee reported in Rickert's speech of 12 March 1878, *Verhandlungen des Reichstags,* 3 Leg. Per., II Sess., 1878, 19 Sitz., XLVII, 472.

[34] Tirpitz, *Memoirs,* I, 21-26.   But for favorable appraisals of Stosch, see Koch, *Stosch,* pp. 70-73; Hassell, *Tirpitz,* pp. 1-2, 26-27, 29, 31, 62, 92-93, 115-16; Persius, *Menschen und Schiffe,* p. 7; Poschinger, *Bismarcks Bundesrat,* II, 399, and III, 158-59; Batsch, "Stosch," *Deutsche Revue,* XXI, 38-39; Admiral von Tirpitz, "Albrecht von Stosch: Zum 100. Geburtstag am 20. April," *Norddeutsche Allgemeine Zeitung,* Friday, 19 April 1918.

[35] To Freytag, 11 March 1872, Memoirs, II, 3; to Freytag, Wilhelmshaven, 13 Nov. 1872, *ibid.,* II, 18.

[36] To Freytag, Berlin, 23 Feb. 1873, *ibid.,* II, 35.

[37] Freytag to Stosch, Leipzig, 30 Jan., 10 Feb., 1872, Helmolt, *Freytag an Stosch,* p. 87.

him when Frederick William became Prussian King and German Emperor. His friend's political future would best be furthered, Freytag thought, by a post in the Army.[38] Many viewed the separation of the Navy from Army administration as a temporary expedient, until Roon retired, and Stosch could become Minister of War and of Marine. Kameke's appointment in 1873 as Roon's successor helped scotch these rumors.[39] As a matter of fact, with the passage of each year, Stosch became more and more wedded to the Navy. The demands of his position and the conflicts with Bismarck took their full toll on his nervous system and he often looked, not for other posts, but yearningly for rest.[40]

As he grew older his thoughts turned to the region of his birth, the Rhineland. In his fifty-seventh year, in 1875, he purchased a villa close to the village of Oestrich im Rheingau with the money given to him by the Emperor for his services in the war.[41] Situated on the right bank of the Rhine between Wiesbaden and Coblenz, with the *Weingebirge* and the Metternich "Schloss Johannisberg" in the background, "Haus Stosch" offered him an idyllic refuge from political conflict and administrative business and a home for his old age.[42] Here his friends often gathered over a glass of his own vintage to exchange the latest political news.[43]

However, thoughts of rest occurred only intermittently amid great activity. In 1871 Freytag had urged Stosch to use every effort to sway public opinion in favor of the Navy and himself. It was necessary, he felt, to overcome the popular mistrust of the Navy, which had arisen from its inactivity in the Franco-German

---

[38] Freytag to Stosch, Leipzig, 21 Nov. 1872, *ibid.,* p. 89; same to same, Siebleben, 30 June 1874, *ibid.,* p. 99.

[39] Batsch, "Stosch," *Deutsche Revue,* XXI, 31. It is incorrect to infer, as does Schröder, *Stosch,* p. 87, that Stosch had great ambitions of becoming War Minister and that these ambitions were killed by Kameke's appointment. In fact, Stosch favored the choice of Kameke and supported him with the Crown Prince. Memoirs, II, 22-25.

[40] Stosch to Freytag, Oestrich, 13 July 1875, *ibid.,* II, 101-2.

[41] To Frau von Stosch, Mainz, 31 March 1875, *ibid.,* II, 95; Werner Kratz, *Oestrich und Mittelheim im Rheingau* (Arnsberg, 1953), p. 48, erroneously places its purchase in the early eighties. The weather vane still bears the date "1875," and probably marks Stosch's purchase.

[42] Cf. Freytag's comment in a letter to Salomon Hirzel, Siebleben, 16 June 1876, in *Freytag an Hirzel,* p. 217.

[43] The present writer visited "Haus Stosch" in September 1953 and May 1954 and had the pleasure of sampling the Stosch wine. On Rheingau wines, see S. F. Hallgarten, *Rhineland Wineland* (London, 1952), pp. 73-84.

War. "A trusted officer" should be placed in charge of relations with the press. Freytag put his own political journal, *Im Neuem Reich,* at his friend's disposal and promised to use his influence with the Hamburg *Korrespondent* and the *Börsenhalle.* Good relations with the Reichstag were "very necessary." As members particularly interested in the Navy, Freytag listed the later National Liberal President of the Reichstag, Max von Forckenbeck, *"unconditionally the best person as a parliamentary adviser,"* and Wilhelm v. Freeden, director of the North German Naval Observatory. For technical advice on the merchant marine, he felt that the merchant Droege would be useful in dealings with the English, and H. H. Meier, a National Liberal official of the North German Lloyd, would also be of service. Stosch should preserve a "mild and tolerant mien" toward parliamentary efforts to show shrewdness. Popularity with the Reichstag would result in respect from the Chancellor and renown throughout the country. The meetings of Reichstag committees were more important than the sessions themselves, noted Freytag, himself a former member of the Reichstag. In the committee meetings frankness and friendliness would work wonders. The most important thing was to let people know of his work, so that there would be no objection to him as a General. To that end Freytag desired Stosch to inform him of reform projects so that they might be given publicity.[44] The General was quick to avail himself of Freytag's periodical, *Im Neuem Reich.* Freytag, an experienced journalist, who took particular pleasure in writing pro-Navy articles for his friend, advised him to make his technical memoranda simple and clear for the benefit of Reichstag members, and encouraged him to build ships, so that the people would see some tangible results from their contributions to the Navy. He even composed toasts for Stosch to deliver on public occasions.[45] Stosch did not place his reliance upon Freytag's articles alone, but attempted to publicize the Navy in all possible ways.[46]   It is

[44] Freytag to Stzosch, Leipzig, 4/5 Dec. 1871, Helmolt, *Freytag an Stosch,* pp. 82-85.
[45] *Ibid.,* pp. 88, 92, 94, 98.
[46] It is of interest in this connection that Stosch believed that there was great need for the Government to control the press during the Kulturkampf (Stosch to the Crown Prince, 3 April 1874, Memoirs, II, 74). Presumably he altered his opinion when Bismarck unleased the official press and set it on his trail.

significant that an officer in the Naval Ministry was intrusted with "literary matters."[47] Manoeuvers and reviews, and a visit by the Reichstag to the fleet kept the Navy in the public eye. The discussions of the annual naval budget, both in the Reichstag and the Bundesrat, served to further this goal.

The Bundesrat or "Federal Council" was the unique institution designed by Bismarck to maintain the federal character of the German Empire. German sovereignty rested in the "totality of allied governments" represented in the Bundesrat.[48] The Bundesrat possessed not only legislative functions, but had judicial and administrative duties as well. Its members were the representatives of the twenty-five German states and possessed diplomatic immunity. They could vote only on instruction from their home governments. The Imperial Constitution gave the chairmanship of the Bundesrat Committee on Naval Matters to Prussia.[49] This chairmanship Stosch received when he became a Prussian representative to the Bundesrat in 1872. He used his position to gain support for his maritime program (see Chap. V below) and to take the lead in any proposal concerning naval and maritime affairs. He enjoyed such success that, "in the course of years," the representatives of Lübeck, Bremen, and Hamburg always approached him with their projects. In this manner he was able to put his mark upon both naval and maritime legislation. He made it his practice "never to attend the Committee on Naval Affairs without previously informing myself completely about the matter at hand."[50] As a Prussian representative to the Bundesrat, he had the task of defending the Bundesrat's decisions on naval legislation before the Reichstag.[51]

Bismarck had the support of the National Liberal and Liberal Imperial parties in the Reichstag of the early seventies. The particularistic Conservatives opposed him because of his nationalistic

---

[47] *Almanach de Gotha*, 1882, p. 69.   [48] This was Bismarck's view.
[49] Howard, *German Empire*, chap. iv.
[50] Stosch to Tirpitz, 25 Dec. 1895, Hassell, *Tirpitz*, p. 105.
[51] Constitutionally he did not, and could not, appear in the Reichstag as Minister of State or Chief of the Admiralty. Members of the Reichstag, Bundesrat representatives, and specially designated Imperial officials alone could speak in the Reichstag. The Bundesrat representatives and Imperial officials were restricted to defending the views of their departments or those of the Bundesrat. They could not freely express their opinions nor vote. For references to Stosch's actions in the Bundesrat, see Poschinger, *Bismarcks Bundesrat*, II, 106, 125-29, 397-98. Cf. Walter Hubatsch, *Der Admiralstab und die obersten Marine behörden in Deutschland* (Frankfurt a. M., 1958), p. 35.

policies; the Center party struggled against his anticlerical measures in the Kulturkampf; the Left Liberals *(Fortschrittpartei)* voted against him, because he refused to introduce a parliamentary government on the English model.   The fleet remained relatively unaffected by party struggles until 1877.   It was small, and its expenses were slight.   The liberals of all shades (Liberal Imperials, National Liberals, and Left Liberals) generally upheld their traditional support of the Navy.   The Conservatives supported the Navy reluctantly as a part of their general program of backing national defense, while the Center indifferently voted with the rest of the Reichstag.[52]

The naval budget[53] debate of May 1872 was the occasion for Stosch's entrance upon the parliamentary scene, and he frankly and engagingly admitted that he did not yet possess the knowledge necessary to reach any firm decisions on naval policy.   However, he did state his belief that the Navy should be subordinated to Army needs.[54]   The speakers of the Liberal Imperial party[55] were pleased that he put the interests of the Army before those of the Navy, and approved his demands for ships.[56]   Johannes von Miquel, later Finance Minister under William II and future friend of Stosch, and Robert von Benda, an old friend of the General, spoke for the National Liberals.   Miquel disagreed with Stosch's financial demands and asked for a detailed shipbuilding plan, based on that of 1867.   Benda supported the Admiralty's request for funds and, amid shouts of approval from the deputies, expressed his satisfaction that Stosch was not a Minister who pretended to know all the answers.[57]   The Left Liberals were divided.   Baron von Hoverbeck and Friedrich Harkort echoed Benda's praise of Stosch's modesty and announced their intentions of voting the naval credits. Theodore Schmitt, representing the port of Stettin, took a more

---

[52] Kehr, *Schlachtflottenbau,* pp. 10-14, 17-20, 23.

[53] The naval budget was handled as part of the regular budget and *not* in the exceptional manner of the Army budget.

[54] Speech of 27 May 1872, *Verhandlungen des Reichstags,* 1 Leg. Per., III Sess., 1872, 29 Sitz, XXIV, 559.

[55] Count zu Münster-Ledenburg (Hannover), Dr. Schleiden, and v. Kusserow.

[56] *Verhandlungen des Reichstags,* 1 Leg. Per., III Sess., 27 May 1872, 29 Sitz., XXIV, 556-557, 561-562, and 28 May 1872, 30 Sitz., XXIV 576.

[57] *Ibid.,* 29 Sitz., 27 May 1872, XXIV, 562; 30 Sitz., 28 May 1872, XXIV, 657-59.   For Miquel's attitude, see Herzfeld, *Miquel,* I, 274.

critical view of the expenditures, but also announced his support.[58] No one else participated in the debate and the estimates were approved.

The suggestion that the Chief of the Admiralty should prepare a shipbuilding plan was taken up by Stosch.[59] He put much careful preparation into the plan, writing Freytag from Berlin on May 4, 1873:

> I enclose herewith a copy of the so-called plan for the foundation of the fleet. If you will write about it, I will leave the handling of the matter up to you entirely. I would like to hear new and independent points of view before I enter upon the parliamentary battle. Before the end of the month, I am going to try my hand at bribery and conduct the Reichstag around Wilhelmshaven and entertain it. Many of the gentlemen do not know what water is at all, not to mention a warship. Otherwise the Reichstag is very industrious and fulfils all the expectations of the Government.[60]

The eagle, if somewhat jaundiced, eye of Eugen Richter, leading orator and journalist of the Left Liberal party, detected the monetary motive behind the invitation, but he, with most of his fellow deputies, made the tour of Wilhelmshaven and Bremerhaven. Stosch did not fail to refer to the budgetary needs of the admiralty in one of his toasts. The trip favorably impressed the deputies, as the support of Stosch in the budget debates was to show.[61] Prince Adalbert's death occurred at this time, and Richter's motion in the Reichstag Budget Committee to abolish the post of Inspector General of the Navy received Stosch's strong support and the Committee's approval.[62] The debate of 26 and 27 May 1873 brought a variety of opinions to the fore. The Conservative speakers supported the credits, but deplored the cost.[63] Mosle, who spoke for the National Liberals, declared that the Navy "was a national aim like none other" and complimented Stosch with the

---

[58] *Verhandlungen des Reichstags,* I Leg. Per., III Sess., 27 May 1872, 29 Sitz., XXIV, 555-56, 559-61, and 28 May 1872, 30 Sitz., XXIV 579.

[59] To Freytag, Wilhelmshaven, 13 Nov. 1872, Memoirs II, 18-19.

[60] *Ibid.,* II, 46.

[61] Eugen Richter, *Im alten Reichstag: Erinnerungen* (Berlin, 1894-1896), I, 63-65; Prince Hohenlohe-Schillingsfürst, *Memoirs* (New York, 1906), II, 91-92.

[62] Richter, *Im alten Reichstag,* I, 67.

[63] Von Wedell-Melchow's speech, 26 May 1873, *Verhandlungen des Reichstags,* I Leg. Per., IV Sess., 1873, 39 Sitz., XXVIII, 817, and Baron von Minnergerode's, 27 May 1873, 40 Sitz., XXVIII, 849.

words: ". . . we now have a famous organizer at the head of the Navy, as was necessary (Hear! Hear! left), and we can be sure that the proposals which he makes to us are carefully thought out and will be adhered to in so far as possible." He called for the construction of a Baltic–North Sea Canal.   Eduard Lasker, leader of the left wing of the National Liberals, stressed economy, congratulated Stosch on his knowledge of technical matters, and felt that the shipbuilding plan showed that "clarity" and "decisiveness" would henceforth characterize the naval administration.[64] The Left Liberals introduced a discordant note into this harmony of approval.   Richter expressed his concern at the cost,[65] which also troubled Friedrich Harkort.   The latter felt that German naval development should wait until technical advances became clear.[66] Stosch wrote the Crown Prince of the results of the debate: ". . . so far everything has gone well, and I receive the means to create."[67]

The third reading of the naval budget of 1873 occasioned speeches in support of Stosch's shipbuilding plan by the National Liberals, the Liberal Imperial party, and the Left Liberals.   Dr. Schleiden, of the Liberal Imperial party, who had firsthand knowledge of the French, English, and American navies and had benefited from the advice of Admiral Porter of the American Navy, strongly supported torpedo development.   He deplored the Bundesrat's refusal to vote money for the construction of a Baltic–North Sea Canal, which Stosch had proposed.   An amendment to the budget was passed, which requested the Chief of the Admiralty to encourage German shipbuilding.[68]

The naval debates of the following years until 1877 witnessed willing Reichstag support of Stosch's proposals. Heinrich Rickert, a newly elected member of the National Liberal left wing from Danzig, became *rapporteur* on naval affairs for the Budget Committee.   Holding this position and representing a district which

---

[64] *Ibid.*, 40 Sitz., 27 May 1873, XXVIII, 856-57.
[65] *Ibid.*, 29 Sitz., 26 May 1873, XXVIII, 817.
[66] *Ibid.*, 40 Sitz., 27 May 1873, XXVIII, 847-49.
[67] 29 May 1873, Memoirs, II, 47.
[68] *Verhandlungen des Reichstags*, I Leg. Per., IV Sess., 18 June 1873, 55 Sitz., XXVIII, 1221-23; 23 June 1873, 59 Sitz., XXVIII, 1377-80; Koch, *Stosch*, p. 10.

took a strong interest in maritime affairs, he came into frequent contact with the Chief of the Admiralty. On this tenuous official connection, Bismarck was to base the charge that Rickert and Stosch were the two most prominent members of a liberal shadow "Gladstone Ministry," which was to replace him. Particularly appreciative of Stosch's energy and zeal, even in their criticisms, were retired Commander von Saint-Paul Illaire (Liberal Imperial party), Rickert, and Richter.[69] The only measure which aroused controversy was the proposed construction of a second entrance to the harbor of Wilhelmshaven, opposed by some of Stosch's subordinates in the Navy. However, he managed to convince a majority of the Budget Committee of its utility and practicality, and the Reichstag voted the necessary funds.[70]

An incident in the Budget Committee session in December 1875 was to have delayed repercussions. Here Stosch accepted a National Liberal amendment, sponsored by Rickert, which decreased the estimates, but blocked the adoption of Richter's proposal to strike out various credits for the building of warships. If Stosch had not accepted the amendment, he would have not been able to construct the ships he desired.[71] Bismarck was to force a major domestic political crisis over Stosch's action.

Stosch's relations with the Reichstag showed the success accorded to unfailing courtesy, tactful statements, and a willingness to compromise. As a Prussian representative to the Bundesrat, constitutionally he could only defend the Bundesrat's decisions before the Reichstag, but, within these circumscribed limits, he gave evidence of an ability to work in harmony with the deputies. Jealousy of Stosch's success and fear of his parliamentary influence were probably factors which aroused Bismarck's distrust and determined his tactics of attacking the Chief of the Admiralty in the Reichstag. This attack was to alter greatly Stosch's relations with that body.

[69] *Verhandlungen des Reichstags*, 2 Leg. Per., 11 Sess., 1 Dec. 1874, 22 Sitz., XXXIV, 414; III Sess., 15 Dec. 1875, 28 Sitz., XXXVIII, 683, 686.

[70] *Ibid.*, II Sess., 1 Dec. 1874, 22 Sitz., XXXIV, 417; 14 Dec. 1874, 30 Sitz., XXXIV, 690; Batsch, "Stosch," *Deutsche Revue*, XXI, 203; Memoirs, III, 39, 43-44.

[71] Richter, *Im alten Reichstag*, II, 10-11.

4

The views of Albrecht von Stosch on the political issues of the early seventies shed significant light upon his reputed liberalism, which Bismarck roundly denounced in his memoirs (see Chapter VI below). He linked the General with the court circles of the Empress Augusta, the Crown Prince, and the Left Liberal party, which favored the introduction of a ministry responsible to the Reichstag. Later historians, both nationalistic and liberal, aware of the Chancellor's conflicts with the Chief of the Admiralty, have generally accepted Bismarck's charge as true coin. Detailed examination of Stosch's views seriously modifies this traditional picture. During the seventies, his interest ranged widely and extended from the condition of French war prisoners[72] to the organization of local government.

While his comments on foreign policy are many and varied, they are much the same in general tenor, showing a great admiration for, and understanding of, Bismarck's personality and ability. One example will suffice to show their nature. The Chancellor had encountered opposition abroad to his struggle with the Roman Catholic Church, and, in February 1875, requested the Belgian government to restrain its church leaders and press from interference in Germany's domestic affairs. Concerned about the rapid reconstruction and rearmament of France after the War, Bismarck forbade the export of horses from Germany to France in March. In the following month an article, almost certainly inspired by the Chancellor, appeared in the Berlin *Post* under the headline: "Is War in Sight?" Foreign opinion, distrustful of Germany's motives, grew alarmed, and war was feared.[73] Stosch, accustomed to Bismarck's tactics, refused to become excited. In a letter to Freytag from Berlin on 22 April 1875, he wrote:

I was astonished to find a martial mood here, when I returned after three weeks' absence. I lay no weight at all on the sensational articles and notes. I believed that the Chancellor had had only the intention of

[72] Vicomte de Gontaut-Biron, *Mon Ambassade en Allemagne (1872-1873)* (3rd ed.; Paris, 1906), p. 40.

[73] E. M. Carroll, *Germany and the Great Powers, 1866-1914* (New York, 1938), pp. 110-20; William L. Langer, *European Alliances and Alignments 1871-1890* (New York, 1931), pp. 43-45; A. J. P. Taylor, *The Struggle for Mastery in Europe, 1848-1918* (Oxford, 1954), pp. 225-26; Norman Rich and M. H. Fisher, eds., *The Holstein Papers* (Cambridge, 1955 ff.), I, 93, 117.

showing the French we were not afraid and the Belgians that talk of
the devil makes him appear. However, here danger is seen everywhere;
there is no appreciation of such a calm standpoint. Bismarck was
sick, and I could not get any certain information. Then yesterday the
Chancellor gathered us [the State Ministry] together at a session. His
cold was apparent, but he was unusually active in spirit and in a good
mood. I can tell you that we will remain at peace.[74]

It is significant that Stosch's conclusion "we will remain at peace,"
obviously based upon Bismarck's statements to the Ministry, preceded the British and Russian remonstrances in Berlin in May,
which ended the crisis.[75]　His view of Bismarck's motives agrees
with the best historical appraisal, but he apparently remained unaware of the serious reaction of foreign governments to the crisis.[76]

In domestic politics the great issue of the early seventies was
the Kulturkampf, Bismarck's attempt to destroy the political power
of the Roman Catholic Church. German diplomatic relations with
the Vatican were severed. Imperial legislation expelled the Jesuits
and attempted to control pronouncements from the pulpits. Prussian enactments secularized education, assumed control of church
property, deprived bishops of power over the lesser clergy, offered
appeals to secular courts in ecclesiastical cases, and introduced
obligatory civil marriage. Some of the German Catholic hierarchy
were even jailed. The Chancellor had in his campaign the general
support of most German Liberals,[77] who were much influenced by
the secular tendencies of the day. Stosch's views, while opposed
to those of most parliamentary liberals, were perhaps liberal in the
wider sense. In the forties he had been quartered with many jovial
Catholic priests in the Rhineland and had considered them as
friends. His later study of conditions in Poland, under the tutelage
of General von Brandt, confirmed his tolerant attitude. A deeply
religious Protestant, he may well have found the Roman Catholic
faith more congenial than secular disbelief. To be sure, he felt
that teaching in Catholic schools was directed at the political power
of the state, and, until the day he died, he favored universal public

[74] Memoirs, II, 96.
[75] Taylor, Struggle for Mastery in Europe, p. 226.
[76] Carroll, Germany and the Great Powers, pp. 115, 120-22; Langer, European
Alliances and Alignments, pp. 45-55.
[77] "Liberals" is used throughout to designate the Liberal Imperial, National
Liberal, and the Left Liberal parties.

education under state control.[78]   But he strongly desired, chiefly on practical grounds, the end of the conflict.   He wrote to the Crown Prince on April 19, 1872, of the effort to control Catholic bishops: "Personally I consider the entire struggle a mistake, because the Government always gets the worst of it.   The Government can only act in public.   The bishop does the opposite, plays the martyr, and triumphs in defeat."[79]   After discussing measures for secularizing the schools, he added to a letter to Frederick William on April 23, 1873:

> Up to now the conflict has served state interests.   I believe we should content ourselves with that, for we shall not obtain a positive success.   The struggle remains theoretical and embitters minds.   Both state and religion are harmed.   I would make peace and sacrifice Falk [the Minister of Religious Affairs].[80]

Stosch's opposition to the Kulturkampf brought him into conflict with his friend, Gustav Freytag, who strongly favored the official policy.   In a letter which shows a more critical attitude toward the Chancellor, Stosch wrote:

> Church and State bother me too, as does Freytag's desire for a battle with the Church, which, in my opinion, threatens to destroy the inner springs of our power.   Here also Bismarck says: *Divide et impera*— that does not please me; it strengthens our enemies and particularism.[81]

In a letter of 29 December 1873 he enlarged on his views, and expressed his unwillingness to see Frederick William become King and Emperor in the near future:

> . . . No one can hope more than I that we will keep on with the old ruler.   He is so necessary to win peace with the Church.   If Germany would be powerful, we cannot carry the civil war between Church and State to the knife, for we cut off our own muscles.   Right now the young Prince would mean a weakening of our political situation.
>
> When you [Holtzendorff] say to me: "The State must emerge from this business as the acknowledged victor," you must not take offense, if I consider that a theoretical standpoint.   I want a free and powerful Germany, and, for that, I must have quiet at home.[82]

[78] See especially *Memoirs*, I, 15.   [79] *Memoirs*, II, 7.
[80] *Ibid.*, II, 45-46.
[81] To Holtzendorff, Berlin, 16 Nov. 1873, *ibid.*, II, 59.
[82] *Ibid.*, II, 59.   Cf. his belief that the expulsion of the Jesuits would have little practical result.   Adelheid Constabel, *Die Vorgeschichte der Kulturkampfes* (Berlin, [1956]), p. 260.

As a solution to the divisive effects of the Kulturkampf, Stosch privately proposed the acquisition of colonies to absorb German emigration. Freytag objected that this would bring further conflicts between Stosch and Bismarck and, in any case, was not feasible as long as relations with France remained difficult and demanded the full attention of the country.[83] Stosch replied on 22 April 1875:

I am pained that you oppose public treatment of the colonial question. I completely agree with you that the immediate initiation of a colonial policy would cause many difficulties, but we really have not reached that point yet. Then too the press treatment of the question would be hard to connect with me personally and could hardly affect my relation to the Chancellor. But even if you are right in this, it is another question whether our situation does not make it our duty to support measures which increase German power and the goals attainable by the spirit and which are in opposition to the destructive elements of the Kulturkampf. You have repeatedly said that country people like to fill their idle minds with the overseas world, the emigrants, and foreign conditions. Then the thought of overseas undertakings would exercise a stimulating power over German hearts and would be fundamentally popular. Also the great Chancellor would be won over to my plans much sooner by the press than if I presented them.—All nations have started on their greatest tasks at a time of strong ferment. If we choose to wait quietly at home to make ourselves felt abroad, then we are completely finished. Today if we complete every task which is justifiable in itself, our power will be strained everywhere. Bismarck himself shows us the way. The world will see that Germany has not been weakened by the Kulturkampf; that is the entire substance of the row with France and Belgium. A similar *avis* to the world lies in colonial policy, but, as I said, personally I must stand aloof from literary activity for it, because my person could harm the matter.[84]

This letter reveals Stosch as an early colonial enthusiast, who favored extending German hegemony in Europe to the world. It is significant that he fully realized Bismarck's detestation of him would damage the policies he supported. There is little doubt that German colonial settlement would have been more lasting if German emigration could have been channeled into her overseas pos-

[83] Freytag to Stosch, Siebleben, 18 April 1875, Helmolt, *Freytag an Stosch*, p. 105.
[84] Memoirs, II, 96-98.

sessions.[85]   Stosch made no public statement of his views at this time, though he tried to secure their adoption by Parliament (see Chapter V), and only in retirement did he publish an anonymous article on the subject.

With the passage of time his opposition to the Kulturkampf increased.   In late 1875 he termed a law forbidding Catholic processions an "incalculable error."   Previous governmental measures, he noted, had been directed at the ecclesiastical hierarchy and had received the unwilling acquiescence of the people, but forbidding processions would strike at every Catholic.[86]

A remark of Bismarck's that the forthcoming elections would result in a National Liberal and Left Liberal coalition opposed to a Conservative and Centrist coalition prompted Stosch to comment that this proved that the Chancellor wished to make peace with the Church and the Conservatives, as he (Stosch) had previously recommended.[87]   His appraisal of the Chancellor's ultimate political objective proved to be quite correct.   Indeed, his whole attitude toward the Kulturkampf showed a keen grasp of the realities of the internal political situation and penetrating insight into the aims and methods of Bismarck.

Stosch's views of the internal situation in general also reflected his political perspicacity.   This is illustrated by a letter he wrote to Freytag from Berlin on 23 February 1873:

I have been through highly interesting battles or spasms [*Kampfe oder Krämpfe*].   The Ministry is sick, and its leader . . . is sicker still. Everyone is accustomed to getting the guiding principles of his activity from Bismarck; all stand helpless when this fountain runs dry.—It is the same thing with the Chamber.   Prussia, as leader of the Empire, the King, with the entire nimbus of his deeds and his position, and Bismarck, as the worker of Europe, are so powerful that an individual parliamentary life cannot develop.   This is shown, first of all, in the complaint of all parties that they lack leaders.   We are positively poor in men.[88]

---

[85] On the size of German emigration, see J. H. Clapham, *The Economic Development of France and Germany, 1815-1914* (4th ed., Cambridge, 1951), p. 208.

[86] To the Crown Prince, 1 Nov. 1875, Memoirs, II, 105-6.

[87] To the Crown Prince, 13 March 1876, *ibid.*, II, 115.

[88] *Ibid.*, II, 36-37.

His admiration for Bismarck and his realization of the dangers of his power clearly emerge here and occur frequently throughout his correspondence. He was generally critical of his ministerial colleagues for their lack of independence and strong will.[89]

A friendly feeling for, and admiration of, Great Britain was at this time a characteristic of the liberal parties. Stosch's opinion of that power, gained while on a tour of the factories, shipyards, and naval installations at Plymouth, Sheffield, Glasgow, and Liverpool in 1873[90] certainly was in accordance with the liberals' standpoint. He wrote to his wife from London on 27 September 1873:

It is such an immeasurably rich nation that it cannot be judged by our standards. Care for the common weal is advancing everywhere. What is barely possessed by the rich in Berlin is provided here for everyone. . . . Only Krupp goes further in his installations. . . .[91]

The problems of local administration also attracted Stosch's attention, and revealed another aspect of Great Britain for him to admire. He felt that East and West Prussia, which were poor provinces, little favored by nature, should be divided into as small administrative units as possible.[92] Local administration he believed, should be organized in such a fashion as to facilitate the participation of the landed classes. He wrote to the Crown Prince on 2 November 1874, of the measures of the Minister of Interior, Count Fritz zu Eulenburg, which aimed at altering the organs of provincial administration:

Eulenburg's leveling tendencies appear very serious to me. Even [Finance Minister] Camphausen said that one should not make changes without cause. It will arouse opposition in community, church, and school. The art in such organizational questions is how conservative elements can best be brought to bear. Self-government is a field in which the "gentlemen" [English in the original] can participate from the first. The administrative divisions must therefore be so designed that virtuous and distinguished people can take the lead in the units concerned without becoming too hampered in their private life. . . . It is wrong to create subordinates and bureaucrats for this, instead of

[89] *Ibid.,* II, 35, 37, 86, 117-18, 121; Lucius, *Bismarck-Erinnerungen,* p. 87.
[90] Memoirs, II, 57.   [91] *Ibid.,* II, 56.
[92] To the Crown Prince, 16 Dec. 1873, *ibid.,* II, 62-63. On the local administration, see Lysbeth W. Muncy, *The Junker in the Prussian Administration under William II, 1888-1914* (Providence, 1944), chap. v.

cultivating aristocrats.—Eulenburg is going over to the radicals with his blissful theories. By the way, he is quite astonished to meet resistance.[93]

This letter is one of the few theoretical documents from the hand of a pre-eminently practical statesman. He favored the development of the nation upon a basis provided by the landed classes and looking to local rather than state control. He elaborated this opinion in another letter to the Crown Prince on 21 December 1874:

> The State Ministry sat for four hours on Sunday considering the regulations for the provinces. I got the idea that Camphausen's guiding principles stem from France, where a law spins all the threads of life and brings everything to one homogeneous mass. It is just the opposite in England. The law hardly concerns itself with communes, districts, etc. In France, revolution has a home. In England, the country is untroubled no matter how high the waves of party surge. I hope this organization will . . . come before the Chambers at a time when the pendulum of power is not pushed too far to the left.[94]

Thus Stosch wished, in local affairs at least, the adoption of an administrative system which maintained local freedom and diversity and embodied a conservatism, responsive to change, based upon the feelings of duty and honor of the governing classes. He rejected the centralizing and egalitarian system of France in favor of English diversity and local freedom.

The early seventies give us a clear insight into Albrecht von Stosch's political beliefs and aims. The touchstone of any policy was its practicality; he was in general opposition to the Kulturkampf because he considered it theoretical. While he backed secularized state education, his tolerance and respect for religion forced him to object to Bismarck's actions. The jailing of Bishops and the outlawing of religious processions, moreover, seemed to him to divide, not unite, Germany and to disturb domestic peace, so necessary for the development of the new nation. His solution, besides ending militant anti-Catholic measures, was to divert German energies into colonial expansion. The idea was a logical outgrowth of his intense nationalism.

Stosch's views were predominantly conservative. Like the Liberals, he admired English material prosperity, but he also praised the power of the landed classes in both Great Britain and Germany.

[93] Memoirs, II, 84-85.   [94] Ibid., II, 85.

He, with the Liberals, admired Bismarck's foreign policy, but he had a much clearer appreciation of the Chancellor's aims and political ruthlessness. He deplored the lack of independence in the Ministry and Parliament which resulted from Bismarck's dominance. Far from nursing ambitions of becoming Chancellor, he looked with distrust to the time when Frederick William came to the throne, although he himself might then expect to play a more decisive role. His views remained conservative, nationalistic, and pragmatic throughout the early seventies, and he attempted to influence the Crown Prince in accordance with them.

5

The title of Minister of State conferred upon Stosch by William I made it his duty to attend meetings of the State Ministry. He had no voice in the proceedings, but he greatly enjoyed them, and, from 1872 to 1877, reported on them to the Crown Prince at his request.[95] Stosch occupied the unique position of being the only person who regularly informed the future sovereign of the inner workings of the Prussian-German government.

The heir to the throne greatly appreciated his accounts, and wrote on 8 May 1872 that "no one could . . . be more to my liking as an adviser . . . ; it is, therefore, a particular joy for me to see your handwriting on my desk."[96] On 26 January 1873, Frederick William added:

I owe it to you quite alone that I am oriented on internal ministerial matters. Otherwise, I could only reach conclusions of an uncertain nature from the newspapers and debates of the Chambers. Of course, it cannot be helped, and consequently, we must be quite resigned.[97]

With this last sentence, he forestalled any attempt by his adviser to influence the Emperor or Bismarck to send him regular official reports or to admit him to posts of responsibility. It was his resignation to the powerlessness of his own position which continually hampered Stosch's efforts to persuade him to take a more active interest in public affairs, in preparation for the day when he would ascend the throne.

[95] *Ibid.*, II, 4.   [96] *Ibid.*, II, 10-11.
[97] *Ibid.*, II, 30.

He gave practical expression to his affection for the Admiralty Chief by taking an interest in, and promoting, the Navy. He proposed the naval trip to Sweden in 1873 to the coronation of the King of Sweden and Norway.[98] He had the regulations governing the firing of salutes in the Navy sent to him[99] and generally approved them. He was willing to leave to his father the determination of the number of guns due each rank,[100] joining to these observations a series of remarks characteristic of his concern with external formalities. "The chaos of Empire and Kingdom makes decisions so difficult! In my opinion, the three Kings [of Saxony, Würtemberg, and Bavaria], but no other German ruler or prince at all, take precedence over the Crown Prince of the German Empire!"[101] The Chief of the Admiralty played on his weakness for external display to strengthen his support for the Navy.[102]

Stosch took his responsibilities as adviser to the future monarch seriously and attempted to educate him for his future role. His reports are, for the most part, concise and objective summaries of discussions. When he did give his own opinion, he was usually careful to divorce it from his narrative. The reports, prepared with the reader in mind, were short, and often included humorous and pithy comments to arouse and retain Frederick William's interest. As an example of the humorous touches, the devastating explanation of a Polish woman when asked why she was emigrating to America may be cited. She replied simply: "But there's no Bismarck there."[103]

The Imperial Chancellor was naturally the principal subject of many reports. Stosch was an interested spectator of the indecision of the Ministers when Bismarck was absent and took care to point this out to Frederick William.[104] Bismarck's health was poor during a greater part of his Chancellorship, and each vacation he took seemed to be an indication that he might soon resign or die.

---

[98] Crown Prince to Stosch, Potsdam, 20 July 1873, *ibid.*, II, 49-50.

[99] Same to same, Wiesbaden, 28 Jan. 1873, *ibid.*, II, 31.

[100] Same to same, 16 Feb. 1873, *ibid.*, II, 33-34.

[101] *Ibid.*, II, 34.

[102] *Ibid.*, II, 16, 52-53, 124-25. Prince William (later Emperor William II) also took a strong interest in the Navy; Hallmann, *Der Weg zur Schlachtflottenbau*, pp. 48-49.

[103] Stosch to the Crown Prince, 14 April 1872, Memoirs, II, 7.

[104] 17 Nov. 1872, *ibid.*, II, 19. Cf. Stosch to Freytag, Berlin, 12 June 1872, *ibid.*, II, 15.

Stosch wrote of one such occasion to Frederick William on 7 May 1872, that the Chancellor's successor could only be a "dwarf."[105] Stosch made no attempt to conceal his admiration of the Chancellor. He wrote: "It was again an enchantment to see the Imperial Chancellor in full spiritual activity. His flights of thought can become quite striking, when the task of defending the Empire against Prussian particularism falls upon him."[106] The Prince and his adviser soon became inured to the rumors and threats of the Chancellor's departure to private life,[107] although the General was often disappointed by the failure of the Chancellor to retire. His departure during the lifetime of William I would, Stosch felt, enable the Crown Prince to recall him when he became Emperor and thus "greatly better his position"![108] At a Crown Council in 1876 Stosch's admiration for the Chancellor even caused him to join Bismarck and the Ministry in opposing Germany's participation in the Paris international exposition, although the Emperor and the Crown Prince favored it.[109] He also supported Bismarck against the Crown Prince in a bitter altercation over Heinrich Geffcken. Geffcken, Professor of Constitutional Law at the University of Strassburg, had become a lively publicist in the Kulturkampf and had achieved some contemporary notice with his book *Church and State,* which aimed at reconciling the two institutions.[110] He attempted to present his ideas to Bismarck through Frederick William. The Chancellor responded to the Crown Prince's interference with anger and impertinence. Stosch used his influence without any success to bring Frederick William closer to Bismarck by abandoning Geffcken.[111] The Chancellor's ire did not find an outlet until 1888, when he tried to entrap Stosch in Geffcken's disgrace.

[105] *Ibid.* Cf. Crown Prince's reply, 8 May 1872, *ibid.,* II, 11.

[106] To the Crown Prince, 24 Jan. 1873, *ibid.,* II, 28-29.

[107] *Ibid.,* II, 94.

[108] To Freytag, Berlin, 3 March 1875, *ibid.,* II, 95.

[109] Christoph von Tiedemann, *Aus sieben Jahrzehnten: Erinnerungen* (Leipzig, 1909), II, 94-102.

[110] On Geffcken and the Kulturkampf, see Georges Goyau, *Bismarck et l'Église* (Paris, 1913-1922), II, 29, 314-15, 340, 410, and III, 52, 94.

[111] Memoirs, II, 69, 109; *Anhang zu dem Gedanken und Erinnerungen von Fürst Bismarck* (Stuttgart & Berlin, 1901), II, 477-80; Heyderhoff, *Im Ring der Gegner Bismarcks,* pp. 173-83.

Perhaps the greatest irony of Stosch's whole career was that, while he was usually working to strengthen the Chancellor's position with the Crown Prince, Bismarck feared that he was ambitious to replace him and was undermining his own efforts to be on good terms with Frederick William.[112] It is a tribute to Stosch's objectivity and political realism that he continued to further the interests of a man who sought to destroy him politically, if not indeed personally, because he felt that his country's interests would best be served by Bismarck's continuance in office. At the same time, he tried to instruct the Crown Prince on Bismarck's character, even relaying harsh remarks about the Empress Augusta and Crown Princess Victoria.[113]

The views of the Crown Prince and Stosch approached closest agreement in their nationalism and their opposition to the attempts of the Conservatives to maintain Prussia's predominant position in the Empire. The General's view was briefly expressed: "The ambition of the best people of all Germany . . . must be chained to the Empire; otherwise it cannot prosper."[114] While the Crown Prince viewed the Kulturkampf as a "calamity," he felt that the Chancellor's power, which had grown out of the conflict, could be directed with good effect against "one-sided Prussian particularism."[115] Very characteristic of his nationalistic sentiments is his letter of 26 August 1873:

We return to Potsdam on the 31st to attend the unveiling of the victory column. This angers me deeply because it will have a "purely Prussian character," which one cannot be responsible for at the unveiling of a monument that is also meant for 70-71. New bad blood will be bred.[116]

The opinions of the Crown Prince and Stosch on the military law of 1874[117] revealed their plans for the future development of

[112] On Bismarck's abortive plans for Frederick William's assumption of power made with the idea of providing for a smooth transition, see Stosch to the Crown Prince, 2 May 1872, and 7 May 1872, Memoirs, II, 7-9.

[113] *E.g.*, Stosch to the Crown Prince, 21 Feb. 1876, *ibid.*, II, 112.

[114] To Freytag, Berlin, 12 June 1872, *ibid.*, II, 15.

[115] To Stosch, Wiesbaden, 28 Jan. 1873, *ibid.*, II, 30.

[116] To Stosch, Wyk auf Föhr, *ibid.*, II, 53.

[117] On the considerable constitutional issues involved, see R. Schmidt-Buckeburg, *Das Militärkabinett der preussischen Königen und Deutscher Kaiser* (Berlin, 1933), pp. 129-30; Poschinger, *Bismarcks Bundesrat*, II, 399-400, and III, 161-64.

the Empire. Frederick William desired a law which would give the Emperor the power of appointing and transferring all officers, as he pleased, and would "fetter the Bavarians and Württembergers close to us and improve the abominable treaties at Versailles."[118] These ideas struck at the very character of the Empire, which rested upon the federal rights of the states, guaranteed by treaty. Stosch favored the abortive attempt of Roon to create an Imperial War Ministry, which would in effect, have carried out the Crown Prince's nationalist ideas. Both Stosch and the Crown Prince envisaged a unitary state, with a completely unified army. To achieve this end, Stosch evidently did not shrink from independent ministries, who would be in a measure responsible to the Reichstag.[119] This constitutional change might well have provided the transition to the goal of a ministry responsible to the Reichstag alone.

Stosch's influence over the heir to the throne was always directed to persuading him to participate much more actively in public affairs. Stosch proposed that he become Governor General of the Imperial province of Alsace-Lorraine in 1872, but the Prince objected, replying on 17 November 1872:

> . . . I cannot approve what you say about my independent activity as Regent of Alsace-Lorraine, despite my strong feeling that I was reared for such a task and my belief that a rapprochement with the mother country could best be brought about in this manner. On the other hand, it is impossible to let myself be used as the tool of the Chancellor. . . .
> Such activity would be theoretically conceivable only if I were an independent official with princely rights, who would personify the personal union with the Empire. That is a complete impossibility under the present conditions.[120]

Further attempts by Stosch to influence him to take a hand in public affairs met with no greater success. In 1876 Frederick William denied that his inactivity would result in a lack of initiative or interest in the affairs of state. He felt that his strong feeling for the Empire and the "true German patriotic spirit, which domi-

---

[118] To Stosch, Wiesbaden, 28 Jan. 1873, Memoirs, II, 30.

[119] Ibid., II, 30, 44, 74.

[120] Potsdam, ibid., II, 16-17. William I later blocked the appointment of his son as Governor General of Alsace-Lorraine. Morsey, Die Oberste Reichsverwaltung, pp. 179-80.

nates the South Germans as well as the Alsatians," would save him from that. At the same time, he felt "quite isolated," for there were few men who told him what they "really think."[121] Stosch continued his efforts for the rest of Frederick William's life, but was nearly always routed by his passive resistance.

The critical wounding of William I by an assassin in June 1878 necessitated the proclamation on June 4 of the Crown Prince as Regent, a position he held until December 5. He felt it his duty to govern in accordance with his father's wishes, and, indeed, he was not empowered to alter the personnel of the Government.[122] These six months of limited power were the only real opportunity that he was to have to exercise the prerogatives of a sovereign, for when he eventually ascended the throne he was a dying man.

Stosch had written him on hearing the news of the attack on the Emperor,[123] and the two friends met on June 5. Stosch was "very cordially greeted," and invited to the Crown Council that evening.[124] Far from wishing to exert influence, Stosch wanted only to escape from Berlin to the peace and quiet of his beloved Oestrich. However, Normann and Friedberg, "who are the *intimississimi* of the young Prince," told him that the forty-seven year old Frederick William would consider the General's departure an "offense to his dignity."[125] Stosch was very pleased, however, with the Regent's activity, writing Freytag on June 8:

The Crown Prince works vigorously and is serious and industrious beyond expectation. His youth is a great advantage. He approaches business freshly and is only surprised at the caution which meets him everywhere. The Regency Order put another fortunate check on him, for the question of personnel remains outside his sphere. He feels this chain and that, I hope, will strengthen his power of resistance. As for the old monarch, he will, thank God, . . . recover from his wound.[126]

Stosch was also called in as an adviser by the Empress, the Grand Duke and Duchess of Baden, and their heir. They were concerned about the danger of assassins, and William had suggested

[121] Crown Prince to Stosch, 26 Oct. 1876, Memoirs, II, 123.
[122] Poschinger, *Kaiser Friedrich,* III, 241-49.
[123] Stosch to his wife, 3 June 1878, Memoirs, II, 152-53.
[124] To his wife, Berlin, 5 June 1878, *ibid.,* II, 154.
[125] To his wife, Berlin, 7 June 1878, *ibid.,* II, 155.
[126] *Ibid.,* II, 156. Cf. to his wife, 11 June 1878, *ibid.*

that they receive advice from a "well-informed" and "trusted" man.
Stosch admittedly knew nothing of the matter, but, to insure that
the wounded Emperor would remain undisturbed, he stressed the
strength of the police, the courts, the Army, and the Government,
and the pacific disposition of the people. This seemed to produce
the desired effect.[127]   Indeed, he had no fears of a revolution, as
long as "we do our duty."[128]

    Thoughts of going on vacation were still postponed by the
Crown Prince's request for his advice, which, Normann told him,
was desired on the law against the Socialists.[129]   After reporting
to the Regent, he hoped to be permitted to leave Berlin. However,
Frederick William clasped his hand at parting and declared:
"Always be as frank with me, and, when you have anything to
discuss, come to me."   Stosch was thoroughly nonplussed and
consoled himself with the thought that he could depart when
Frederick William left the capital.[130]   He saw the Regency as a
good preparation for the royal heir's future duties,[131] but had no
desire to have a part in it. He wrote his wife:

You are quite right to be surprised that he keeps me here and yet
does not see me often. He feels a certain insecurity which makes him
want to keep me near him. It is still possible that he wants to ask me
about something.[132]

The General, invited to the Regent's breakfasts,[133] was advised by
Friedberg to remain. However, the Crown Princess was planning to
leave for Hamburg, which "will make him quite restless,"[134]
Stosch predicted. He was able to take his departure at the end
of July.[135]

    His general impression of Frederick William's first months as
Regent were given in a letter to Freytag on August 2:

The young Prince has done better than I expected. He was earnest,
industrious, and retiring. He only lacked method—and for work too.

---

[127] To his wife, 9 June 1878, *ibid.*
[128] To his wife, Berlin, 26 June 1878, *ibid.*, II, 160.
[129] To his wife, Berlin, 17 June 1878, *ibid.*, II, 158-59.
[130] To his wife, Berlin, 20 June 1878, *ibid.*, II, 159.
[131] To his wife, Berlin, 26 June 1878, *ibid.*, II, 161.
[132] To his wife, Berlin, 3 July 1878, *ibid.*, II, 161-62.
[133] To his wife, 17 and 18 July 1878, *ibid.*, II, 162.
[134] To his wife, Berlin, 25 July 1878, *ibid.*, II, 162-63.
[135] To his wife, Berlin, 28 July 1878, *ibid.*, II, 164.

The fulfilment of duties is not an organic part of his life. He practices the art of governing as an industrious traveler studies art, not from his own will, but dependent upon external circumstances.—His questions were not the product of his own mental labor. He spoke of the things which most strongly touched his own heart. He was, and is, in a difficult position, since he is supposed to rule and yet must pay attention to the strict monarch, who is still living. Now he is finished [*sic*] and has been through a good school for the times to come.[136]

A conflict with the Regent developed in autumn 1878. On the advice of Count Münster, German Ambassador to Great Britain, he issued an order to a ship without obtaining Stosch's approval. The order was not obeyed, which "caused a flutter and finally a reconciliation." Stosch remarked that he had a "firmer support" in William than in his son.[137] Frederick William wrote a letter of explanation to the Chief of the Admiralty, declaring that the issuance of the order had seemed to be of immediate importance to him. He defended his right to give such an order, for, with the order, "*I* really assumed further responsibility, and I had my reasons, which others could not know." He declared the incident at an end and rejoiced in the prospect of seeing Stosch soon.[138] This minor conflict apparently had no effect on their friendship, for Stosch was noticed as a guest at the Crown Prince's birthday celebration on 18 October 1878.[139]

The Admiralty Chief continued his efforts to incite the Crown Prince to greater participation in public affairs. Frederick William replied to congratulations on his forty-ninth birthday that he was always delighted to receive one of Stosch's letters, for he always expressed his opinions "bluntly." He thanked him for a memorandum on the proposed revision of infantry regulations in the Foot Guards, but thought they must remain a *"noli me tangere"* during William's life. He expressed his dissatisfaction with the attitude of General Albedyll, Chief of the Military Cabinet, toward improvements in the Foot Guards, and toward the superannuation

[136] *Ibid.*, II, 165-66.
[137] To Freytag, Oestrich, 3 Oct. 1878, *ibid.*, II, 169.
[138] Potsdam, 3 Oct. 1878, *ibid.*, II, 169-70.
[139] Werner, *Erlebnisse*, p. 242.

of army officers, but was resigned to seeing such things continue.[140]
He went on to say:

Now I have arrived at your letter of 18 October, where you speak of the
pressure the years exert on those who stand apart waiting and who easily
lose joy, even because embittered, in their affairs. You want me to
look to the future, which offers such a rich creative field, with a joyful
and good spirit! Do you really believe that I still harbor such thoughts,
that after the blows of fate which have struck my home and the half
century which I have behind me, I still feel a desire in old age to undertake a task which can be carried through only with young, unbroken
strength? What can one do at my age of fifty years? One can barely
sow a few grains, and even their existence is highly questionable. . . . In
the present regime . . . every capable person is subordinated. They can
only obey; they no longer think independently. Moreover, there is
the further consideration that I feel little inclination to do business
through a major-domo [Bismarck]. There you have my innermost
thoughts!

He described the mood which dominated him:

. . . I am resigned; I lack a joyful or assured spirit; I am inspired by no
other wish than to spend the couple of years that yet remain to me as
quietly and as retired as possible in my household and be swiftly placed
in the background by the new sun [Prince William]. . . .

You shake your head and reproach me, but you will find, if you
ask Normann or [my adjutant] Mischke, that they have known this side
of me for a long time and have, honestly, but in vain, tried to talk me
out of it. . . .

The Crown Prince was troubled that "my wife, with such a gifted
nature and whose talents, spirit and reason seek their equal, never
finds a field for developing them, but has to remain retired, exiled
and misunderstood, and, afflicted with grief, must suffer loss after
loss." He concluded this sorrowful letter with the words:

If you add up all that I said, you will easily understand that I will fulfil my duties where I must and will come forward as I have done before, but there can no longer be any question of a joyful state of mind.
May it fall to my children's lot some day to carry out what shall be

[140] Wiesbaden, 23 Oct. 1880, Memoirs, II, 210-12. The changes in the
infantry regulations made by Frederick III in 1888 may have resulted from
Stosch's advice; Frederick III to the War Minister, Charlottenburg, 20 March
1888, in Poschinger, *Kaiser Friedrich,* III, 456.

denied to me. But remain as before my loyal friend in complete frankness, as is always

Your sincere and faithful,

FREDERICK WILLIAM, *Crown Prince.*[141]

This honest, moving, and depressing document did not shake
Stosch from his attempt to rouse the Crown Prince from his apathy.
If he fought a losing battle, he realized that his country's future
might suffer from the passivity of the future monarch. He commented to Freytag:

. . . the heir to the throne is already an old man. Strength that is not
exercised dies away; he keeps aloof from activity and influence. Only
that power which grows from work can live. It is wrong to believe that
we are powerful, because all bow before us.[142]

Nevertheless, military circles, as well as Bismarck, looked upon
the Crown Prince's accession to the throne as disturbing. Waldersee reported in January 1881 that it was rumored that after twenty
years of waiting the German heir showed signs of impatience for
power. He did not fear the effects of the Prince's reign in the
long run, but felt that in its early days it could have a disturbing
character. Waldersee noted that "among the people who could
be feared belongs Admiral v. Stosch, because he could really
cause much damage in the Army."[143] Waldersee's fears of Stosch
may have referred to the Admiral's desire to retire elderly personnel
from the Army and the reports of his liberal sentiments.

The Crown Prince remained Stosch's friend, despite occasional
conflicts. Prince Henry, accompanied by his military governor,
Seckendorff, came to Berlin to attend the marriage of his brother,
Prince William, in 1881, without asking leave from the naval
authorities. Stosch felt it necessary to take official notice of the
incident. The Crown Prince objected in a "very characteristic"
letter of 28 February 1881 that he recognized that the Chief of
the Admiralty had acted according to regulations, but he pleaded
that Prince Henry had come to Berlin only after repeated requests

[141] Memoirs, II, 212-13. Cf. Normann to Freytag, Berlin, 20 Jan. 1882, Julius
Heyderhoff and Paul Wentzcke, eds., *Deutscher Liberalismus im Zeitalter Bismarcks: Eine politische Briefsammlung* (Bonn and Leipzig, 1926), II, 390-91.
[142] Berlin, 26 Dec. 1880, Memoirs, II, 215.
[143] Waldersee, *Denkwürdigkeiten,* I, 206.

from himself. He, the Crown Prince, bore the responsibility. He
promised that his son would observe all naval regulations in the
future and asked that the Prince and his governor be excused from
all blame. He signed himself "Your old friend."[144]

The appointment of General Albrecht von Stosch as Chief of
the Imperial German Admiralty was achieved through the Emperor's favor and the desire of Bismarck to please the Crown
Prince. In his post, Stosch, meeting problems as they arose day
by day, was able to establish a firm strategic doctrine, construct
ships, improve personnel, and ready the fleet for combat. His role
in politics was conditioned by his incessant activity in building the
German Navy.

His political views maintained their conservative tinge. He supported Bismarck's foreign policy, but, in general, because of tolerance, respect for religion, nationalism, and distaste for theory,
opposed the Kulturkampf. The purpose of state policy, he thought,
should be the strengthening of the landed classes. He backed
Bismarck because of an intense nationalism, which led him into
colonial ambitions, but felt that the Chancellor's dominance suppressed individuality in the State Ministry and the Reichstag.

He played a unique role as adviser to the Crown Prince from
1872-1877, being the only person who informed him on the inner
activities of the Government. Frederick William reveals himself
in his relations with Stosch, not as a liberal champion, but as a
weak, passive individual, prematurely aged and resigned to playing
no part in public affairs. He distrusted Bismarck, was strongly
nationalistic, and took a persistent interest in the external attributes
of power. At the same time, he welcomed Stosch's frank reports,
even if he did little to follow them. It is small wonder that the
Admiralty Chief showed no desire to see the Crown Prince become
King and Emperor in the immediate future and betrayed no
ambition to assume an important post in his government. He
worked to educate Frederick William to his future duties, presenting reports in such a way as to retain his interest and to arouse in
him a desire to play a more active role in government. Stosch
met scant success. His basic aim was to bring the Crown Prince
to co-operate with Bismarck, not by concealing his faults, but by

[144] Memoirs, II, 216-17.

revealing his character and the foundation of his policy, and by removing sources of friction.

The Chancellor, on the other hand, was beginning to regard the Admiralty Chief with distrust.   Stosch's tactful relations with the Crown Prince and with all groups in the Bundesrat and Reichstag came to be viewed by Bismarck as a plot to replace him. Thus, at a time when Stosch wanted only to continue as Admiralty Chief and was supporting the Chancellor with the Crown Prince, Bismarck was seeking to weaken his influence by nursing criticism of the Navy and was using the uncertain delimitations of Stosch's duties to shove him from office.

V

THE ROAD TO CONFLICT

General and Admiral Albrecht von Stosch, Chief of the Imperial Admiralty, Minister of State, Prussian Representative to the Bundesrat, and life member of the Prussian Chamber of Peers, followed an active and appreciated career until 10 March 1877. Then Bismarck's public attack brought him into open conflict with the Iron Chancellor and altered his entire position. The widely publicized struggle which ensued was preceded by an almost unknown conflict which was no less spirited. One of its main causes was the uncertainty of Stosch's position in the German constitutional framework.[1]

The Navy had a complicated constitutional history. Naval business had been separated from the Prussian War Ministry in 1853, because Frederick William IV felt "army officers always reported incorrectly on naval affairs." A civilian was made Chief of the Admiralty for command and administrative matters, and he countersigned royal orders. The King received reports on the Navy from the Chief of the Admiralty, the Commanding Admiral, and the privy councilor intrusted with the affairs of the Civil Cabinet. When William assumed royal powers the organization of the Navy was altered, and the civilian element was excluded. Naval command matters were placed directly under the ruler, while the Prussian War Minister countersigned royal orders and thus assumed responsibility to the ruler for them. Command matters included "all proposals concerning appointments, promotions, transfers, dismissals, decorations, pardons, and furloughs." As a

[1] For a brief discussion of the constitutional position of the Navy, see Huber, *Heer und Staat,* pp. 353-57.

matter of practice, command matters were channeled to the King through the Prussian Military Cabinet. The North German Constitution amended this arrangement. The King still controlled naval command matters independently of Parliament[2] as *Bundesfeldherr*, and the Military Cabinet continued to report on them. However, the Confederation Chancellor assumed responsibility for naval administrative matters and countersigned administrative orders, while the War Minister actually administered the Navy. Upon the outbreak of War in 1870, the naval section of the War Ministry assumed responsibility for command matters as well.[3] The Imperial Constitution continued the authority granted to the Chancellor in 1867 and placed the naval organization completely under the Emperor. The first portion of the section entitled "Navy and Navigation" read:

The Imperial Navy is a unitary one under the supreme command of the Emperor. Its organization and composition are in the province of the Emperor, who appoints the naval officers and officials, and to whom they, together with their crews, take an oath of obedience.[4]

Bismarck's aim was to have, in fact, only one Imperial Minister, himself, to whom the other Ministers would be responsible, or, in his own words, he would not "ask eight jackasses when he wanted to eat a spoonful of soup." He considered himself the only Imperial Minister responsible for naval administration. In addition, he desired *at first* that the Prussian Ministers become Imperial Ministers in name, but, of course, with responsibility to the Imperial Chancellor, not directly to the King-Emperor.[5] His views of the function of the Chief of the Imperial Admiralty were in accord with these more general opinions. When Stosch's appointment had been decided upon, Bismarck and Roon, then Prussian War and Naval minister, reached agreement on Stosch's functions at a meet-

---

[2] I.e., the Bundesrat and Reichstag.

[3] Schmidt-Bückeberg, *Das Militärkabinett*, pp. 79-80, 105, 114, 117; Morsey, *Die Oberste Reichsverwaltung*, pp. 127-29; Hubatsch, *Der Admiralstab*, pp. 17-32.

[4] Wilhelm Altmann, ed., *Ausgewählte Urkunden zur Verfassungsgeschichte seit 1806* (Berlin, 1898), II, 15. Paul Laband, *Le Droit Public de l'Empire allemand* (Paris, 1904), V, is the authoritative account of the military and naval provisions of the Imperial Constitution. Howard, *German Empire*, relies heavily on Laband.

[5] Hans Goldschmidt, *Der Reich und Preussen im Kampf um die Führung* (Berlin, 1931), pp. 7-10.

ing of the State Ministry on 11 November 1871. The whole Ministry, including Roon, approved the Chancellor's proposal that Stosch become "President of the Admiralty with the character of a Minister of State and with the right to participate in the State Ministerial sessions after the manner of the President of the Imperial Chancellery, State Minister Delbrück." Bismarck thus saw Stosch as much his subordinate as the President of his own chancellery, who sat in the ministry only as an observer at this time.[6]

Under this constitutional arrangement, Stosch became the responsible official for command and personnel matters of the Navy and reported on them directly to the Emperor. He was also charged with the naval administration under the "real Naval Minister," Bismarck.[7] However, as we have said, just where command stopped and administration began, no one knew. Stosch wrote in his memoirs of the appointment:

Up to this time [1872], the administration had been subordinated to the War Ministry; Prince Adalbert had held the high command. The latter was named Inspector General of the Navy. I had to conduct the high command according to the Emperor's orders, but was responsible for the administration to the Imperial Chancellor. I became "Chief of the Admiralty" and a Minister, but this latter only *in partibus*.[8]

His post as Minister of State had little practical significance. He had no voice in ministerial discussions, except as requested on technical matters, and was only a "silent observer."[9] He commented in his memoirs on the difficulties of his constitutional position:

That could not be arranged differently according to the Imperial Constitution, but from the start it was a source of endless nuisances, because of the quite unavoidable conflicts over authority. The Navy was supposed to serve three masters [William I, Bismarck, and Stosch]

[6] *Ibid.,* pp. 12-13; Joachim Lehment, *Kriegsmarine und politische Führung* (Berlin, 1937), p. 30; Schmidt-Bückeberg, *Das Militärkabinett,* pp. 117-18; Morsey, *Die Oberste Reichsverwaltung,* p. 130.

[7] Lehment, *Kriegsmarine,* p. 29; *Memoirs,* I, 271.

[8] *Memoirs,* II, 1.

[9] Stosch to Freytag, Wilhelmshaven, 13 Nov. 1872, *ibid.,* II, 18. The Ministry of State functioned *in practice* as both the Prussian and Imperial Ministry. For a general discussion of it, rather poor for the period of the Empire, see Otto Hintze, "Das preussische Staatsministerium im 19. Jahrhundert," *Festschrift zu Gustav Schmollers 70. Geburtstag: Beiträge zur brandenburgischen und preussischen Geschichte* (Leipzig, 1908), pp. 403-93.

or even four, since the Imperial Chancellor's representative [Delbrück] also came into the reckoning [on budget matters].[10]

At first harmony rather than conflict was the dominant mood. Stosch wrote:

The Chancellor, who united all imperial departments in himself, was not at all in the position to trouble himself with details. As occasion offered, he gave his essential instructions at social gatherings by word of mouth. He said that my chief task was to free myself from the [particularistic] Military Cabinet and, as an Imperial Minister, to bring my influence to bear upon the Emperor. This was quite right and was in agreement with the Chancellor's basic principle of putting aside all particularism in favor of the Empire. But for me it meant that I was to sacrifice the most powerful support of my position, quite uncertain whether I could gain a new one in the Empire. Thus dependent upon first gaining success as a Minister, I had to let further developments take care of themselves.[11]

Stosch here shows himself in agreement with the Chancellor's desire to diminish the influence of the Prussian military in the affairs of the Empire. To achieve this aim he had to forsake his position as a Prussian General and seek a new one in his duties as imperial Naval Chief. The ambiguity of his constitutional position was enough in itself to lead to clashes with Bismarck.

2

Uncertain constitutional rights, which stemmed from the fact that many details of the new government had not been decided, were not the basic cause of the antagonism between Stosch and Bismarck. They only fixed the battleground. Politically, the reason for the conflict lay in the Chancellor's growing suspicion that Stosch was working to hinder his program by influencing William I and was seeking to supplant him as Chancellor when

[10] Memoirs, II, 1.
[11] Ibid., II, 2. Since Bismarck did not often go into society (his presence at the wedding of Prince William in 1881, for example, was regarded as a sign of great favor; see Sir Frederick Ponsonby, ed., Letters of the Empress Frederick [London, 1928], p. 184), the question arises: What were these social gatherings? Stosch probably means the social gatherings after the meetings of the State Ministry. He was also a visitor at Bismarck's Bierabende for officials and parliamentarians, the Emperor's and the Empress', as well as the Crown Prince's. Bismarck also gave an occasional dinner for the State Ministry and the Bundesrat, at which Stosch would be present. In general, the General had little love for large social gatherings.

Frederick William became Emperor. Personally, the cause lay in the very similarity of their natures. Both were strong men who loved power and who sought their goals with complete independence. Neither would submit long to the other.[12]

Throughout the protracted struggle William I showed great satisfaction with Stosch's administration of the Navy. Stosch became a life member of the Prussian Chamber of Peers in 1872. In 1874 the Emperor renamed Fort Jägersburg near Kiel in his honor. In March 1875 he promoted him to the rank of Lieutenant General [General der Infanterie], and in September of the same year made him an Admiral and the highest ranking officer of the German Navy. H. M. S. Stosch joined the Moltke and Bismarck in the fleet. On 18 January 1878, Stosch received the Grand Cross of the Order of the Red Eagle and, in 1881, the Order of the Black Eagle. These signal honors were the symbol of the trust the Emperor placed in his Chief of the Admiralty, which he further expressed in his continued refusal to accept Stosch's frequent letters of resignation, despite Bismarck's constant pressure.[13]

Stosch's administrative capabilities even aroused the Chancellor's grudging admiration, and his growling remarks about the Admiral stand in contrast to the utter contempt he had for most of his opponents, real and fancied. He once said: "Stosch was only useful as Commissary [General], as Naval Minister he was good for nothing."[14] As time passed, his remarks grew more pointed. In the eighties he noted that Stosch's predecessor, Roon, and successor, Caprivi, were also infantry generals and moaned: "If one could only have a Hussar lieutenant as Admiral at least once; but always infantrymen."[15] It remained for England to follow his advice when Winston Churchill became First Lord of the Admiralty. On another occasion Bismarck sarcastically observed: "We have a fleet that is unable to sail, so we cannot be injured in distant

---

[12] See especially Hassell, Tirpitz, pp. 19, 32-33; Richter, Im alten Reichstag, II, 9-10. Morsey, Die Oberste Reichsverwaltung, p. 131, traces Stosch's feeling of independence to his friendship with the Crown Prince. It was more probably the result of support by William I and financial independence since the "donation" of 1872, as well as being an innate part of his character.

[13] Hermann von Petersdorff, "Albrecht von Stosch," A. D. B., LIV, 604.

[14] Undated, Heinrich von Poschinger, Neues Bismarck-Jahrbuch (Vienna, 1911), I, 296. Cf. Bismarck, Gesammelte Werke, XV, 534.

[15] Undated, Poschinger, Neues Bismarck-Jahrbuch, I, 189.

parts of the world."[16] As a matter of fact, it was Bismarck's failing and Germany's tragedy that the Chancellor could not abide the company of able, independent-minded colleagues. The complaints of the lack of competent officials on the higher levels in the time of William II can be traced to Bismarck's extirpation of independence and initiative in his subordinates. Bismarck met in Stosch an opponent who, if not his match in unscrupulousness, was not afraid to defend himself. They clashed almost at once.

In the spring of 1872 the draft of a military code was laid before the Reichstag, after approval by the Ministry and the Bundesrat. The Naval Chief asked his friend, the National Liberal deputy Robert von Benda, to introduce amendments to the bill, which he felt were necessary in the interest of the Navy. Bismarck got wind of his action and wrote a stiff note to the Chief of the Admiralty on 11 April 1872, reprimanding him. "No imperial official," the Chancellor declared, had the right to take independent measures to alter a measure approved by the Government. He asked Stosch to withdraw his proposals and inform him when this was done. This Stosch apparently did, for the incident occasioned no further comment. He was definitely at fault here and had exceeded his powers.[17] Another incident soon followed.

A Hamburg merchant in Haiti called upon the Navy for support in his claims on the government there. Captain Batsch, who commanded the two corvettes cruising in the Caribbean, seized two Haitian ships, and, on July 13, 1872, Haiti agreed to the merchant's demands. The German Foreign Office was displeased at Batsch's assumption of the initiative without prior consultation and declared that such requests for naval support could be honored only by the Foreign Office itself or by the German consul in Haiti. The merchants of Hamburg surprisingly objected that Batsch's action disturbed their relations with Haiti, and they were upheld by the German consul there. Stosch noted that the merchants objected only because they were not accustomed to seeing German authority exercised abroad and that the Navy had not yet learned how to act in such circumstances. He proudly wrote in his memoirs that a year later the consul asked for German naval aid, and the citizens

[16] Poschinger, *Bismarcks Bundesrat,* II, 126.
[17] Hassell, *Tirpitz,* pp. 33-34.

of Hamburg soon sought the protection of the German Navy. Although the prominent National Liberal orator, Eduard Lasker, attacked the brutal use of German force against a defenseless republic, Stosch remained loyal to Batsch, and the Captain did not suffer for his action.[18]

Another dispute developed over Stosch's labor policies. A strike over wages broke out in the Danzig Naval Yards. Stosch discussed the workers' demands with two of their representatives, the strike was called off, and he raised wages, after the laborers agreed to longer hours of work. The newspapers, in reporting the incident, stated that Stosch had increased wages without condition during the course of the strike. Acting on this intelligence, Bismarck directed a letter to the Admiralty Chief on 5 September 1872, declaring that it was poor policy for departments of the Government to take personal notice of workers' agitation, and inexcusable to make concessions to them. No intervention between capitalists and workers was permissible, he insisted, for it weakened the bargaining power of taxpaying private interests in their wage policies. In any case, the different branches of the State Ministry, he maintained, should be co-ordinated on labor policy. As Imperial Chancellor and Chairman of the Prussian State Ministry, he requested that Stosch refer any further demands to the Imperial Chancellery, which would dispatch them to the State Ministry.[19] There is no evidence to show that Stosch had intended anything more than the practical solution of a current problem. Indeed, his conservative views in general and his attitude toward the Social Democrats (see Chapters VI and VIII below) in particular made prolabor action on his part unthinkable.

Bismarck's increasing friction with Stosch gained some notoriety, for a National Liberal deputy wrote the President of the Reichstag in September that the Chancellor had made "violent scenes" with various officials including Stosch.[20] The Crown Prince's private secretary and Stosch's old friend, Karl von Normann, wrote to Freytag in November:

[18] Memoirs, II, 51-52; Bethcke, Politische Generale!, pp. 103-4; Mantey, La Marine allemande, pp. 122-23.
[19] Hassell, Tirpitz, pp. 34-35; Poschinger, Neues Bismarck-Jahrbuch, I, 264-66.
[20] Wilhelm Wehrenpfennig to Eduard von Simson, Berlin, 22 Sept. 1872, in Heyderhoff and Wentzcke, Deutscher Liberalismus, II, 59-60.

Our friend, in my opinion, is becoming much too active in politics, is flatly thinking of many adventurous and impossible plans especially *contra* Varzin [i.e., Bismarck], and is very angry when one remains cool and prefers to depend upon proven greatness. It is wrong in every way that that he does not remain aloof and apart.[21]

It is not stated what his political plans may have been, but they may have had to do with extending his competence over the merchant marine (see below).

Bismarck's conception of the powers of Stosch as Chief of the Admiralty found expression in an inspired article in the *Kölnische Zeitung* on 10 January 1873. After discussing various legislative measures and the rumors of Bismarck's plans concerning the Prussian Ministries,[22] it read:

Like the navy, the Foreign Office, the Ministry of Communications, the army seemed fated to fall within the jurisdiction of the Imperial Chancellor, so that the head of the War Office would, as Minister of State, occupy the same position towards the Imperial Chancellor as General Stosch in his capacity of Chief of the Admiralty, and Herr Delbrück as President of the Federal Chancellerie [*sic*].[23]

This conception of Stosch's subordinate position was put to the test in his first serious conflict with Bismarck in February 1873, on the question of countersignature.

On 28 January 1873 William I approved Stosch's proposal to grant the same rights of employment to deck officers leaving active service as those given to active Army officers separated from service. Stosch countersigned this order, thus assuming responsibility for it. The order was published in the official naval gazette on 31 January. Bismarck wrote to the Chief of the Admiralty pointing out that, by Article 17 of the Imperial Constitution, the Chancellor alone could countersign imperial orders. In his reply of 11 February Stosch merely explained the circumstances in which the countersignature had been given and made no mention of the constitutional issue involved. Bismarck complained verbally to the Emperor and, on 21 February he addressed a memorandum to him on the subject. He noted that Article 17 of the Constitution gave him alone the right to countersign imperial orders and,

---

[21] Neues Palais, Potsdam, 14 Nov. 1872, *ibid.,* II, 66.
[22] Busch, *Bismarck,* II, 227-34.   [23] *Ibid.,* II, 230.

since the Navy was an imperial organization by Article 53, the right to countersign naval orders clearly came within his competence. Moreover, Stosch had, Bismarck insisted, already submitted countless orders of a similar nature for his countersignature. He also called attention to the imperial order of 1 January 1872, which made Stosch responsible to the Emperor in command matters and to the Chancellor in administrative affairs. Article 17 of the Constitution declared that responsibility was assumed by countersignature, and Bismarck thus had the right to countersign naval administrative orders. While he conceded the Emperor's rights in command matters, he argued that a royal order of 14 March 1859 made clear that naval command matters did not require countersignature. He requested the Emperor to disapprove countersignature in these matters, since it was an infringement of the royal power of command. The order concerning deck officers lay within his province, he concluded, and he requested that the Emperor make this clear to Stosch.[24]

The Chief of the Admiralty reported to the Crown Prince, in a letter of 25 February 1873 on the continuing conflict:

I have had the misfortune to countersign an imperial order which was the Imperial Chancellor's business. On the other hand, the Chancellor has interfered in my department through his deputy [Delbrück]. The conflict stemming from that led yesterday to a very stormy scene, when the State Ministry met for a so-called private session at the Imperial Chancellor's. Before the beginning of the session, the Prince invited me to his room, told me that I lacked every ministerial qualification and had to subordinate myself to him unconditionally no matter whom he employed as his representative. I replied with spirit, and we both had flushed faces when we entered the session. Today I asked H. M. to make me the deputy of the Chancellor in naval matters, instead of Delbrück, or dismiss me.[25]

The position of the Emperor between two such determined men as Stosch and Bismarck was hardly to be envied. It is possible that Stosch precipitated the crisis over countersignature to win his right to represent the Chancellor in naval affairs. He wrote to the Crown

---

[24] Schmidt-Bückeberg, *Das Militärkabinett,* pp. 118-20. Cf. Freytag's comment on the crisis in his letter to Stosch, Leipzig, 24/25 February 1873, in Helmolt, *Freytag an Stosch,* p. 93.

[25] Memoirs, II, 37-38. Cf. Hubatsch, *Der Admiralstab,* p. 38.

Prince on 2 March that no official decision had yet been reached, but "H. M. is on my side for the present, and the Chancellor seems to want to give in."[26] The Crown Prince's standpoint sheds light on his relation to both Stosch and Bismarck. He wrote from Wiesbaden on 4 March:

. . . I come in writing to counter an error, which Normann has probably already explained verbally. I refer to your belief that I find your move against Bismarck too harsh.

This is not so. On the contrary, I consider it fortunate that someone decisively opposed him and defends the office entrusted to him. I should certainly be sorry for the Navy's sake if you left it, but you cannot sacrifice your personal worth to the Chancellor. I do not know how far you can go without putting yourself in the wrong, since I do not know the text of your instructions, but I can only hope that men who do not understand technical matters will not determine naval business, and that, therefore, the right you demand will be recognized as soon as possible.[27]

On 5 March Stosch informed the Crown Prince that Delbrück had visited him, which was a sign that the Chancellor was inclined to compromise.[28] The issue was finally settled by the Emperor on 8 March 1873. He wrote to Stosch:

(1) I must recognize as proved the Imperial Chancellor's view that my order of 28 January should have been signed, not by you, but by the Imperial Chancellor, since the question raised in this order concerns an administrative matter, which falls under the responsibility of the Imperial Chancellor.

(2) I reserve further decision on the countersignature of orders concerning command matters. The countersignature of this order is to be deferred until then.

(3) Your further statements in your communication of the 25th ultimo lead me to believe that you do not know of my order of 16 June 1868,[29] which governs the representation of the Imperial Chancellor in his functions with regard to the Army and Navy.

I am having a copy of this order sent to you herewith and remark that it is apparent from its provisions, without a doubt, that the Imperial Chancellor can only be represented in naval matters by the Chief of the Admiralty and that your *orders* in naval affairs can only go through the Imperial Chancellor himself.

[26] *Memoirs*, II, 38. [27] *Ibid.*, II, 40.
[28] *Ibid.*
[29] For its text, see *ibid.*, II, 44, and Goldschmidt, *Der Reich und Preussen*, p. 10 n.

... I can take even less notice of your desire ... to be relieved of your office, since you have filled it ... to my complete satisfaction. I can expect that you, in a just recognition of the interests of the service and of progress in the Navy, ... will resolve the difficulty which has arisen between you and the Imperial Chancellor. ... .[30]

William informed Bismarck on 8 March that the Emperor had the right to have the Chief of Admiralty countersign orders in command matters, except in monetary questions.[31] William had acted to keep both Bismarck and Stosch aware that he alone made the final decisions. In fact, he was very jealous of his rights in military matters and viewed with suspicion encroachments on them, even by the Chancellor.

Stosch was fully aware of the significance of the Emperor's decision. He wrote to the Crown Prince on 9 March: "I am very grateful to His Majesty ... for the ... Cabinet order. By that I receive the same competence that Roon had and can therefore calm myself, for I now have a support in the monarch's word."[32] This first serious conflict with the Chancellor had resulted in a victory for Stosch, although he was defeated on the immediate point at issue. He had established his constitutional rights in naval matters and had remained in office despite the Chancellor's onslaught. Another soon followed.

A revolt in Spain of the followers of Don Carlos necessitated the dispatch of German ships to the Spanish coasts to protect national interests. A part of the Spanish fleet declared for Don Carlos and separated itself from the ships of the Republican fleet. In the summer of 1873 Captain Werner captured two of the Carlist vessels and declared them pirates. Bismarck, as Foreign Minister, objected to Werner's independent action, and the Emperor recalled him. He was placed before a court martial. In Werner's defense it should be noted that Stosch had not yet drafted instructions for overseas squadrons, and each commander still acted on his own.[33]

Stosch had both to defend his subordinate and punish him for his action, since the Chief of the Admiralty agreed with the

---

[30] Memoirs, II, 42-44.
[31] Schmidt-Bückeberg, *Das Militärkabinett,* p. 121.
[32] Memoirs, II, 44.
[33] *Ibid.,* II, 50-51; Tirpitz, *Memoirs,* I, 16-18. Cf. Walter Hubatsch, *Die Ära Tirpitz* (Göttingen [1955]), pp. 28-29.

Foreign Minister that Werner had acted precipitately. He wrote to Holtzendorff on 7 August 1873:

Naturally I take every step to back him up, since I must support my officer's thirst for action under all circumstances. But when the Imperial Chancellor says: "Werner has committed a great political error and has acted against instructions," I cannot contradict him. Werner has acted in opposition to orders without any pressing reason and therefore is not to be saved. Bismarck says: "I can give ever so many assurances that we want peace, but I will not be believed or trusted when the German soldier pushes himself forward at every opportunity to make his power felt. Only recall will make my political action possible again."—The Emperor could not contradict that, but the behavior of the Navy greatly pleased him. Therefore nothing further will happen to Werner.[34]

The Crown Prince informed Stosch on 26 August that he could not understand what "crime" Werner had committed and did not see any reason for punishing him. He wished Germany to emulate England's free action in similar cases.[35] Stosch liked Freytag's article defending Werner, but could not free him from all blame, because he had acted against definite orders. No one was dissatisfied with Werner, the General wrote Holtzendorff, "even the great Bismarck." He was pleased by Werner's action and "suddenly recognized the maritime power of Germany; the Emperor is simply delighted."[36] Nonetheless, the Chancellor wanted to sentence Werner to twelve years in prison, but William wished him freed.[37]

The Werner affair embittered the relations between the two antagonists for a year,[38] for not until the summer of 1874 did the court martial reach a decision. Werner's independent action seems to have rankled in Bismarck's mind. While Stosch wrote Freytag on 28 February 1874, that the Chancellor was not troubling him,[39] he added:

In the last few days I have again had the feeling that I am standing on very soft ground; it is odd that Werner always offers the opportunity for the Chancellor to try to fall upon me. At an audience with Albedyll

[34] Berlin, Memoirs, II, 54.   [35] Wyk auf Föhr, ibid., II, 53.
[36] Berlin, 31 Aug. 1873, ibid., II, 54-55.
[37] Freytag to Salomon Hirzel, Siebleben, 19 Sept. 1873, in Dove, ed., Freytag an Hirzel, pp. 205-6.
[38] See letter to Freytag, 29 Dec. 1873, Memoirs, II, 64.
[39] Berlin, ibid., II, 73.

four days ago, the old Emperor said: "Bismarck's always attacking Werner, but he means Stosch." It has become that heated.[40]

Judging from Bismarck's references to his control over the Navy in the spring of 1874, he may well have wished to assure himself and others that such control was his.[41] When Werner was freed by the court martial in late summer 1874 and this decision was approved by the Emperor,[42] the Chancellor, then in conflict with Stosch over their mutual ministerial competence, at least tacitly approved a strong article attacking Stosch in the officially inspired *Norddeutsche Allgemeine Zeitung*.[43] Werner felt no gratitude for his defense by the Admiralty Chief and later was one of the most violent critics of the "Stosch System."[44]

Stosch and Bismarck seemed to find a temporary point of agreement in the civil marriage question. As part of the Kulturkampf, the Minister of Religious Affairs, Falk, wished to make civil marriage compulsory throughout the Empire. The Chief of the Admiralty reported to the Crown Prince on 8 February 1873 that the Chancellor had decided to leave the question to be settled by the states within the Empire.[45] Civil marriage was again discussed by the State Ministry on 7 November. Falk proposed now to make civil marriage compulsory only throughout Prussia. The Ministers of Finance, Commerce, Interior, and War supported Falk. Delbrück, the President of the Imperial Chancellery, remained silent, and the "Justice Minister hedged." Bismarck was not present, but his views were presented by his assistant von Bülow. He disliked the measure and, in Stosch's words, "again opposed the doctrinaires." The Chancellor did not consider the theoretical merits of the question, but held it to be a "purely political question." The State, at war with the Roman Catholic Church, should not strengthen its

[40] *Ibid.*

[41] 21 March, 10 April, Freiherr Robert Lucius von Ballhausen, *Bismarck-Erinnerungen* (Stuttgart and Berlin, 1921), pp. 46, 51.

[42] Memoirs, II, 51.

[43] Freytag to Salomon Hirzel, Siebleben, 22 Aug. 1874, in Dove, *Freytag an Hirzel*, p. 211.

[44] Stosch's defense of Werner was generally known in the Navy; Tirpitz, *Memoirs*, I, 16-18; Batsch, "Stosch," *Deutsche Revue*, XXI (1896), 37.

[45] Memoirs, II, 32. Schröder, *Stosch*, pp. 88-89, conjectures (giving no documentary basis for his view) that Bismarck intended to incite Stosch to express his opinions in the civil marriage question.

enemy, as civil marriage would by arousing opposition in every family. Moreover, Bismarck maintained that the Emperor was not well enough to decide so important a matter before the opening of the Prussian Chamber.[46] In a report to the Crown Prince, Stosch commented: "I completely agreed with the Chancellor. The battle cannot be drawn to a close by radical doctrinaires, who prefer a civil war to every compromise. The Chancellor's defeat of the Conservative party in now being avenged."[47] By the latter remark, Stosch meant that Bismarck's liberal allies were getting out of hand. Evidently he spoke his mind in the session, for Normann was disturbed that he had done so, when Delbrück, occupying an analogous constitutional position in the Ministry, had remained silent.[48] Moreover, Normann feared that the Crown Prince would become involved in the civil marriage question, since his friendship with Stosch was well known. Normann urged the Admiralty Chief to keep silent, but his reply was uncompromising.[49] Normann wrote to Freytag on 14 November: "One can often say hard things to his face; he maintains a calm silence and remains peaceful and conciliatory. But when one writes, he does not see the joke."[50] He gathered from the reports of the session that Bismarck's opposition was only temporary and tactical, while Stosch was an "opponent of civil marriage on principle." He feared that his friend had ruined the "political future of which he still dreams,"[51] but Stosch's speaking out in the State Ministry apparently had no repercussions. He informed the Crown Prince on 7 December that hostility to the measure had delayed the Emperor's approval.[52] The Crown Prince replied on 12 December that he had remained silent on the "whole disease of civil marriage," on the advice of Wilmowski, Chief of the Civil Cabinet. He found it surprising that "this regime" would sponsor a measure of "such a deeply revolutionary character" in its effects on the life of the people and the state.[53] The measure,

[46] To the Crown Prince, 8 Nov. 1873, Memoirs, II, 57-58.
[47] Ibid.
[48] To Freytag, Neues Palais, Potsdam, 10 Nov. 1873, in Heyderhoff and Wentzcke, Deutscher Liberalismus, II, 91.
[49] To Freytag, Neues Palais, Potsdam, 14 Nov. 1873, ibid., II, 92.
[50] Ibid.   [51] Ibid., II, 92-93.
[52] Memoirs, II, 59. Stosch had also spoken up in the Ministry in 1872; Constabel, Die Vorgeschichte des Kulturkampfes, p. 260.
[53] Memoirs, II, 62.

nevertheless, was adopted in Prussia, and, in 1875, it became imperial law.[54]

In the meantime, Stosch had been attempting to extend the constitutional competence of his office. His aim was stated as early as 12 June 1872:

At the present, I am working to make my department a real Imperial Naval Ministry. Besides the Navy, it should include pilot, tonnage, and lighthouse matters, which are subordinated to the Prussian Ministry of Commerce. However, the opposition of Prussian particularism hinders such an extension of Imperial power.[55]

His ambitions grew even greater and soon encountered much opposition. He wrote in November 1872:

All powers fight against the foundation of an [Imperial] Ministry of Commerce, which is necessary for the coasts and for all overseas trade. The coastal states, especially Hamburg and Prussia, above all, struggle most violently against the embrace of the Empire. But the Imperial Chancellery also does not want to let go of such a rich department.[56]

He persisted in his attempt to enlarge his powers as Chief of the Admiralty and obviously used his position as Chairman of the Bundesrat Committee on Naval Affairs to further his views. He stated in December 1873:

We must represent our maritime interests more strongly in the Empire . . . , as well as educating our trading captains better. I am fighting for that, and I have the Hanseatic cities [Lübeck, Bremen, and Hamburg] on my side.[57]

Stosch's exact aim in extending the Navy's competence over the merchant marine appears most clearly in a lengthy letter to Freytag dated 2 February 1874:

The percentage of sea accidents has steadily climbed with the development of iron ship construction. Up to now the Navy has controlled all branches of scientific work which sought to remedy this. . . . I consider it my duty to support this developing world trade and to create a Supreme Maritime Authority. But it cannot be conjured up by magic,

[54] Poschinger, *Bismarcks Bundesrat*, III, 86-90.
[55] To Freytag, Memoirs, II, 14-15.
[56] To Freytag, Wilhelmshaven, 13 Nov. 1872, *ibid.*, II, 19.
[57] To Freytag, Berlin, 29 Dec. 1873, *ibid.*, II, 64.

especially since all the particularist states, with Prussia at the head, vote against it. However, the power of the Empire must be concentrated. The Imperial Chancellery, which has so many great and power-consuming projects in progress, can spare little time and interest; the Admiralty has more feeling for it. Therefore, I would wish to form a Department for the Merchant Marine and hope slowly to draw the particularist's rights into it. The interests of the merchant marine and Navy never collide and could be combined in one Ministry for a reasonable period.

The votes in the Reichstag for such a department have increased recently. At the present, the naval observatory at Hamburg is being formed under the Admiralty, with offices in all harbors. I believe that will lay an egg in the particularists' nests, which they will hatch out themselves with all their strength.—I have learned a great deal from the preliminary work on this and already astonish the landlubbers.[58]

His plan to become Chief of the Merchant Marine, as well as the Navy, testifies both to his nationalism and to his personal ambition. Bismarck's increasing opposition to him made such a plan impractical, for the Chancellor was not inclined to approve the extension of the powers of a man he regarded primarily as a military official of the Emperor and whom he detested. Indeed, Bismarck's indifference to German naval expansion and colonial development in this period may well have been conditioned by his hatred of Stosch.

3

A six months' struggle with the Chancellor over the competence of the Navy began in July 1874 and reached only an uneasy truce in January 1875. A German journalist in Spain, Captain Schmidt, was shot by the Carlists as a spy. When Bismarck received the report, he asked the Emperor to send the German Channel squadron, which was outfitted and manned only for a summer maneuver, to the Carlist capital, Bilbao. The order was communicated to Stosch via the Foreign Office, instead of by the regular route of a command order of the Emperor.[59] Stosch declared in his memoirs:

The squadron had been in commission for only six weeks and therefore was not yet capable of action. Several of the ships needed repair; the

[58] Berlin, *ibid.,* II, 70-71. For Freytag's reply, see Helmolt, *Freytag an Stosch,* p. 97. Stosch first mentions the supreme maritime authority in a letter to Holtzendorff, 16 Nov. 1873, Memoirs, II, 58.

[59] *Ibid.,* II, 78.

Spanish harbors on the north coast were unsuitable for reception of large ships; the Bay of Biscay is one of the most stormy of the waters of the earth; the only harbor in which our ships could take on provisions or make repairs was the French Bordeaux, which could not be considered a suitable port of refuge for us. So I refused the Chancellors's dispatch of the squadron as military inadmissable. The Chancellor complained to the Emperor, and, following this, the squadron, which was on its way home, was ordered to await the Emperor's decision.[60]

Stosch reported to the Emperor on 30 July 1874 on the conflict.[61] He repeated the arguments he had given Bismarck and added a few more. He stated that the squadron was manned by recruits, and the ships were not prepared for war. Moreover, the training of naval personnel would be disturbed by the action. In the report he used language which was to arouse Bismarck's ire. He contended that, if the Chancellor's request were granted,[62]

. . . a military power would be employed which is quite useless for this task . . . . This maritime power could not achieve the object sought, because the coasts concerned are considered to be so unapproachable for these armored ships that they cannot even come into sight of them.[63]

He developed his conception of his authority and that of Bismarck and denied that the Admiralty had approached the Foreign Office in a "purely negative way." It only desired to inform the latter's officials that it was not their business "to determine which part of the Navy would be employed, but the task which was to be performed." He explained that different tasks required different ships and he would be glad to ask the Emperor's approval for the dispatch of ships when their mission was communicated to him.[64] William I supported Stosch's viewpoint,[65] but the conflict did not end there.

A mistake which fanned Bismarck's wrath is described by Stosch in his memoirs.

---

[60] *Ibid.,* II, 78-79.

[61] The full text of the report is given in Koch, *Stosch,* pp. 45-46. The date and shortened text appear in Hassell, *Tirpitz,* pp. 35-37. The order of events is taken from Memoirs, II, 78-79. For a summary of his arguments, see Freytag to Salomon Hirzel, Siebleben, 22 Aug. 1874, in Dove, *Freytag an Hirzel,* pp. 211-12.

[62] Koch, *Stosch,* pp. 45-46.   [63] *Ibid.,* p. 45.

[64] *Ibid.,* p. 46.   [65] Memoirs, II, 79.

Then another incident occurred which strengthened the Chancellor's ire. The Imperial Order [halting the squadron until a decision was reached] was delivered to the consul in Dover to give to the squadron. However, it did not see the consul's signal and calmly steamed past without receiving the order. The Chancellor now assumed that I had ordered the squadron to return without running into Dover. An enquiry was undertaken, but could produce nothing. But all guilt was mine, and he [Bismarck] loudly proclaimed that he could not stand my rudeness.—Then a small ship was sent to the Spanish coasts which was quite able to perform the allotted task.—If the Chancellor had come to terms with me on the ships to be sent before he reported to the Emperor, the affair would have gone quite smoothly. But even after many years he reproached me in writing for always seeking to disturb his political undertakings and cited this affair as evidence.[66]

Bismarck soon resorted to new tactics. Stosch informed Freytag on 28 September 1874:

I have a little rest again and, with the Emperor's support, have even made myself somewhat freer of the Chancellor, but you cannot let him out of your sight for a minute. The document which I sent to the Emperor from Gotha[67] is the burning cause of his anger. It has given material for his utterances about me to Stephani, [the National Liberal deputy,] and others. I am rude, I interfere in politics, etc.—The freeing of Werner has filled his cup to the brim and resulted in that unheard of article in the Norddeutsche [Allgemeine] Zeitung . . . and other vehement attacks on me. But the worst is a dreadful interference in my naval budget. He has struck out everything that would bring, or assure, new life to the Navy and even tells me what ships I should build. I am submitting my counterproposals tomorrow. If he sticks to his orders, I shall declare that I cannot defend the budget.—The Emperor wants to keep me in all circumstances and recently told the Crown Prince that it was on this account that he had recently expressed his public satisfaction with me.[68] In itself resignation would not be difficult for me, but it would greatly pain me now to let the work which I started pass into other hands. At the present, none of my officers has progressed enough so that I can turn it over to him.[69]

[66] Ibid. Stosch was in Oestrich when the telegram was sent to the consul at Dover ordering the squadron to stop. Batsch, "Stosch," Deutsche Revue, XXI (1896), 40. Cf. Roggenbach's advice to Stosch in the event of a serious crisis developing; Bonn, 30 Aug. 1874, in Heyderhoff, Im Ring der Gegner, pp. 159-62.

[67] It is not clear to what this refers. The place of the report of 30 July 1874 was given as "Berlin," but it may well have been written in Gotha.

[68] In the redesignation of Fort Jägersburg as Fort Stosch.

[69] Memoirs, II, 81-82.

This letter showed that Bismarck was undeterred by the Emperor's support of the Naval Chief and intended to carry on the fight by hamstringing the naval budget, while Stosch indicated his defensive strategy of appealing to William for support.

His admiration for the Chancellor remained undiminished, despite personal attacks. It says much for his objectivity that he could write on 2 November 1874 of Bismarck's conversation in the State Ministry that the "clarity of his thought and expression exercises a perennially new charm on me."[70] Indeed, Stosch even attended two of Bismarck's evening parties in late December, although the Chancellor was privately complaining of his "court intrigues."[71]

Meanwhile, the Chief of the Admiralty had dispatched the gunboats *Nautilus* and *Albatross* to the Spanish coast under the command of Commander Zembsch. The instructions to Zembsch shed light on Stosch's view of the role of the Navy in foreign affairs. Zembsch was ordered to station himself near Santander and report on the extent of German interests in Northern Spain and the naval power of the Carlists. He was told to keep in contact with the German diplomats in Madrid, but to act on his initiative when necessity demanded. Stosch enclosed a copy of the Foreign Office's letter, which enjoined the commander merely to display his flag and instructed him that neither an armed intervention nor a crusade was intended. The small squadron fulfilled its tasks with success and even came off the victor in a small engagement.

It soon became apparent that the murder of Captain Schmitt was a single act of fanaticism and that the minor German interests in Spain did not require the presence of ships. The autumn storms threatened the German vessels, and they drew nearer to the French coast. Fearful of storms, Stosch proposed to the Foreign Office that the ships be sent first to another Spanish port and then winter in Argentina. Bismarck countered that Zembsch had not complained of the conditions at Santander and that the departure of the ships to another Spanish port would give the impression that Germany had only two gunboats capable of action. He also observed

[70] To the Crown Prince, *ibid.*, II, 82.

[71] Heinrich von Poschinger, *Fürst Bismarck und die Parlamentarier* (Breslau, 1894-1896), I, 80 n.; Lucius, *Bismarck-Erinnerungen*, pp. 57-58.

that apparently the Navy did not have enough light ships suitable for political and security goals. The last remark was apparently what Stosch had been waiting for. He replied that the Navy had just been effectively started. Lack of manpower was the difficulty, and this resulted from the short term of service. Moreover, Germany devoted less money to its Navy than any other Great Power including Austria. To fulfil the demands placed upon it by the Foreign Office, it had to exercise great economy of force. Thus, when the ships had served their purpose, as they had at Santander, the Foreign Office should release them from service. Zembsch's report supported Stosch, and the ships were recalled to Germany. Just before the squadron departed for home, a German brig was robbed by the Carlists, but Zembsch did not hear of the incident. Bismarck took great pains to ask the Admiralty how was it possible for the German squadron to be ignorant of an event in its vicinity when the whole German press was full of it.[72] The dispute now became more acrimonious.

The Chancellor evidently felt that the time was ripe to resume his attack, for he wrote Stosch a long letter on 4 January 1875 with the avowed purpose of determining the respective duties of the Navy and the Foreign Office in the employment of ships overseas. He noted that neither the Werner court martial, at which the Foreign Office was *not* represented, nor the correspondence on the dispatch of ships to the Spanish coast had settled the question of ministerial competence. The latter correspondence gave "proof that not only had I to make out without the will to assist where I would have expected a desire to oblige," but also "I found Your Excellency little susceptible to the political goals and motives laid down by myself." He observed that "where . . . I believed I could count on joyful co-operation and even stimulating initiative I encountered difficulties" which could not be attributed entirely to technical reasons. He admitted that he was dependent upon the Chief of the Admiralty for technical advice, but he could not accept Stosch's interference (in a report to William) with political matters, "for which I alone am responsible to His Majesty." He claimed that Stosch had exceeded his authority when, in his letter to the Foreign Office, he had characterized the *"entire undertaking*

[72] Koch, *Stosch,* pp. 45, 47-51. He gives no dates.

as inopportune" and in his report of 30 July 1874 when he said
the ships, which would not be visible from shore, were useless.
The mere show of force by a Great Power would make an impression. Bismarck announced his willingness to let pass the question whether or not the dispatch of ships to the Spanish coast
would have had the same effect, but he could not ignore Stosch's
repeated proposals to withdraw them. His suggestions must have
originated from other than technical reasons, Bismarck contended,
because the other powers had stationed ships at the same spot.
He then noted that when he signed the order for their recall, the
ships left the coast at a moment when their instructions called
for action.[73] He followed this reference to the Carlist plundering
of a German brig with the left-handed compliment that he did not
doubt the zeal and good intentions of the commanding officer. However, Your Excellency could hardly consider me wrong, if I have
misgivings about assuming political responsibility for missions of warships to foreign countries, as long as I do not find the Naval High
Command accessible to the political motives and arguments represented
by me. . . . In the public discussion which perhaps is imminent, I would
find it difficult to defend the way in which our interests and the appearance of our flag have been maintained against the Carlists.[74]

Bismarck concluded by stating that the future employment of the
Navy would have to be decided by the Emperor and by requesting
Stosch to send him a list of ships and an estimate of the time they
would need to prepare for an expedition to Spain.[75] This savage
attack was clearly made with the intention of forcing Stosch out
of office.

The Chief of the Admiralty evidently thought out his defense
carefully because he did not take action until 9 January 1875.
On that day he sent the Chancellor's letter to William I and added
his comments to it. He wrote that he could only conclude that the
Chancellor considered his continuance in office as "prejudicial to
the interests of the Emperor and an obstacle to the performance
of that policy which he has conducted with such great success to
the glory of Your Majesty." Stosch insisted that he had fulfilled
his duties to the "best of my knowledge and conscience" and

[73] Hassell, *Tirpitz*, pp. 38-39.   [74] *Ibid.*, p. 39.
[75] *Ibid.*

had sought to meet Bismarck's demands, as far as the technical
state of the Navy permitted. He argued that "no Navy on earth
has so many ships on foreign service, in relation to its strength
and its budget, as does the German Navy." These demands created
even greater difficulty because the German Navy was the only
one that had both universal military service and a short term of
service. As a result, training problems were acute, and ship complements had to change once every two years. Germany had
the third largest merchant marine and, next to England, the
greatest number of citizens in foreign countries. Overseas employment of the Navy was thus continually necessary, but the naval
budget had remained the same as the demands on the Navy had
increased. These factors had resulted in the conflict with the
Chancellor, Stosch maintained. He declared that it was possible
that he put too much emphasis on naval interests, because he
wished the Navy to be strong before it assumed overseas tasks.[76]
He then made a subtle appeal to William's jealousy of his military
prerogative, stating:

It goes against my military opinions and experience to maintain that
something can be accomplished with a force which lacks a reserve, or
that one is able to conquer an enemy through demonstrations. When,
for example, my approval is expected of the demand to impress the
enemy by the appearance of a few ships which cannot approach the
coast, then, supported by the first principles of military science, I must
certainly label that as quite impossible. But the Imperial Chancellor
makes this demand and even disputes my right to express my views
about it, because it is a political demand. However, I believe that the
judgment as to which element of power lies in a military measure really
can be correctly viewed by a soldier as falling within his province. The
Imperial Chancellor has not only rejected military-technical claims,
but has also interfered in them. In this year's budget, he has, without
further inquiry, decreed which ships will be built.[77]

Stosch further complained that, while the Imperial Chancellor gave
many directives to the Navy on technical matters, he did not wish
the Admiralty even to co-operate in the preparation of its budget,
which lay within the Chancellor's competence. The General disclosed that the proposals which aimed at saving money by putting
the Navy on an equal basis with the Army were rejected, and Army

[76] *Ibid.*, pp. 40-41.   [77] *Ibid.*, p. 41.

increases were not applied to the Navy. To obtain consideration of a proposal to raise the marines' pay by six pfennigs, he had to act through a member of the Reichstag, and he received cognizance of the naval budget only when it was printed and sent to him as a member of the Bundesrat. These incidents left no doubt in his mind that Bismarck wanted his departure. This did not surprise him after all that had happened, but he did not believe that he need take any notice of Bismarck's wish until "it was positively told to me." This had now taken place, and Stosch asked William to accept his resignation. To remain in office would only damage the Navy. He could not work "in harmony" with the majority of the Ministry and perceived that "if the youthful portion of Your Majesty's armed strength, the Navy, would prosper, it needs not only demands upon its performance but, first of all, benevolent attention." He concluded that he resigned only in the interest of the Navy and in the belief of the necessity of his action, with "unconditional faithfulness" to the Emperor. He added that he was sending a copy of the letter to the Chancellor.[78]

Having submitted his resignation to the Emperor, Stosch continued his offensive by addressing a somewhat shorter letter to Bismarck on the same day, 9 January 1875. He repeated his conclusion that the Chancellor had wished him to resign, but Stosch had left it up to Bismarck "to take the necessary steps." Since the Emperor had appointed him Chief of the Admiralty and had "expressed his satisfaction with my activities," he was not resigning on his own account; he believed that his departure would aid the Navy.[79] He observed:

Therefore, I rest content with the principle which holds good for every Prussian officer, to keep firmly to his post as long as that is agreeable to the War Lord and as long as the officer feels his own powers are sufficient. However, I must simply characterize as false the charge, which Your Highness made in your honored letter of 4 January, that I used a report to the Emperor to interfere in political matters against Your Highness' intentions.[80]

Having made this uncompromising statement, he said that he could only consider the charge as offensive and asked Bismarck to ex-

[78] *Ibid.*, pp. 41-42.   [79] *Ibid.*, p. 42.
[80] *Ibid.*

plain himself.[81]   He continued: "I am conscious of being without fault in the matter and will find the best-informed judge of my complaint in His Majesty.   I look forward to Your Highness' further communications on this matter."[82]   He concluded this biting note by referring to the heavy duties put on the infant Navy, which was not given adequate funds for overseas service.

Stosch had picked up Bismarck's gauntlet and struck him in the face with it.   He had chosen his ground carefully, had taken a leaf from the Chancellor's book, and had threatened resignation to get his way.   William refused the Admiralty Chief's offer of resignation and evidently told Bismarck to accept Stosch's view of his competence.[83]

The Chancellor submitted to the Emperor's decision with very bad grace, as his letter to Stosch of 10 January 1875 indicates.   He declared that the Admiralty Chief had been mistaken when he believed that Bismarck wished his resignation, and he, the Chancellor, had not forgotten that he had no right to information about Stosch's naval activities, which the Emperor had publicly praised.   However, Bismarck could not quite bring himself to say that he approved Stosch as Chief of the Admiralty, for he wrote: "Even less have I expressed a wish about Your Excellency's remaining or not remaining in your present position, with which I have nothing to do."   He declared that he had only raised the question of how far Stosch had made difficult his duties as Foreign Minister. To the General's demand for an explanation of the "false" charge that he had used a report to the Emperor to express political opinions, Bismarck took refuge behind the rather lame excuse that his health did not permit him to consult the documents on the question.[84]   The sting of Bismarck's letter lay in the tail.

However, since Your Excellency has combined the removal of the existent difficulties for the foreign service with thoughts of a change in personnel, I cannot fail to express my conviction that Your Excellency's behavior would also make the position of my successor in the Chancellery more difficult, if he wishes to satisfy his duty and his responsibility.[85]

[81] *Ibid.*   [82] *Ibid.*, p. 43.   [83] *Ibid.*
[84] *Ibid.*, pp. 43-44.
[85] *Ibid.*, p. 44.   Cf. Bismarck's statements of 16 Jan. (Hubatsch, *Der Admiralstab*, p. 38, n. 14) and 4 Apr. (Hubatsch, *Die Ära Tirpitz*, pp. 29-30).

This letter apparently ended the "Carlist crisis." Stosch, content with his victory, was not foolish enough to expect his opponent to apologize, and the budget seems to have been revised to his satisfaction, judging by the lack of references to the contrary. The "Carlist crisis" between the two adversaries was decisive for the future development of their relations. The Chancellor, who made no distinction between his personal opponents and those of the Empire, had finally encountered a Minister who did not tamely submit to attack. He had forced Stosch to offer his resignation, but the Admiralty Chief had effectively gained the Emperor's support. There can be no doubt that the defeat rankled in Bismarck's mind. Thereafter, the State Ministry was too small to contain them both for long.

4

An uneasy truce now ensued. Bismarck, who suffered frequently from nervous attacks, was ill and apparently lacked the energy and the opportunity to carry on the battle. When Stosch harbored thoughts of inciting an active colonial policy in the spring of 1875, Freytag apparently persuaded him to abandon the idea which could only lead to further conflicts and his resignation.[86] Normann told Freytag in August 1875 that Roggenbach and Stosch had met and were confident of Bismarck's resignation. "The War Ministry," he felt, "would be the most suitable post for our friend, who nevertheless follows quite different plans."[87] What these "different plans" were can only be conjectured; probably, Stosch's wish to extend his competence to embrace the merchant marine is meant. In October he wrote his wife from Berlin that the Imperial Chancellor had once again struck out his budget proposals and his worries over the Navy's future kept him from sleeping. To gain his point would mean a new conflict, but "I take the field with new powers and am not afraid of battle." He noted later in the day that Bismarck had now accepted his proposals, and he could again sleep soundly.[88] Bismarck, having been

[86] Freytag to Stosch, Leipzig, 24 Feb., Siebleben, 18 April 1875, in Helmolt, *Freytag an Stosch,* pp. 103, 105.

[87] Neues Palais, Potsdam, 31 Aug. 1875, in Heyderhoff and Wentzcke, *Deutscher Liberalismus,* II, 136.

[88] 12 Oct. 1875, Memoirs, II, 103-4.

defeated once on the budget issue had apparently abandoned any further attempts to dictate to Stosch in the matter, but he looked for new grounds of attack. The Chief of the Admiralty wrote to his friend Roggenbach on 31 January 1876:

My relation to the great Chancellor remains unchanged; he recently told a member of the Reichstag: "Stosch does very well as commander of the Navy, but as a Minister he lacks logic." I was greatly pleased by this remark. Recently the fellow complained to the Emperor about a newspaper report concerning me. You should have seen his rage when the report proved to be unfounded.[89]

Bismarck's most vicious attack on Stosch was made about this time.[90] He asked the Imperial Justice Office to draw up a bill of particulars indicting the Chief of the Admiralty for treason. The charge was based upon Stosch's independent action in concluding the Convention of Ferrières in 1871 (see Chapter III). The Imperial Justice Office pointed out that the Chancellor had made himself responsible for the Convention when he signed the definitive Treaty of Frankfort, which incorporated the provisions. Bismarck quickly abandoned the prosecution.[91]

In the meantime, Bismarck and Stosch had clashed over their respective powers with regard to ships in service. In late December 1875, the German Minister to Athens was asked by von Bülow, Secretary of the Foreign Office, whether conditions in Turkey did not warrant the presence of German ships in Near Eastern waters. Under this prodding, Radowitz responded that he thought the local outbreaks of Moslem fanaticism made the dispatch of ships by all the Great Powers desirable; he suggested that Germany send two warships, one to be stationed at Salonika. He was astounded to receive the reply that he would do better to await an occasion for sending ships before making proposals for their employment. Bismarck's confidant Busch told Radowitz privately the reason for the Chancellor's rebuke. Bismarck himself had ordered the question

---

[89] Heyderhoff, *Im Ring der Gegner,* p. 175.

[90] Helmolt (*Freytag an Stosch,* p. 324) places it in March 1876, producing no evidence for his view. Stosch (*Memoirs,* I, 242) merely relates that "in the year 1876," when he "came into great conflict with the Chancellor," the move was made. It may have been the result of the "Salonika affair" or perhaps Stosch's memory betrayed him and it was really made after Bismarck's speech of March 1877. His informant was very likely Friedberg.

[91] *Memoirs,* I, 242.

raised, but Stosch had stolen a march on him. He had reported to the Emperor that the ships should not be sent before Bismarck discussed the question with William. An angry correspondence between the Emperor and Chancellor ensued, and Bismarck felt that Stosch had only used this opportunity to attack him. He could not touch the Chief of the Admiralty, so his wrath fell upon the unsuspecting Radowitz.[92]

The threatening situation in the Near East did not escape Stosch, who, on 22 January 1876 issued secret orders to one of his ships to sail immediately to Portugal and hold itself in readiness for an outbreak in the Eastern Mediterranean. On 6 May 1876 the German and French consuls were murdered by Moslem fanatics at Salonika.[93] The Emperor approved the dispatch of a squadron to the Near East, and Stosch worked hard to send a fleet "to document our position as a World Power," but was concerned that there was no reserve left for future action.[94] He wrote his wife on May 18: "I have a great desire to get away, for the Chancellor is pressing me hard again. Nothing will come of it, because I would have to offend the old Emperor to reach my goal [of resignation]."[95] He had informed the Foreign Office of the difficulties in instructing recruits if they were placed on active service and had received Bismarck's reply that he should call up the reserves to meet the emergency. He objected that the reserves were on duty with the merchant marine and could not be mobilized immediately.[96] Stosch reported to Freytag on 29 May that public reaction to the swift dispatch of a squadron to Salonika was favorable and the Emperor had praised him for it. However, William had expressed his dissatisfaction over some details.[97] Stosch continued:

The path of power is really practical only for young people. Thus my thoughts are pleasantly occupied with quiet life in Oestrich. I have a constant desire for that, but I also want to stay on here with honor as long as duty demands. Nonetheless, my private worries do not disturb

[92] Hajo Holborn, ed., *Aufzeichnungen und Erinnerungen aus dem Leben des Botschafters Joseph Maria von Radowitz* (Berlin and Leipzig, 1925), I, 354-55.
[93] Koch, *Stosch*, pp. 51-52.
[94] To his wife, Berlin, 14 May 1876, Memoirs, II, 119-20.
[95] Berlin, *ibid.*, II, 120.
[96] Koch, *Stosch*, pp. 52-53. He gives no dates.
[97] Memoirs, II, 119.

my delight in the Chancellor's deeds. His performances in the realm of foreign policy are as delightful as the most beautiful works of art.[98]

The passage of time did not dim Stosch's admiration of the Chancellor's genius, but their antagonism continued.

As soon as the German squadron, in conjunction with the fleets of other powers, had quieted the Moslems, Stosch asked that the fleet be withdrawn, pointing out that it was needed for duty elsewhere and the budget made no provision for further duty in the Near East. The Foreign Office reluctantly permitted the withdrawal of a few of these ships. Stosch was careful not to furnish Bismarck with occasion to attack him. When the Emperor proposed that the German captains in the Mediterranean send separate reports on the situation there, he objected that this matter lay within the competence of the Foreign Office and would have to be approved by Bismarck.[99] Although the "Salonika affair" had ceased to cause friction between the two statesmen by August 1876,[100] Stosch's constant efforts to secure the withdrawal of the greater part of the squadron met with success only in December.[101]

The mutual relations between Stosch and Bismarck continued, however, on a "war footing," as Roggenbach described it to the Empress Augusta in October.[102] When Stosch appeared at Bismarck's parliamentary soirée on 2 December they merely exchanged bows without shaking hands, as was the custom.[103] The relations of Bismarck with Stosch were thus already embittered by 1877. Their ambition and independence clashed, and the Chancellor sought to remove his opponent from his post. These repeated efforts failed because of the trust William I put in his Admiralty Chief. Bismarck, deeply suspicious of Stosch's influence on both the Emperor and the Crown Prince, was obsessed with the idea the Admiral aspired to be his successor. Having failed to weaken the Emperor's resolve to keep Stosch, the Chancellor now turned to public opinion as the force necessary to shake the Admiral from the tree of office.

[98] *Ibid.*   [99] Koch, *Stosch,* p. 53.
[100] Stosch to Freytag, Berlin, 31 July 1876, Memoirs, II, 121.
[101] Koch, *Stosch,* p. 53.
[102] Ehnerfahrnau, 24 Oct. 1876, in Heyderhoff, *Im Ring der Gegner,* p. 131.
[103] Heinrich Eduard Brockhaus [Hermann Michel, ed.], *Stunden mit Bismarck 1871-1878* (Leipzig, 1929), p. 162.

5

During the Reichstag budget debate of 10 March 1877,[104] the Left Liberal orator Eugen Richter referred to the Admiralty's complaisance during the budget discussions of 1875. Prince von Bismarck in his reply observed that Richter's success with the Admiralty had astounded him. He declared: "I myself sought in vain to obtain a similar success from the Navy in the months that preceded the bill. (Hear!)." He stated that he had to accept as correct the demands the departments presented to him, but he had a conflict with the Navy over the budget which was "conducted with much dialectical flow of language." He had finally decided for a lower sum than the Navy demanded, and thus "could not expect that the authority or the persuasive powers of Herr Richter (Hagen) would have greater effect than mine on the Navy department." This open attack on Stosch, coupling him with the liberal opponents of the Government, aroused great excitement.[105]

Stosch was totally unprepared for this assault, for just the evening before he had shaken the Chancellor's hand in apparent friendliness. He had left the Reichstag shortly before Bismarck spoke, after he had been informed that the naval budget would not be discussed that day. An Admiralty official brought him the first report of the attack, and he did not see the full account until

[104] For general accounts of the Chancellor crisis of spring 1877, see Erich Eyck, *Bismarck: Sein Leben und Werk* (Erlenbach-Zürich), 1941-1944, III, 195-200; Johannes Ziekursch, *Politisches Geschichte des neuen deutschen Kaiserreiches* (Frankfurt a. M., 1925-1930), II, 314, 410. Oskar Klein-Hattigen, *Geschichte des deutschen Liberalismus* (Berlin-Schöneburg, 1912), II, 209-14, contains many inaccuracies. Cf. the account in Klein-Hattingen, *Bismarck und seine Welt* (Berlin, 1903), II, Pt. I, 288-300. Constantin de Grunwald, in his excellent brief biography, *Bismarck* (Paris, 1949), pp. 404-5, and in a letter to the writer (Paris, 16 Sept. 1953), maintains that "following" Bismarck's attack, Stosch "was retired despite all the objections of the old Emperor." Even accepting M. de Grunwald's explanation that this "nearly corresponded to reality even if this . . . means a delay of six years" (as he states in his letter), Stosch's resignation of 1883 was apparently the result of his own desire and only indirectly of Bismarck's pressure on William.

[105] Hagen was Richter's district. For the text of Bismarck's attack, see *Verhandlungen des Reichstags*, 3 Leg. Per., I Sess., 1877, 6 Sitz. XLIV, 70, or more conveniently, Horst Kohl, ed., *Die Politische Reden des Fürsten Bismarcks* (Stuttgart, 1892), VII, 20-21. For a critical appraisal, see Richter, *Im alten Reichstag*, II, 7, 11-12. Bismarck's charge had been made previously, but only to his intimates, Tiedemann, *Aus Sieben Jahrzehnten*, II, 44 (26 May 1876).

the evening papers arrived.[106]   He wrote of the basis for Bismarck's charge:

> The truth was that I had approved a National Liberal amendment for the decrease of an item which had never been objected to by the Chancellor. The only error I committed was not asking his express approval. This procedure, to be sure, was not in order, but it in no way justified this public attack.[107]

On the following morning, Sunday, 11 March, Stosch gave the documents proving his contention to his friend War Minister von Kameke and asked him to explain to the Chancellor that his account was based on error. He requested Bismarck to make a statement to that effect in the Reichstag on Monday, but "Kameke did not receive a satisfactory reply." When Monday's Reichstag session passed without the Chancellor's taking any action, Stosch submitted his resignation to the Emperor, detailing his reasons.[108] The next day he was unofficially informed that William would not accept it, and, on 14 March, the Chancellor was requested to document his account for the Emperor. Bismarck, Stosch notes, "said that I was persecuting him and sought to overthrow him."[109]

The official press was treating Stosch as a "dead man."[110] Freytag wrote angrily from Wiesbaden that he should not resign and expressed the hope that the Emperor would support him. Bismarck's action outraged Freytag's sense of decency.[111] Roggenbach was just as outraged. In a letter of 21 March to Stosch, he declared that the assault was the "result of a premeditated plan and not the emotion of the moment." The fact that the whole Ministry had supinely submitted to Bismarck's attack on a colleague showed the "degree of moral degradation which the pressure of his personality has produced on his weak-minded collaborators." He thought Stosch would be in a better position if he left. In retire-

---

[106] Memoirs, II, 134.   [107] Ibid., II, 134-135.

[108] Ibid., II, 135. Lucius, Bismarck-Erinnerungen, p. 104, probably on Bismarck's authority, says that Stosch gave illness as his reason for resignation. Both Stosch's own statement and the Emperor's reply of 24 March disprove this statement.

[109] Memoirs, II, 135.

[110] Richter, Im alten Reichstag, II, 13.

[111] To Stosch, 15 March 1877, in Helmolt, Freytag an Stosch, pp. 119-20.

ment, he could hope that the end of Bismarck's misgovernment would bring a "day of new activity."[112]

The Chancellor openly discussed his attack on Stosch at a soirée he gave to a large group of Reichstag deputies. He spoke of Stosch's request for an apology and declared that it was impossible. Those present were certain Stosch would fall.[113] Stosch wrote the Chief of the Military Cabinet, Albedyll, on 18 March that he felt his position was suffering because everyone believed that he was a "dying man," whose authority was at an end. He noted that the press seemed to think that since Bismarck wished him to, "I must weaken." Under these circumstances he thought it would be better for him to go on vacation until the question was settled and he asked Albedyll to submit his request to the Emperor.[114] Bismarck was complaining to his intimates at the time that Stosch was a "spy and an intriguer, who did not open his mouth in the Ministerial councils, but then told tales to the Crown Prince and His Majesty."[115] On 22 March the Chancellor expressed the wish for a long vacation to observe how his opponents would like the way the Government was conducted in his absence.[116] Three days later Stosch received the Emperor's refusal of his resignation.[117]

The Emperor's letter of 24 March 1877 was a masterpiece of tact. He said that there was no need for an alteration in the Navy; "I recognize with lively satisfaction the great progress which the Navy has made under your direction. . . ." He could see no

[112] Segenhaus bei Neuwied, in Heyderhoff, *Im Ring der Gegner,* pp. 183-85.
[113] Poschinger, *Bismarck und die Parlamentarier,* I, 129.
[114] Hassell, *Tirpitz,* pp. 44-45. Cf. Memoirs, II, 135. In January 1877 Stosch complained to Albedyll of the "uninterrupted interferences of Bismarck in the military sphere of the Navy." The Chief of the Military Cabinet asked General von Manteuffel's advice about the letter. Manteuffel apparently misunderstood Stosch's protest and thought it directed against the Military Cabinet (Schmidt-Bückeburg, *Das Militärkabinett,* pp. 124-25). However, Ludwig Dehio ("Eduard von Manteuffel und der Kaiser," *Deutsche Rundschau,* CCVI [Jan.-March 1926], 44) notes that Stosch thanked Manteuffel for his "good counsel" after the crisis of 1877 and conjectures that Manteuffel intervened with the King to save Stosch. The *Magdeburgische Zeitung* of 30 June 1884 (Helmolt, *Freytag an Stosch,* p. 327) maintained that Moltke had used his influence with William to prevent Stosch's dismissal in 1877. Schröder, *Stosch,* p. 92, states (citing no evidence) that both Manteuffel and Moltke, as well as the Empress Augusta, intervened to save Stosch. If either General used his influence, it was more probably Moltke, with whom Stosch was in closer contact.
[115] Lucius, *Bismarck-Erinnerungen,* p. 105.
[116] *Ibid.,* p. 106.   [117] Memoirs, II, 135.

important contradictions in the accounts of the affair that he had received from the two antagonists and noted that Stosch had admitted his error in making the concession to the Reichstag without obtaining the Chancellor's approval. William did not doubt that Stosch had acted in the best interest of the service. Bismarck had not meant to attack him, but was merely responding to a remark made by an opposition deputy. William, however, wrote that he could take no action to correct the mistaken interpretation that Stosch had conceded something to Richter. The Emperor's continued trust would show the falsity of the reports, which had already been discounted in the press. He expressed his pleasure that the Navy would continue to receive "your challenging and prudent leadership." William sent a copy of the letter to Bismarck with a covering note which stated that Stosch was at fault in making the budget concession, but the Chancellor should have informed him long ago. William directed on 7 April that the Ministry be informed of his letters to Stosch and Bismarck.[118] He had decided the technical question at issue in favor of Bismarck, but it was Stosch who triumphed by remaining in office. Neither the Chancellor's attack nor the inspired press campaign had shaken the Emperor's trust in the Chief of the Admiralty.

Nonetheless, the Chancellor did not forsake the offensive. He decided that Stosch need not be invited to the session of the State Ministry on 29 March because he "tells tales to the Emperor or the Crown Prince about everything that occurs in his presence." At this session, Bismarck announced that he was determined to resign, but if he were refused, he would go on vacation. He told one of his subordinates that he was worn out and was particularly troubled by the "passive resistance of Ministers" to his tax and economic proposals and to his measures to rid himself of the particularists.[119] The Chancellor's offer of resignation raised a great storm in the press, but it was finally refused on 10 April with William's famous word: "Never!"[120]

[118] The text of the letter to Stosch is given in Tiedemann, *Aus sieben Jahrzehnten*, II, 130-32. The text in Memoirs, II, 135-38, is *exactly* the same, except that a few words are abbreviated and, in one instance, transposed.

[119] *Ibid.*, II, 124-28. Cf. Goldschmidt, *Das Reich und Preussen*, p. 27.

[120] Eyck, *Bismarck*, III, 197-99, reaches the interesting conclusion that Bismarck was so afraid that his resignation would be accepted that he did not put it into writing.

What was Bismarck's intention? Was he merely displaying his extreme hatred of Stosch and the bitterness he felt at being defeated? An inspired article in *Die Grenzboten* of 7 April, written by Busch, throws light on his motives. Busch stated that the Chancellor seriously meant to resign, but not because of his health or the "Stosch affair," "though it can hardly have been a matter of particular satisfaction to him." The underlying cause lay in "friction," which came from a "certain exalted lady [the Empress Augusta]," who supported the Ultramontanes. Busch pursued this idea through several more "friction articles," paying special attention to Geffcken.[121] The Berlin *Post* of 7 April carried an even more significant article which maintained that the Chancellor would stay, if he received the authority to introduce measures concerning social, tax, and railway reform.[122] Bismarck's bitterness against Stosch was strong, nevertheless. On 10 April he told a subordinate that he could not work under "Stosch circumstances."[123] The following day he informed the representative of Württemberg that he had resigned both because of his health and his relations with the State Ministry and said he approved of the Emperor's attitude toward Stosch. Contradictorily, he repeated his charge of "spy" and promised that, when he returned from vacation, Stosch "would have little pleasure in remaining in office."[124] The real reason for Bismarck's attempted resignation probably lay in his remark on 29 March and the Berlin *Post* article on 7 April. He was tired, in ill health, disappointed that Stosch remained, and disturbed by opposition at court, but his real aim was to force the Emperor to give advance approval to his new economic policy. If he were upheld by William, he could initiate his program. Politically he was drawing away from the free-trader National Liberals and looking to the Conservatives for support. To reach his goal of social insurance, protective tariffs, and more taxes, he wished to dismiss the Ministers who had been appointed when he was working with the Liberals. This program took some years to

---

[121] Busch, *Bismarck*, II, 270-72.

[122] Poschinger, *Bismarck und die Parlamentarier*, I, 130.

[123] Lucius, *Bismarck-Erinnerungen*, p. 108.

[124] Freiherr von Mittnacht, *Erinnerungen an Bismarck* (4th ed.; Stuttgart and Berlin, 1904), pp. 59-60.

accomplish, but his attempt to resign in March 1877 was a step in that direction.[125]

Indeed, it is extremely doubtful whether the Chancellor seriously meant to leave the Government. His statement to the State Ministry on 29 March that he would go on a long vacation if his resignation were not accepted seems to substantiate this view. This was the opinion not only of shrewd critics like Richter[126] and Lasker,[127] but of the Emperor as well.[128]

The "Chancellor Crisis" of early 1877 had a definite effect on Stosch's career. He had been publicly branded by Bismarck and the press as the Chancellor's opponent, and he could count upon the opposition of the Chancellor's many supporters and admirers to his naval program. Moreover, Bismarck excluded him from the sessions of the State Ministry. Stosch inquired on 30 March 1877 why he had not been invited to the previous day's session. He received the reply that a "private discussion," and not an official session, had taken place. On 6 April Bismarck signed an order stating that Stosch had been receiving the reports and votes of the Ministry illegally. He was entitled to attend only those sessions "which concerned the affairs of the German Empire." Bismarck concluded: "What affairs are to be characterized as such will be determined in every single case by the President of the State Ministry [Bismarck]." This order was constitutionally unjustifiable and was merely one of Bismarck's constant efforts to incite Stosch.[129] He also wished to stop the Admiral's reports to the Crown Prince on the sessions. Stosch recorded in his memoirs:

[125] On Bismarck's change in economic policy, see Adalbert Wahl, *Deutsche Geschichte, 1871-1914* (Stuttgart, 1929), I, chap. vii. On his political shift, see P. H. Block, *Die Parlamentarische Krisis der nationalliberalen partei, 1879-1880,* (Münster i. W., 1930).

[126] Richter, *Im alten Reichstag,* II, 13.

[127] Mittnacht, *Erinnerungen an Bismarck,* p. 85.

[128] William I to Roon, 17 April 1877, in Erich Brandenburg, ed., *Briefe Kaiser Wilhelm des Ersten* (Leipzig, 1911), pp. 285-86.

[129] Goldschmidt, *Das Reich und Preussen,* pp. 27, 179-80; Memoirs, II, 138; Lehment, *Kriegsmarine,* p. 33. Schröder, *Stosch,* p. 92, states that Stosch could not object, since there were no constitutional precedents. Morsey, *Die Oberste Reichsverwaltung,* p. 132n. 31, agrees with this view. On the other hand, Stosch's right to be present at such meetings was clearly stated in the Emperor's order appointing him Chief of the Admiralty (Priesdorff, *Soldatisches Führertum,* VIII, 314), and he had exercised this right since 1872.

From this day on I no longer attended the private sessions of the State Ministry . . . . I had a right to complain and make a new cabinet question of it. However, I perceived that I would gain nothing for myself, but would create much trouble for the Emperor. It is a platonic and purely decorative honor to attend the most important proceedings without having the right to speak. Kameke kept me continually informed. I did not miss the Ministers' speeches; I only found it difficult to be denied the enjoyment of the Chancellor's utterances, especially on foreign policy. This direct overflow of his greatness always charmed me into complete admiration, even when my own little lamp burned dim. I lived therefore only in my position as Chief of the Admiralty, avoiding every collision, but feeling the great man's resistance in all business relations and also in the press. Love of the Navy held me firm to the battleground, since at the time the likelihood of binding the sphere of the merchant marine to mine seemed to be a possibility. This was the goal for which I had strived for six years. I would have considered that the greatest success of my career.[130]

Despite continued conflicts with Bismarck and his followers, the Admiral, then almost sixty, was to remain at his post until 1883.

6

The fourteen months from the crisis of March 1877 to the sinking of the *Great Elector* in May 1878 were relatively quiet ones for Stosch. This lull may be partially attributed to Bismarck's absence in Friedrichsruh for the greater part of the period. Of course, Stosch was frequently attacked by the press, but he did not come into any direct political conflict with the Chancellor. Bismarck had not yet persuaded any members of the Reichstag to try to limit seriously the naval budget, although, on 14 April 1877 Rickert, for the Reichstag Budget Committee, reported an amendment to strike out an appropriation for a naval transport. Eugen Richter spoke in favor of the amendment and was supported in the vote by the Center, the left wing of the National Liberals, and his party of Left Liberals. Besides Stosch, the National Liberals, Jacobs, a retired Admiralty official, Benda, Stosch's friend, and Mosle spoke against it. Robert Lucius, one of Bismarck's intimates, and a member of the Liberal Imperial party, also spoke against the amendment, and the Conservatives voted in

[130] Memoirs, II, 138-39. In May Bismarck seems to have suspected Stosch of misusing his right to countersign orders, but apparently Stosch was innocent. Morsey, *Die Oberste Reichsverwaltung,* p. 132.

opposition to it. The ship was struck out of the naval budget by the narrow margin of 124 to 102.[131]   This was a defeat, but a minor one.

Both the Emperor and the Crown Prince continued to show their trust in Stosch. A visible sign of their approval was the entrance of Frederick William's second son, Prince Henry, into the German Navy in the middle of April.[132]   Although Stosch must have christened the corvette *Bismarck* with mixed feelings in July,[133] his relations with the Chancellor showed a temporary improvement the following month. The two antagonists agreed that the continued presence of German ships in the Mediterranean served no useful purpose. William, on the other hand, did not wish "to recall the symbols of our power from the theater of operations."[134] Bismarck even seemed to have reached the point of tolerating Stosch. The National Liberal leader, Rudolf von Bennigsen, told Stosch that Bismarck had discussed with him a plan for an Imperial Ministry.[135]   Stosch related to Roggenbach that when asked about the Naval Chief, Bismarck replied:

"He will be an independent Minister in the Imperial Ministry." Isn't that nice? The fellow thinks he can first trample me and then dispose of me at will. I believe I am quite free of the thought of coming into a close relationship with the Chancellor. . . .[136]

As a result of Bismarck's attacks, Stosch encountered increasing resistance to his projects. Despite Freytag's advice to stay within his province and avoid conflict with the Chancellor,[137] he continued to push his plan to extend his powers to include the merchant marine. Initially he found support from the National

---

[131] *Verhandlungen des Reichstags,* 3 Leg. Per., I Sess., 1877, 21 Sitz., XLI, 472-76. There was no roll call. The attitude of the parties is inferred from the party affiliations of the speakers and of the recorded votes of Reichstag officials.

[132] Poschinger, *Kaiser Friedrich,* III, 218.

[133] Bethcke, *Politische Generalen!,* p. 109.

[134] Stosch to Freytag, Berlin, 9 Aug. 1877, Memoirs, II, 143. A few ships were still retained in the Mediterranean after the Salonika affair. For advice on Stosch's future course, see Normann to Roggenbach, Wiesbaden Schloss, 22 Nov. 1877, in Heyderhoff, *Im Ring der Gegner,* p. 187; Freytag to Stosch, Leipzig, 14 Dec. 1877, in Helmolt, *Freytag an Stosch,* pp. 123-24.

[135] Stosch to Roggenbach, 27 Dec. 1877, Heyderhoff, *Im Ring der Gegner,* pp. 190-91.

[136] *Ibid.,* p. 191.

[137] Wiesbaden, 10 Jan. 1878, in Helmolt, *Freytag an Stosch,* p. 125.

Liberal deputy and merchant, Alexander Georg Mosle. But Mosle, who represented Bremen in the Reichstag, was a staunch champion of Bismarck. In fact, in 1879 he was to change from ardent advocacy of free trade to a strong protectionist policy under the Chancellor's influence.[138]   Stosch wrote to Freytag on 18 January 1878:

I have taken many steps for my plans . . . and have had the most astonishing experiences.   One learns again and again how much one must reckon with Prussia, if one would reach the goal.   Earlier Mosle was especially favorable to the extension of the Naval Ministry.   Now he is vacillating, believes in the possibility of an Imperial Ministry, and thinks the union of the merchant marine with the Imperial Ministry would do better.   The solution of the puzzle is that he wants to become Minister of Commerce himself, when the great division [of offices to the National Liberals] takes place.

Bismarck's attacks also affected Stosch's relations with his naval officers.   In the same letter to Freytag, Stosch continued:

In my six years as Chief of the Admiralty, I have striven to preserve all maritime singularities and make the Navy a militarily reliable weapon. There has been no system up to now.   Every commandant can carry out training for service . . . as he sees fit . . . . My wish to create one law for all would meet great resistance, especially from the senior naval officers, who have lost a part of their independence.   The manifold attacks on me in the official press increase this spirit of resistance and awaken the officers' desire to give their own views space in the papers. For the moment, the Emperor continues to keep me and the nation has given me money, so I must remain faithful.   But I am glad to go into winter quarters.[139]

The project to combine the merchant marine with the Navy never succeeded, and Stosch did not obtain the support of the officer corps until he dismissed a number of high officers, including Admirals Werner and Henk, during the investigation of the sinking of the *Great Elector.*

Surprisingly enough[140] Stosch's competence was apparently extended early in 1878.   The Chancellor's frequent and extended absences from Berlin necessitated the passage of a law establishing

---

[138] Poschinger, *Bismarck und die Parlamentarier,* I, 108, II, 330-32, III, 14.

[139] Memoirs, II, 146-48.

[140] Stauffenberg, a leader of the National Liberal left wing, predicted it would not happen.   Poschinger, *Bismarck und die Parlamentarier,* II, 270.

representation for him in his various functions under the direction of a "Vice Chancellor." By this law, Stosch was empowered to countersign all orders concerning the Navy and maritime interests. He exercised for, and with responsibility to, the Chancellor, all the latter's powers over naval administrative matters.[141] In reality, this seems a further confirmation and slight extension of his rights gained in the conflict over countersignature in 1873.

During the debate on the naval budget on 12 March 1878, Rickert, for the Reichstag Budget Committee, charged that warship building was proceeding too swiftly, but the Committee wished to leave Stosch "a free hand." Stosch replied to this "attack" with the argument that demands on the Navy had greatly increased and ship construction had to be expedited. Rickert retorted that no attack had been made, for the Admiralty Chief was, in fact, less extreme in his demands on the Reichstag than the other department heads.[142]

Bismarck looked with a jealous eye upon Stosch's popularity with the Reichstag, particularly since the liberal majority was at odds with him. When Stosch projected another visit of the Reichstag to the fleet in April 1878, Bismarck attached to the Admiralty Chief's invitation the request that the Reichstag vote its expenses for the trip. The leaders thereupon decided to send only a delegation.[143] During the tour of naval bases, Stosch "had the pleasure of being only praised."[144] His harmonious relations with the Reichstag were soon to be shattered by a great naval disaster, which was to give Bismarck a further opportunity to dislodge his rival.

The ambiguity of the constitutional position of Albrecht von Stosch, Chief of the Imperial Admiralty, resulted in bitter conflict with Otto von Bismarck, the German Chancellor. The constitutional struggle stemmed from Stosch's dual responsibility to both William I and Bismarck. Neither the Admiralty Chief nor the

[141] Poschinger, *Bismarcks Bundesrat*, III, 391-92; Wahl, *Deutsche Geschichte*, I, 577-81; Lehment, *Kriegsmarine*, p. 31; Hubatsch, *Der Admiralstab*, p. 37. See Bismarck's repetition of the Ferrières charges on 20 February 1878. Lucius, *Bismarck-Erinnerungen*, pp. 129-30.
[142] *Verhandlungen des Reichstags*, 3 Leg. Per., II Sess., 1878, 19 Sitz., XLVII, 477.
[143] Richter, *Im alten Reichstag*, II, 59.
[144] Stosch to his wife, Berlin, 17 May 1878, Memoirs, II, 149-50.

Chancellor was willing to surrender to the other. With the passage of time, Bismarck, observing Stosch's extraordinary position of favor with the Emperor and the Crown Prince and his popularity with the Bundesrat and Reichstag, concluded that the General was an opponent who sought to become Chancellor. Once Bismarck arrived at this view, he held to it with bulldog tenacity and used every means at his disposal to rid himself of Stosch.

There is no evidence that Stosch, in the seventies, had any ambitions of becoming Chancellor. He did disregard the limitations of his post, early in the decade, by persuading National Liberal members of the Reichstag to introduce alterations in military legislation and the budget. Such matters were clearly within the competence of the Chancellor. Stosch also exceeded his powers as Minister of State, but with no visible repercussions, by vocally supporting Bismarck in the civil marriage question. As the split with the Chancellor widened, Stosch assumed a more reserved attitude and was careful to stay within his constitutional sphere. At the same time, he evinced great personal ambition and intense nationalism by persistent attempts to attach the merchant marine to the Admiralty.

Serious conflict between the two antagonists did not erupt until two years after Stosch asumed office. Prior to this time, there were minor collisions on military legislation and intervention in Haiti, and a misunderstanding over labor policies in the Danzig dockyards, but no fundamental disagreement. Even the clash in 1873 over the question of countersignature did not embitter the two. Here the Emperor chided Stosch for a technical error, but refused his resignation and confirmed his right to be the Chancellor's deputy in naval affairs.

The real struggle between Bismarck and Stosch began in the years 1874-1875 over the employment of ships in Spanish waters, a contest made more heated by the Chancellor's resentment at the failure to punish Captain Werner for ignoring his instructions in 1873. The question at issue was whether Bismarck or Stosch should determine the duties of the Navy. The future pattern of the Chancellor's efforts to dislodge the Admiralty Chief emerged clearly for the first time. The Bismarck-inspired press was unleashed, official enquiries were initiated, the Chancellor expressed his fury privately to influential individuals, and efforts were made to weaken the Emperor's support of Stosch. Moreover, Bismarck engaged in an acrimonious correspondence with the Admiralty Chief, accusing him of interfering with matters of policy. Stosch met this challenge with consummate skill. He refused to back down, but, following the Chancellor's example, offered his resignation to the Emperor. He made a carefully calculated appeal to William's jealousy of any infringement of his military prerogatives. The Emperor refused the resignation and supported Stosch's stand. The Carlist affair was the decisive event in the relations between the Chancellor and the General, for it determined their hostile nature in the future.

Bismarck now decided upon open warfare. He attempted to try Stosch for treason, but was unsuccessful. He sought to slash the naval budget, until the Admiralty Chief showed his determination not to yield. Having failed to shake Stosch's position by using the considerable governmental powers at his disposal, the Chancellor attempted to arouse public opinion against his opponent. Characteristically, he based his attack, not on the fact that Stosch had been complaisant to the National Liberals on the naval budget of two years before, but on the false charge that the Admiralty Chief had surrendered to the Left Liberals, a party in opposition to the Government. The Chancellor, sure of success, announced to the Reichstag in 1877 that he was in strong disagreement with the General. Stosch had no choice but to submit his resignation. William rebuked him for not securing the Chancellor's prior approval of a concession to the National Liberals, but kept him in office. The Chancellor countered with his resignation, but this too was refused. While the desire to secure the Emperor's advance approval for a switch in internal policy probably was the prime motive for the Chancellor's action, he had clearly attempted to overthrow Stosch. In the Reichstag and the press, Bismarck publicly expressed his distrust of Stosch's relations with party leaders. Conversations, scarcely more private, betrayed the Chancellor's fear of the General's contacts with the Emperor and the Crown Prince. He even chided Stosch for not speaking out in the sessions of the State Ministry, which constitutionally was impossible.

The open attack of 1877 meant that Stosch was viewed by the world as the inveterate opponent of the strongest man in Europe. He could expect only official obstruction and constant criticism from the semi-official press and the Chancellor's admirers. Any weakness the Admiralty Chief showed would be exploited to force him from office. Bismarck's opportunity came with the great naval tragedy of 1878.

VI

CRISIS AND RESIGNATION

1

The "catastrophe of Folkestone" of 31 May 1878 was a hard blow to Stosch's prestige. The ironclad battleships *King William, Great Elector,* and *Prussia* were placed in commission on 6 May 1878. Together they were sent to represent German interests in the Mediterranean. The newly built *Great Elector,* captained by Count v. Monts, had been tested and pronounced fit for service by Rear Admiral Batsch, the chief of the squadron.[1] The political decision to steam for the Mediterranean was not made known to Stosch until after 20 May, and speed was necessary to get the squadron underway.[2] It departed from Wilhelmshaven for Gibraltar on 29 May and reached the English Channel on 31 May at 3:00 A.M. without special incident.[3] It passed Dover at 9:00 A.M., the three ships steaming in close formation about one hundred metres apart. Shortly before 10:00 A.M., when the squadron was in the vicinity of Folkestone, Rear Admiral Batsch on the *King William* went below after seven hours of duty, accompanied by his second-in-command. Lieutenant Commander Klausa, the officer of the watch, took command of the ship. Meanwhile, aboard the *Great Elector* Count v. Monts had received the official—and false—report that all compartment doors were closed below. A bark approached the squadron, and the *King William* altered course to avoid it. Klausa suddenly perceived that this maneuver endangered the *Great Elector,* and he excitedly ordered the men at

---

[1] Koch, *Stosch,* p. 61.
[2] Stosch to his wife, 20 May and 26 May 1878, Memoirs, II, 150-51. In the former letter he notes that no decision had been reached on the port of destination of the squadron; in the latter he writes that the order to sail would go to the squadron "tomorrow."
[3] Koch, *Stosch,* p. 61.

the wheel to return to the former course. The order was misunderstood, and the *King William* rammed the *Great Elector*. Badly damaged itself, the *King William* could only pick up survivors as water poured into the hold in the *Great Elector*, which sank fifteen minutes later.[4]

The "catastrophe of Folkestone" on 31 May 1878, with the loss of two hundred and seventy men and a material damage of seven million marks, offered an opportunity for Stosch's opponents to attack his "System."[5] The moment the news of the disaster reached Germany, the sinking of the "Great Elector" ceased to be a question of naval discipline and technical knowledge alone. The reports of the accident commission and the courts martial became fuel for press attacks and Reichstag criticism. Against Stosch was ranged a curious combination of dissatisfied naval officers, disgruntled politicians, both liberal and conservative, and last but most important of all, Bismarck.

The attack on Stosch, both from within the Navy and without, centered on the question whether the tragedy of Folkestone could be attributed to the faults of the officers in command or to the "Stosch System," which the critics were careful never to define. Under the cloak of this all-inclusive term, Stosch's opponents gathered all they found objectionable in the Navy and in Stosch himself. Many were inspired by Bismarck, who did not hesitate to exploit a national disaster to rid himself of a dangerous political rival. The three main lines of attack on Stosch were that he had put too heavy demands on German shipbuilding, that he tried to train his officers and seamen as though they were "infantrymen," and that he was an autocrat, never consulting his own subordinates.[6] Stosch summarized the effects of the catastrophe in his memoirs:

> The unhappy business of the *Great Elector* made wider and wider circles. The press was filled with attacks on me, and the officers especially put all the blame on me and my "System." They strove to butcher me also in three repeated courts martial, as well as in preliminary investigations, but without success. In spite of that, the attacks increased daily, and the Reichstag also joined in them. All parties were

[4] *Ibid.*, pp. 61-64.
[5] Petersdorff, "Stosch," *A. D. B.*, LIV, 601; Hassell, *Tirpitz*, p. 28.
[6] Hassell, *Tirpitz*, pp. 28-29, 45, 92; Batsch, "Stosch," *Deutsche Revue*, XXIII, 353.

united against me. I was saved, oddly enough, by the left and not from love of me, but from hatred of the Chancellor, for it was realized how he had fanned the flames. They had not forgotten how he had similarly treated [Finance Minister] Camphausen, by drawing with him the opposition, which later deeply regretted its complaisance.[7]

For the moment, Bismarck was too affected by the severe wounding of William by an assassin, too occupied with instructing the Crown Prince on his duties as Regent, and too concerned with internal and foreign affairs to bother himself about Stosch. Before it was known whether the Emperor would recover, he appears to have feared the immediate accession of Frederick William, for he took special notice of Stosch at an evening meeting in early June and even shook hands.[8]

The Admiral was deeply disturbed by the sinking of the *Great Elector* and laid awake nights seeing "horrible pictures of sinking ships." Suffering from extreme nervous tension, he wished to escape from Berlin, but was occupied with reports on the tragedy and his duties with the Crown Prince. On 8 June he privately expressed the fear that the chief of the squadron, Admiral Batsch, bore the principal burden of guilt, which was unfortunate, for "he is such an able man." There could, however, be no question of preferential or easy treatment.[9] Attacks on Stosch mounted. He noted that "complaints are heaped upon Batsch to strike at me," adding: "We will see who laughs best."[10] He wrote Freytag from Oestrich in 2 August that he would gladly "leave the Navy, if it would not be so terribly cowardly." He particularly felt the attacks from men "for whom I have done the most personally." He had often taken steps to defend Admiral Werner, who now led the assault. Stosch reported that the accident commission which had investigated the disaster complained of no one, but limited itself "to pointing out that the Stosch system alone, i.e., myself, bore the guilt."[11]

One of the first acts of the Reichstag when it met was to discuss the sinking of the "Great Elector." Perhaps at Stosch's suggestion,

[7] Memoirs, II, 166-67.
[8] Stosch to his wife, Berlin, 7 June 1878, *ibid.*, II, 155.
[9] To Freytag, *ibid.*, II, 155-56.
[10] To his wife, Berlin, 25 July 1878, *ibid.*, II, 164.
[11] *Ibid.*, II, 164-65. Cf. Stosch to Roggenbach, Haus Stosch, Oestrich, 12 Aug. 1878, in Heyderhoff, *Im Ring der Gegner*, p. 192.

so that he could immediately counter the attacks in his own way, the National Liberal Mosle sponsored an interpellation of the Admiralty Chief on 13 September 1878. The deputy's speech was conciliatory; he even declared that such disasters were *"part of the price that a nation pays for a fleet."*[12] Stosch entered the Reichstag at 1:00 A.M., his head filled with memories of the engagement at Loigny-Poupry in 1870, where he had also been "calm in battle." As he delivered his forty-minute speech in the overly warm chamber, he "read on their [the deputies'] faces that I had won them for me."[13] Restricted by the law governing publication and not wishing to open himself to the charge of influencing the court martial, he refused to discuss the technical reasons for the sinking of the *Great Elector.* He confined his remarks to personal criticism, since the whole press insisted that "I alone am guilty." These assaults he traced to disgruntled senior officers who could not adjust themselves to his command. Justifying the record of his administration, he pointed out that great demands were made on the small means at his disposal and, as a result, "I have expected more militarily than was perhaps the case earlier." He concluded with a spirited defense of Admiral Batsch.[14]

These statements came under heavy fire. The Left Liberal orator, Albert Hänel of Kiel, denied that criticism was aimed at Stosch personally, praised his energy and attention to detail, but charged him with ignoring technical advisers and the council of admirals, failing to train ships' complements properly, and overburdening his officers. Hänel's concluding request for full publicity on the affair was greeted with cheers. Stosch admitted that he had not called the Admiralty Council, for, new to his duties, he felt "to let himself be directed in his business by majorities is the surest guarantee of accomplishing nothing." The Right accompanied this Bismarckian phrase with "Bravo" and "Very Good." Stosch was unable to say whether official reports on the disaster would be published or not, but "the Admiralty has nothing to hide" and he would work to secure their early dissemination. Another assailant, the Chairman of the North German Lloyd and National

---

[12] *Verhandlungen des Reichstags,* 4 Leg. Per., I Sess., 1878, 3 Sitz., LI, 14-15.
[13] To his wife, Berlin, 14 Sept. 1878, Memoirs, II, 167-68.
[14] *Verhandlungen des Reichstags,* 4 Leg. Per., I Sess., 1878, 3 Sitz., LI, 15-18.

Liberal deputy H. H. Meier, asserted that strict discipline had caused dissatisfaction within the Navy and called for a return to the old organization with an Inspector General to curb Army influence on the fleet. He also implied that periodic meetings of the Admiralty Council would help to control the General. Perhaps unaware of Meier's old acquaintance with Bismarck[15] and remembering only his former support of the naval estimates, Stosch professed surprise at this assault, combatting it with a reference to a recent accident of a vessel of the North German Lloyd.[16] With this, the interpellation ended.

Nonetheless, the attacks on "Stosch's Infantry System" persisted. Freytag wrote on 26 September that Stosch, formerly a "favorite" of the press, was now suffering from the reaction to his popularity and urged his friend to publish the court martial records as soon as possible. If there were no publication, onslaughts would be resumed in the Reichstag, and Bismarck would be able to force Stosch out of office with both William's and Frederick William's approval.[17] Stosch replied that he earnestly desired full publication. He noted the bitter criticism of the Left Liberal *Kieler Zeitung* and attributed this to the inspiration of senior naval officers. He would not assail them in the Reichstag, but he was in a pugnacious mood; "I am certainly an old fellow, but, before I leave the field, I can still strike powerful blows." Bismarck, he believed, had not intervened in the struggle.[18] Later in October Stosch stated that, while he had worked to leave his post in 1877, now he wanted to stay. If he were forced to resign, he would remain silent, and, indeed, it did not matter in what year he was able to tend his vineyards in Oestrich.[19]

The Chancellor, in fact, seems at first to have taken a reserved attitude toward the attacks on Stosch and was probably content to let others pull his chestnuts out of the fire. When Princess von

[15] Poschinger, *Bismarck und die Parlamentarier,* II, 332.

[16] *Verhandlungen des Reichstags,* 4 Leg. Per., I Sess., 1878, 3 Sitz., LI, 19-24. Schröder, *Stosch,* pp. 94-95, speaks of Stosch's "curt explanations," which aroused the opposition of the deputies.

[17] Siebleben, in Helmolt, *Freytag an Stosch,* pp. 128-29. Strong rumors circulated that Stosch would resign and assume the command of an army corps. Priesdorff, *Soldatisches Führertum,* VIII, 316.

[18] Oestrich, 3 Oct. 1878, Memoirs, II, 168.

[19] To Freytag, Berlin, 18 Oct. 1878, *ibid.*

Bismarck, even more partisan than her husband, returned from a trip to Kiel in October 1878 with tales of Stosch's unpopularity, he merely listened with a grin and made no comment.[20] However, in November a press official in the Chancellery privately disclosed that a recent article in the *Kölnischer Zeitung* denouncing the Admiralty Chief was inspired by the Chancellor, "who will not rest until Stosch is dismissed." Bismarck was said to have called Stosch to account for concluding a treaty for the raising of the *Great Elector* without his consent.[21] William was rather doubtful of his Naval Chief's abilities in December, but, fortunately for Stosch, Roggenbach was at hand to defend his friend. William was pleased to hear Roggenbach's statements and admitted that he knew only what he read in the newspapers.[22] The Chancellor's animosity grew. In a letter of 11 December from his retreat in Friedrichsruh, he put as the first of his reasons for seeking retirement the desire to be relieved from the "further responsibility for colleagues like Stosch."[23]

The assaults on Stosch in the press and the Reichstag[24] from Bismarck's friends and the left now grew more intense. The first court martial on the sinking of the *Great Elector* reached a decision on 1 February 1879, and sentenced the officer of the watch of the *King William* and Captain Count Monts of the *Great Elector* to imprisonment for a month and two days. William reserved judgment on the approval of the sentences.[25] When the Reichstag considered the naval budget on 11 March 1879, the Left Liberal orator, Hänel, opened the onslaught by expressing surprise that Stosch, despite vehement criticism, had made no public explanation

[20] Bismarck, *Gesammelte Werke*, VIII, 286.

[21] Robert Bosse, "Erinnerungen," *Die Grenzboten*, LXIII (1904), 400 (entry of 13 Nov. 1878). On the unsuccessful attempt to raise the ship, see Koch, *Stosch*, pp. 68-69. This incident is perhaps connected with Bismarck's insistence, on 22 Nov. 1878, that the Navy had no rights in financial questions. Morsey, *Die Oberste Reichsverwaltung*, p. 132.

[22] Karlsruhe, 3 Dec. 1878, in Heyderhoff, *Im Ring der Gegner*, pp. 195-97.

[23] To Count von Stolberg-Wernigerode, in Bismarck, *Gesammelte Werke*, VIc, 127.

[24] See Freytag's offer to secure National Liberal support for his friend, Wiesbaden, 4 Jan. 1879, in Helmolt, *Freytag an Stosch*, pp. 129-30. Typical of the press attacks is "Marine Minister von Stosch und die Katastrophe bei Folkestone, fachmännisch beleuchtet, von einem vormaligen Seeoffizer [Admiral Werner?]," *Deutscher Revue*, III Jg. (1879), vol. II, 67-75.

[25] Koch, *Stosch*, p. 64.

of the catastrophe which had taken place nine months before. He implied that Stosch was keeping silent until the affair passed out of the public eye, and he threatened action by the Reichstag to secure the documents of the court martial. "Representative of the Bundesrat, Chief of the Admiralty, Minister of State von Stosch," as he is designated in the proceedings, replied that he could not discuss the legal action which was then in progress and refused to defend himself further. He concluded, while the right cheered him, "I believe I have done my duty, and I will do it as long as I am at my place." Lasker, the leader of the National Liberal left wing, expressed unwillingness to accept Stosch's statement about the court martial and called for complete publicity. Bismarck's intimate, Dr. Lucius of the Liberal Imperial party, confirmed Stosch's statement on the legal proceedings, but believed that the naval administration was at fault through concentrating too much power in Stosch's hands. Lucius favored Hänel's proposal to strike out the first title of the naval budget, but this was defeated after Lasker had spoken out against it.[26]

This debate had a such depressing effect on Stosch that he submitted his resignation to William on 14 March. He was shaken by the opposition of the Left Liberals, National Liberals, and Liberal Imperials, who, he felt, had declared that "I was a misfortune to the Empire as Chief of the Navy." He was also influenced in his action by the widespread support of this view in "military circles," the press, and the general public.[27] He wrote to William:

My authority in the Navy is, and will be, undermined and will be lost entirely. I, who undertake so many new projects, can no longer work to the advantage of the Imperial service without complete authority and the firm belief of my subordinates in my knowledge and my continuance in my position.—I have striven in previous years to make Your Majesty's Navy a military power. This was not to be achieved without extreme strain, for continually increasing tasks had to be demanded with the almost daily increasing employment of the Navy. Such demands were new, but they were borne with willingness to make sacrifices, until the misfortune of the preceding year changed enthusiasm to ill-humor. Senior officers gave expression to this feeling, which, at first, resulted in

[26] *Verhandlungen des Reichstags,* 4 Leg. Per., II Sess., 1879, 18 Sitz., LII, 376-81.
[27] Memoirs, II, 173.

almost twice the number of convictions for offenses against discipline in the lower ranks. The dismissal of Rear Admiral Werner brought a certain calm, but, with the present mood of the Reichstag and press, discipline must suffer again. The general report runs that I exercise unlawful tyranny and misuse my power only to remain in office.—I can no longer be useful to Your Majesty's service in such a situation. . . .[28]

The Admiral said that his resignation was even more pressing because of the court martial's decision. He had been informed that the Judge Advocate had advised William to set aside the decision, "because it was too mild," and to order a second trial. The lack of high naval officers would necessitate "soldiers" taking part in this trial, and they would bring in a "harsher" penalty; the foreseeable result was that the Army would "free the General [Stosch]" and "punish the Admiral [Batsch]," which was directly contrary to what the naval officers had decided. The conflicting decisions would diminish the credit of military justice in the eyes of the public, just at the moment when its amendment was being proposed in the Reichstag. If Stosch departed, the decision of the first court martial could be upheld, and the Navy would be rendered a "great service." Moreover, if the decision of the first court martial were approved, Batsch, the "only possible leader in case of war," would be preserved unpunished to the Navy.[29] Stosch concluded:

My departure would satisfy the common conception of justice, retain that very able and strong man for the Navy, and would release the Army from the role of exercising punitive power on the naval officers.

To judge by the speech of deputy Lucius, the Imperial Chancellor again harbors the wish to separate the command and the administration of the Navy in the future. After the Navy has gained a certain stability in its organization, I can only consider that as correct. As Army experience shows, administration and command are often at odds in their demands. The compromise of both certainly follows easiest when they are combined in one person, but I myself doubt whether that is always in the interest of the service.—The question of money is the most decisive for the administration, while performance is for command. If command and administration exist side by side, performance, the higher element, will certainly triumph in the end; the monetary question very easily wins the upper hand in the union. Therefore, I submissively ask Your Majesty to return to the earlier organization on the occasion of my departure. None of the senior naval officers is yet fit to direct

[28] *Ibid.*, II, 173-74.   [29] *Ibid.*, II, 174-75.

the administration; I can cite only Rear Admiral Batsch as thoroughly suited for the command.[30]

Stosch was informed that the Emperor wished him to continue as though his resignation of 14 March 1879 had never been sent.[31] There is little doubt that Stosch meant his offer of resignation seriously. However, the sincerity of his expressed opinion that the command and administration of the Navy should be separated is open to suspicion. It is in direct opposition to his earlier and later views. Most probably he was trying to forestall the Chancellor's attempt, through Lucius and other Reichstag members, to divide command from administration. William's refusal of the resignation showed his satisfaction with the organization of the Navy, and Stosch could continue with the knowledge that the Emperor was alerted to the attempts to divide his naval authority.

Criticism of the "Stosch System" continued unabated. Freytag wrote on 17 March 1879 that the assaults on Stosch in the press and the Reichstag exceeded in virulence anything he had experienced in his long journalistic career. He had decided to take up his pen in defense of his friend, although the very "extravagance" of the charges had produced a reaction.[32] At the second reading of the naval budget on 19 March Rickert stated that it was the opinion of the Budget Committee that too many ships were in commission in proportion to the number of naval personnel, but that it had decided not to hamper Stosch. However, he offered an amendment to strike out one large armored vessel. Stosch spoke against the amendment, but it was adopted.[33] The onslaught was renewed in the Reichstag debate of 28 March. The Left Liberal Hänel, and the National Liberals, Lasker and H. H. Meier, pressed again for complete publicity on the sinking of the *Great Elector.* Bismarck's intimate, the Liberal Imperial Lucius, avowed his surprise at the press opinions that his speech of 11 March was an attack on Stosch and denied that he spoke for the Chancellor.[34] The Admiralty Chief evidently attempted to combat parliamentary criticism with social weapons, for he gave a dinner for the deputies

[30] *Ibid.,* II, 175-76.   [31] *Ibid.,* II, 176.
[32] To Stosch, Wiesbaden, in Helmolt, *Freytag an Stosch,* pp. 130-31.
[33] *Verhandlungen des Reichstags,* 4 Leg. Per., II Sess., 1879, 22 Sitz., LII, 498-501.
[34] *Ibid.,* 4 Leg. Per., II Sess., 1879, 28 Sitz., LII, 685-87.

on 3 May. Bismarck's parliamentary soirée of the same date may have been held to woo away some of Stosch's guests.[35]

The legal proceedings dragged on. On 16 May William decided to try Admiral Batsch by a court of Army officers, much to Stosch's concern, but, as a "fellow defendant," he was powerless. Despite encouraging statements to Batsch,[36] he was made nervous and ill by the criticism of himself.[37] On 13 June he was delighted to hear a little praise of the Navy during a debate on the Samoan Treaty; "I have not heard that sound for a long time."[38] He was depressed[39] again by the decision of the second court martial, which sentenced Batsch to six years in prison, but freed Count Monts of all blame.[40] Confiding to Frau von Stosch that "it is high time I go; I feel completely exhausted," on 29 June he submitted a memorandum to the Emperor on the court martial's findings.[41] Stosch asked approval of its decisions for "practical reasons," although he did not agree with them. He also requested that Batsch be restored to favor after serving his sentence which should be commuted to fortress detention and that Count Monts, whom Stosch considered chiefly at fault, be retired. He also wished to publish the court martial proceedings. William shared Stosch's view of Monts's guilt and on 12 July announced in a letter to the Admiralty Chief that he had ordered a retrial. He reserved judgment on whether to publish the records of the court martial and to distribute them to the naval officer corps, which "seems to be very necessary in order to resolve the manifold differences which emerge in your report."[42] A few days later he commuted Batsch's sentence to fortress detention.[43] Thus, while William did not accept all of Stosch's recommendations, he was in general agreement with him on the causes of the *Great Elector* tragedy.

[35] Poschinger, *Bismarck und die Parlamentarier,* I, 170; Siegfried von Kardorff, *Wilhelm von Kardorff* (Berlin, 1936), p. 150. On the other hand, Stosch may have been challenging Bismarck. There is no evidence to show who acted first.

[36] Stosch to Batsch, Berlin, 17, 21, 22 May, Oestrich, 26 May, 1879, Memoirs, II, 182-84.

[37] To Freytag, Berlin, 22 May 1879, *ibid.,* II, 177.

[38] To his wife, Berlin, 15 June 1879, *ibid.,* II, 179.

[39] Inferred from Roggenbach to Stosch, London, 17 June 1879, in Heyderhoff, *Im Ring der Gegner,* p. 197.

[40] Koch, *Stosch,* pp. 64-65.

[41] To his wife, Berlin, 15, 17, 22 June 1879. Memoirs, II, 179-81.

[42] *Ibid.,* II, 184-87.   [43] Koch, *Stosch,* p. 65.

Meanwhile, the Admiralty Chief had persistently demanded to be dismissed. His memorandum of 29 June 1879 reached William before the records of the court martial, and Chief of the Military Cabinet Albedyll informed Stosch that he was acting counter to regulations by discussing a matter of which His Majesty was officially ignorant. On 5 July Stosch, feeling his right of direct communication with the Emperor was being denied and his naval advice rejected, presented his resignation. Twice he reiterated his request to be relieved; twice he was told to wait until William reached a decision on the legal proceedings.[44] Finally, Stosch expressed his firm determination to retire in a letter from Oestrich of 14 July which declared:

I grew up in obedience to my War Lord and would persevere in the same unconditionally, if I did not feel myself to be disturbed in the chief duty of a Prussian officer, the maintenance of personal honor, which I uphold in inexorable strictness. I have been banished from Your Majesty's councils by General Albedyll's letter of the 3rd instant. It is no longer to be my duty to express my convictions to Your Majesty and to seek Your Majesty's decision in all important naval business.[45]

William speedily replied from Coblenz on 16 July 1879 that he regretted to see the Admiral in opposition to him and to a general who had his confidence. Stosch's action was based upon a misunderstanding of the "actual circumstances." The Emperor continued: "It has never entered my mind to limit you in the slightest in your previous rights and duties as Chief of the Admiralty, and I do not know where a limitation is supposed to exist. . . ." He contended that, as "judge of my officers," he could take no action until a matter was officially before him. When he ordered a regular presentation of legal reports, he had restricted his own power to act independently, and Stosch had no reason to consider the Emperor's refusal to receive his memorandum as "an affront to yourself." He argued:

Besides, you should certainly know me well enough to realize that I would never say a word to the contrary, if a relaxation of the regulation took place through extraordinary circumstances, and that I would also have accepted your report without further question, if you had at least waited until I had received the report of the Judge Advocate. But you

[44] Memoirs, II, 184-87.   [45] Ibid.

have discussed, under the date of 29 June, a report . . . which was only completed on 1 July, and which only reached me on 5 July!

He declared that he had always wanted only "trustworthy, complete, and truthful reports" from Stosch, even if he could not always accept their recommendations; Stosch was not to believe that "in the future I wish less honest opinions!" He concluded:

Believe me, my good Stosch, that in this affair you really have no reason to feel offended. Keep firm your trust that I have always wished you well! However, in fact, it is not a correct point of view . . . to feel offended when *one* of *very many* proposals is disapproved by your King.

May these words serve to calm you; that is actually my hearty and sincere wish.[46]

Stosch responded from Oestrich on 17 July that he was "deeply ashamed to have doubted the benevolence" of the Emperor "for a moment." He added that nothing could have disturbed him as much as the possibility that he had "lost the trust of my high War Lord."[47] With this letter, the correspondence on Stosch's fifth recorded resignation attempt, his second of 1879, ceased. Whether this incident aroused the enmity of the Chief of the Military Cabinet, which could have influenced Stosch's sixth and successful effort in 1883, is not recorded. It is, indeed, possible that Albedyll had really attempted to circumscribe the Admiral's right to report directly to the Emperor.

The legal proceedings for the trial of Count Monts were now initiated. To prove one of the technical points of the case, Stosch went to great pains to have a simple model of the *Great Elector* constructed. The court refused to accept the demonstration of the model as evidence, and it may have worked in the sense opposite to that which Stosch intended. The president of the court, Prince August of Württemberg, averred that the Admiral was attempting to influence the court's proceedings illegally, but the Emperor did not share this view. The court decided to free Monts.[48] Meanwhile, the attacks continued.[49] Roggenbach wrote from London that the English press was filled with "lies against the Stosch

---

[46] *Ibid.*, II, 188-90.   [47] *Ibid.*, II 190-91.
[48] Koch, *Stosch,* pp. 65-67.
[49] Cf. Treitschke's bitter comments on Stosch in his letter to Friedrich von Weech, Felsonegg bei Zug, 20 Aug. 1879, in Willy Andreas, ed., *Briefe Heinrich von Treitschkes an Historiker und Politiker vom Oberrhein* (Berlin, 1934), p. 40.

System."[50] The Emperor did not falter in his support of Stosch, telling him on 21 August that "I congratulate myself that I have kept you." When the Admiral mentioned the effects of the assaults on his nerves, William replied that he could see that, but "keep your chin up."[51] The approval of the report of Monts's court martial was so long delayed that Bismarck even threatened to use his influence to speed a decision.[52] William finally concluded on 18 December 1879 that Count Monts bore the responsibility for the doors to the compartments of the *Great Elector* standing open, but felt that a fourth court martial would serve no useful purpose. With this decision, which supported Stosch's view, the legal proceedings ended,[53] and the Naval Chief was officially cleared of all blame in the disaster. Stosch's Reichstag critics were unappeased.

During the first reading of the naval budget on 24 February 1880, the National Liberal H. H. Meier and the Conservative Baron von Maltzan-Gültz did defend Stosch's proposed alteration of technical regulations against the objections of the Left Liberal Rickert. However, both Lasker, a leader of the National Liberal left wing, and the Left Liberal Hänel, Stosch's leading assailant, found inadequate the "unofficial" account of the sinking of the *Great Elector,* which had appeared in the official naval gazette and placed the blame on Monts. They favored an official report to the Reichstag, and Hänel promised to present at the next meeting a motion to secure it.[54] The Admiralty Chief actually desired an official publication before the next debate, but the Emperor deferred decision[55] and finally did not approve the request.[56] Bismarck now intervened.

Bismarck seems to have been inclined at first to abandon his efforts to dislodge Stosch. He remarked on 28 January 1880:

. . . I am not bothering about *its* [the Navy's] budget at all. I fear that the naval administration is not directed as it should be or as the Im-

[50] To Stosch, 10 Aug. 1879, in Heyderhoff, *Im Ring der Gegner,* p. 198. The London *Times* from 30 July to 20 Aug. 1879, contains only reports on Stosch, with no comment.
[51] To his wife, Berlin, Memoirs, II, 192.
[52] Stosch to the Crown Prince, Berlin, 7 Nov. 1879, *ibid.,* II, 200-201.
[53] Koch, *Stosch,* p. 67.
[54] *Verhandlungen des Reichstags,* 4 Leg. Per., III Sess., 1880, 7 Sitz., LVIII, 87-91.
[55] To Freytag, 2 March 1880, Memoirs, II, 202.
[56] This emerges clearly from the debate of 4 March 1880.

perial interests demand—but I desist from all steps against Stosch. The Emperor always takes his side, and I am too old and weak to undertake the struggle again. I desire, therefore, to remain completely aloof from naval affairs and take absolutely no responsibility for them.—By virtue of the law [of 1878] governing my representation I can do that too. I want to leave it like that.[57]

However, his interest in the Navy increased when he learned that Stosch, as a Prussian representative to the Bundesrat, had, on 21 February, introduced into the Reichstag a bill whose mundane aim was the "double calculation of the service time of naval personnel at Yokahama." When a copy of this measure reached Bismarck, he was outraged; the Admiralty Chief, he declared, was usurping the Chancellor's prerogative of submitting bills to the Reichstag. He forbade any repetition of the incident and replaced Stosch's bill with another.[58] Bismarck's mood now became more violent and belligerent.

At a dinner on 26 February 1880 Bismarck used expressions against Stosch which one of his guests did not dare put into his memoirs thirty years later for fear of a libel suit.[59] His raging temper was expressed in the parliamentary maneuvers he was planning against Stosch. The Chancellor approached his frequent spokesman in the Reichstag, the protectionist Wilhelm von Kardorff of the Liberal Imperial party, and asked him to propose an amendment to the naval budget authorizing an appropriation for the salary of an Inspector General of the Navy. Kardorff, who was impressed by Stosch's abilities, refused to have any hand in this attempt to limit his powers by stripping him of control of command matters. Kardorff not only would not support the Chancellor's move, he braved his ire by actively opposing the measure in the Reichstag Budget Committee. Bismarck then approached the obscure protectionist deputy von Ohlen und Adlerskron, a friend of his son Wilhelm. Ohlen, who represented the district of Nam-

[57] Adolf von Scholz, *Erlebnisse und Gespräche mit Bismarck* (Stuttgart and Berlin, 1922), pp. 24-25.

[58] Morsey, *Die Oberste Reichsverwaltung*, p. 133. Not only were the powers of the Chancellor as presiding officer of the Bundesrat involved, the question of his representation and the right of countersignature also entered into the question. See also Poschinger, *Bismarcks Bundesrat*, II, 127-28. Later in the year, Bismarck refused to countersign naval documents and thus assume responsibility for them. Morsey, *Die Oberste Reichsverwaltung*, p. 133.

[59] Werner, *Erlebnisse*, p. 182.

slau, undertook the Chancellor's task and was thereafter derisively referred to in debate as "Admiral von Namslau."[60] According to Stosch, Bismarck intended the post of Inspector General for the Emperor's nephew, Prince Frederick Karl, whom he chose in order to render the scheme palatable to William. The deputies knew of the plan, and "everyone found it ridiculous that an infantryman in naval affairs would be improved by a cavalryman." One of Stosch's most hostile critics, Admiral Henk, was to be made Naval Chief.[61] It is indicative of the esteem in which the Reichstag held Stosch that all the Chancellor's blandishments could not conjure up a more impressive parliamentarian to mount his attack. Thus, two motions, one from Bismarck's supporter Ohlen introducing an Inspector General into the budget, and the other from the Left Liberal Hänel demanding from the Chief of the Admiralty an official report on the catastrophe of Folkestone, threatened Stosch during the second reading of the naval budget on 4 March 1880.

In response to Hänel's request to take a stand on his motion, Stosch contended that the account of the *Great Elector* tragedy in the official naval gazette was "unofficial" in name only. It emanated from the Admiralty, was "written from the documents," and examined both the questions of guilt and the measures taken to prevent any recurrence of the disaster. Excluded from it were only command matters, which, "by old tradition," were the concern of the monarch alone. The Conservative spokesman, Udo, Count zu Stolberg-Wernigerode, supported the Admiral's stand against interference in command matters and announced his party's opposition to the Hänel motion. The fiery Eduard Lasker, leader of the National Liberal left wing, censured Stosch's "completely autocratic domination" of the Navy, which tolerated "no control and no opposition." Speed, overburdening of personnel, and disregard of advice would lead inevitably to a repetition of other accidents like the sinking of the *Great Elector,* for which Stosch

[60] Kardorff, *Kardorff,* pp. 173-75.
[61] To Freytag, 14 March 1880, Memoirs, II, 202-3. Stosch attributed the defeat of Ohlen's motion to the Chancellor's choice of Frederick Karl. He told Freytag on 8 April (*ibid.,* II, 204-5) that after the debate was over, Bismarck had changed his candidate for Inspector General to Prince Ernest of Leiningen, who, as an English Admiral, brother-in-law of the Grand Duke of Baden, and cousin of the Crown Princess, stood high in royal favor.

alone bore the guilt. Lasker called for the adoption of the Hänel motion.[62]

The Chief of the Admiralty, in reply, defended himself from the attacks from the left and anticipated the assaults of Bismarck's supporters. He stated that apparently the account in the official naval gazette was sufficiently detailed, since it had provided his opponents with their arguments. Lasker had spoken of the honor of the Navy; those who had put "stain after stain" upon the fleet had not considered its honor. Divided command of the Navy had shown many faults both in the sixties and the Franco-German War, while Prince Adalbert, as Inspector General, had filled only a "post of honor." It was the Reichstag which had abolished the post on his death. He knew of no instance of constructive support from those who proposed sessions of the Admiralty Council, a suggestion which rested "alone upon complete ignorance of men and affairs." A newspaper article had said that his son-in-law had been responsible for the helm of the *King William,* when it struck the *Great Elector.*[63] This false intelligence, like all the criticisms of the press, was directed at him personally. He maintained that no officers then in the Navy opposed his administration, and he was proud to see the honor with which German ships had performed their duties abroad. He was not disturbed by the charges that there was too much haste and overburdening of personnel; the Navy must be ready to do its duty, if it would be successful.[64]

Georg von Bunsen, a member of the left wing of the National Liberals and a friend of the Crown Prince,[65] declared that he spoke for the majority of his party. He proposed referring the Hänel motion to the Budget Committee, and then launched into a spirited defense of the "Stosch System," as an "effort to do the possible with strong measures in a very limited time in order to make a

[62] *Verhandlungen des Reichstags,* 4 Leg. Per., III Sess., 1880, 12 Sitz., LVIII, 240-48

[63] The charge of nepotism is repeated in Karl Friedrich Nowak, *Germany's Road to Ruin* (London, 1932), p. 2, but apparently nowhere else. His source is William II. Stosch's son Ulrich was connected with a marine battalion, and his son-in-law, Hollen, later became an Admiral.

[64] *Verhandlungen des Reichstags,* 4 Leg. Per., III Ssess., 1880, 12 Sitz., LVIII, 248-49.

[65] On Bunsen, see Theodor Barth, *Politische Porträts* (Berlin, 1923), pp. 65-67; Adolf Rubinstein, *Die Deutsch-Freisinnige Partei bis zu ihrem Auseinanderbruch, 1884-1893* (Berlin, 1935), p. 37.

moderate-sized European fleet out of a very small one." Stosch and Batsch were popular in the Navy. Doubtless their measures had aroused some opposition, but the Reichstag "must not be the tool of these dissatisfied elements (Bravo!)." Hänel returned to the attack, but disclaimed any intention of assailing Stosch. As befitted one of Germany's leading constitutional theorists, he now stressed the constitutional issue at stake: passage of his motion would establish the control of the Reichstag over the fleet. Windthorst, the wily leader of the Roman Catholic Center party, contended that by naming Stosch instead of the Chancellor in his motion Hänel was attacking the Chief of the Admiralty. The motion was, in any case, meaningless, for it left the Government free to submit what it pleased to the Reichstag. The competence of the Reichstag did not extend to court martial matters, and it was useless to raise the theoretical question of its rights. He took no position for or against the Navy; he proclaimed: "I have no ambition to become a Grand Admiral of the German Fleet (Laughter)." Hänel rose and changed his motion to read that the Chancellor, instead of Stosch, be requested to submit a report on the tragedy of Folkestone. The Hänel motion was defeated.[66]

Stosch had triumphed over the attempt of the left to win Reichstag support of a motion which expressed distrust of his administration and command of the Navy. He had received the support of the Conservatives, the Liberal Imperial party, the Center, and the majority of the National Liberals. He had been opposed by Lasker[67] and the Left Liberals. He now had to counter Bismarck's attempt to interfere in the organization of the Admiralty.

The protectionist[68] von Ohlen und Adlerskron rose to champion his amendment which provided a salary for an Inspector General of the Navy. The Inspector General would have the principal duty of correcting poor training and lack of combat readiness and

[66] *Verhandlungen des Reichstags,* 4 Leg. Per., III Sess., 1880, 12 Sitz., LVIII, 249-57.

[67] Lasker's opposition to the Admiral apparently affected his decision to lead the "secession" of the National Liberal left wing from its party. See Max von Forckenbeck to Franz von Stauffenberg, Berlin, 14 March 1880, in Heyderhoff and Wentzcke, *Deutscher Liberalismus,* II, 302.

[68] He belonged to the Gruppe Schauss-Volk, originally the extreme right wing of the National Liberals, which had formed its own party in 1879. See Block, *Parlamentarische Krisis,* pp. 48-53.

would assume control of command matters. Stosch would retain the administration of the Navy, which would handle shipbuilding, and he would be obligated to call together an Admiralty Council. Ohlen pleaded with the Reichstag to approve his amendment and not wait until another catastrophe made it imperative. Stosch's friend, the National Liberal Robert von Benda, denounced Ohlen's amendment as "extraordinarily unusual," impossible to incorporate in the current budget. Lasker favored the amendment as a protest against the "Stosch System." The Liberal Imperial leader, Wilhelm von Kardorff, despite Bismarck's request, rose and defended Stosch. The naval administration had been, in general, "excellent." While he favored the separation of naval administration and command for the distant future, he did not think it up to the Reichstag to take the initiative in such matters.[69] The amendment, which struck not only at Stosch, but also at the Emperor's power over command matters, was defeated by a nearly unanimous vote of all parties.[70]

A last echo of the Ohlen motion was heard during the third reading of the naval budget on 18 March. Ohlen plaintively expressed surprise that he had received so little support. With obvious reference to Stosch's friendship with the Crown Prince and Crown Princess, he ascribed the defeat of his amendment to "unhealthy Byzantinism, which was formerly the custom of courtiers." Eugen Richter, the Left Liberal leader, saw no "Byzantinism" in the question and countered with a thinly veiled reference to Bismarck's support of the Ohlen amendment. He announced his support of the unitary organization of the Navy and shrewdly pointed out that, if the Reichstag created an Inspector General, it would be establishing an official with no responsibility to it.[71] Here the debate ended.

The debate of March 1880 closed the discussion on the sinking of the *Great Elector*. Stosch had achieved a triumph. Opposition from the press, high ranking naval officers, Left Liberals, and

---

[69] *Verhandlungen des Reichstags,* 4 Leg. Per., III Sess., 1880, 12 Sitz., LVIII, 257-61. H. H. Meier, the National Liberal, declared on 5 March that the Admiralty Council should meet more frequently. *Ibid.,* 13 Sitz., LVIII, 568-69.

[70] Kardorff, *Kardorff,* p. 174.

[71] *Verhandlungen des Reichstags,* 4 Leg. Per., III Sess., 1880, 22 Sitz., LVIII, 488-90.

Bismarck had failed to shake the belief of the Emperor or the majority of the Reichstag in his capabilities. His most consistent supporters had been the Conservatives, who had applauded his rejection of the principle of majority rule and voted against any attempt to weaken the authority of the Emperor over command matters. His most persistent critics had been the Left Liberals and some leaders of the allied left wing of the National Liberals. If the Liberals were backing Stosch as Chancellor, which Bismarck believed, their means were extremely devious.

Bismarck made no attempt to conceal his ire at the miscarriage of his plans. On 9 March he gave a long audience to Moritz Busch, furnishing him with material for an inspired article in *Die Grenzboten*. The Chancellor roundly cursed Stosch in terms which in German editions of Busch's reminiscences are rendered by a blank space and in the English versions as "a vain, incapable fellow." The Chancellor even praised his archenemies Lasker and Hänel for their hostility to Stosch, and assailed his supporters of the Liberal Imperial party, because of Kardorff's stand. He ascribed the action of that party to the belief that the Admiral was high in favor with the Crown Prince, which, he said, was not the case, and maintained that Stosch "was retained only because he is a Freemason of high degree."[72] He denounced Stosch for the conclusion of the Saxon military convention and that of Ferrières and could not "help wondering what he got from the Saxons and Thiers." He further stated that the fleet "is quite worthless," and Stosch "is a servile creature." On the next day Count Herbert Bismarck presented Busch with additional materials for his article. Entitled "On the Reichstag," it duly appeared in *Die Grenzboten* and was widely copied. Busch praised the Hänel amendment, but censured its "lame" defenders. The latter were chided for not fulfilling their "right and duty" of condemning the "impractical," "wretched," and "reckless" Stosch administration, which was "ruinous" to the Navy. The Admiral's "infantry system" had "cost much precious money," just as his conventions with Saxony and France had done. Busch noted that Stosch had promised to inform the Reichstag of the causes of the catastrophe, but now went

[72] The present writer has seen no evidence of Stosch's membership in the Masons, who were one of Bismarck's favorite subjects of attack.

back on his word.   The article demanded the appointment of an experienced officer as head of the Navy.   Busch saw Bismarck on 20 March and asked what he thought of the article.   The Chancellor replied: "Anything one likes may be said about him.   He cannot come in my way."[73]   Earlier, he had scornfully remarked that Stosch "ought to write a biography of the Great Elector; that is his subject."[74]   The Chancellor never took defeat lightly, if indeed he ever accepted it.

Stosch was hardly more elated.   On 14 March 1880 he asked Freytag not to pen articles defending him, but to write "poetical works for the world."   He desired rest, and even ordered his house at Oestrich enlarged for his retirement, but his officers told him he was still useful.[75]   Three weeks later he was "quite prepared to fall," and, referring to reports of William's ill-health, "only implored the Crown Prince, who probably will officiate as the priest at my sacrifice, not to let the Navy suffer through my successor."   He recognized Bismarck's inspiration of Busch's *Die Grenzboten* article by the condemnation of his diplomatic activity in the sixties and 1871.[76]   Stosch's success in repelling attacks in the Reichstag did not greatly raise his spirits, for he saw realistically the forces operating against him and realized that as long as Bismarck held power there would be no peace for the Chief of the Admiralty.

It is to the period 1878 to 1880 that Bismarck referred, when he wrote in his memoirs of a "Gladstone Ministry," composed of Stosch, Friedenthal, Camphausen, Rickert, and Windthorst, backed by the "Roman Catholic court influence" of the Empress Augusta. The purpose of this ministry was to supplant him.[77]   While the National Liberal, and later Left Liberal, leader Heinrich Rickert

[73] Busch, *Bismarck,* II, 413-14, 416-17, 421-22; Moritz Busch, *Tagebuchblätter* (Leipzig, 1899), II, 569-74, 577-78.   The German edition dates the second interview on March 22.

[74] 13 March 1880.   Bismarck, *Gesammelte Werke,* VIII, 351.   The Chancellor was playing upon the two meanings of "Great Elector": the sunken vessel and the Prussian ruler of the seventeenth century.

[75] Memoirs, II, 202-3.

[76] To Freytag, 8 April 1880, *ibid.,* II, 204-5.

[77] Bismarck, *Gesammelte Werke,* XV, 338, 373, 379.   Cf. Frederic B. M. Hollyday, "Bismarck and the Legend of the 'Gladstone Ministry,'" in Lillian P. Wallace and William C. Askew, eds.   *Power, Public Opinion, and Diplomacy* (Durham, N. C., 1959), pp. 92-109.   Holstein conjectured that Secretary of State of the Interior Bötticher and Stosch were intimates.   Rich and Fisher, *Holstein Papers,* II, 17.   Cf. *ibid.,* pp. 76, 117.

may have possibly harbored such an idea, as Bismarck charged in 1884,[78] there is not a shred of evidence, beyond the Chancellor's statements, to suggest that Stosch had any such notions. During these years he was at odds with a large portion of the Liberals over the investigations attending the sinking of the *Great Elector*. His expressions during the debates were, quite significantly, applauded by the Right. His connections with Rickert resulted from the latter's position as *rapporteur* on the Navy budget for the Reichstag. Moreover, Stosch's ambition, or what little ambition remained, was directed at executing his naval duties. Bismarck's attack was doubtless inspired by the fear that Stosch was weaning both the Emperor and the Crown Prince away from him and by violent hatred for his independent rival.

2

During the years 1880 to 1883 Stosch's mood was conditioned by increasing weariness, a desire for rest, and illness. The Imperial Naval Maneuvers of September 1881, which took place in the presence of the Russian Tsar and as a result of which Stosch was decorated with the Order of the Black Eagle, the highest decoration in William's gift, struck a deep blow at his health. He "completely collapsed and remained for many weeks entirely unable to perform the slightest task." His nervous system did not recover for years.[79] He explained to Freytag on 16 February 1882 why he did not resign, troubled as he was by political attacks and physical weakness: ". . . I often wish to shake off the burden of office in order to live for myself and the moment. But, and you may call me weak, I cannot go as long as the Emperor lives. He continually shows me signs of his favor and satisfaction."[80] Thus he remained at his post, not in order to step from there to the War Ministry or Chancellorship during the reign of the Crown Prince, but through devotion to William I. The desire for rest also

[78] Poschinger, *Bismarck und die Parlamentarier*, III, 34; Poschinger, *Bismarcks Bundesrat*, II, 127-28, IV, 134. Rickert denied this charge in the Reichstag (*Verhandlungen des Reichstags*, 5 Leg., Per., IV Sess., 1884, 42 Sitz., LXXVI, 1083), in his journal, the *Danziger Zeitung* (Helmolt, *Freytag an Stosch*, p. 326), and in private (Hermann Pachnicke, *Führende Männer im altem und neuen Reich* Berlin, [1930], p. 35).
[79] Memoirs, II, 214-15, 216, 220-22.
[80] *Ibid.*, II, 225.

fought with the love of power.[81]   The struggle between the two
emerges most clearly in a letter of 5 January 1883:

As a man becomes older and older, solitude becomes easier and easier
for him. I am curious just how I will create a permanently quiet life in
Oestrich. I long for rest, but am afraid of it. The great responsibility
I bear often weighs upon me; yet I greatly like the power connected with
it. Thus man struggles constantly with himself and the world, until
he finally becomes quite still . . . . Great men are born, not made.[82]

In the end, desire for rest was to be one of the factors which
brought his final resignation.   Another was the continuing combat
with Bismarck.

The conclusion of the investigations and debates on the sinking
of the "Great Elector" ended neither Stosch's conflict with Bismarck nor the assaults of the press.   However, the budget debate
of early 1881 took place in an atmosphere more cordial than that
of the previous three years.   The tone was set by Rickert, leader
of the secessionist left wing of the National Liberals, the "Liberal
Union," at the first reading on 28 February.   He complimented
the Admiralty Chief for including an appropriation for the Naval
Observatory.[83]   The Budget Committee met and Stosch, as usual,
presented the Navy's case, but with astonishing results.   He wrote
the Crown Prince on 10 March 1881:

I find myself in the quite extraordinary position that, in the Budget
Committee, the Conservatives make life quite difficult for me, while the
extreme Left spiritedly stands up for me. That is not unpleasant in so
far as the Werner indictment against me, which formerly was backed
only by them, now finds no support. However, I feel extremely misplaced politically and hope for a *rapprochement* with the Right in the
regular session.[84]

This was written while Bismarck was speculating on Stosch's
friendliness to the left.

The second reading of the naval budget took place on 11
March.   Rickert, reporting for the Budget Committee, told the
Reichstag that Stosch's demand for two more ironclads had been

[81] Cf. to Freytag, 12 July 1882, *ibid.*, II, 230.
[82] To Frau von Rosenstiel, *ibid.*, III, 1.
[83] *Verhandlungen des Reichstags*, 4 Leg. Per., IV Sess., 1881, 6 Sitz., LXII,
p. 77.
[84] Memoirs, II, 217.

defeated by a tie vote of the Committee members. Stosch spoke and insisted that if the ships were struck out, the reserve ships he had planned could not be built and the defense of the Baltic Sea would be weakened. He remarked, in anticipation of H. H. Meier's attacks, that the Navy was dependent upon German ship-yards, while the North German Lloyd built in England. The National Liberal spokesman, Kiefer, and Kardorff, the Liberal Imperial deputy, moved the restoration of appropriations for one ship. Kiefer announced that the whole National Liberal party favored this motion in the interest of national defense. Robert von Puttkammer, the Minister of Religious Affairs, who doubtless represented Bismarck's views,[85] spoke against the motion in the name of the majority of the Conservative party. He declared that Conservative hostility to the amendment was based upon technical and financial considerations, not on "inspiration from above," as the press had maintained. Kardorff, representing the Liberal Imperial party, thought Puttkammer's love of the Navy "very platonic" and contended that the ship had been lost in the Budget Committee only because two members were absent. If the Kiefer-Kardorff amendment were defeated, the German shipbuilding in-dustry would suffer. The National Liberal Meier felt shock, he stated, at Stosch's "unprovoked attack" on the North German Lloyd. He asserted that he would not consider the attack a per-sonal one, for, he ironically observed, perhaps the Admiralty Chief was unaware that he was connected with the company, which was building three ships in German yards. In fact, he backed the amendment to restore one ship to the budget, and the Reichstag so decided.[86] The Liberal Imperials, the National Liberals, and the Left Liberals barely carried the motion over Conservative and Centrist opposition.[87]

The third reading of the naval budget on 23 March 1881 was concerned with the condition of the dock workers. The Social Democratic leader, Hasenclever, objected that the naval dockyard workers had not been given their work certificates when they re-

[85] That Bismarck took a strong interest in the result emerges from Kardorff, *Kardorff*, p. 175.

[86] *Verhandlungen des Reichstags*, 4 Leg. Per., IV Sess., 1881, 13 Sitz., LXII, 262-67.

[87] Kardorff to his wife, 12 March 1881, in Kardorff, *Kardorff*, p. 175.

fused to pay the Prussian stamp tax. This was the triumph of Prussian particularism over the Empire. Hasenclever asked Stosch to request the Prussian Finance Ministry to permit stamp-free certificates. He also noted that the Navy refused to employ workers over forty. Stosch replied with marked courtesy that the tax was purely a Prussian affair, and neither he nor the Reichstag had any control over it. It was legally impossible to pay the workers' tax from naval funds. He did not employ older workers because they were soon pensioned and younger workers performed dockyard duties better. Rickert, the orator of the "Liberal Union," upheld the Admiral's statement on the stamp tax. The Left Liberal leader, Albert Hänel of Kiel, recognized the validity of his position on the employment of older workers, but thought that it placed great hardship on non-Social Democratic workers. Stosch explained that the Navy wished to build up a steady worker population and thus employed young and healthy people, who did not wander from job to job. He expressed his willingness to investigate the policy if it brought hardship. Rickert announced his satisfaction with this reply. Although the members of the Reichstag denied Stosch one of the ships that he demanded,[88] the speakers had greeted him with cordiality. This was in marked contrast to the attacks of previous years.

The year 1881 marked a great change in German politics. Bismarck's swing toward protection, his dismissal of officials inclined to liberalism, and his dictatorial ways had split the National Liberal party, which had supported him. The right wing of the party, which favored protection, broke off in 1879. The left wing of the National Liberals seceded in 1880 and took the name of the "Liberal Union." Their leaders included Max von Forckenbeck, Eduard Lasker, Ludwig Bamberger, Georg von Bunsen, and Heinrich Rickert. They fused with Eugen Richter's Left Liberals in 1884. The "Liberal Union" was particularly hostile to the Chancellor's ecclesiastical policy, his military demands, and, above all, his protectionist and paternalistic program. During the year preceding the end of the Reichstag session in June 1881, many of the governmental proposals were defeated. Bismarck was in an angry mood

[88] *Verhandlungen des Reichstags,* 4 Leg. Per., IV Sess., 1881, 20 Sitz., LXII, 463-66.

and worked to exterminate his liberal opponents in the elections of October 1881. In the course of the campaign, which began in the summer of 1881, Bismarck strove mightily to influence the electorate, but an oppositional majority was returned for the first time in the history of the Empire.[89] The Chancellor's rage at these events found a vent in attacks on Stosch.

The relations between the two antagonists seemed to improve early in 1881. Stosch, perhaps on Roggenbach's advice,[90] accepted social invitations from Bismarck. There was a sensation when the Naval Chief appeared at the Chancellor's soirée of 4 April 1881 for the first time in five years, but Bismarck was particularly courteous to him.[91] This incident received due notice in the press, and Freytag hoped that it signalized the conclusion of an armistice between the two opponents.[92] This sanguine view was not justified by events. Bismarck complained to Agricultural Minister Lucius on 12 June 1881 that Rudolf von Bennigsen, the leader of the National Liberals, and Stosch were intriguing with the Finance Minister for the formation of a ministry with Stosch as War Minister, Bennigsen as Chancellor, and Forckenbeck as Minister of Interior. The Chancellor claimed that the Crown Princess favored the idea, but that Frederick William opposed it. Bismarck contemplated a signed letter to the newspapers attacking the Admiralty Chief, because Stosch "would have Rickert elected in Danzig by the dockyard workers and conspired with Hänel in Kiel." Moreover, he would complain to William that he could not "serve with such a ————." Lucius did not know how much truth and how much fiction lay in Bismarck's remarks, but noticed that he was ill and upset.[93]

---

[89] Willy Kremer, *Der Soziale Aufbau der Parteien des deutschen Reichstags von 1871-1914* (Emsdetten, 1934), pp. 25-26; Eyck, *Bismarck*, III, 309-24, 351-54, 377; Rubinstein, *Deutsch-Freisinnige Partei, passim;* Ludwig Bamberger, *Gesammelte Schriften* (Berlin, 1894-1898), V, 39-134; Block, *Parlamentarische Krisis,* pp. 33-37, 93-96; Friedrich Naumann, *Die Politischen Parteien* (Berlin-Schöneburg, 1910), p. 108. For biographies of the liberal leaders, see Barth, *Politische Porträts;* Pachnicke, *Führende Männer;* and August Stein, *Es war alles ganz anders. . . .* (Frankfurt a. M., 1922).

[90] Roggenbach to Stosch, Segenhaus, 1 Feb. 1881, Heyderhoff, *Im Ring der Gegner,* pp. 210-11.

[91] Poschinger, *Bismarck und die Parlamentarier,* I, 215.

[92] Freytag to Stosch, Leipzig, 19 April 1881, in Helmolt, *Freytag an Stosch,* p. 134.

[93] Lucius, *Bismarck-Erinnerungen,* pp. 209-10.

The Prussian Minister of Interior, Robert von Puttkammer, wrote Stosch about supporting Rickert. The Admiral replied that the allegation was untrue, and that the Navy had received more support from the Conservatives than from the Liberals. Puttkammer forwarded the letter to the Chancellor, who replied on 29 July. Bismarck instructed the Minister of Interior to send the Chancellor's message to Stosch directly or write him as though the message came from himself. The latter method "would perhaps be more pleasant to Herr von Stosch" and might succeed in obtaining the result desired. He questioned the truth of the Admiral's assertion that the Navy had found more support with the Conservatives than with the Liberals. In his communication to be passed to Stosch, Bismarck stressed the necessity of depriving the extreme liberals of the claim that they represented the real interests of the Navy. This could be accomplished if the Admiralty used its influence in the Naval dockyards at Danzig to defeat Rickert and to elect a Conservative deputy.[94] Stosch followed these instructions to the letter.[95] The mutual bitterness between Bismarck and Stosch was noted by the press in August 1881, when neither took any notice of the other when they traveled on the same railway train.[96] The Chancellor did not cease to work for Rickert's defeat. At the close of fleet maneuvers at Danzig in honor of Alexander III, William I, doubtless under Bismarck's prodding, told the mayor of Danzig that he "would consider the re-election of Rickert as a personal attack on himself."[97] Stosch wrote in his memoirs:

Since the existence of the Reichstag, Rickert had been a member of the Budget Committee on the Naval estimates and had used his power in handling budget details to put the dockyard workers and the lesser Naval officials in a friendly mood. For example, he had induced the Reichstag, against the arguments that I repeatedly presented [in the Committee], to give dockyard engineers a higher rank . . . . This gained votes for Rickert with the workers. When soon thereafter he was re-elected with a great majority, it was established that a number of dock-

[94] Puttkammer's letter and Stosch's reply are referred to in Bismarck to Puttkammer, Kissingen, 29 July 1881, in Bismarck, *Gesammelte Werke,* VIc, 220.

[95] Memoirs, II, 222-23.

[96] Poschinger, *Bismarcks Bundesrat,* II, 127 n.

[97] Memoirs, II, 222. Cf. Poschinger, *Bismarck und die Parlamentarier,* III, 34.

yard officials and the greatest part of the dock workers had voted decisively for him. The dutiful countermeasures of the dockyard administration had been completely unsuccessful.

The Chancellor ordered a disciplinary investigation of the political engineers [sic], gave a long speech in the Reichstag about it [sic], pushed the matter through two courts, was not satisfied with the last decision, but instituted a new charge and let the whole matter drop as soon as I received my dismissal.—I was supposed to be compromised somehow for [allegedly] furthering Rickert's election, but the investigation discovered nothing, because I was not even there at the time. It lasted 18 months and produced no evidence at all, and yet three years later [1884], when I had long since been living here [Oestrich] in complete retirement, the Chancellor, in the Reichstag, charged that I had elected Rickert. Despite all this activity, he was certain that I, contrary to my duty, had conspired with the Left Liberals against Emperor and Empire. *Habeat sibi.*[98]

This supposed connection between Rickert and Stosch eventually stimulated further press onslaughts.[99]

The Reichstag struck out, without discussion, the second ship requested by Stosch earlier in the year, during the naval budget debate of 7 December 1881. Rickert reported that the Budget Committee was pleased with the Admiral's explanation of the regulations governing the care of ill dock workers, and felt that he had made a special effort to remove injustices in pensioning older workers. It was divided on the general policy of not employing workers over forty, but was gratified by Stosch's express orders to accept these workers when they were otherwise qualified. Hirsch of the Left Liberals, a founder of workingmen's benefit societies, did not doubt Stosch's good intentions, but he desired legal definition of the workers' rights and duties. The dockworkers' benefit association, he noted, was run by the Navy, not by the workers themselves, and the amount of their contributions was not sufficient to guarantee effective liability insurance. He asked Stosch to correct the latter evil, inquired why workers' wages had been lowered, and added that state taxes were particularly burdensome on workers'

[98] Memoirs, II, 222-23. Cf. Lucius, *Bismarck-Erinnerungen,* pp. 255-56; Eyck, *Bismarck,* III, 310.

[99] To his wife, Berlin, 17 May 1882, *Memoirs,* II, 228. Schmidt-Bückeberg, *Das Militärkabinett,* p. 115, notes Stosch's question on 18 September 1881 concerning the Chancellor's right to countersign orders conferring decorations, but this does not seem to have led to any conflict with Bismarck.

communities. He felt, in general, that a sound social policy was not being followed. Stosch answered that the workers' welfare association had been in existence for only two years and that he had to work for practical goals, not meet idealistic conditions. Naval dockyard wages were determined by the wages in private dockyards, but were somewhat higher. He recognized that the small amount of workers' contribution to liability insurance was justified only by existing conditions. He added that he could not grant self-government to the association, because that was against general state policy. Hirsch, in reply, conceded that the Navy had always done its best for the workers. He acknowledged that his own aims, which were practical, could not be put into effect immediately. Rickert expressed his regret that, as *rapporteur* of the Budget Committee, he could not comment on the conditions in the dockyards, which he had discussed many times with Stosch.[100] Bismarck's reaction to this statement can only be imagined.[101]

Newspaper accounts that increased appropriations would be demanded for the Navy provoked Bismarck's wrath in September 1882. He wrote the Secretary of State of the Interior that "I know nothing about it, but . . . the practice of earlier years gives me no reason to doubt these reports." It was possible that the Chief of the Admiralty had spoken to the Emperor on financial, as well as command, matters and would inform the Finance Minister only after the Emperor's approval had been received. While disclaiming any inclination to object to William's decisions in military matters, Bismarck declared that he could not let pass any such action by the Admiral. The Chancellor asked the Secretary of State of the Interior to inquire of the Finance Ministry whether Stosch had asked, or apparently planned, to increase naval appropriations. If there was ground for the report, he was to inform Stosch in the Chancellor's name that he would not tolerate interference in fiscal questions. Should Stosch hold to his intentions, Bismarck said he would be unable to remain in office with his naval colleague and

[100] *Verhandlungen des Reichstags,* 4 Leg. Per., I Sess., 1881-1882, 12 Sitz., LXVI, 257-61.

[101] Freytag refers to a crisis Stosch was facing in February 1882. This probably has to do with the Danzig election affair. Freytag to Stosch, Wiesbaden, 11 Jan. 1882, in Helmolt, *Freytag an Stosch,* p. 139.

would explain the affair to the Emperor and to the Reichstag.[102]
The newspaper report was either unfounded or Stosch capitulated,
for Bismarck never carried out any of his drastic threats.

Stosch spoke in the Reichstag for the last time during the
naval budget debate of 23 January 1883. The Social Democratic
deputy, Blos, complained that naval regulations ordered the dismissal of any worker who belonged to a Social Democratic, nihilist, or other organization which supported the "overthrow of the
existing state order." Stosch announced that the Navy had and
would continue to oppose any revolutionary elements among the
workers. Rickert, reporting for the Budget Committee, stated
that, while Stosch's great accomplishments were recognized, the
Committee could not vote another ironclad. The Committee was
gratified that Stosch had stayed within the limits and financial
requirements of the shipbuilding plan of 1873 and had promised to
submit a new one.[103] The debate then ended.

The mood of all parties in the Reichstag had been friendly to
Stosch until the Chancellor's public assault on him in 1877. When
it was followed by the sinking of the *Great Elector* in 1878, the
Left, dissatisfied by his failure to account to the public for the
causes of the catastrophe, assailed him vigorously. The Conservatives and National Liberals, probably realizing that the Emperor
had not approved such a report, saved the naval budget. When
the Conservatives and supporters of Bismarck attacked him, the
Left championed his cause because of its hatred for the Chancellor.
The courtesy with which he treated the Reichstag and his evident
willingness to co-operate with it won him a certain popularity in
that body.[104] Moreover, the majority seemed thoroughly persuaded
of his administrative capabilities. When Heinrich Rickert spoke
on the first reading of the naval budget on 18 March 1884, he
paid tribute to Stosch, "who had always worked in harmony"

[102] Bismarck to von Bötticher, Varzin, 24 Sept. 1882, Secret, in Bismarck,
Gesammelte Werke, VIc, 261-62.
[103] *Verhandlungen des Reichstags*, 5 Leg. Per., II Sess., 1882-1883, 37 Sitz.,
LXIX, 1026-29.
[104] See Richter, *Im alten Reichstag*, II, 9-10, 59. Cf. Rickert's praise of
Stosch in 1892 for his economy and willingness to co-operate with the Reichstag,
which Rickert believed was the cause of Bismarck's hatred of Stosch. *Verhandlungen des Reichstags*, 8 Leg. Per., II Sess., 1892-1893, 7 Sitz., CXXVII, 106c,
2 Dec. 1892.

with the Reichstag for the development of the Navy, praised his administration for creating a war fleet with moderate funds, and acclaimed his "decision and energy." The Admiral's friend, Robert von Benda, repeated Stosch's frequent remark to the Reichstag members: "If you want to mould the Navy, Gentlemen, you must act on your best judgment; but whatever you do, do it properly." He spoke warmly of the "highly honored man, with whom we have worked for so many years."[105] Doubtless he expressed the opinion of the majority of the house. Stosch could not, of course, give free expression to his own opinions in the Reichstag. He had to defend the decisions of the Bundesrat. However, his views of the crippling power of majorities, expressed in the debate of September 1878, and the necessity for fighting the Social Democrats by economic means, stated in 1883, have a certain spontaneity which testifies to his adherence to these conservative opinions.

3

The resignation of Stosch on 20 March 1883 was the direct result of a constitutional crisis of the first magnitude,[106] which decided the extent of the powers of the Prussian War Minister. The Admiral's part in the crisis was apparently a secondary and completely voluntary one, but shows him to have been a defender of the prerogatives of the War Minister.

The struggle between War Minister von Kameke and Chief of the Military Cabinet von Albedyll reached its height in the early

[105] *Verhandlungen des Reichstags*, 5 Leg. Per., IV Sess., 1884, 8 Sitz., LXXV, 119-20, 122. Cf. "General von Stosch and the German Navy," *Journal of the Royal United Service Institution*, XXVIII (1884), 205-11.

[106] The writer's principal reliance has been on the discussion in Schmitt-Bückeberg, *Das Militärkabinett*, pp. 136-51, and Friedberg's Memorandum, "Resignation Attempts of the Ministers von Kameke and von Stosch," in Lucius, *Bismarck-Erinnerungen*, pp. 258-61. See also Craig, *The Politics of the Prussian Army*, pp. 217-32; Morsey, *Die Oberste Reichsverwaltung*, pp. 236-39; Eberhard Kessell, "Die Tätigkeit des Grafen Waldersees als Generalquartiermeister und Chef des Generalstabs der Armee," *Die Welt als Geschichte*, XIV (1954), 195-96; Kessel, *Moltke*, pp. 693-703. The memoirs of Albedyll's wife, Julie v. Albedyll-Alten, *Aus Hannover und Preussen: Lebenserinnerungen aus einem halbem Jahrhundert* (2nd ed., Potsdam, 1914), contain no information on the crisis. Stosch's memoirs are completely silent on the immediate cause of his resignation. The documents may have been destroyed during the Geffcken investigation or have been considered too secret to reproduce. His grandson, Herr Ulrich von Stosch, possesses no papers which bear on this case. Some interesting details appear in Rich and Fisher, *Holstein Papers*, II, 15, 17, 31-32, 34, 44. For a confused and inaccurate press appraisal, see Johannes Penzler, *Fürst Bismarck nach seiner Entlassung* (Leipzig, 1897-1898), I, 227-28.

eighties. The artificial separation of command and administrative powers had been the source of constant friction, for neither William, Bismarck, Albedyll, Moltke, Kameke, Stosch, nor their subordinates could clearly say what measures fell in the category of command and which in the sphere of administration. Each case was decided upon its separate merits, with due regard for the personalities involved. Albedyll fought to secure the independence of the Military Cabinet from the War Ministry, the right to report directly and regularly to the Emperor, the separation of his personnel bureau from the Ministry, and—a factor considered by many to be the determinant in his calculations—to receive seniority rights over the War Minister. The right to report directly to the Emperor, without the mediation or the presence of the War Minister, was of the greatest practical importance. The eighty-five-year-old William, whose growing weakness in resisting the views of his subordinates had been noticed by Stosch, made final decisions in military matters. If his ear were gained, Albedyll could expect to find his own proposals accepted. He met the strongest opposition from Kameke.[107]

The Prussian Constitution made the War Minister the responsible official for all military matters, both of command and administration. To him the Military Cabinet and the General Staff had been subordinated since the Wars of Liberation against Napoleon. This organization had demonstrated its success; it incorporated the practical advantage of making one man accountable to the King for military matters, instead of three, who might present conflicting views. Kameke vehemently defended his rights as War Minister against the encroachments of the Military Cabinet.[108]

The Military Cabinet, unlike the War Ministry which had only a few legal rights in Imperial matters, was both a Prussian and Imperial organization. However, its chief function, that of personnel, was subordinated to the Prussian War Minister. In his efforts to free himself from this restriction, Albedyll found a powerful ally in Count Waldersee, who in January 1882 was appointed Army Quartermaster General and designated Moltke's eventual successor as Chief of the General Staff. Waldersee, a man

[107] Schmidt-Bückeburg, *Das Militärkabinett*, pp. 136-37, 141, 144.
[108] *Ibid.,* pp. 145-46.

of consummate ambition, saw that to rise in the Army it behooved him to be on excellent terms with the chief of personnel, Albedyll. The previous poor relations of the General Staff with the Military Cabinet soon changed to a close alliance between Albedyll and Waldersee. The Quartermaster General was preparing war plans which affected the railways and the Army finances. These lay within Kameke's competence, and a battle was soon joined between the General Staff and War Ministry. Waldersee, backed by Albedyll, sought to win the independence of the General Staff from the War Ministry and to achieve the right to report directly to the Emperor. Here he met opposition from Moltke, who, at the time, held that he could approach William only when his presence was requested. In April 1882 Moltke departed on extended leave, and the way lay open for Albedyll and Waldersee to push their projects. Their first goal was to dispose of their chief obstacle, War Minister von Kameke. Albedyll seized upon an order of Kameke's extending complimentary payments of a deceased officer's salary to his heirs from a month to three months as infringing the Emperor's power of command. A spirited correspondence ensued between the two men, which the Chief of the Military Cabinet kept alive until the beginning of 1883.[109]

The opportunity to force Kameke's dismissal, for which Albedyll and Waldersee had been waiting, came early in 1883. The Reichstag had expressed a desire to abolish, or at least to limit, the exemption of officers from municipal taxes. Kameke, desirous of securing approval of his Army program, wished to make a token concession to the Reichstag. On 22 January 1883 William called a conference composed of[110] Count von Moltke, General von Pape, von Albedyll, and von Stosch to advise him on the matter. Stosch and Moltke supported Kameke's desire to make a slight concession, while Albedyll stressed his view that it would be an invasion of the Emperor's power of command. On 1 February Albedyll went to

---

[109] *Ibid.*, pp. 137-39; Waldersee, *Denkwürdigkeiten*, I, 218-20; Walter Görlitz, *Der Deutsche Generalstab: Geschichte und Gestalt 1657-1945* (Frankfurt a. M., n. d.), pp. 141-42. Kessel, *Moltke*, p. 694, maintains that Kameke was responsible for the continuance of the struggle.

[110] Friedberg (Lucius, *Bismarck-Erinnerungen*, p. 259) relates that Kameke was also present, but Kameke complained to Lucius (*ibid.*, p. 249) that he was not. At the meeting, held on 28 January, Stosch is said to have spoken "like a Republican." Kessel, *Moltke*, p. 699.

Bismarck. The Chancellor, who had long desired to make the War Minister completely his subordinate and who objected to any Reichstag meddling with the Army, agreed with Albedyll's suggestion that Kameke be dismissed, but proposed Waldersee as his successor. The embarrassed Albedyll objected that Waldersee did not "expect" this post, and the idea was dropped. The Chief of the Military Cabinet told Waldersee the next day that he believed that he had won over the Chancellor for their project. After a second conference on 11 February in which Stosch alone supported Kameke, the Emperor ordered Kameke to block any concession and to inform the Reichstag that it could exercise no "interference in command matters" and that the War Minister "bore no responsibility for assisting in command matters." Kameke made a statement to that effect on 12 February. The incident seemed closed.[111]

However, Albedyll had no intention of letting the matter rest there. He issued orders which fell within Kameke's competence and used his protests to convince William that he was interfering in command matters and was surrendering the Emperor's rights over the Army to the Reichstag. The Emperor, probably at Albedyll's suggestion, asked Bismarck for his opinion on Kameke's activity. The Chancellor replied that the War Minister was permitting the Reichstag to gain control over the Army. Governed by the advice of the Chancellor and the Chief of the Military Cabinet, William wrote Kameke on 24 February, stating that the Reichstag had no rights over command matters, and it must be so informed. The Army must have no doubts as to who held the command. William aimed at reaching an "understanding" with Kameke, but, under the circumstances, no agreement was possible. Kameke, embittered by the attempt of the "Bismarck-Albedyll-Waldersee Triumvirate" to make him a War Minister "of the second class," departed from the War Ministry on 3 March, declaring: "With me the last Prussian War Minister leaves this house."[112]

The aim of Bismarck, Albedyll, and Waldersee was achieved. Kameke's successor, Paul Bronsart von Schellendorff, was persuaded

[111] Lucius, *Bismarck-Erinnerungen*, pp. 249, 259; Schmidt-Bückeberg, *Das Militärkabinett*, pp. 139-42; Kessel, *Moltke*, pp. 699-700.

[112] Schmidt-Bückeberg, *Das Militärkabinett*, pp. 142-43, 151; Lucius, *Bismarck-Erinnerungen*, pp. 249-61; Waldersee, *Denkwürdigkeiten*, I, 224-25; Bismarck to William, 24 Feb. 1883, *Gesammelte Werke*, VIc, 273-76; H. O. Meisner, *Kriegsminister, 1814-1914* (Berlin, 1940), pp. 33-34.

to approve the right of both the General Staff and the Military Cabinet to report directly to the Emperor and also submitted to the separation of the Army personnel bureau from the Ministry, although in the budget it was still carried as part of the Ministry. The change was thus masked from the eyes of the people's representatives. Bronsart further recognized the independence of the Military Cabinet in general and Albedyll's rights of seniority in particular. He told the Cabinet Chief that he did not wish to bear the odium of appearing to yield to force on his acceptance of office, so he asked and received Albedyll's willing permission to present the changes to the Emperor. On 8 March 1883 William approved the Military Cabinet's demands and on 24 May, the General Staff received the right to report directly and regularly to the Emperor, although it remained technically under the War Minister. The constitutional crisis of 1883 had the practical result of dividing military functions among the War Ministry, the Military Cabinet, and the General Staff. In fact, the War Ministry lost control of military policy, which the Military Cabinet and the General Staff, accountable to the King-Emperor alone, henceforth determined. Divided command was one of the contributing factors to Germany's defeat in World War I. Bismarck's power was also enhanced. He was no longer faced with a powerful War Minister or with attempts to establish an independent Imperial War Ministry. The generally undistinguished men who followed Kameke could not effectively challenge the predominance of the "Imperial War Minister," von Bismarck. Thus after 1883, the War Minister occupied a subordinate place in the military and governmental organization and the powers of Bismarck, Albedyll, and Waldersee were correspondingly increased. Parliamentary control over the Army was effectively hindered by placing command matters in the hands of officers who were not forced to seek the Reichstag's support.[113]

Stosch, who had strongly supported Kameke throughout, felt that he no longer possessed the Emperor's confidence, and on 7 March he submitted his resignation, ostensibly because of his

[113] Görlitz, *Der Deutsche Generalstab,* p. 142; Schmidt-Bückeberg, *Das Militärkabinett,* pp. 143-48; Meisner, *Kriegsminister,* pp. 49-50; Huber, *Heer und Staat,* pp. 363-66. For a different interpretation of Bronsart's actions, see Friedrich von Bronsart, "Das alte Kaiser und sein Kriegsminister von Bronsart," *Historische Vierteljahrschrift,* XXXI (1937-1939), 293-306.

health.[114] William refused it on 11 March, stating that he saw no reason for it. Stosch repeated his resignation giving his arguments in detail, and William approved it on 16 March, while expressing his displeasure at Stosch's disobedience. In a letter of 3 April 1883 to the Ministry, William, greatly disturbed by the departure of Kameke and Stosch, explained that they had been dismissed because of disagreement over the Emperor's control of command matters. He termed Stosch's second request for dismissal "a sort of political covenant," which "necessitated the approval of his resignation."[115] William further declared:

I believe I must realize that the actual reason for General von Stosch's resignation attempt [lies] in a certain wounding [of his feelings] in the municipal tax business and in his political convictions, which decisively deviate very much further from the measures of my Government than I had previously believed and assumed.[116]

He concluded with a denial that Bismarck had any hand in Stosch's departure.[117] Stosch had complained in March that

. . . they were bringing him into discredit as a liberal and were seeking to surround the Crown Prince with as conservative a company as possible. He had chiefly striven to bring him out of himself and sought to surround him with able people.[118]

It is obvious from this remark that Bismarck, supported by Albedyll and Waldersee, worked to secure Stosch's dismissal, because of his supposed liberal influence on the Crown Prince. It is equally apparent, from the Emperor's letter of 3 April, that Stosch had supported Kameke in his wish to make a limited concession to the Reichstag and had fought for the supremacy of the War Ministry in Army affairs. Doubtless feelings of personal friendship for Kameke influenced his attitude. It is probable that he raised strong objections to the separation of Army command and administrative matters. He may well have objected openly to William's

---

[114] Officially Stosch could only receive his dismissal; in fact he resigned. Cf. the excellent discussion in Morsey, *Die Oberste Reichsverwaltung*, pp. 132, 268.

[115] Schmidt-Bückeberg, *Das Militärkabinett*, pp. 144-49; Lucius, *Bismarck-Erinnerungen*, p. 260.

[116] Schmidt-Bückeberg, *Das Militärkabinett*, p. 149. Cf. Kessel, *Moltke*, p. 700.

[117] Priesdorff, *Soldatisches Führertum*, VIII, 317.

[118] Lucius, *Bismarck-Erinnerungen*, p. 255 (March 18).

policy[119] of retaining senior officers in command long after they had reached retirement age.[120]   It is also probable that he defended the practical necessity of working with the Reichstag in military matters and opposed the breach in constitutional practice. Whether, as an article, "apparently inspired" by Bismarck, in the *Deutsche Tageblatt* maintained, Stosch was the "leader" in the wish to make a concession to the Reichstag, and Kameke only followed "in his wake," remains unproved.[121]

Stosch was embittered by the whole affair, for when William invited him to a farewell audience, he offered the specious excuse in writing that he had already sent his uniform home.   The Emperor, though deeply hurt,[122] warmly expressed gratitude for Stosch's services to himself and to the Navy.[123]   The Crown Prince and Princess were greatly angered by the way Stosch had been treated.[124]

His retirement on 20 March 1883 was the result of his own voluntary action in a matter which was not directly a part of his duties.   It resulted from a combination of circumstances and was not solely the consequence of his championing of the powers of War Minister.   In June, he replied to a letter from the National Liberal leader, Rudolf von Bennigsen, who had written him three months before to persuade him to remain in office. He stated that he could say no more than "I had no single reason whatsoever which motivated me, but I could not remain with the best will [in the world]."[125]   He contended:

[119] Schmidt-Bückeberg, *Das Militärkabinett,* pp. 149, 160.   On the general trend toward co-operation between the Ministers and the Reichstag, see Morsey, *Die Oberste Reichsverwaltung,* pp. 311-12.

[120] This inference is based upon his continual references to the "old age of [the personnel of] the state," his objection to the age of the officers in the Foot Guards (which emerges from the Crown Prince's letter of 23 Oct. 1880), and his later expression of disgust with Albedyll's personnel policy (Stosch to Normann, Oestrich, 22 Dec. 1887, Memoirs, III, 132).

[121] Quoted in the *National Zeitung,* 10 March 1883, Poschinger, *Bismarcks Bundesrat,* II, 135. Cf. Holstein's remark, Morsey, *Die Oberste Reichsverwaltung,* p. 237 n. 54.

[122] Lucius, *Bismarck-Erinnerungen,* p. 258. Schröder, *Stosch,* p. 98, implies (citing no evidence) that William was cool in the final interview, which never took place.

[123] Hassell, *Tirpitz,* pp. 46-47.

[124] Waldersee, *Denkwürdigkeiten,* I, 226; Rich and Fisher, *Holstein Papers,* II, 37, 39-40.

[125] Haus Stosch, Oestrich im Rheingau, 12 June 1883, in Oncken, *Bennigsen,* II, 500.

A man has the right to demand that he can aim at the success of his activity and that he can enjoy his work within himself. When one feels every day that . . . he is no longer progressing, then his duty to his country ceases and he is freed. . . . May others be luckier and have better success.[126]

He wrote Admiral Batsch on 16 March 1883: "You may imagine that the separation from the Navy will not be easy for me, and that I have taken this decisive step only after the most mature deliberation." He noted that he had recommended Batsch to the Crown Prince as his successor, but Frederick William "has decisive influence only occasionally," and he concluded by saying that Batsch would find him a "lonely and forgotten man."[127] He wrote on 15 April:

I have really lost the center of my life and my activity, but not a single friend. All who stood close to me had long since departed, and the new race was reserved toward me, as politically dangerous. I was so lonely that an infinite longing to become free seized me. I was certain I would retire as soon as I decently could. That has happened, and I feel cheerful in my innermost heart. You would object that the attempt is not yet two weeks old, but when one reaches my age and has enough of the world behind him, one has a trustworthy feeling that one needs to live as a spectator.[128]

The constitutional crisis of 1883 was only the immediate cause of Stosch's departure. Worn by official and public attacks, realizing that his presence damaged the Navy, whose ship construction was completed according to plan, feeling the weight of his years and the infringement of his independence by the Chancellor, he decided to resign as soon as occasion offered. When that came, he retired from official, but not political, life to the home the nation had given him in Oestrich.

The sinking of the newly built German battleship the *Great Elector* brought Albrecht von Stosch under heavy fire from all sides. Until 1881 he had, as a loyal servant of the Emperor and a defender of the imperial military prerogatives, the support of the Conservative party. The liberal parties, after the *Great Elector* catastrophe, had combined with his harshest critics, the supporters of the Chancellor, to attack Stosch. The debate of 1880 was the

[126] *Ibid.*   [127] Berlin, Memoirs, III, 2.
[128] To Frau von Rosenstiel, *ibid.*

zenith of these assaults. The Liberals of the left sought to secure an official report to the Reichstag on the tragedy, but were defeated by admirers of the Admiralty Chief, enemies of Bismarck, followers of the Crown Prince, and those who felt such a report could not constitutionally be demanded by the Reichstag. The other attack came from the supporters of Bismarck, who attempted to take command matters from Stosch's control. The Chancellor could find only an extremely obscure deputy to be his spokesman, a fact strongly indicative of the opposition to Bismarck and the popularity of Stosch. This motion received almost no backing. During the following years, the Conservatives, who were moving closer to the Chancellor, opposed the naval budget, while the Liberals, refusing to be Bismarck's lever in forcing Stosch out of office, rallied to the Admiralty Chief's support. In general, the Reichstag demonstrated a strong belief in his capabilities and was won over by his conciliatory stand.

Until 1883, when his control over command matters seemed challenged, William I supported Stosch. Wavering slightly in 1878, the Emperor proved amenable to Roggenbach's advocacy of his friend's case. The Admiralty Chief insured the Emperor's backing by two offers of resignation and he continued to receive unusual signs of imperial favor. Jealousy of his command prerogatives probably prevented William from permitting an official publication of the results of the courts martial on the tragic sinking, but a semi-official report did appear. Throughout the protracted official investigations, he championed the Admiralty Chief's contention that the "Stosch System" was not at fault.

The battle over the "Stosch System" would never have been so fierce nor so protracted had it not been for the inveterate hatred of Bismarck. He expressed his violent anger in a brutal fashion through private conversations, the inspired press, and the speeches of his supporters. He used all means at his command to rid himself of his rival, but always met William's resistance. Bismarck came to believe that Stosch was a prime mover in the formation of a "Gladstone Ministry" to replace him as Chancellor. He contended, mistakenly, that Stosch worked to secure the re-election of another member of this "shadow cabinet," Heinrich Rickert.

Whether Bismarck could have ever forced Stosch from office, if he had been unwilling to go in 1883, is extremely problematical.

Throughout the struggle the Admiralty Chief gave every sign of adhering to his basic conservatism. In his resignation attempt of July, 1878, he sought to maintain his honor as a Prussian officer and, later in the Reichstag, announced his opposition to the revolutionary Social Democrats. Supported by the Left Liberals in 1881, he felt himself "misplaced politically," and he felt no compunction at using official powers to secure Rickert's defeat in Danzig. He constantly sought to win the Crown Prince over to Bismarck's policy. Nevertheless, he was not in total agreement with the Chancellor's views. He believed, unlike Bismarck, that the Crown Prince should have able advisers and that the War Minister should possess full accountability and independence. Moreover, he showed himself conciliatory toward the Reichstag. He believed that a responsible official was forced to make concessions to the majority to reach the practical goal of securing appropriations. These differences coupled with Bismarck's fear of Stosch's popularity with the Reichstag, the Crown Prince, and the Emperor were the root causes of the Chancellor's enmity and suspicion that Stosch worked to overthrow him. The departure of the Admiralty Chief in 1883 left Bismarck's fury unabated, and Stosch was soon to find himself once again the subject of public controversy.

VII

STOSCH AND THE EMPEROR FREDERICK III

1

Resignation from office left Stosch with only the dying embers of his old ambition. In 1883 he disclaimed any desire for further official activity, but admitted that "I like to talk politics, but only with men of independence." Unfortunately, "all the great people whom I have seen up to now view me as the victim of the Chancellor and that determines their words."[1] Reports in the *Kölnische Zeitung* that he had an audience with William only brought a "hearty" laugh from him.[2] The last flickerings of his ambition came in 1885. The news of Manteuffel's death reawakened Stosch's desire, dormant since 1871, to become Governor General of Alsace-Lorraine. Bismarck, he felt, might appoint him to do the Crown Prince a favor, while simultaneously separating the royal heir from Stosch. Although Stosch told Freytag that the whole idea was nonsense,[3] he asked the Crown Prince to intervene for him with Bismarck. At the same time, he confessed that "greed for power has clouded my horizon."[4] The Crown Prince met the Chancellor but did not raise the question.[5] The matter was apparently pursued no further. In a letter to Freytag on 22 August 1885 Stosch admitted:

[1] To Frau von Rosenstiel, Oestrich, 6 Oct. 1883, Memoirs, III, 3.

[2] To Frau von Rosenstiel, Oestrich, 20 Dec. 1883, *ibid.*, III, 4.

[3] To Freytag, 26 June 1883, *ibid.*, III, 25. On the proposal to appoint a Governor General of Alsace-Lorraine in 1871, see Morsey, *Die Oberste Reichsverwaltung*, p. 176 n. 76.

[4] To Freytag, 11 July 1883, Memoirs, III, 29. Stosch was not considered as a candidate and the Crown Prince backed the successful aspirant Hohenlohe. Morsey, *Die Oberste Reichsverwaltung*, p. 192.

[5] To von Normann, Oestrich, 14 July 1883, Memoirs, III, p. 31. For Freytag's reaction, see his letter to Stosch, Siebleben, 17 July 1885, in Helmolt, *Freytag an Stosch*, p. 163. Cf. Rich and Fisher, *Holstein Papers*, II, 208-9.

A short while ago I let myself be seduced into pursuing ambitious plans, but that was stupidity, originating in old dreams. I lack any ambition on the eventual change of monarch, and, in fact, I am seized by fear of it; a fear, which becomes more oppressive the closer the time approaches, and the more distinctly the dreams and phantasies of the heir to the throne become clear.[6]

His fears of the accession of the Crown Prince were shared by Bismarck, who acted to smooth the transition.

The Chancellor could not rely upon continued tenure in office unless he secured the support of the future monarch, for William I, who was eighty-seven in 1884, was expected to die at any time. Bismarck viewed with disfavor the supposed liberal ideas and anti-Bismarckian tone of the Crown Prince's entourage. In the early eighties Count v. Radolinski was appointed as Court Marshal to Frederick William to report to the Chancellor and to dispose of the independent advisers of the Crown Prince.[7] The chief adviser who was replaced during this period was Karl von Normann, intimate counselor of the royal couple for nearly twenty years. Stosch urged Normann to remain with Frederick William[8] and viewed with alarm Bismarck's efforts to remove him by appointing him Prussian Minister to Oldenburg. In a letter of 7 July 1884 Stosch pressed Frederick William to retain Normann, while striving at the same time to preserve his own influence.[9] He wrote sarcastically:

To be sure, I am a dangerous man, the candidate of the Left Liberals for the Chancellorship, as the Chancellor, according to the best informed sources, recently maintained, but I believe that Your Imperial Highness has known me to be a faithful man and knows that I am free from egotistical goals and party motives. It occurs to me in this connection that, when Sommerfeld assumed his position [as new private secretary to the Crown Prince], the gossip was reported to me that he had said one of his duties was to paralyze my influence upon Your Imperial Highness. The expression is too foolish to be true, but the

[6] Memoirs, III, 38.
[7] Ponsonby, *Letters of the Empress Frederick*, pp. 192-93; Rich and Fisher, *Holstein Papers*, II, 146, 148, 150. Stosch wrote Normann on 14 Dec. 1887, Memoirs, III, 127, that Radolinski was in regular communication with the Chancellor.
[8] Stosch to Normann, Oestrich, 26 April 1884, *ibid.*, III, p. 8. On the Stosch-Normann friendship, see Rich and Fisher, *Holstein Papers,* II, 46, 47-48, 99, 106.
[9] Oestrich, Memoirs, III, 11-12.

tale shows what thoughts are active in the circles in question. I am firmly convinced that the same opinion is given today upon the departure of Normann.[10]

The Crown Prince explained in reply that Normann accepted the Oldenburg appointment to become familiar with state procedures, "until the moment comes when I am able to utilize his unusual capacity of work." Moreover, Normann desired the post and it was in "his and my interest" to separate him from court life. Frederick William believed that Bismarck's offer of the position was in accord with "his completely altered attitude toward me," for he showed a desire to co-operate and secure the Crown Prince's good-will. Bismarck was certainly not appointing Normann "to trip him up at his pleasure," nor had he surrounded the Crown Prince with "his people." Frederick William repulsed the suggestion that Sommerfeld was intriguing against Stosch; "he is not like that, and, in the second place, I do not allow myself to be lectured on my trust in my friends."[11] Despite these assurances, Stosch remained convinced that Normann's career was endangered and believed he would be dismissed when the opportunity came.[12] Here the Admiral was mistaken, for Normann remained in his post until his death in 1888. The Chancellor doubtless wished to make the entourage of the Crown Prince dependent upon him and to establish his influence over the heir to the throne, but he was also pleased to be able to win Frederick William's favor by appointing an intimate adviser to an inconspicuous post. Bismarck's personal ambition did not exclude the statesmanlike desire to bring the Crown Prince into contact with his future duties.

When Bismarck revived the Prussian State Council to give advice on legislation, he had Frederick William made its President.[13] The project doubtless resulted from the wish to bind the future monarch to the Government's program, the desire to prepare him for his future duties, and the wish to revive in altered form

[10] *Ibid.*, III, 11.
[11] Potsdam, 20 July 1884, *ibid.*, III, 16-18.
[12] To Freytag, 30 July 1884, *ibid.*, III, 20-21. Cf. Rich and Fisher, *Holstein Papers*, II, 146-49.
[13] Poschinger, *Kaiser Friedrich*, III, 390-94; Müller-Bohn, *Kaiser Friedrich*, pp. 511-12; G. Schuster, *Briefe, Reden und Erlasse des Kaisers und Könige Friedrich III* (Berlin, 1907), pp. 296-98.

the abortive plan for an economic advisory council.[14]   The National Liberal leader Miquel told Stosch he favored the idea, because "it would keep the Crown Prince from giving rein to his leftist policies."[15]   Stosch commented to Normann on April 26, 1884:

I was able to reassure him about that, for we know that, in reality, the inner nature of the Prince is in clearest opposition to the left . . . . I cannot yet get it through my head that the Crown Prince will preside over the State Council.   I fear that he will not be able to understand the decisive points in the debate . . . . —I certainly wish that he would come out for the Military Pension Law now, so that the Army would get its rights, and the middle parties would be reconciled.   The Chancellor, as well as most other men who make decisions, looks to him now.   He could accomplish a great deal.[16]

It is significant that Stosch doubted the Prince's capabilities in public affairs.   He wrote him on 16 July that the Empress Augusta believed that the Council had been created only "to shackle" her son, but she wished him "to look, and take a part, in the future with happiness and confidence."   Stosch heartily agreed with this view and added that "It is my daily and continual prayer that Your Imperial Highness will participate more in the life of the state, and following the natural course, acquire immediately a field of activity and influence."[17]   The Crown Prince, in his reply of 20 July, recalled that he had long hoped for a legislative advisory committee, which could prepare ministerial bills better than the "time-consuming methods of the Chambers' and Reichstag committees." He had been surprised to be named head of the Council, for he had previously discounted the rumors of his appointment as a "necessary evil" of being Crown Prince "at the present time."[18]   He concluded:

The chief activity will take place in the 7 sections and full sessions may be the exception.   There it can easily happen, in view of the [Bismarkian] composition of the members of the State Council, that I will be in a splendid minority . . . ; after 20 years of silence I find occasion to give my opinions openly in a way which gives me little pleasure.[19]

[14] On this project, see Julius Curtius, *Bismarcks Plan eines deutschen Volkswirtschaftrat* (Heidelberg, 1919).

[15] To Normann, Oestrich, 26 April 1884, Memoirs, III, 8.

[16] *Ibid.*

[17] *Ibid.,* III, 13.

[18] *Ibid.,* III, 18.

[19] *Ibid.,* III, 18-19.

Bismarck eyed with suspicion anyone who could possibly desire to replace him. He was particularly fearful of the Left Liberal party, which had been augmented by the National Liberal left wing in March 1884. The Crown Princess Victoria was known to favor this party, which sought to establish the Chancellor's responsibility to the Reichstag. Bismarck, fearing the dominance of Victoria over her husband, tried to break the party.[20]   Part of this campaign was a speech he made in the Reichstag on 26 July 1884, in which he combined his detestation of the Left Liberal leader Heinrich Rickert with his virulent hatred of Albrecht von Stosch.

The Chancellor stated that "the Navy is more popular . . . with the opposition than the Army," and he expressed his pleasure that the liberals backed at least part of the armed forces. However, he hoped their support was lasting and "not tied to the Stosch regime."[21]   He asserted:

I have frequently heard talk—I do not know whether or not to the satisfaction of my former colleague in the Naval Administration—that my colleague Herr v. Stosch was viewed as my successor in the Imperial Chancellery. . . . On this account, I always observed this gentleman with particular interest. . . .[22]

He had believed that the Navy would lose the backing of the opposition headed by Rickert, "the essential prop of Minister v. Stosch," but this, he was glad to say, had not proved to be the case. The Left Liberal leader, Eugen Richter, denied hearing anyone suggest Stosch as Bismarck's successor. The Chancellor replied blandly that Richter was not in the inner circle of those who propounded the idea. He claimed that in 1877 the plan was worked out in detail for a future ministry to succeed him; "I do not know whether with the knowledge of Herr von Stosch, but they still counted on his co-operation, his power, and his connections to give support to the future cabinet."[23]   This attack provoked a lively press agitation, in which the principal protagonists

[20] Eyck, "Empress Frederick," *Quarterly Review,* no. 589, pp. 362-63; Dorpalen, "Frederick III," *American Historical Review,* LIV, 24-25.
[21] Kohl, *Bismarck Reden,* X, 209. For Rickert's statement that provoked this attack, see *Verhandlungen des Reichstags,* 5 Leg. Per., IV Sess., 1884, 42 Sitz., 26 June 1884, LXXVI, 1059.
[22] Kohl, *Bismarck Reden,* X, 209-10.   [23] *Ibid.,* X, 210, 212-13.

were the National Liberal *Magdeburgische Zeitung* and the officially inspired *Norddeutsche Allgemeine Zeitung*.[24]

The National Liberal *Magdeburger Zeitung* of 30 June 1884 maintained that the opposition between Bismarck and Stosch stemmed not from the Liberals, but "originated from the basic differences in the natures of both statesmen," which came to light "long before 1870." The Admiral was not the candidate of the Liberals for the Chancellor's position, but the choice of the Conservatives. The crisis of 1877 had ended through the intervention of the Conservative deputy Count von Moltke. For two years the antagonists worked in "visible peace" with each other because of Kameke's mediation. The article confessed that the Liberals had co-operated with Stosch, because "he was a very competent man, who was always open to practical suggestions and to whom the German Navy owes great thanks." The Liberals "never proposed" Stosch as future Chancellor, because they knew that Bismarck preferred the National Liberal leader von Bennigsen to a "Lieutenant General, who, with great services to the Empire, yet had grown old in one-sided Conservative ideas."[25]

The officially inspired *Norddeutsche Allgemeine Zeitung* of 5 July 1884 took a strong stand against this "first attempt" to create a legend. It termed as "characteristic" the implication of the *Magdeburgische Zeitung* that the Liberals would never propose a general as Chancellor, which might indeed be the attitude of the Left Liberals in 1884. The *Norddeutsche Allgemeine Zeitung* inquired: "How does one become a Reichstag deputy in Danzig?" The answer to this question showed that the "former Chief of the Admiralty was influenced at least enough by liberalism to wish to see it represented in parliament." It continued: "Herr von Stosch not only associated with the so-called Court Liberals, Rickert, v. Bunsen, v. Forckenbeck, etc. . . . , he upheld them in the political sphere. He was ready to place his relations with the Court at their disposal." It claimed that the "heterogeneous elements, the National Liberals, Left Liberals, the Secessionists

---

[24] The articles are reprinted in [Dr. Robolsky], *Unsere Minister seit 1862* (Berlin, 1890), pp. 238-45, and Helmolt, *Freytag an Stosch*, pp. 326-32.

[25] Quoted from the *Norddeutsche Allgemeine* Zeitung, 5 July 1884, in Helmolt, *Freytag an Stosch*, pp. 326-27.

[the "Liberal Union"], and the Ultramontanes" had banded together to form a ministry to displace the existing Government, just as the coalition of diverse elements led by Gladstone had assumed office from the Tories. In this Ministry, the "Chief of the Admiralty was intended for the role of Mr. Gladstone." The Bismarckian journal termed the statement of its rival about the crisis of 1877 and Moltke's intervention "inspirations of the Left Liberal's phantasy." The resignation of Stosch had resulted not from differences with the Chancellor, but from disagreement with the Emperor over the "principles" of naval administration. The journal chided the Left Liberals for abandoning "their candidate," after they considered him as "politically dead," and for accusing him of being a Conservative, unfit to become Chancellor because he was a general. Replying to another article in the National Liberal *Magdeburgische Zeitung,* which had held fast to its opinion of Moltke's intervention in 1877 and termed the talk of a "Gladstone Ministry," "a bandit's tale," Bismarck's organ, the *Norddeutsche Allgemeine Zeitung* of 14 July 1884 insisted that the crisis of 1877 was the result of a difficulty between Stosch and Delbrück over a concession to the Reichstag in the budget and repeated the denials and assertions of the article of 5 July.[26]

Stosch would not accept tamely the imputation that he had aspired to be "Gladstone" for the liberals. He felt that he had become the target of the Chancellor, because of opposition to the separation of Normann and the Crown Prince. He wrote on 8 July 1884:

The attacks on me are continued by the marvelous article in the *Norddeutsche Allgem. Zeitung* . . . . The intention decidedly is to kill me morally before the change in monarchs takes place. I have written to Berlin to obtain the stenographic report of the Chancellor's speech and the newspaper articles in question; then I will see what I will do. In no case will I conduct a press war, but I have always insisted upon fighting back when I am attacked. He has certainly struck upon my opposition somewhere in his operations against Normann, and that has aroused his anger.[27]

Freytag considered the article of the *Norddeutsche Allgemeine Zeitung* an attack on Stosch's honor which justified either legal

[26] *Ibid.,* pp. 326-32.
[27] To Freytag, Oestrich, Memoirs, III, 12.

action, or, at least, a complaint to the editor. Freytag suggested that as a general Stosch could call upon a military court of honor to protect his position with the Emperor and the Crown Prince. He could approach the Minister of Interior and ask him to use his influence on the editor and send a copy of the letter to Frederick William, or he could seek the support of the Emperor and his heir independent of such action.[28]

Stosch now took defensive measures. He wrote War Minister Bronsart on 15 July 1884 complaining of the attack of the "official newspaper" of 5 July on "an old general." The journal sought to establish his "connection with the parties in enmity to the Government," and he asked Bronsart to take steps to prevent any further attacks.[29]   A copy of the letter was dispatched to the Crown Prince.[30]   Stosch wrote Freytag of his appreciation for his advice. Not only had he informed Frederick William of the measures taken to defend an "old general, flooded with honors by His Majesty," against the charge of being a "revolutionary and an opponent of the Government," but he had also asked Albedyll to give a copy of his letter to the Emperor.[31]   These expressions are conclusive proof that Stosch did not favor the Left Liberals and even considered their moderate program "revolutionary."   Stosch wrote further to Freytag:

The Crown Prince told Normann that I was right in everything; only the interpretation that the Chancellor's attacks were aimed at me was false. I am only the cloak; it is the Crown Prince who is meant.—That view may be quite right, but it only makes the Prince's weakness, in letting it all fall on me, more marked.[32]

The Crown Prince informed him that he had been "very angered" by the attacks on his old friend.[33]

The efforts to silence the press were ultimately successful. The War Minister stated that the *Norddeutsche Allgemeine Zeitung* was not an official journal, so he could do nothing. Stosch retorted that it "was accessible to ministerial approaches." Bronsart

---

[28] To Stosch, Siebleben, 9 July 1884, in Helmolt, *Freytag an Stosch,* pp. 151-52.
[29] Memoirs, III, 14.   [30] *Ibid.*
[31] Oestrich, 17 July 1884, *ibid.,* III, 14-15.
[32] *Ibid.,* III, 15.
[33] Potsdam, 20 July 1884, *ibid.,* III, 19.

then expressed his regret at the attacks, but still felt he could take no action. Albedyll wrote Stosch that since William knew nothing of the affair, it would be better for Stosch to present his case in person. Although a letter to the editor elicited no reply, Stosch felt it "still must have reached the right address, for since then all has been quiet."[34] The press agitation ceased, but there were echoes of the incident. In the Reichstag debate of 26 November 1884 Rickert denied that any Left Liberals had tried to replace Bismarck with Stosch. The Chancellor replied that he had heard of other colleagues besides Stosch who had aimed at supplanting him.[35]

Like much of Bismarck's opposition to Stosch, his attempt to destroy him and the Left Liberals by associating them in the public mind had its tinge of irony. The old General was resolutely opposed to the influence of the Left Liberals on the Crown Princess. In 1885 he expressed his pleasure at the Chancellor's assaults in the Reichstag on the Left Liberal orator Eugen Richter and declared that he was sure the attacks would hit their mark in the Crown Prince's palace. He remarked: "To be sure, it will not bring an improvement; the feelings there are not governed by reason."[36]

Bismarck had attempted, without success, to break the back of the opposition parties in the election of 1884. His aim was to destroy the Left Liberals, Center, and Social Democrats, so that whatever ideas Frederick William may have harbored about coming to an agreement with them could be quashed. He used the device of pushing premature adoption of a military bill to run for seven years. The majority of the Reichstag opposed it, but he was able to create, with a minimum of manipulation, the illusion of danger from abroad. For a time it seemed that he would present Russia as "the enemy," but France became the scapegoat. The vociferous agitation of the French League of Patriots and the popularity of General Boulanger were dressed up by Bismarck as an immediate threat to Germany. The Chancellor refused to com-

---

[34] To Freytag, Oestrich, 30 July 1884, *ibid.*

[35] Kohl, *Bismarck Reden,* X, 264-65; *Verhandlungen des Reichstags,* 6 Leg. Per., I Sess., 1884-1885, 3 Sitz., in LXXIX, 36-37. Cf. Bismarck's speech of 11 Jan. 1888, in Kohl, *Bismarck Reden,* XII, 214.

[36] To Freytag, Oestrich, 25 March 1885. Memoirs, III, 23.

promise on the military measure and magnified the danger from France in the press. In January 1887 the Reichstag amended the military bill by limiting the credits for three years. Bismarck immediately dissolved the body. A bitter election campaign was conducted by him, supported by the "Cartel," a coalition of Conservative, Liberal Imperial, and National Liberal candidates, who favored the Chancellor's protectionist and paternalistic policy. Their overwhelming victory ended the Reichstag threat to Bismarck's domination.[37]

Despite his belief that the fear of France was unfounded,[38] Stosch worked to secure Frederick William's approval of the military bill. At the same time, he aimed to separate the Crown Prince from the oppositional Left Liberals and to bring him into alignment with the National Liberals, who supported the military estimates, Bismarck's policy, and, in general, the status quo. Stosch's two main channels of contact with the National Liberals were their leaders, Rudolf von Bennigsen and Johannes von Miquel. The acquaintance with Bennigsen stemmed from associations in the Reichstag; the friendship with Miquel, the Mayor of Frankfort, resulted from common membership in the Prussian Chamber of Peers, where they found a community of political interest.[39] While Stosch felt that Normann was the man best suited to the task of helping the Crown Princely couple escape from their "unclear" position, resulting from the Left Liberal belief in their support, he visited Potsdam himself and had long conversations with Frederick William.[40] The Crown Princess' close friend, Henriette Schrader, whom she had met in her welfare work, had introduced the Crown Prince to her husband, the Left Liberal deputy, Karl Schrader.[41] Stosch bluntly told the Prince that "nothing could be more dangerous for his position than the reports of Herr Schrader . . . about his

[37] Carroll, *Germany and the Great Powers*, pp. 227-50. Langer, *European Alliances*, pp. 365-88, maintains that the French danger was a real one. See also Eyck, *Bismarck*, III, 296, 377, 431-32, 445, 448-59; Joseph V. Fuller, *Bismarck's Diplomacy at its Zenith* (Cambridge, Mass., 1922); Heinz Trützschler von Falkenstein, *Bismarck und die Kriegsgefahr Jahres 1887* (Berlin, 1924).

[38] To Normann, Oestrich, 2 Feb. 1887, Memoirs, III, 83. Cf. to Freytag, 17 Feb. 1887, *ibid.*, III, 85.

[39] Herzfeld, *Miquel*, II, 114, 384.

[40] To Normann, Oestrich, 2 Feb. 1887, Memoirs, III, 83.

[41] Feder, *Bismarcks grosses Spiel*, p. 45. On 3 March 1887, Stosch told Normann that Schrader "is a complete stranger to me." Memoirs, III, 87.

intimate wishes and thoughts." This dumfounded Frederick William, who remained silent for a long period. However, Stosch secured his support for the military bill, and he was able to assure Bennigsen that the "Crown Prince will act correctly." The National Liberal leader believed that this would insure victory for the Cartel in the elections. Stosch then wrote the Prince that he "must let the world know of his interest in the Army," remarking to Normann: "You will laugh at me and believe I look for the impossible; then I delude myself for King and Fatherland." His intervention was observed, for Windthorst, the leader of the Center party, spoke to him at great length, obviously, the General thought, so that Windthorst's remarks would be repeated to Frederick William. The Centrist leader felt that the Chancellor was a power abroad, "but the opposite at home." No member of the Reichstag was suitable to be his successor. If the late ultrareactionary Field Marshal Wrangel were living in his vigor of 1848, Windthorst would support him for Chancellor. Internal and external danger necessitated placing at the "head a soldier whom the Army trusted."[42] The Centrist leader seems to have been hinting at his party's support of Stosch, if Frederick William appointed him Chancellor.

After the election Stosch continued his efforts to bring closer contact between the National Liberals and the Crown Prince. At the same time he was rather critical of his National Liberal allies. He considered them "dramatizers," for Miquel had handed him a letter from Bennigsen, in which he proposed to demand of Bismarck the advance approval of his party. Stosch dryly commented: "One can demand a great deal, but a lion will not let himself be chained with such threads." He advised Miquel to work toward a reconciliation of his party and the heir to the throne.[43] He had been actuated, in his efforts to bring the National Liberals closer to Victoria, by the "great national upsurge" of the election and by Bismarck's remark to Miquel that he "could only progress with the National Liberals." Miquel had talked with the party leaders and their co-operation seemed assured. Difficulties lay, the National Liberal leader thought, in Bismarck's "ruthlessness" and in

[42] To Normann, Oestrich, 2 Feb. 1887, ibid., III, 80-82.
[43] To Freytag, Oestrich, 3 March 1887, ibid., III, 86.

the Crown Princess, who, "as everyone knows, is in close contact with the Left Liberal party through Herr Schrader." Stosch warned the heir to the throne that "a further move to the left in the Reichstag would deprive him of the support of the German princes." He advised the Crown Prince on 3 March 1887 to receive Miquel and to have the Crown Princess talk with him. Stosch's purpose was to secure mutual co-operation.[44]

The Admiral continued his agitation in a letter to Normann of 13 March 1887. To secure the "cooling of the Crown Princess' love for the Left Liberals," he suggested that Normann point out to her that her attitude would lead Bismarck into the lists against her husband.[45] He wrote:

. . . Germany's strength rests upon the unity of Emperor, Princes, and Reichstag majority. All can yet go well, if the Crown Prince gains a firm footing in political life, but only his wife is in the position to bring him to that.[46]

While he desired to bring about the union between Frederick William and the National Liberals, he was careful to avoid any undue pressure. He decided not to attend the March opening of the Chamber of Peers in Berlin, for he feared that the Prince would think: "He now comes at every moment; there must be some reason for that." At the same time, Stosch disclaimed any personal ambition; he "wanted nothing whatever from him," but worked "only to serve the future."[47] He repulsed Normann's suggestion that he become the Prince's chief adjutant; "I would be made to leave my quiet life without the conviction that I would be serving the common good." He informed his friend on 4 April 1887 that the Crown Prince had wanted to meet Bennigsen and Miquel, but that he dared not for fear of his wife. Stosch had "continually felt" her opposition "through all her friendliness"; if the Prince insisted upon following her advice, there was no place for him. The only possible way to check her domination was to surround the Crown Prince with strong advisers who would persuade him to reach a speedy decision and then face her with a *"fait accompli."*[48] In

---

[44] To Normann, Oestrich, 3 March 1887, *ibid.,* III, 86-88.
[45] Oestrich, *ibid.,* III, 89.   [46] *Ibid.*
[47] To Freytag, Oestrich, 25 March 1887, *ibid.,* III, 90.
[48] Oestrich, *ibid.,* III, 90-91.

short, Stosch admitted the defeat of his attempt to wean Victoria from the Left Liberals and to lead her into co-operation with Bismarck's supporters, the National Liberals. When Miquel gave him a memorandum on the tax question to present to Frederick William, he was forced to advise him that it should not be communicated, because of the "lack of discretion at the Court."[49] Stosch might continue to denounce Schrader's influence on Victoria,[50] but he was able to effect nothing.

2

The main interest of the eighties to Stosch, besides his attempts to defend himself against Bismarck and to bring the Crown Prince closer to the Chancellor through the National Liberals, was the policy of Frederick William when he became Emperor. Like Bismarck,[51] Stosch was concerned, as he had been in the past, to stimulate the Crown Prince's interest and activity in public affairs. His influence was brought to bear through letters, but especially through personal encounters. Frederick William continued to express his gratitude toward Stosch for his advice[52] and sought to bring the General into more regular contact with himself.[53]

The increasing age of William I, eighty-eight in 1885, caused Stosch to prepare a memorandum on the measures to be taken when Frederick William became King and Emperor.[54] His particular concern was the future relationship between the prospective ruler and the reigning German monarchs. Judging by the information he received of the attitudes of the Duke of Coburg through Freytag and of the Baden and Swedish monarchs through Roggenbach, he feared that Frederick William would clash with the

[49] To Normann, Oestrich, 26 April 1887, ibid., III, 94.
[50] To Normann, Oestrich, 1 Dec. 1887, ibid., III, 125.
[51] Freiherr von Mittnacht, Erinnerungen an Bismarck, Neue Folge (4th ed.; Stuttgart and Berlin, 1904), p. 43.
[52] E.g., Crown Prince to Stosch, Potsdam, 3 July 1885, Memoirs, III, 26-27.
[53] In 1883, for example, he asked Stosch to accompany him on an official visit to Spain, but this fell through. To Frau von Rosenstiel, Oestrich, 20 Dec. 1883, ibid., III, 4. Cf. Rich and Fisher, Holstein Papers, II, 46, 148. Holstein's belief that Normann was responsible for the suggestion is probably true, although Stosch's presence on the trips to Italy and the opening of the Suez Canal made him a likely choice in any case. For Stosch's and the Crown Prince's views of the Battenberg Affair, see Memoirs, III, 29, 65, 70.
[54] To Freytag, Oestrich, 14 April 1885, ibid., III, 24.

German princes.[55]   He remarked on July 1885: "The Prince is becoming better known among the princes.   One of them speaks of the unconditional domination of the wife and of the pride of the husband."[56]   The main difficulty arose from Frederick William's vision of himself as the direct heir of the medieval German Empire and not as the lineal descendant of the Prussian Kings.   He wished to assume the title "Frederick IV," instead of Frederick III.[57]   An important constitutional question was at stake.   The German Crown was not given by the Constitution to the Hohenzollern family, but to the King of Prussia.   The line of succession was determined by Prussian law.   Frederick William could, by the Constitution, only become King of Prussia as "Frederick III," and then be proclaimed German Emperor.   If he became "Frederick IV," he would be setting himself above the Constitution and his fellow princes, who were very jealous of their remaining rights.[58]

The peaceful solution of this issue and the insurance of a smooth transition between reigns were the aims of Stosch and his friends in preparing three documents for the Crown Prince to sign when he became Emperor.[59]   Roggenbach, who was deeply disturbed by reports of William's bad health, asked to be invited to "Haus Stosch" in Oestrich at the end of July 1885 and suggested that Justice Minister Friedberg be summoned to the conference. Geffcken wrote Stosch that Roggenbach had invited him also, but the Baden statesman, when showed the letter, categorized it as "simply a lie."   In any event, Friedberg, Roggenbach, and Geffcken gathered at Stosch's house to discuss the policy of the future government.   Geffcken held to the position that he had presented to the Crown Prince in "long documents," which aimed at "immediately" overturning everything.   Roggenbach desired that the Crown Prince take "a position toward the Chancellor."   Stosch was for the "status quo [das Conservieren], but, from the first, remained in the minority in the Crown Council."   The four men agreed upon the

[55] To Normann, Oestrich, 22 July 1885, *ibid.*, III, 31.
[56] *Ibid.*, III, 34. Cf. the King of Saxony's remark on the Crown Prince's pride, Stosch to Normann, Oestrich, 8 Sept. 1885, *ibid.*, III, 40.
[57] Samwer, *Roggenbach,* p. 151; Roggenbach to Stosch, Schopfheim, 18 July 1885, in Heyderhoff, *Im Ring der Gegner,* p. 228.
[58] The constitutional position of the King-Emperor is discussed in Howard, *German Empire,* pp. 29-38.
[59] See Samwer, *Roggenbach,* pp. 150-54.

drafts of a proclamation to the people and a letter to the Chancellor. The proclamation was prepared by Geffcken, revised by all four men, and given the final touches by Roggenbach and Geffcken. Stosch thought these drafts "contained worthwhile thoughts," though none were "beautiful, warm, or really shrewd." He realized that the policy of the future reign would not be determined by manifestoes, but thought it did no harm to prepare the Crown Prince in advance. More important, Stosch felt, were letters to be sent to the Kings of Bavaria, Württemberg, Saxony, and the princes most closely related to Frederick William. They were to be individually prepared, but were to contain the same general opinions. Their purpose was to calm the fears that Frederick William intended to infringe the constitutional rights of the princes. Stosch thought they should be drawn up immediately or the Crown Prince would never adopt them. Friedberg and Roggenbach promised to influence him to accept all the documents; Stosch tried to persuade Normann to do the same. Friedberg advised Roggenbach that the "Crown Princess puts great weight on your opinion and no one brings the Prince to a decision as surely as she does"; he counseled the Baden statesman to gain her support.[60]

After two contentious days with Roggenbach and the Grand Duke of Baden, Frederick William, who championed "his Frederick IV and plans for the subjection of the princes," approved the three documents and had them copied at once. Stosch warned Roggenbach that "he should always remember that the Crown Prince was a man of emotion, who . . . succumbed to a momentary intellectual impulse, but always returned to his first thoughts. Therefore you cannot let go of the Prince now." Stosch cautioned Normann to remember that Roggenbach was to remain the "sole adviser, otherwise the Prince will become mistrustful."[61] Indeed, the Admiral had no expectation that "so weak a man can hold to . . . [a decision] for 24 hours, and only the high-flown sound of the documents makes them agreeable to him."[62]

[60] Stosch to Normann, Oestrich, 8 Aug. 1885, Memoirs, III, 33-36.
[61] To Normann, 20 Aug. 1885, ibid., III, 36-37; Roggenbach's letter of 18 August upon which Stosch bases his information is printed in Heyderhoff, Im Ring der Gegner, pp. 229-31.
[62] To Freytag, Oestrich, 22 Aug. 1885, Memoirs, III, 39.

The proclamation "To My People" and the letter to Bismarck, the first drafts of which had been prepared in Stosch's study in Oestrich, were issued by the Crown Prince when he became the Emperor Frederick III in 1888.[63] The letter to the Princes, the acceptance of the title of "Frederick III," and the references in his address to the Reichstag to upholding the rights of the federal states embodied Stosch's main aims.[64] The proclamation "To My People" spoke of the "unforgettable inheritance of the Hohenzollern dynasty," Frederick's desire to work with the federal governments for the welfare and peace of the land, and his wish to maintain the "inseparable bond between the Prince and the people." His letter to Bismarck thanked the Chancellor for his services to William I and announced his intention of supporting the Constitution and the laws without great changes. He wished to protect the constitutional rights of the federal governments, the Reichstag, and the Emperor under the "highest law" of the "improvement of the public welfare"; to maintain the armed forces; to preserve religious toleration; and to reform finances.[65] This program was liberal only in the sense that Frederick III apparently wanted to curb Bismarck's misuse of power and keep him within constitutional bounds. Parliamentary control of the Army was anathema to him.[66] Stosch and his friends had saved Frederick from coming into instant conflict with the Chancellor and the German princes over his constitutional prerogatives.

However, the Crown Prince accepted the advice of Stosch and his friends only when he became Emperor. Prior to 1888 he continued to announce his adherence to the title of Frederick IV. Stosch remarked in 1885 of Frederick William's speech at Aachen: "He indicated that he felt himself to be the heir of Charlemagne;

[63] Stosch noted no differences of substance in the decrees issued and those drafted. Stosch to Normann, Oestrich, 17 March 1888, *ibid.*, III, 153-54.

[64] The proclamation "To the German Reichstag," Charlottenburg, 19 March 1888, is given in Schuster, *Friedrichs Briefe*, pp. 348-49. Cf. Bismarck's statement in the Bundesrat, in Poschinger, *Bismarcks Bundesrat*, V, 272. The only reference I have found to the letter to the Princes is Freiherr von Marschall's report to the Baden Government, Berlin, 13 March 1888. Otto Gradenwitz, *Bismarcks letzter Kampf, 1888-1898* (Berlin [1924]), p. 61.

[65] Schuster, *Friedrichs Briefe*, pp. 339-43.

[66] Hans Delbrück, *Erinnerungen, Aufsätze und Reden* (3rd ed.; Berlin, 1905), pp. 75-76.

he now wants to shout that out to the world."[67]   Even in December 1887, only four months before his accession, he announced to the appalled Roggenbach that he meant to be proclaimed "Frederick IV, German Emperor,"[68] saying further:

. . . I alone created the German Empire.   My father considered it a matter of secondary importance and still treats it like that.   I intervened; when Bismarck spoke to me after Sedan about crossing the line of the Main River, I bound him to [the idea of] the German Emperor. —When I left Berlin last May, Bismarck came to speak with me about the death of the Emperor.   He said: "I must know what title you will assume."—I answered as above.   He said no word in reply and therefore agrees; with that all the expert, scholarly, and juristic opinions which I have gotten in the matter lose their meaning . . . .   The Crown Princess explained to Roggenbach: "All my arguments do not help a bit here; he insists on it."[69]

Stosch realized that the practical measures the future government of the Crown Prince would institute depended, to a large extent, upon personnel.   In an interview in June 1886 Stosch told Frederick William that a change in program was not necessary if he retained Bismarck.   However, he should work to replace the reactionary Minister of Interior Puttkammer[70] and the Minister of Finance Scholz by such men as the Liberal Imperial Count von Arnim-Boitzenburg, former President of the Reichstag, and the National Liberal Rudolf von Bennigsen.   Stosch related: "This thought was very sympathetic to him; it was likewise agreeable to him to hear that he should not proceed against Bismarck."[71]   The Admiral apprised the National Liberal Miquel that he favored him as successor to Puttkammer.[72]   He wrote Normann on 28 July 1886 that the Crown Prince has "not an atom of will or action . . . or any reliability either."   In other letters Stosch urged Normann to become Minister of the Household or accept the "most discreet position of trust" so that he might "give the Prince occasional backbone."   He hoped that in this position Normann would be-

[67] To Freytag, Oestrich, 22 Aug. 1885, Memoirs, III, 39.
[68] Stosch to Normann, Oestrich, 22 Dec. 1887, ibid., III, 130.
[69] Ibid., III, 130-31.
[70] Stosch had earlier favored the entrance of Puttkammer into the Ministry. Entry of 24 April 1876, in Lucius, Bismarck-Erinnerungen, p. 87.
[71] Stosch to Normann, Oestrich, 15 June 1886, Memoirs, III, 57-59.
[72] Oestrich, 26 June 1886, in Herzfeld, Miquel, II, 56-57.

come as quietly powerful as Lehndorff, Emperor William's Adjutant-General. As for himself, he wanted only "freedom to look for a rest and to enjoy life."[73] It is obvious from his candidates for office in the new reign that, while he opposed a liberal revolution, he worked to replace the more reactionary members of the Government by men of greater independence and respect for the law. He had no desire to force Bismarck out of office, for his attitude toward the Chancellor remained the same as it had been in the past. His statement to Normann on 8 February 1888 may be considered the final estimate of his own feelings toward the Chancellor.[74] He declared: "I cannot love him, but I have to admire him with all my intellectual powers."[75] Holding these views he felt it a patriotic duty to support Bismarck with the Crown Prince, while warning him against the Chancellor's abuse of power.

During the eighties Frederick William's heir, Prince William, began to take a more active interest in public affairs. As a result, relations with his father, who was very jealous of his prerogatives, worsened. As early as 1884, Frederick William was "very bitter" that both Prince William and Herbert Bismarck, the "hereditary Chancellor," had been summoned to Gastein for the "glorification" of the Austro-German Alliance, while he had been ignored.[76] Stosch used this antagonism in an attempt to rouse the Crown Prince from his continued apathy. He wrote to Normann on 2 February 1887:

—I do not need to tell you anything about the Prince's complaints. My aim was to bring him out of the negative role towards people and affairs into which he has fallen. He has repeatedly sent away the Chancellor and treats Herbert as though he did not exist. He said: "I really believe I must let the throne go right to William."—I remarked that the world was beginning to think the same; that struck a spark. I developed the matter in more detail and showed him how the Chancellor could ask himself whether his work would not be on more secure foundations with Prince William . . . .—This had a powerful effect.— Then I lifted him up with the remark that he had been a decisive power to all leading men for a long time.—He: "I could not interfere in

---

[73] Oestrich, 26 June, 9 Aug. 1886, Memoirs, III, 60, 64.

[74] This is suggested by his son, Ulrich, in ibid., I, 273-74.

[75] Oestrich, ibid., III, 143.

[76] Stosch to Freytag, 14 April 1888, ibid., III, 8. For other testimony to this see, e.g., Rich and Fisher, Holstein Papers, II, 46-47.

business."—I: "But you must say what you do not want. They would pay attention to that . . . ."[77]

As Frederick William's fatal illness (see below) progressed, Prince William was naturally proposed as the Emperor's representative in official affairs. Stosch foresaw that if Prince William assumed these duties of his father, "the Crown Prince would be beside himself."[78] The Crown Princess was disturbed by her son's thirst for power and by his relations with the anti-Semites. The Crown Prince declared: "William does intentionally what he knows is disagreeable to me."[79]

The personality of the young Prince was well known to Stosch through his many acquaintances in Berlin. Characteristic of the comments made to him during these years was that of Naval Minister Caprivi, who was angry at William for absenting himself from a ship launching.[80] He declared:

The Prince thinks he knows everything and is always there with his information. He has a big mouth in naval matters too, but he is still surprising, because he knows everything—ship construction, artillery, torpedos . . . . The naval officers are enthusiastic about him.[81]

Despite these and other reports which were hardly favorable, Stosch's thoughts turned, in early 1888, to the idea of effecting a *rapprochement* between Prince William and the National Liberals. He urged Normann to accept the invitation of Liebenau, a member of the young Prince's entourage and later his Chief Court Marshal, to come to Berlin. He noted that, while the Conservatives were well represented among William's associates, the National Liberals were not. This group, he thought, should "form the party capable of governing," because of its "opposition to particularism." He asked Normann to become the intermediary between Liebenau and the National Liberals. Both Miquel, who "had ambition and a wide vision," and Bennigsen, who "lacked initiative," wished to

---

[77] Oestrich, Memoirs, III, 79-80.
[78] To Normann, Oestrich, 15 Aug. 1887, *ibid.*, III, 109.
[79] To Normann, Oestrich, 22 Dec. 1887, *ibid.*, III, 129.
[80] To Freytag, 10 Oct. 1887, *ibid.*, III, 113.
[81] *Ibid.* For additional comments, see especially Stosch to Normann, Oestrich, 15 Dec. 1887, *ibid.*, III, 125-28.

come into contact with Prince William.[82]   Stosch's interest in the
young Prince stemmed partially from his realization that Frederick
William was fatally ill, but also had its roots in the almost complete
disillusion with him.

Meetings and correspondence with Frederick William throughout the eighties saw Stosch continually defeated by a wall of
apathy and indifference.   As early as 1885 the Admiral wrote:

The future monarch is today a rudderless ship dependent upon the tow
line of his wife and her moods.   This is known everywhere in informed
circles . . . . Since Normann's departure the Crown Princely Court
lacks all reasonable people; the Chancellor's belief that he can accomplish more with tools is one of his weaknesses.[83]

Later in the year he described a meeting with Normann to Freytag:

We talked of many things, but could not take a happy view of the
future.   You know the old prophecy which circulates in Berlin, that
the Emperor will live to be over 90 and his successor will be one-armed.
The wretched conclusion of our discussion was that Germany will be
lucky if things turn out that way.

You pained me when you said our attempt to influence the Prince is
a waste of time.   Even if you are right that cannot stop me from following
the beaten path.[84]

The Crown Prince's persistent inertia depressed the aging Admiral.
On 4 May 1886 he saw the Crown Prince and informed Normann:

. . . he began to unburden his heart.   Bismarck, father and son, treat
him simply with scorn.   He feels so isolated; only Albedyll has taken
up with him, because he is in bad with Prince William.—What could
I reply?   I feel sympathy for the Prince in the depths of my soul.   You
must have attended the Good Friday lamentations in a Catholic Ca-
thedral.   They have always deeply moved me; I had exactly the same
feeling at the unending laments of this poor weak soul.   I do not know
of any help for it. . . .[85]

The Crown Prince spoke of the general situation, "naturally with
the bitterest pessimism."   He thought that Bismarck's concessions

[82] Oestrich, 8 Feb. 1888, *ibid.,* III, 143.   On Liebenau and the liberals, see
Bülow, *Memoirs,* I, 87; Rich and Fisher, *Holstein Papers,* II, 47-48.

[83] To Freytag, 11 July 1885, Memoirs, III, 29.

[84] To Freytag, 26 Sept. 1885, *ibid.,* III, 42-43.   Cf. to Normann, Oestrich, 7
Dec. 1885, *ibid.,* III, 47-48.   Older readers will recall "Kaiser Bill's" stunted left
arm.

[85] Oestrich, 5 May 1886, *ibid.,* III, 55.   Cf. pp. 21, 51-53.

to the Catholics would bring difficulties to his reign, while Stosch resolutely maintained the opposite opinion.[86]   He described the conclusion of the interview:

Our conversation on war and peace became lively. He said: "I will not fight a war." I thought that was quite a false philosophy. He must have clear goals for his policy and be aware that he must also use the sword to achieve it. I elaborated on this to him, and he returned repeatedly to it. In short, at the end he was surprisingly lively, and I took my leave once more under the illusion that the Prince would think further of the conversation.[87]

His hopes of the Crown Prince, never high, vanished in the grave.

Early in January 1887[88] the Crown Prince began to suffer from a sore throat and hoarseness, which alarmed his surgeon, who consulted Dr. Gerhardt, Holtzendorff's son-in-law. An operation was performed, but there was little improvement. Professor Bergmann, another specialist, was then called in. Gerhardt and Bergmann decided upon an operation, but Bismarck persuaded the Emperor to forbid it. In May other doctors diagnosed cancer. Bismarck determined that the best specialist in Europe would be summoned, and Dr. Morrell Mackenzie, the British throat specialist, was accordingly brought to Berlin. He suggested that the growth on the Prince's larynx be examined by Rudolf Virchow, the noted pathologist. Virchow declared that the examination showed no signs of cancer, while Bergmann and Gerhardt insisted that their royal patient was suffering from that disease. The controversy over treatment continued until the death of Frederick William and afterward. The Crown Princess was accused in the official press of summoning Mackenzie because he was an Englishman, and Bismarck used this lie to discredit Victoria in the eyes of the German people.[89]

---

[86] *Ibid.*, III, 56.   [87] *Ibid.*

[88] Heyderhoff, *Im Ring der Gegner,* p. 258, contains the first reference (4 April) to the illness in the Stosch-Roggenbach correspondence.

[89] The clinical details of the illness appear *ad nauseam* in Stosch's memoirs and Roggenbach's letters to him. See Ponsonby, *Letters of the Empress Frederick,* pp. 224-316; Eyck, *Bismarck,* pp. 507-10; Sir Morell Mackenzie, *The Fatal Illness of Frederick the Noble* (London, 1888). R. Scott Stevenson, *Morell Mackenzie* (London, 1946), is a modern treatment of the case. He conjectures (pp. 94, 145, 164-67) that Frederick's cancer may have resulted from syphilis, perhaps contracted on the trip to the opening of the Suez Canal. If so, this disease might account, in part, for the Crown Prince's depression, his uneasy attitude toward his wife, and his general weakness of will.

A meeting between the Crown Prince and Stosch took place on 13 and 14 May 1887. Stosch wrote Normann that the Crown Prince had said:

"What does it matter if I die; it is agreeable to me. I feel only one more duty in life: to leave something behind for my daughters. . . ."—With that I describe to you his entire condition. In all the many hours which I passed alone with him, I was never happy for an instant, but, in fact, often had tears in my eyes.—The Prince is helpless, and one feels completely helpless toward him.[90]

Deceived by the official press and his confidants, Stosch thought that the Crown Princess was the "curse of the country," who through support of Mackenzie would make her husband a cripple or a corpse before the end of the year.[91] Learning that the Prince had been told that he had cancer and had decided against an operation, Stosch observed: "It was the greatest moment of his life and all his best qualities came into play. Now he wants a clergyman, but he will not get one [, because of the anticlerical Crown Princess]."[92] His memory returned to his long associations with Frederick William, and he wrote Normann on 30 November 1887:

I have thought back over the many difficult and dangerous days in which I saw the Prince and remembered how I always marveled at his total calm and cold-bloodedness in such situations. That was completely true no matter whether the shot whistled or a difficult responsibility had to be assumed. Only once did I see him lose his head and then on the childish occasion when his camel stampeded. The danger of a fall immediately passed, but it had overpowered his spirit, and he screamed like a child until he sat upon a donkey. The thought of danger is completely foreign to him, but when it thrusts itself upon him without warning, then it masters him; he believes he is upheld by the angels, until he feels the devil's claws in his own flesh.—From this point of view, the behavior of the Crown Princess is perhaps quite correct. He must be prevented from looking death in the face and from that it follows that every operation, even the smallest, can endanger his life.—May the Prince have a speedy end and keep the reputation of

[90] Oestrich, 16 May 1887, Memoirs, III, 94.
[91] To Normann, Oestrich, 10 Oct. 1887, *ibid.*, III, 113.
[92] To Normann, Oestrich, 13 Nov. 1887, *ibid.*, III, 117. Cf. Stosch to Freytag, Oestrich, 13 Nov. 1887, *ibid.*, III, 118.

a courageous and fine man. He was always a handsome and lovable person, and he will remain one to the end.[93]

While Stosch was critical of Victoria's conduct, he defended her against the bitter remarks of the Empress Augusta, not "from a feeling of justice, but from pity"; "after all, she still has the most to lose."[94]

The long-awaited moment finally arrived. On 9 March 1888 the Crown Prince Frederick William was proclaimed Frederick III, King of Prussia, German Emperor. Stosch's thoughts turned first, not to the new monarch, but to his old sovereign, William I. He wrote to Normann the same day:

For the last 30 years, all my thoughts and deeds were closely bound to the Emperor; I owe the splendor and richness of my life to him alone. How often have I felt his goodness and favor and was proud in my innermost heart. When I knelt before him to receive the Order of the Black Eagle, he softly said to me: "You have been true to me and have proved yourself wherever I have placed you."—Believe me, those words ring in my ears today and move my soul.[95]

Since the first days of his friendship with the Crown Prince, Stosch's efforts had been directed at educating him for his future duties and at bringing him in harmony with his father's Government. During the final years of Frederick William's life, the Admiral had tried to stimulate in him an interest in public affairs and attempted to reconcile him with Bismarck. One of Stosch's chief goals had been to protect the constitutional settlement of 1871 and the rights of the German princes. His efforts encountered Frederick William's passivity, indifference, and mystic belief in the inheritance of the Holy Roman Empire. Victoria, who exercised a predominant influence over her husband, opposed him. Hating Bismarck with good reason, she desired a ministry responsible to the Reichstag. Stosch hoped to direct her into a more conservative course and wished to curb her influence, but, with no plan of action, and it is difficult to imagine any plan that would have succeeded, he could do very little. It was certain by 1888

[93] Oestrich, *ibid.*, III, 121-22.
[94] Stosch to Normann, Oestrich, 19 Nov. 1887, *ibid.*, III, 121.
[95] Oestrich, *ibid.*, III, 149.

that the Empress would not turn to him for advice and that he did not look to the new reign for power or honors.

3

The hopes of an entire generation were blasted when a dying man ascended the throne on 9 March 1888. Since his father had become King of Prussia in 1861, Frederick William had been the focal point of opposition hopes and aspirations. Fatally ill and speechless, the fifty-six-year-old monarch had no opportunity to put into effect any sweeping program of reforms. Indeed, it is doubtful that he had intended any. It is certain that his wife, the talented and energetic Victoria, wished the government to be chosen by the Reichstag. Her husband's weakness of will and lack of firm political conviction place in real doubt any belief that he would have energetically carried out such a program, even if he had been physically able. It is true that he dismissed the reactionary Minister of Interior Puttkammer, as Stosch had desired, and decorated some prominent Left Liberals, but there is a strong suspicion that Bismarck approved Puttkammer's departure and merely wished to escape the responsibility for it, while the decorations were given for professional activities, not for political opinions. The Empress, secretly advised by Ludwig Bamberger, the Left Liberal leader, was powerless, and the official press attacked her openly. It seems probable that, had he lived, Frederick III would have maintained the status quo and ruled in accordance with the existing constitutional organization, while taking a strong interest only in increasing imperial powers over the twenty-five states. There would have been no sweeping changes, but Bismarck's ruthlessness might well have been curbed and the more reactionary and subservient ministers might have been replaced by less conservative and more independent statesmen.[96]

Stosch discussed his relations with the Emperor Frederick and the Empress Victoria in a letter to Normann on the day of the ac-

[96] Eyck, *Bismarck,* III, 512-30; Ponsonby, *Letters of the Empress Frederick,* chap. xi; Dorpalen, "Frederick III," *American Historical Review,* LIV, 1-31; Feder, *Bismarcks grosses Spiel,* pp. 51-59, 340-405. Stosch also attributed Puttkammer's dismissal to Bismarck's intrigues. To Normann, Oestrich, 8 June 1888, Memoirs, III, 166.

cession. He recalled that his friendship was closer with Frederick III than with his father[97]

. . . but he completely lacks inner and outer resolution. A short time ago, when Seckendorff left [San Remo], the present Emperor said with great warmth: "Stosch is my friend." He knew that, but then asked his wife for permission to send me his greetings.—Roggenbach tells me that the Crown Princess [sic] said of me during his recent visit to San Remo: "I treasure his good characteristics, but he has made much trouble for us."—She has felt my opposition, and for years his [Frederick's] power has extended only far enough to let himself be led by her.[98]

Stosch was concerned to see who would be appointed to represent the Empress and the *"mystique* of Empire" in Frederick's councils. He was surprised and pleased that the Crown Prince had been proclaimed "Frederick III," instead of "Frederick IV," and would be proclaimed King of Prussia before he became German Emperor.[99] Berlin gossips believed that Stosch had been summoned to the capital by the new Empress,[100] and on 13 March Waldersee noted rumors of the presence of "General Stosch, one of the candidates for Chancellor."[101] As a matter of fact, Stosch had come to Berlin only for William I's funeral. He apprised Normann on 15 March that the new Emperor, who "had often pictured to me how he would march to music into the hall to receive the oaths of allegiance," was prevented from having a coronation. Now "music will only accompany his path to the grave, a terrible irony of fate." He recorded that the "liberal appearance" of Frederick's beliefs was already waning.[102]

Thus he went to Berlin, but did not see the Emperor nor did he want to see him. He only regretted that he could not recommend Normann to him as an adviser. He found everyone in Berlin bitter at Frederick for making no decisions, and at Victoria for her treatment of her husband. The only signs of the Emperor's

---

[97] Oestrich, *ibid.,* III, 149.   [98] *Ibid.,* III, 149-50.
[99] *Ibid.,* III, 151-52.
[100] Kiderlen-Wächter to Ambassador von Radowitz, 12 March 1888, in Ernst Jäckh, *Kiderlen-Wächter, der Staatsman und der Mensch: Briefwechsel und Nachlass* (Berlin and Leipzig, 1925), I, 104.
[101] Waldersee, *Denkwürdigkeiten,* I, 373.
[102] Oestrich, Memoirs, III, 152-53.

political views were the decorations that he had bestowed and the proclamations he had issued. Stosch recalled that the first drafts had been prepared in his own home and was curious to see how soon Geffcken would make known "to the world" his participation in the preparation of these "empty words." It had been planned in 1885, he told Normann, to have Frederick make Bismarck "Duke of Lauenburg," and he felt the Emperor had acted wrongly in not doing this. He feared that Bismarck would come into conflict with Frederick.[103]

Stosch's presence in Berlin was widely noticed and produced a crop of unfounded rumors. The diplomat Stolberg believed that the Empress had refused to approve an appointment, because Stosch was said to favor it. Agricultural Minister Lucius reported that Bismarck was not displeased by this friction in the ranks of his opponents, while he felt that the General had not acted to his own best interest, for it had long been expected that he would become Frederick's Minister of the Household. Caprivi, Chief of the Admiralty, asserted that Stosch had long wished to be Frederick's chief adjutant so that he could play a powerful political role behind the scenes. The Naval Chief thought Stosch had encountered the opposition of Bismarck to his plans, and knowingly stated that Stosch had aroused Victoria's hatred by strongly opposing her wish to give precedence to English newspaper correspondents at a fleet review. Bismarck, on 22 March, was "visibly satisfied to know that his old opponent was out of action," and that he could remain the "unchallenged master of all transactions."[104]

The course of the new reign was anxiously watched by Stosch. He reported that Friedberg had opposed Frederick's wish to grant a general amnesty. Stosch favored it, as well as the release of the Social Democrats and the ennoblement of many individuals.[105] He continued to regret that the Emperor did not appoint Normann a member of his household. The press attacks against the Empress,

[103] To Normann, Berlin, 17 March 1888, and Oestrich, 29 March 1888, *ibid.*, III, 153-55. William II later conferred this title on Bismarck.

[104] Entries of 22 and 23 March 1888, in Lucius, *Bismarck-Erinnerungen,* pp. 439-40. Schröder, *Stosch,* p. 96, again without citation, repeats Caprivi's story of the English newspaper correspondents and places it during the Danzig Fleet Review of 1881. This tale seems more the product of malicious Berlin gossip, which seldom spared Victoria, than of an actual incident.

[105] To Normann, Oestrich, 29 March 1888, Memoirs, III, 154-55.

inspired by Bismarck, were not "sharp" enough for Stosch, for she "works behind the scenes against the general welfare and undermines monarchial power." She was not to be controlled by "smiles and courtesies, and she often told me that she was to be led only by fear." She had been misused by the press, he claimed, but, if Germany had the English press, it would not have acted with greater discretion.[106] Stosch wrote on 17 May of the Emperor's physical condition and inability to speak:

It is a heart-rending situation.—Misfortune has robbed the Empress of her reasoning powers.—Everyone . . . speaks with the greatest appreciation of the tenderness with which Bismarck handles everything and agrees to guide. All eyes are turned to the Crown Prince [William], but yet no one is sure of him, even Bismarck. He [William] said of Frederick the Great that he would never have become great, if he had had the misfortune to inherit a minister like Bismarck. No one believes in lasting harmony between the two.[107]

Stosch asked Miquel to instruct the future sovereign in a real program of reform in order to "calm the liberal elements."[108]

On 18 May Stosch received an invitation from Frederick III to come to Berlin and witness the marriage of his son, Prince Henry. Stosch was pleased, but did not expect to stay long in the capital.[109] As soon as he arrived at the Hotel Kaiserhof in the middle of May 1888, he received the order to report to the Emperor before noon. He was informed when he arrived at Charlottenburg Palace that Frederick had gone through extreme suffering, but would be pleased to be told that he was looking well. Stosch was summoned to him. Frederick "sat half-reclining by an open window, stood up, kissed and embraced me, sat down again, took up his pad and wrote: 'You look splendid.' " He was pale and thin and "death looked from his eyes." They discussed Prince Henry's future and the Emperor's own plans. This last interview between the old friends lasted fifteen minutes, and Stosch was "quite broken up" by it. He was advised to see the Empress and was received by her with "beaming heartiness," but when she discussed "her hard fate," she "seemed as if she were going to burst into tears." They

[106] To Normann, Oestrich, 16 April 1888, ibid., III, 157-58.
[107] To Frau von Rosenstiel, ibid., III, 159-60.
[108] Miquel to Bennigsen, Frankfurt, 5 May 1888, Oncken, Bennigsen, II, 542.
[109] To Normann, Oestrich, 18 May 1888, Memoirs, III, 160-61.

were interrupted and she pressed him to return. However, after witnessing the marriage, he immediately left the capital. Stosch believed that she was excluded from Frederick's councils by his advisers and now sought to regain her husband's ear by calling in old friends.[110] He wrote to Normann on 28 May: "She has carefully removed anyone who could give the Emperor power to rule alone. Now she is astonished that there is no help at hand. How often she must look longingly for you."[111]

When articles appeared in the press speculating on his appointment to some post, Stosch termed them nonsense.[112] He explained:

The people desire a sign of liberal convictions, which they, without knowledge, expected from the new Emperor. Alterations in the highest regions are the first requirement . . . . Of all the men who stood near the Emperor in former times, I hope to be the only one who receives no sign of favor now; in Berlin, I worked with all my strength to that end. I want nothing more from the world than a peaceful existence here in Oestrich.[113]

While the press speculated, the Empress was writing to her secret adviser, Ludwig Bamberger:

Herr von Normann is unfortunately so National Liberal, and Stosch swears by Bennigsen and Miquel . . . . Stosch is *so* venomous against me, hates England with so blind a fury, is, in general, vehemently clumsy and tactless, and, at the same time, unfortunately *so tyrannical,* that it is not advisable to allow him any influence. Normann and Stosch are one . . . . Stosch has turned back very much to Bismarck.[114]

Under these circumstances Stosch might well term the newspaper articles "nonsense." He had no desire to serve under the Emperor Frederick, both because he was in complete disagreement with the Empress and because such a position could have no permanent influence. He had no ambition for such a post and realized that neither Victoria nor Bismarck would permit him to return to office.

[110] To Normann, Oestrich, 28 May 1888, *ibid.,* III, 161-63.
[111] *Ibid.,* III, 163. [112] *Ibid.,* III, 164.
[113] To Frau von Rosenstiel, Oestrich, 5 June 1888, *ibid.,* III, 164-65.
[114] N.d., *ca.* 21 May 1888, in Feder, *Bismarcks grosses Spiel,* pp. 322-23. Cf. Egon, Count Corti, *Wenn . . . : Sendung und Schicksal einer Kaiserin* (Graz, Vienna, Cologne, [1954]), p. 488.

His political ambitions were for others. He even wondered about the possibility of Miquel's becoming Bismarck's successor.[115]

The news of Frederick's death on June 15, 1888, after a reign of ninety-nine days, came as a great relief to Stosch. He promised "to forget the Empress' madness," for "she has received her sentence and cannot escape punishment, but I will leave the execution of it to others."[116] He attended the Emperor's funeral.[117] For over twenty years he had striven to prepare Frederick William for his reign. He had sought to develop in him an interest in public affairs and a reliance on independent men. His efforts had met with failure. Frederick William, whose only real function in life would begin after he became King and Emperor, became depressed as his father lived on, and he lost himself in fantastic dreams of medieval splendor. His wife's superior talents and greater activity were a constant reproach to him. Attempts to rouse him from his dreams and apathy were unsuccessful. Only the external attributes of royal power appealed to him. Dying he could have no real influence on the course of events, even if he had desired to exert any. He had placed high value on the outspoken opinions of his old friend Stosch, who had ridden into battle with him. Stosch's advice to Frederick was the result of ambition for power and a feeling of duty to his country and his royal house. As time passed, his ambition flickered out, but motivated by patriotic feeling, he continued his futile efforts to influence the Crown Prince. Only death dissolved their old friendship in 1888. However, Bismarck had a long memory, and he forgave Stosch neither his friendship with Frederick nor his independence. Bismarck seized the opportunity to strike at his rival late in 1888.

4

The *Deutscher Rundschau* published on 20 September 1888 a short anonymous article entitled "Selections from the Emperor Frederick's Diaries." Heinrich Geffcken had read Frederick's war diary 1870-1871 years before and had copied portions of it.

[115] To Normann, Oestrich, 8 June 1888, Memoirs, III, 166. Cf. Herzfeld, *Miquel*, II, 123-24.

[116] To Normann, Oestrich, 15 June 1888, Memoirs, III, 166.

[117] *Ibid.*; Normann to Freytag, 11 July 1888, in Gustav Freytag, *Briefe an seine Gattin* (Berlin, 1912), p. 177.

He now published those sections which criticized Bismarck, attested to Frederick's liberal views, and emphasized his desire to proclaim the Empire.[118]   Bismarck in a conversation with Busch said, "I myself consider the diary even more genuine than you do," but he proposed to treat it as a forgery.[119] He reported to Emperor William II on 23 September that the diary in its published form "was not genuine." He asserted that he had not been permitted by William I to inform Frederick of state policy during the Franco-German War, because the Emperor feared his son would betray secrets to the Francophile English court, and because of Frederick's "political advisers of doubtful capacity." Bismarck charged that the publication contained errors both of fact and of chronology. If the diary were genuine, its editor could be punished under the law against disclosing state secrets. Since it was not, the editor could be brought to trial under the law of libel. This mendacious report was approved by William II, though it slandered his own father, and was published in the official gazette on 27 September.[120] Bismarck's aim was manifestly to discredit Frederick and his friends. The Empress Frederick wrote her mother, Queen Victoria, on 29 September, that she could call Blumenthal, Stosch, and others to attest to the authenticity of the diary selections, but she did not desire to see them ruined.[121]   Geffcken was arrested the next day and brought to trial.[122]

The relations between Stosch and Geffcken[123] had been cool from their first encounter, more than twenty years before, and the Admiral received little enjoyment from Geffcken's unsolicited visits.

[118] On the Geffcken affair, see Eyck, *Bismarck,* III, 531-40; Herbert Richter, "Heinrich Geffcken und seine Veröffentlichung des Tagebuches Kaiser Friedrichs," *Festschrift Martin Bollert zum 60. Geburtstag* (Dresden, 1936), pp. 240-54; Ponsonby, *Letters of the Empress Frederick,* chap. xiii; *Deutscher Geschichtskalender,* 1888, II, 43-76; 1889, I, 1-13, 364-66; Wahl, *Deutsche Geschichte,* II, 485-92; Meisner, *Friedrichs Tagebuch 1870-1871,* Foreword.

[119] Busch, *Bismarck,* III, 194-95.

[120] Friedrichsruh, 23 Sept. 1888, Bismarck, *Gesammelte Werke,* VIc, 395-97.

[121] Ponsonby, *Letters of the Empress Frederick,* p. 349.

[122] Eyck, *Bismarck,* III, 337.

[123] Stosch's reaction to Ernest II of Coburg's pamphlet, *Another Program of the 99 Days* gives an indication of his attitude toward the Geffcken affair; see Helmolt, *Freytag an Stosch,* pp. 211-12; Freytag, *Briefe an seine Gattin,* p. 265; *Deutscher Geschichtskalender,* 1889, I, 17-18; Arthur G. Lee, ed., *The Empress Frederick Writes to Sophie* (London, 1955), p. 56; Stosch to Freytag, 4 Oct. 1888, Memoirs, III, 183.

His last visit to Stosch before his arrest was apparently on 13 September 1888, when he came to ask his opinion of an article on naval warfare of the future. The Admiral observed: "It is amusing with what impudence and assurance he writes about things which must remain completely foreign to him." With rather malicious glee, he showed the retired professor Admiral Batsch's comment on his recent article on the English fleet maneuvers, which read: "It must have been written by a merchant."[124] Although Stosch thought that Geffcken would be freed, he believed him "guilty of a breach of trust." He had no right to publish the diary, but he had gotten an "itchy pocket" and "wanted to make a journalistic coup."[125] Stosch concluded: "It has always been his ambition to acquire secrets and his particular joy to boast and show off about them. That is avenged now. You [Freytag] are quite right: 'The moth has flown into the flame.' "[126]

Events now came in rapid succession. Roggenbach wrote Stosch that the police had broken into his house and seized his correspondence with Geffcken. Fortunately, he had already burned the Admiral's letters to himself. He knew nothing about the publication of the diary, but Bismarck planned to destroy all the Emperor Frederick's intimates and his hate was particularly directed against Roggenbach, whose influence he feared on William II and the Grand Duke of Baden. Justice Minister Friedberg was in the ironic position of prosecuting his former associates. Victoria wrote: "These thing are allowed and sanctioned by William against his father's most trusted and oldest friends!!!"[127]

The Admiral was outraged by the Chancellor's action. Bismarck, he maintained, could have simply asked Roggenbach whether he had assisted Geffcken, but, "blind in his anger," he had ordered the police search. He thought that the Chancellor was perhaps proceeding against Victoria by these means and decided to burn his correspondence with Frederick, for "it alone could

---

[124] To Freytag, Oestrich, 15 Sept. 1888, *ibid.*, III, 182.
[125] *Ibid.*, III, 183-84.   [126] *Ibid.*, III, 184.
[127] Roggenbach to Stosch, Mainau, 26 Sept. 1888, in Heyderhoff, *Im Ring der Gegner*, p. 294; same to same, Schopfheim, 16 Oct. 1888, *ibid.*, pp. 294-96; Empress Frederick to Queen Victoria, 30 Oct. 1888, in Ponsonby, *Letters of the Empress Frederick*, p. 356; Stosch to Freytag, Oestrich, 20 Oct. 1888, Memoirs, III, 184.

give the great man a headache and it is my duty to spare him."[128]
He related that Roggenbach was cited as a witness in the Geffcken
trial and was questioned about the people mentioned in his confiscated letters, "particularly searchingly about me." Fortunately
for Stosch, the "St." referred to in the letters was "in most cases"
Stockmar. Both Stosch and Freytag were summoned as witnesses.
Stosch had been called by Geffcken to testify to his "respect for the
Chancellor." The old general was asked by the prosecutor what
he knew of the diary and what had prompted Geffcken to publish
it. He testified that Frederick's diary "was, in general, only the
reworking of his daily letters to his wife,"[129]   and that Frederick
had told him in 1886 or 1887 that he could not show him his
diary because it contained too much personal material, and that he
did not wish it published because it touched upon too many
political matters. Stosch declared that Geffcken was aware that
its publication would endanger the welfare of the Empire.[130]   The
Admiral did not disclose, if he remembered, that he had read a
version of the diary in 1875.[131]

Stosch returned from Berlin, the "parade ground of passions,"
after being forced to attend the trial under the threat of a penalty
of three hundred marks. He had been called, he wrote, to "en-
tangle" Geffcken; "this aroused my especial anger and made me
bull-headed." He considered it "comical that the Chancellor again
wishes to show the world that I am a criminal."[132]   The draft of
Frederick's proclamation to the people had been found in Geffcken's
papers, and the Chancellor was outraged by this new information.
In late November Stosch saw Bismarck's actions as attempts to
destroy his supposed successor, Roggenbach. The Chancellor had
gone to the Emperor with extracts from Roggenbach's confiscated
correspondence and had convinced him that he harbored a "viper
in his bosom." Stosch had escaped unscathed, but said that he

---

[128] Stosch to Freytag, 20 Oct. 1888, Memoirs, III, 184-85. It is certain that
he did not burn all of Frederick's correspondence with him and doubtful that he
burned any. His letters to Frederick had been returned by Victoria earlier in the
year. Empress Frederick to Stosch, Friedrichskron, 18 July 1888, ibid., III, 174.
[129] Stosch to Freytag, 11 and 24 Nov. 1888, ibid., III, 185-86.
[130] Deutscher Geschichtskalender, 1888, II, 59, 71.
[131] Stosch to Freytag, Oestrich, 13 July 1875, Memoirs, II, 101.
[132] The first attempt in the seventies to accuse Stosch of treason over the
Treaty of Ferrières is referred to here.

had burned "all letters of importance."[133]   The whole business was "horrible" to him, and the reports that the trial would continue before the Supreme Court at Leipzig disturbed his rest.   The press had treated Roggenbach "basely."   He had been totally innocent, but "they have succeeded in blackening him."[134]   Bismarck now proceeded to even greater lengths.   An attack in the *Kölnische Zeitung* of 15 December on the British Ambassador to Russia, Sir Robert Morier, accusing him of betraying German state secrets to the French in 1870 and of representing "English interests" at the Crown Princely Court, offered further evidence to substantiate the belief that Bismarck was attacking both the Empress Frederick and the memory of her husband.[135]   Stosch observed to Freytag:

> That now the young Emperor dishonors his father and mother by the attacks upon his name and lets lying filth be thrown at the noble figure of the Crown Prince, who was loved by the people like none other, has been detrimental to his own authority and to monarchial feeling.[136]

Sir Robert Morier published on 31 December his correspondence with Herbert Bismarck, which disproved the Chancellor's charges and placed Herbert in a very unfavorable light.   Geffcken was freed on 5 January 1889.   The Bismarck-inspired *Kölnische Zeitung* of 6 January charged that the trial had coincided with an attempt to displace the Chancellor and declared that the decision would help perpetuate the legend that the Emperor Frederick had been "guilty" of supporting the Left Liberal program.[137]   Stosch viewed the outcome of the Geffcken and Morier affairs as a "profound defeat of the Chancellor."   He considered the conclusion of the *Kölnische Zeitung* article, which accused men behind Geffcken of trying to force Bismarck's resignation, as "classic," and he noted

[133] To Frau von Rosenstiel, Oestrich, 29 Nov. 1888, Memoirs, III, 186-88. Stosch did not burn the major portion of Roggenbach's letters to him, for they are published in Heyderhoff, *Im Ring der Gegner*, pp. 155-447.   On the other hand, Stosch's letters to Roggenbach appear in his memoirs only after the Geffcken trial started, except for a mere handful printed in *Im Ring der Gegner*.   However, Roggenbach became Stosch's most trusted correspondent only after Normann's death in July 1888, and the loss of his correspondence with Roggenbach previous to that time is thus not as serious as it might otherwise have been.

[134] To Freytag, Oestrich, 6 Dec. 1888, Memoirs, III, 183-84.

[135] Stosch to Freytag, 20 Dec. 1888, *ibid.*, III, 190; *Deutscher Geschichtskalender*, 1888, II, 56-57.

[136] 20 Dec. 1888, Memoirs, III, 190.

[137] *Deutscher Geschichtskalender*, 1889, I, 1-2, 13-14.

that the journal had produced no proof. He believed that both he and Roggenbach were the targets of the attack, which resulted from Bismarck's *"cauchemar des conspirations,"* to quote Schuvalov, Russian Ambassador to Berlin.[138] In a letter of 21 January the Admiral disclaimed any close connection with Geffcken and declared that he had been "very outspoken" with him. It was a "puzzle" to Stosch why Roggenbach had maintained relations with Geffcken, who was "an entertaining man from the versatility of his knowledge and connections, but his offensiveness and his desire to surpass everyone causes distrust."[139]

Bismarck continued his attacks. On 17 January 1889 Justice Minister Friedberg was dismissed. Eugen Richter's Left Liberal *Freisinnige Zeitung* noted that Friedberg had taken part in the preparation of Frederick's decrees. The press in general ascribed his fall to the failure of the Geffcken trial and to the disclosure of his connection with the late Emperor. On 19 January the bill of particulars against Geffcken was published, his correspondence with Roggenbach was given to the Bundesrat, and selections appeared in the *Kölnische Zeitung.*[140] There was a strong reaction against Bismarck in the Reichstag, but the National Liberals held to a reserved position, since Miquel feared that a defense of Bismarck's victims might rebound to the discredit of Stosch and Roggenbach.[141] The Princess of Wied suggested that Stosch persuade Roggenbach to emigrate.[142] Stosch was able to change her mind from this "mad idea to punish himself, because he was treated basely."[143] Stosch asked Hahnke, Chief of the Military Cabinet, to protect the interests of his officer son. This letter was shown to

[138] To Roggenbach, Oestrich, 6 Jan. 1889, Memoirs, III, 192. Schuvalov's statement usually is given as *"cauchemar des coalitions,"* and in reference to foreign, not domestic, policy.

[139] To a "young friend," Hermann Oncken, in "Zur 'Erinnerungen an Franz von Roggenbach' von Karl Samwer," *Historische Zeitschrift,* CVIII (1912), 623. When this article was reprinted, Oncken changed "young friend" to "military friend." Hermann Oncken, *Historisch-politische Aufsätze und Reden* (Munich and Berlin, 1914), II, 272.

[140] *Deutscher Geschichtskalender,* 1889, I, 5-8, 365-66.

[141] Herzfeld, *Miquel,* II, 122.

[142] Segenhaus, 28 Jan. 1889, in Heyderhoff, *Im Ring der Gegner,* pp. 312-13.

[143] Stosch to Freytag, 29 Jan. 1889, Memoirs, III, 194-95. Cf. same to same, 7 Feb. 1889, *ibid.,* III, 195.

William II, who sent his thanks to Stosch.[144]   The whole Geffcken affair, coupled with the Morier incident, may have first aroused William II's distrust of his Chancellor. William II may have been also influenced by the mediation of Roggenbach's patron, the Grand Duke of Baden, and by Stosch's letter to Hahnke.[145] Stosch's final summary of the affair appears in a letter to Freytag of 13 February:

> I follow with anxious attention the battle of the Chancellor against the consequences of the Geffcken trial. I know my great friend; he cannot get over it. He begins to see ghosts and hunts them, and yet no other man can overthrow him. He is his own enemy. One realizes that, from the report to the Emperor on, anger has been his counselor, and now when all parties in the Reichstag express their disapproval, if only by silence, he upbraids the National Liberals for not helping him![146]

His friendship with Frederick III was one of the most decisive factors influencing Stosch's career and his relations with Bismarck. Had Frederick William come to the throne in the seventies or early eighties, it is probable that Stosch would have played a key role in the government. As it was, the friendship helped shorten the period of his public activity and disturbed his life even after Frederick's death.

Albrecht von Stosch's belief that the German Government should rest upon a cordial alliance between the Emperor, the confederated princes, and the Reichstag emerges clearly in the eighteen-eighties. Friederick William, in Stosch's opinion, should work in close friendship with his fellow princes and not shatter the constitutional settlement of 1871 by the impractical, romantic

---

[144] To a "young friend" (see n. 139), in Oncken, "Bericht," *Historische Zeitschrift*, CVIII, 633.

[145] Historians merely surmise that the Geffcken affair must have aroused William's distrust of Bismarck. E. Gagliardi, *Bismarcks Entlassung* (Tübingen, 1927-41), I, 10; Wilhelm Schüssler, *Bismarcks Sturz* (Leipzig, 1921), pp. 28-29.

[146] Memoirs, III, 195-96. The Geffcken affair helped restore relations between Stosch and Victoria and they were outwardly cordial, if not really friendly, until his death. See *ibid.*, III, 166, 169, 171-75, 197-98, 206-7, 229, 234, 255-56, 309, 330; Ponsonby, *Letters of the Empress Frederick*, pp. 386, 389, 445; Hassell, *Tirpitz*, p. 21. Stosch considered Freytag's sketch of Frederick III a faithful one, as did the Grand Duke of Baden. Stosch deplored the break between Freytag and Roggenbach, which resulted from its publication. See Gustav Freytag, *Der Kronprinz und die deutschen Kaiserkrone: Erinnerungsblätter* (6th ed.; Leipzig, 1889); Helmolt, *Freytag an Stosch*, pp. 223, 227; Freytag, *Briefe an seine Gattin*, p. 305; Heyderhoff, *Im Ring der Gegner*, pp. 335-36, 341-42; Memoirs, III, 203-5.

gesture of proclaiming himself the heir of Charlemagne.   The
Crown Prince should also seek a prop in the National Liberals, who
were rallying behind Bismarck and the status quo, and even appoint them and Conservatives as ministers of state.   Stosch was
thus willing to go further than Bismarck in co-operating with the
Reichstag.   However, parliamentary co-operation, not Reichstag
control, was Stosch's aim.   He strongly opposed the "revolutionary" Left Liberals, who desired a ministry chosen by the Reichstag,
and came into serious conflict with Victoria.   He envisaged as
the most powerful official a figure like William's Adjutant-General,
not a ministry responsible to the Reichstag.   Frederick should retain and uphold Bismarck, but should bridle his power with the
support of the confederated princes, able, independent, and conservative ministers, and a willing Reichstag.   Stosch's views of
government were to find more explicit expression in the closing
years of his life.

VIII

THE CLOSING YEARS

1

The closing years of Albrecht von Stosch's life brought no lessening of his keen interest in politics, the Army and the Navy, and the world about him. His long career in the service of Prussia and Germany had brought contact with the leading statesmen, soldiers, and admirals of the day, who kept him informed of developments. During these years of retirement, he had more time for theoretical speculation, and his conservatism found clear expression.

The progress of the German Navy, to which he had devoted the concluding years of his active career, continued to stimulate his concern and criticism. Freed of the restraints of his official position, he was able to state his views more openly. He wrote an article entitled "German Colonization," which, polished by Freytag, was published anonymously in the *Kölnische Zeitung* of 22 July 1883. In it he examined the question: What group—missionaries, merchants, or peasants—was best suited to settle German colonies?[1] The missionaries were not good colonizers, he felt, because they were "strong Christians, but weak Germans." The German merchant abroad had little national feeling, because he had been dependent until recently upon the English fleet for protection. The German peasant did emigrate, as a rule, with his entire family and thus with the germ of a state. If the hundred thousand Germans who emigrated yearly could be channeled to one spot, a self-sufficient colony could be established. However, they were composed of too many diverse elements to make this possible, and be-

[1] Freytag to Stosch, Wiesbaden, 8 June and 20 June 1883, in Helmolt, *Freytag an Stosch*, pp. 142-43, 308 n. 219.

sides, their goal was usually the United States. The chief cause of emigration lay in military service. The Government should lighten this burden in the colonies and perhaps rely on the Landwehr for the training and defense of the colonists. Country people were the best settlers and they could be directed to one spot by the Colonial Society. A colony, however, should be settled only by the free choice of voluntary emigrants. If the colonists looked to the state or the Church for continual assistance, they would not prosper. Colonies founded by such means were always a mistake; "We need only to think of Texas [sic]."[2]

The Admiral also wrote and planned to publish an article entitled, "The German Navy and Colonization" through the medium of his friend Freytag. He prepared it during September and November 1884, but it was refused by the Kölnische Zeitung. He then submitted it as a memorandum to his successor as Chief of the Admiralty, General v. Caprivi.[3] The memorandum opened by noting that the German Navy had already taken the first steps toward a colonial policy. The German trader, formerly dependent for his security on the small scope of his operations or on a foreign power, could now look to the German fleet for protection. The Navy would have to be increased. The Germans should re-conquer both world trade and the European carrying trade which the English had captured at the time of Napoleon. German ships and machine construction were superior to the English, and the Admiralty had fostered them by building warships in German yards and by training technicians. The North German Lloyd ought to follow this example. Caprivi's plan for the fleet, with its emphasis on the torpedo and the protection of the coasts, was based on false premises. Domination of the high seas would reduce attacks on the coasts to a minimum; if the fleet tried to de-fend everything, it would protect nothing. In any case, defense of the coasts was the Army's duty. Besides commanding the seas, the Navy should defend "our world interests." Turning to coloni-

[2] [Albrecht von Stosch,] "Deutsche Colonisation," Kölnische Zeitung, Sunday, 22 July 1883, zweite Blatt. Stosch's final remark perhaps alludes to the abortive "Texas-Verein." See Heinz Gollwitzer, Die Standesherren (Stuttgart, [1957]), pp. 322-26, for a brief account.
[3] Stosch to Freytag, Oestrich, 30 Sept., 12 Nov. 1884, 1 Jan. 1885, Memoirs, III, 21-22; Freytag to Stosch, Wiesbaden, 30 Nov., 20 Dec. 1884, 26 Jan., 4 Feb. 1885, Helmolt, Freytag an Stosch, pp. 156-58.

zation, Stosch noted that emigrants left Germany largely because of
military service and the country lost their present and potential
capital.[4] Worthwhile colonies could be created only by lightening
the military service in them. The emigrant should be considered
no longer as a "criminal" but rather as the "propagator of German
interests in the world and the conquerors of new German lands."
Educated in the "strict school of universal obligation to serve,"
the Germans "will be called to be a dominant power in the world."[5]

These views on the colonial question and the mission of the
German Navy were held by Stosch until his death.[6] His enthusiasm
for colonial development led him to push the foundation of a German state in the Brazilian province of Rio Grande do Sul. He had
the idea presented to the Emperor, but he was told that it was too
visionary even for William II. Stosch argued that "if one would
found colonies, one must also make a plan of determined German
colonization."[7] His ambitions extended to the partition of China,[8]
and he welcomed the acquisition of Helgoland, which he had desired in 1865. It was secured in 1890, by a treaty with Great
Britain, in exchange for German colonial interests in East Africa.
Stosch advised Admiral Hollmann, head of the Imperial Naval
Office, to make sure that the Navy gained control over it.[9] He
wrote Roggenbach:

I am extraordinarily pleased by the acquisition of Helgoland. Helgoland in our hands opens the connection to the North Sea and over-
comes an enemy fleet in only moderately bad weather—and there are
few waters on the whole earth as treacherous to leave. I am of the
opinion that it is [Chancellor] Caprivi's work. As for the African
partition, I am not well enough informed to report on its full meaning,

---

[4] Cf. to Freytag, Oestrich, 31 Jan. 1892, Memoirs, III, 267.

[5] Batsch, "Stosch über die Marine und die Kolonisation," *Deutsche Revue,*
XXII (1897), 53-64.

[6] Stosch to Batsch, 7 Jan. 1885, in Batsch, "Stosch," *Deutsche Revue,* XXI, 205;
Koch, *Stosch,* p. 79; Stosch to Tirpitz, 25 Dec. 1895, 25 Feb. 1896, in Hassell,
Tirpitz, pp. 31-32, 105, 113-14.

[7] To Roggenbach, Oestrich, 2 Nov. 1893, Memoirs, III, 299.

[8] To Roggenbach, Oestrich, 5 Dec. 1894, *ibid.,* III, 319; to Freytag, Oestrich,
6 Dec. 1894, *ibid.,* III, 320; to Spenser Wilkinson, Oestrich, 14 Oct. 1894, *ibid.,*
III, 317; to Frau von Rosenstiel, 13 Oct. 1894, *ibid.,* III, 315; Koch, *Stosch,* p. 78.
He even proposed to the German Government in 1894 that Germany occupy
ports to guarantee payments on Chinese loans, but was "ridiculed." To Freytag,
Oestrich, 6 Dec. 1894, Memoirs, III, 320.

[9] Koch, *Stosch,* pp. 80-81.

but I have the impression that the separate conditions are taken somewhat lightly; we could have gotten more during the momentary weakness of England. An inner progressive element, and individual power lies in the pact for Germany . . . . Caprivi is the representative of German world power and that benefits his position.[10]

Stosch was happy for the Navy's sake that he had been dismissed.[11] When Caprivi, as Admiralty Chief, sent him a copy of the naval budget in 1885, he observed that all of the items he had previously requested which had been denied by Bismarck were included. He had proposed an increase of salary amounting to nine hundred marks for one official and had been assured by Bismarck that it would mean "ruin for the Imperial Finances and would disturb every calculation." The same official received over four thousand marks in Caprivi's budget. This incident proved to Stosch that "I departed entirely in the interest of the Navy and am as satisfied with the decision as I was 2 years ago."[12]

While the naval policy of his successor was in opposition to his views, Stosch remained on friendly terms with Caprivi. He spoke with him late in 1883 and found that "he had no love for the business and, for this reason, will understand it only with difficulty."[13] In 1884 Stosch, who had suggested the separation of the Naval Ministry between command and administrative heads on his resignation,[14] favored making Prince Henry Inspector General of the Navy when he became thirty in 1894. He felt that the Chief of the Admiralty was too "powerful and independent" to make all decisions.[15] Crown Prince Frederick William was in complete agreement with this plan to put his son in control of naval command matters and discussed it with Caprivi.[16] The whole question of the organization of the Navy came to a head in 1888.

[10] To Roggenbach, Oestrich, 20 July 1890, Memoirs, III, 228. Cf. to Roggenbach, Oestrich, 6 July 1890, ibid., III, 230.
[11] Stosch to Batsch (?), 3 May 1885, in Batsch, "Stosch," Deutsche Revue, XXI, 204; same to same, ? January 1885, ibid., XXI, 207. However, he expressed a desire to be Chief of the Admiralty again, if war occurred. Stosch to Freytag, Oestrich, 14 April 1885, Memoirs, III, 24.
[12] To Normann, Oestrich, 7 Dec. 1885, ibid., III, 48.
[13] To Frau von Rosenstiel, Oestrich, 6 Oct. 1883, ibid., III, 4.
[14] Stosch to ?, ? Dec. 1883, in Batsch, "Stosch," Deutsche Revue, XXI, 322.
[15] Stosch to the Crown Prince, Oestrich, 7 July 1884, Memoirs, III, 10.
[16] Crown Prince to Stosch, Potsdam, 20 July 1884, ibid., III, 15.

The fall of Caprivi from his naval post took place in the first months of William II's reign. He resigned because of the Emperor's interference in the Navy and especially because William wanted to separate the naval administration and command.[17]   The Cartel majority in the Reichstag, wishing to co-operate with the Emperor, supported the division of functions.[18]   The Left Liberal leader, Eugen Richter, opposed it on the basis of past experience in divided naval command and declared that Stosch had compared divided command to two hostile brothers performing the same business.[19]   Richter was merely recalling a phrase Stosch had let fall, probably in the Reichstag Budget Committee sessions, and had no personal contact with the Admiral, as some were eager to believe.[20]

As a matter of fact, Stosch favored the change.   At first glance, his position seems inconsistent with his attitude toward the Army organization, where he had opposed the divisive influences of the Military Cabinet and the General Staff and had supported the authority of the War Minister.   Examination of the details of his proposal shows that his position with respect to the Navy and the Army was the same.   He sent a memorandum on the subject to the influential Admiral Hollmann, an old friend and subordinate.   He accepted the division of Naval functions into an Imperial Naval Office, a Naval Cabinet, and a Commanding Admiral, but he foresaw that the Naval Cabinet might gain predominance just as its Army counterpart had.   To prevent this, he suggested that the Chief of the Naval Cabinet be a junior officer who would be subordinated to the Imperial Naval Office.   The Commanding Admiral was to be given all rights of a commanding general as well as supply duties, but he was to be forbidden direct communication with the other departments, including the Foreign Office.   The Secretary of State, at the head of the Imperial Naval Office, was not only to determine all administrative and budgetary affairs, but also, and here Stosch returned to one of his favorite ideas, he

---

[17] Stosch to Normann, Oestrich, 4 July 1888, *ibid.*, III, 170; Hassell, *Tirpitz*, pp. 54-55; Lucius, *Bismarck-Erinnerungen*, pp. 471-72.

[18] Herzfeld, *Miquel*, II, 121-22.

[19] *Verhandlungen des Reichstags*, 7 Leg. Per., IV Sess., 21 March 1889, 44 Sitz., CVI, 1012.

[20] Cf. Richter, *Im alten Reichstag*, I, 67.

was to have all merchant marine matters and the colonies in his department. The Commanding Admiral was to be the senior officer in the fleet, but the Secretary of State was to be the "most gifted and suitable officer" in order that he would be the most powerful one.[21] Stosch thus upheld the powers of the Secretary of State against the Naval Cabinet and the Commanding Admiral, but his views were not adopted. The Secretary of State of the Imperial Naval Office, the Commanding Admiral, and the Chief of the Naval Cabinet were soon established independent of one another. Neither of the last two were responsible to the Secretary of State, who was, indeed, subordinated to the Chancellor. This system, which was further altered in 1899, resulted in the predominance of the Naval Cabinet as Stosch had predicted and led to great and continued friction. The arrangement has been almost universally condemned.[22]

Many of the officers in the Navy, including Admiral von Tirpitz, kept in touch with their old Chief.[23] William II was impressed by Stosch's naval ability. He noted in his memoirs that the German Navy had been "spurred on" by Stosch to build ships in German yards, but the "German mercantile marine had not dared to follow the path courageously blazed by Admiral von Stosch."[24] They had a long conversation during the first months of William's reign. The Emperor was urged by Stosch to use the Navy for further scientific investigations, and William promised to speak to Bismarck about it.[25] William told his later Chancellor Prince Hohenlohe that he wished ships to be built in completion of Stosch's

[21] Koch, Stosch, pp. 78-80.

[22] Schmidt-Bückeberg, Das Militärkabinett, pp. 182-83; Huber, Heer und Staat, pp. 353-57, 362-63; Tirpitz, Memoirs, I, 44-45, 158-60. Cf. Stosch to Roggenbach, Oestrich, 20 January 1890, Memoirs, III, 211; and Hubatsch, Der Admiralstab, pp. 50-53.

[23] See especially Memoirs, III, 6, 240, 266, 337; Koch, Stosch, pp. 75-77; Henry Spenser Wilkinson, Thirty-Five Years 1874-1909 (London, 1933), pp. 125-26. For the Stosch-Tirpitz correspondence, see Hassell, Tirpitz, pp. 30-32, 56-57, 102-15; Tirpitz, Memoirs, I, 60-65. For summaries of the continuance of the Stosch naval tradition by Tirpitz, see Walter Hubatsch, "Realität und Illusion in Tirpitz Flottenbau," Schicksalswege Deutscher Vergangenheit (Düsseldorf, [1950]), pp. 387-518; Hans Hallmann, Krügerdespesche und Flottenfrage (Stuttgart, 1927).

[24] William II, My Memoirs, 1878-1918 (London, 1922), p. 46.

[25] Stosch to Normann, 4 July 1888, Memoirs, III, 170-71.

shipbuilding plan.[26]   The Emperor's plans for the enlargement of
the fleet were supported, in turn, by Stosch.[27]   William was very
friendly to the old Admiral during the ceremonies which attended
the opening of the Kiel Canal in June 1895.   When Stosch remarked to Prince Henry on his departure that he had often felt
warmhearted during the celebration, the Prince replied: "Then we
have achieved what we wanted; you were supposed to feel how
grateful the Navy is to you."[28]

He performed two last services to the fleet before his death
in February 1896.   Hohenlohe told him that the Emperor wished
to increase the naval budget, but he had dissuaded him.   However,
he feared that William would refer to an increased budget in one
of his many speeches.   The Chancellor gave Stosch the task of
persuading Commanding Admiral von Knorr that the sum he
asked was too large and that as much could be accomplished with
less.   Stosch also worked on plans for a naval war with England[29]
some years before the German Navy prepared official plans for
such a conflict.[30]   In his letter to Admiral von Tirpitz on this plan,
Stosch's old bellicose nature came once more to the fore.[31]   Well
might Tirpitz write when he received the news of his "old master's"
death, "There was a man!"[32]

2

The major domestic political event of Stosch's later years was
doubtless the dismissal of Bismarck.   His views of this occurrence
illuminate his basic conservatism.   He traveled to Berlin in January 1890 for Empress Augusta's funeral, where he met and talked
with many old acquaintances.   Waldersee, the Chief of the General
Staff, told him that the Emperor and the Chancellor were in each
other's way, but Bismarck took care not to oppose anything openly.

[26] Entry of 1 Feb. 1896, Berlin, in Fürst Chlodwig zu Hohenlohe-Schillingsfürst, *Denkwürdigkeiten der Reichskanzlerzeit* (Stuttgart and Berlin, 1931),
p. 164.
[27] Hassell, *Tirpitz,* pp. 62-63.
[28] Stosch to Frau von Rosenstiel, Oestrich, 27 June 1895, Memoirs, III, 332-
33; Stosch to Roggenbach, Oestrich, 2 July 1895, *ibid.,* III, 334-36.
[29] To Roggenbach, Oestrich, 23 Jan. 1896, *ibid.,* III, 342; Wilkinson, *Thirty-
Five Years,* p. 219.
[30] Tirpitz, *Memoirs,* I, 68.   [31] See n. 23.
[32] Hassell, *Tirpitz,* p. 117.   For honors paid by the Navy to Stosch's grave in
1900, see Kratz, *Oestrich,* p. 77.

Waldersee believed that the "Emperor regards the Prince as capital which must be fully exploited, but also consumed." Stosch was sure, despite his denials, that Waldersee desired to become Bismarck's successor, "not from inner impulse, but from his spirit of resistance—just because Bismarck does not want it."[33] On 30 January 1890 Stosch wrote to Waldersee that he had recently visited Roggenbach and Miquel and had reached certain conclusions regarding the choice of Bismarck's successor: he must be a soldier, he must assume both of Bismarck's offices of German Chancellor and Prussian Minister-President, he must possess the Emperor's confidence, and he must keep Bismarck's "capital in balance" by announcing in the Reichstag and the Prussian chambers that he planned to continue in the path Bismarck had set.[34]

In support of the necessity of the new Chancellor's assumption of the two major offices Bismarck had filled, Stosch used a lengthy constitutional argument. "The totality of the German princes must form the basis of German unity," and they would bear a powerful Chancellor with greater ease than a powerful Emperor. If they were in accord with the Imperial Government, it could assume a position of independence toward the Reichstag, the "best and most heard voice of the country." The Princes were satisfied with the Empire. Although allies of the King of Prussia, they were subordinated to the Empire by membership in the Bundesrat under the leadership of the Chancellor. He must be strong in the Bundesrat or "the process of dissolution begins." It was his duty to solve the problems of the individual states by imperial action. The protective tariff would strengthen the policy of gaining support from the separate states. The Emperor should seek to preserve his hegemony over the princes, while only the Chancellor should represent him in public, except in military matters, to prevent particularist attacks. The Chancellor's position would have to be strengthened by his serving as Prussian Minister-President. Prussian desires and imperial interests would have to coincide, since Prussian particularism was the greatest danger to imperial unity. Controlling the Prussian votes in the Bundesrat, the Chancellor

[33] To Roggenbach, Oestrich, 20 Jan. 1890, Memoirs, III, 208-10.
[34] H. O. Meisner, ed., *Aus dem Briefwechsel des General-Feldmarschalls Alfred Grafen von Waldersee* (Berlin and Leipzig, 1928), I, 335-36.

could prevent the "destruction of the Empire" by the "particularist
and revolutionary elements, with which the Center seeks to ally
itself." For this reason the idea of an Imperial Ministry should be
abandoned; one man would have to bear the responsibility of
effectively checking the "enemies of unity." While the establishment of an Imperial War Ministry would insure imperial control
by constitutional means, it would cause trouble; an Imperial
Army Command would bring imperial dominance without provok-
ing the opposition of the separate war ministers. The independence
of the Foreign Office was necessary to maintain the "power and
unity of the Empire" both abroad and toward the individual states.
In short, "the present position of power is an imperial necessity."[35]

Stosch based the appointment of a soldier as Chancellor upon
the historic preponderance of the "warrior caste." Germany's
reputation abroad had always been essentially military; "Bismarck
has, not without reason, shown himself as a soldier to the world."
A soldier could stand above factions in the Reichstag, Bundesrat,
and Ministry. His power should "stem not from the power-seeking
parliamentary or bureaucratic elements," but "only from the
Emperor's people"; it could be exercised only if he enjoyed the
Emperor's trust. The Chancellor, the "keystone of German unity,"
and the Emperor should follow in Bismarck's path to secure "wide
support in public opinion." Without this their power would be
illusory. Bismarck had lost popular and ministerial support,
despite all his achievements, because "he had become a bottleneck
in the inner development of the Empire and Prussia." "Egotistical and lazy" in his old age, he had dropped all measures which ran
counter to his own interests, such as the income tax, or which were
not of pressing importance, such as the codification of civil law.
If the new Chancellor acted energetically, he could count on the
backing of the country.[36]

A long list of practical measures to be adopted followed.
Miquel, Stosch reported to Waldersee, was certain that if the new
Chancellor introduced legislation for the workers in the Reichstag
and, as Minister-President, took immediate action in the Prussian
Chambers to push an income tax bill, to turn over real estate and
land taxes to the districts, and to introduce a new organization of

[35] *Ibid.*, pp. 336-37.   [36] *Ibid.*, p. 338.

the districts, he would be upheld by the nation. Miquel felt that the most important law concerned the reorganization of the districts. The Junkers, who feared new burdens, could be won over by entrusting the assessment of real estate taxes to the districts. Stosch asked Waldersee to discuss the matter with Miquel. He thought the question of the peasants particularly important because, "despite everything, I consider the bloody suppression of Social Democracy as imminent." The Social Democrats could be put down only by the Army, whose soldiers were drawn largely from the peasant class. Emigration showed that the peasant was dissatisfied with his burdens and, under existing conditions, he might well combine with the Social Democrats. Stosch observed: "If I can oppose the peasant to the manual laborer, who is continually raising the prices of the necessities of life, I command the stronger element."[37]

The final question which Stosch considered was the status of the Ministers and the Secretaries of State to the Chancellor and the Emperor. In Prussia, the Chancellor, as Minister-President, could work through the State Ministry. Stosch believed that "a revitalization of the Ministers' character," that is, the appointment of independent-minded Ministers, would be in the interest of the new Chancellor. In the Empire, the Imperial Office of the Interior had attempted to co-ordinate the work of the Secretaries of State. This latter arrangement should be altered by making the Chancellor responsible for the co-ordination of Imperial Affairs and by holding regular sessions of the Secretaries of State. In conclusion, Stosch declared that all his observations pointed to Waldersee himself as Bismarck's most suitable successor. Stosch was writing "to serve Emperor and Empire" and expected no extensive reply, only an acknowledgment.[38]

Waldersee briefly replied on 3 February 1890, thanking Stosch for his letter, which contained "many things new to me," and he declared that he would give it serious thought. Much could be discussed only orally. Circumstances had altered since he had seen Stosch. A change was still possible, although he believed the

[37] *Ibid.,* pp. 338-39.   [38] *Ibid.,* pp. 339-40.

"break" would be bridged. He expressed the hope that he would see Miquel soon.[39]

The letter of 30 January has puzzled historians, who cannot reconcile the opinions expressed in it with Stosch's "Victorian-minded"[40] views, his supposed support of the Empress Victoria and the Left Liberals. It has been suggested that he was not a supporter of the Left Liberals.[41] As a matter of fact, Stosch had never favored the ideas of the Left Liberals nor those of the Empress Victoria. On the contrary, he had tried to guide Frederick III along more conservative lines. This letter, written under the influence of the advice of Roggenbach and Miquel and devised to affect Waldersee and provide a program for the future Chancellor,[42] stated Stosch's essentially conservative policy. He viewed Germany as resting not upon the people, but upon the union of the German reigning princes, represented in the Bundesrat under the chairmanship of the Chancellor. In short, he accepted Bismarck's federal solution of the German question. The strength of the state he saw in the military and landed caste, supported by a loyal peasantry. His program was in its broad outlines the acceptance of the status quo. However, he also aimed at future development within the limits imposed by the existing organization of the state. He approved Bismarck's goals, but deplored his methods. In Stosch's program, a Chancellor, strongly backed by the Emperor, would be the responsible minister in the Prussian State Ministry and the imperial councils. He would appoint capable, strong-minded officials, and govern in co-operation with the Reichstag. Bismarck's blocking of initiative and independence was to be brought to an end. The peasants and the Junkers[43] were to be bound more securely to the state, while the workers' lot was to be

---

[39] Berlin, 3 Jan. [sic—Feb.] 1890, Memoirs, III, 213-14.

[40] This term is used in Stadelmann, Moltke, "Vorwort." Frau Dr. Stadelmann, on the authority of Professor Hans Rothfels, writes that her husband meant to designate the views of the group around the Emperor Frederick, when he used the term "viktorianisch gesinnte." Frau Dr. Stadelmann to the present writer, Tübingen, 30 Nov. 1954. But cf. his use of the term in Stadelmann, 1848, p. 188.

[41] Meisner, Waldersees Briefwechsel, I, xiv.

[42] Cf. Herzfeld, Miquel, II, 171-72.

[43] He wrote in 1886 of the Junkers: "I view with great distress the Junker's decline, for they are worth gold in our state organization." To Normann, Oestrich, 16 Feb. 1886, Memoirs, III, 52.

improved by social reform. If the workers proved recalcitrant, they were to be suppressed by the Army, which was to be made more of an imperial institution. The Emperor was to remain master here, but to be publicly reserved in other matters. Stosch's views, practical as they were, if the existing organization of the state and the impossibility of replacing Bismarck with a man of equal stature were accepted, contained one underlying flaw. He presupposed an Emperor who was sincerely and consistently devoted to public affairs and his duties. William I seems to have been in his mind, not William II. The letter, written to a particular man for a specific purpose and stating the views of Stosch's later years, is remarkably consistent with his earlier opinions.

Meanwhile, a struggle was in progress in Berlin. Bismarck believed, as did Stosch, that the workers should, if necessary, be suppressed by force. He objected to the Emperor's decrees of 4 February 1890, which called for an international congress on labor conditions in the mining industry and a Crown Council to consider legislation to protect the workers, and secretly sought to render them fruitless. He refused to limit himself to his Prussian offices and the conduct of foreign policy. The gulf widened between the Chancellor and the Emperor, who was influenced by Miquel, Waldersee, and the Grand Duke of Baden. An election was called in which the Cartel Majority battled an opposition composed of the Center, the Left Liberals, and the Social Democrats.[44]

The changing scene was of great interest to Stosch. The Emperor's appeal for an international congress on worker's legislation appeared impractical to him, because of the "great differences in economic relations in the various states." Moreover, "life cannot be regimented," he declared with singular lack of prescience. He wrote of the second decree concerning assistance to German workers:

I am in thorough agreement with it, for only in this way can we succeed in controlling somewhat the brutal power of this force [the urban proletariat] and make *divide et impera* practical. Securing that control appears to me to be the first duty of statesmanship today. Powder and

[44] Herzfeld, *Miquel*, II, 167-72; Carroll, **Germany and the Great Powers**, pp. 280-84.

lead must inevitably help to keep domestic peace, but this means is only at my disposal when the soldier recognizes the justice of the battle.[45]

Miquel was summoned by William to Berlin to attend the Crown Council, which opened on February 14.[46] Stosch advised him not to go because of his poor health, but he persisted.[47] The Emperor appointed him reporter to the Council, and Stosch twice appealed to Waldersee to see that he was spared great work.[48] On 20 February 1890 the elections resulted in a resounding defeat for the Cartel. The National Liberals lost heavily, while the Left Liberals and Social Democrats, despite the anti-Socialist law, made great gains. An opposition majority faced the Government.[49] Stosch wrote to Waldersee that the Emperor must not find himself at odds with the masses. The Government should not make any new demands for money, but wait for the Reichstag to make an error. When it had done so, it could be dissolved and the "working masses" could be "organized, i.e., divided." He remarked: *"Divide et impera* is one of the most important rules of government."[50]

Waldersee replied to Stosch on 23 February. He accepted Stosch's four requirements for the new Chancellor, who, he agreed, would not have a difficult task. The antagonism between William and Bismarck was fundamental and could not remain long concealed. He felt another dissolution of the Reichstag would not alter its composition. Moreover, an increased military budget was needed. The Emperor's wish to assist the workers would not alter the situation; force would have to be used against them. Bismarck's retirement was imminent, but Waldersee believed that he would not be chosen to succeed him, and, indeed, he professed himself satisfied with his position as Chief of the General Staff. The Chancellor was seeking his successor everywhere, but could not find him. The Ministry was dissatisfied, and Bismarck was said to be looking for "auxiliary troops."[51]

---

[45] To Roggenbach, Oestrich, 10 Feb. 1890, Memoirs, III, 211, 212.
[46] Herzfeld, *Miquel*, II, 172.
[47] Stosch to Freytag, Oestrich, 14 Feb. 1890, Memoirs, III, 212-13.
[48] 15 Feb., 22 Feb. 1890, in Meisner, *Waldersees Briefwechsel*, I, 342-43, 345.
[49] Ludwig Bergsträsser, *Geschichte der politische Parteien in Deutschland* (5th ed.; Mannheim, 1928), p. 121.
[50] Meisner, *Waldersees Briefwechsel*, I, 345-46 (22 Feb. 1890).
[51] Memoirs, III, 214-18. The version in Meisner, *Waldersees Briefwechsel*,

Apparently on the basis of Waldersee's communication, Stosch wrote Freytag on 24 February that the Chancellor's fall was expected. He noted that his old friend General von Loë, the Emperor's adjutant, and Miquel had departed for Berlin. The Emperor, Stosch thought, lacked "self-control." This flaw, compounded as it was by "disorder" in the Reichstag and the Government, would "make salutary co-operation with him impossible." The man who became Chancellor "is either stupid or bold, frivolous or very patriotic." Stosch disclosed that he had refused the suggestion that he assume the task, because he was too old. He inquired: "Can more be offered to me than the titillation of my vanity and a hopeless martyrdom without canonization?"[52] He reported on 27 February that Bismarck was doing all in his power to obey the Emperor. He recalled that the Emperor Frederick had told him that the Ministers always voted down projects disagreeable to Bismarck and Stosch wondered whether these sycophants would support William or the Chancellor.[53]

The wish of Roggenbach and Loë to await Bismarck's self-destruction did not win Stosch's applause. The monarch, he felt, must dismiss the Chancellor. Stosch still felt that Waldersee was the most suitable choice, but Loë said that "the best horse in the stable is Caprivi." The Admiral backed Waldersee because he thought the handling of the Emperor the most important factor; Waldersee could do this, but Caprivi could not. Moreover, Caprivi's "odd old-maidish vanity and susceptibility" and "wilfulness," shown when he was Chief of the Admiralty, made him a poor selection.[54] Stosch wrote to Roggenbach on 9 March: "Waldersee must have gained a wide horizon throughout his whole career. I consider it out of the question to propose another man for the position; I have lived in isolation for seven years."[55] Miquel, Stosch felt,

---

I, 346-48, based on Waldersee's adjutant's copy, has a shortened opening, different paragraphing and wording, and, most significantly, omits the last two paragraphs criticizing Bismarck, which appear in the copy of the original in Stosch's memoirs.

[52] Oestrich, Memoirs, III, 219.   [53] To Roggenbach, Oestrich, *ibid*.
[54] To Roggenbach, Oestrich, 9 March 1890, *ibid*., III, 220-21. Cf. Stosch to Miquel, in Herzfeld, *Miquel*, II, 182.
[55] Memoirs, III, 221-22.

was needed to support the Government in the Reichstag.[56] Waldersee could overcome the difficulty of his former connection with the anti-Semite leader Stöcker in his first speech.[57] Freytag thought Stosch the last man suited to be Chancellor and recorded that the offer to make him Bismarck's successor had not come from influential quarters.[58]

The final break between William II and Bismarck came in March 1890, and the Chancellor left office on 20 March. Prince Chlodwig Hohenlohe wrote of the dinner of the Black Eagle Order of 23 March:

At half-past one dinner, at which I sat between Stosch and Kameke. The former told me about his quarrel with Bismarck, and was as chirpy as a wren that he could now speak openly and that the great man was now no longer to be feared. This comfortable feeling is universal here. Here again it is true that the meek inherit the earth.[59]

"Meek," even in the Biblical sense, is hardly an adjective that applies to Stosch. In fact, he seems to have regretted Bismarck's departure once it became fact. He wrote Freytag on 29 March of Bismarck: "One suddenly feels now how securely one lived under his roof; only the Emperor sees things rosily and feels very sure of himself." The Emperor meant to be his own Chancellor and had no understanding of his Ministers. Caprivi entered upon his office with a "heavy heart," Stosch, who had spoken with him, reported. Stosch hoped that the expectations placed on William would not be disappointed,[60] but he complained that William did not understand the Reichstag.[61] Stosch summarized his view of the change:

The Emperor lacks will and clarity and consequently is weak and unsteady. He acts with his tongue and holds back from deeds. I prefer the late Chancellor to that.—You say that he is starting to become a traitor in his speeches. His speeches always have the same character. Today, as formerly, he has only one goal: . . . always to do what is

[56] Stosch told Miquel on March 6 that he had charmed William. Herzfeld, *Miquel,* II, 180.

[57] To Roggenbach, 9 March 1890, Memoirs, III, 221-22.

[58] To Frau A. Strakosch, 17 March 1890, Freytag, *Briefe an seine Gattin,* p. 458.

[59] Hohenlohe-Schillingsfürst, *Memoirs,* II, 423.

[60] Berlin, Memoirs, III, 222-23.

[61] To Roggenbach, 5 April 1890, in Oestrich, *ibid.,* III, 223-25.

right for the moment. On this account, he always acts clearly and ruthlessly. There is no reason to reproach him for his speeches. He is
now no different than he always was and the world, which has paid
homage to him before, must do it now too. He still stands today in the
forefront of action.[62]

Bismarck's name was linked with Stosch's at least twice in
1890. A pamphlet attacking Bismarck entitled *Videant consules*
appeared in 1890, and Stosch was said to be the author. He denied
in the pages of the *Rheinischen Kurier* having "written or read" it.[63]
The Left Liberal *Breslauer Zeitung* claimed on 24 August that
Bismarck and William I had often been at odds and cited the
"Chancellor crisis" of 1877 as an example. The Berlin *Tägliche
Rundschau* of 27 August maintained that Stosch's resignation in
1883 had resulted from a similar "Chancellor crisis." This the
Bismarck-inspired *Hamburger Nachrichten* denied.[64] Bismarck's
last public mention of Stosch seems to have been during an address
to the board of directors of the Hamburg-American Line on 30
April 1891. The former Chancellor genially declared:

I have always been on a good footing with salt water people—with the
exception of Stosch. As Imperial Chancellor I really stood above the
Naval Minister; since, however, I do not like to speak of matters which
I do not understand, the gentleman should have found me quite good to
deal with. Not so Herr von Stosch, who besides the Navy, loved to
occupy himself with politics, I mean politics in Berlin.[65]

The Admiral's admiration of his old opponent did not diminish
with the years.[66] The hearty ovation given to Bismarck during
1892 brought tears to his eyes; "Bismarck has tyrannized mankind, but has . . . done great things and no one forgets that."[67]
Freytag wrote of Stosch's attitude toward Bismarck:

. . . at times unwilling astonishment predominates. The dominant mood
is violent aversion because of personal conflict of long standing, in which
he was sorely pressed by the detestable qualities of his opponent. His
nature is far more similar to his, in weaknesses as in great qualities, than
he himself realizes. Bismarck is by far superior to him, as to all other

[62] *Ibid.*, III, 227-28.
[63] Poschinger, *Bismarcks Bundesrat*, II, 129n.
[64] *Deutscher Geschichtskalender*, 1890, I, 126-29.
[65] Bismarck, *Gesammelte Werke*, IX, 144.
[66] To Roggenbach, Oestrich, 11 April 1892, Memoirs, III, 272.
[67] To Frau von Rosenstiel, Oestrich, 24 June 1892, *ibid.*, III, 278.

men, in intellect, in sovereign judgment of great circumstances, and perhaps in unscrupulousness in choice of means. Stosch was impeded by the lack of a university education and diplomatic schooling, but he has two characteristics of a strong man in an unusual degree: a massive common sense, which almost instinctively fastens securely upon the simple and correct—and in that he is perhaps superior to Bismarck— and further in his virtues as a general, not embarrassed by a dangerous situation, but dominated by clear will power. He is the born general as Bismarck is the statesman. Both can be violent, pitiless, and hard, but Stosch, who has less richness of spirit, is also less free of moral scruples. Both are immoderately ambitious and desirous for power. Bismarck conducted the battle against Stosch with evil weapons. He was right . . . in the knowledge that Stosch's favorable position as Naval Minister was untenable. Stosch understands that too.[68]

3

Annual visits to Berlin for the chapter meeting and dinner of the Black Eagle Order and the opening of the Prussian Chamber of Peers kept Stosch in touch with the events of the new reign. The personality of William II, upon whom the future course of government depended, particularly interested him.[69] He described his impressions of the Emperor at a chapter meeting of the Black Eagle Order in 1891.

. . . I had the Emperor right before me during the investiture of the knights, and therefore possessed complete freedom to study him: a pretty round face with a lively glance; no feature betrays any thought whatsoever. The old Emperor [William I], when he placed the chain around [the knight's neck], said a few words explaining what had got one the order, and his eyes showed how deeply the heart of the monarch was moved at the investiture. Here everything remains cold, trumpet blasts replace feeling, and only the Emperor shows himself to be especially moved by the foolery.[70]

The relations between the Emperor and the new Chancellor were anxiously watched by Stosch. Caprivi, he felt, was acting "like a chief of staff under a general." William II seemed to believe that he could manage everything but finance, the only field in

[68] To Frau A. Strakosch, Siebleben, 13 Sept. 1890, in Freytag, *Briefe an seine Gattin*, pp. 550-51.

[69] Cf. to Roggenbach, 6 July 1890, Memoirs, III, 320; to Freytag, Oestrich, 12 July and 22 Nov. 1890, *ibid.*, III, 231-32, 236.

[70] To Freytag, Oestrich, 31 Jan. 1891, *ibid.*, III, 243-44. Cf. to Freytag, Oestrich, 23 Jan. 1892, *ibid.*, III, 265.

which he gladly accepted advice.[71] Caprivi's acquiescence to
William's interference in the Army, Navy, and particularly foreign
affairs, greatly displeased Stosch.[72] He strongly favored a reconciliation between Bismarck and William II and considered Caprivi
a "small nature and a disgrace to his post," for his attitude toward
the former Chancellor.[73] He remarked in June 1892: "How quickly
we have declined at home and abroad." He deplored again Caprivi's
refusal to take the responsibility of opposing the Emperor and
thought he had the "standpoint of an adviser to the Crown of
1806."[74] He wrote in 1893: "Our Emperor seems called to destroy
what his grandfather built. He and his assistants lack the calm
decision, the clarity of thought, and the security of execution,
which we need so very much."[75] Complaints of the refusal of the
Ministers and the subordinate officials to take responsibility run
through all his comments on the governmental circles of the
nineties.

Stosch's parliamentary connections were largely with members
of the National Liberal and Liberal Imperial parties. He frequently saw the National Liberal deputy and industrialist Ochel-
häuser and the Liberal Imperial industrialist, Baron von Stumm.[76]
The National Liberal leader Bennigsen often visited him,[77] while
his friendship continued with the National Liberal Miquel, whom
he and Roggenbach apparently persuaded to accept the post of
Finance Minister.[78] Stosch was, in any case, well pleased with this
choice and Miquel's subsequent activity.[79] He reported in 1893
that only two men in Berlin, William II and Miquel, looked with
"confidence into the future"; the Emperor from "complete naïveté,
the other from knowledge."[80] When the reformation of the district

[71] To Roggenbach, Oestrich, 9 Feb. 1891, *ibid.*, III, 246.
[72] To Roggenbach, Oestrich, 5 April 1891, *ibid.*, III, 247-50.
[73] To Roggenbach, Oestrich, 11 April 1892, *ibid.*, III, 272; entry of 29 May
1892, in Waldersee, *Denkwürdigkeiten,* II, 241.
[74] To Roggenbach, Oestrich, 21 June 1892, Memoirs, III, 276.
[75] To Roggenbach, Oestrich, 17 April 1893, *ibid.*, III, 292-93.
[76] *E.g.,* Stosch to Roggenbach, Oestrich, 12 Sept. 1890, *ibid.*, III, 233; Stosch
to Freytag, Oestrich, 7 Sept. 1892, *ibid.*, III, 280-81.
[77] Oncken, *Bennigsen,* II, 619. See Stosch to Bennigsen, Oestrich, 3 July 1894,
ibid., II, 590-92, which contains an interesting analysis of the characters of
Philipp Eulenburg and Bernhard von Bülow.
[78] Herzfeld, *Miquel,* II, 396.
[79] *E.g.,* Stosch to Roggenbach, Oestrich, 26 Jan. 1891, Memoirs, III, 246.
[80] To Roggenbach, 8 June 1893, *ibid.*, III, 293.

government in Prussia was projected, both Miquel and Interior Minister Herrfurth summoned him to vote for the bill in the Chamber of Peers.[81] Toward the Social Democrats, Stosch felt no sympathy whatsoever. In 1891 he said that the proper policy toward them was to give them full freedom of speech, but "bloodily repress all excesses."[82] Nonetheless, he opposed the Subversives Bill [*Umsturzvorlage*], which aimed at placing restrictions on the Social Democrats.[83]

I consider the Subversives Bill a mistake. It is the product of fear. One should not [only] strongly care for the workers, but also permit them as much freedom as possible. A state whose *ultima ratio* is lynch justice is stronger than one under the best bureaucratic domination. The fear of the propertied and middle classes, who all are under the pressure of the nihilist spectre today, is the only source of our governmental power. Our responsible men lack the capability to act, while the Emperor, who perhaps wants to be energetic, lacks every instinct for proper action, both where *he* has taken a hand and where he has not.[84]

The struggle between Caprivi and the Reichstag over military legislation[85] naturally engaged Stosch's keen attention. He felt that the Army was strong enough to quell internal insurrection and its numbers did not need to be increased. He favored a reform of military justice to gain Reichstag support of the Army, and, although he opposed annual Reichstag control of the Army budget, he did back Caprivi's concession of having a vote on the military estimates every five, instead of every seven, years. Stosch also agreed with the Chancellor's willingness to reduce the length of the term of service from three to two years. In January 1893, Caprivi authorized Stosch to make the former's wish for compromise known to the National Liberals, and the Admiral was able to

---

[81] Stosch to Frau von Rosenstiel, Oestrich, 2 May 1891, *ibid.*, III, 252; to Roggenbach, Oestrich, 9 May 1891, *ibid.*, III, 253; to Freytag, Oestrich, 11 June 1891, *ibid.*, III, 255. On the reform, see Erich Eyck, *Das Persönliche Regiment Wilhelms II: Politische Geschichte des deutschen Kaiserreiches von 1890 bis 1914* (Erlenbach-Zürich, [1948]), pp. 49-50.

[82] To Frau von Rosenstiel, Oestrich, 22 Oct. 1891, Memoirs, III, 261-62.

[83] See Eyck, *Wilhelm II*, pp. 105-7.

[84] To Roggenbach, Oestrich, 13 Feb. 1895, Memoirs, III, 325-26.

[85] On this complex question, see especially, Robert Geis, *Der Sturz des Reichskanzlers Caprivi* (Berlin, 1930), pp. 53, 64-65; Georg Gothein, *Reichskanzler Caprivi: Eine kritische Würdigung* (Munich, 1918), pp. 46-72; Eyck, *Wilhelm II*, pp. 64-73; Waldersee, *Denkwürdigkeiten*, II, 123; Memoirs, III, 229-30, 279, 281, 294-95, 318, 341; J. Alden Nichols, *Germany After Bismarck* (Cambridge, Mass., 1958), pp. 192-264.

obtain their firm support. To counter the Emperor's adamant attitude against changes in the Army and to help Caprivi, Stosch suggested to Bennigsen that the National Liberals publicly criticize William II. He got a positive refusal in reply.[86] His proposal to reform military justice was endorsed by Caprivi's successor as Chancellor, Prince Hohenlohe, who had Stosch persuade the King of Saxony to win the Emperor's approval of the measure.[87]

Characteristic of Stosch's conservatism is his remark to Roggenbach about Hohenlohe's weakness:[88]

A Chancellor must have his *own* coloring. In general, I am coming more and more to the view that today where personal interests alone lead men, only tyranny in the good sense will maintain the governance of the state. Bismarck exercised it and all the world followed him; what is still more remarkable, it is precisely the personal autocratic element in our Emperor which wins him more and more admiration. . . . I believe in a great future for Germany and also that we will find the man we need. Therefore, forward with courage![89]

Stosch's national feeling and regard for individual responsibility, so pronounced in this letter, also pervades his opinions of the problems of the Polish minority in Prussia and of religious legislation.

The governmental policy toward the Prussian Poles had interested Stosch since the fifties, when he had discussed the problem with General von Brandt. Stosch published, anonymously, an essay entitled "The Prussian Poles" in the October 1891 number of the *Deutsche Revue*.[90] He felt that the government should win the Poles to Germany not by forcing the alien German language

[86] Memoirs, III, 225-26, 256, 262, 286-88, 291-92; Oncken, *Bennigsen,* II, 579-83.

[87] To Roggenbach, Oestrich, 23 Jan. 1896, Memoirs, III, 341. Cf. Hohenlohe, *Denkwürdigkeiten,* p. 214.

[88] Cf. Memoirs, III, 318 and 325.

[89] Oestrich, 8 March 1895, *ibid.,* III, 320-27. In this connection another comment of Stosch on dictatorship is of interest. He wrote to Freytag from Oestrich on 14 Oct. 1894 (*ibid.,* III, 317) about a book by Constantin Rössler: "He suffers from a mild delusion in believing he can make history with books, but I also believe that events push on to a dictator. But it will not result from a trial of bureaucratic wisdom, but from murder and homicide. How can Rössler think that the many-headed Bundesrat is suited to be a dictator? That demonstrates a lack of clear judgment."

[90] Stosch to Freytag, Oestrich, 28 July, 5 Aug. 1891, *ibid.,* III, 256, 258; Freytag to Stosch, Wiesbaden, 11 July, 25 July 1891, Blankenberge, 29 Aug. 1891, Helmolt, *Freytag an Stosch,* pp. 249, 250, 252.

upon them, but by striking at the great Polish nobles and Roman Catholic hierarchy with a policy benefiting the lesser nobles and, particularly, the peasants. While German would remain the language of the courts, the administration, and the higher schools, use of Polish by army officers and civil officials and in the elementary schools would encourage the peasant to trust the Government. The peasant should be aided in gaining and cultivating the land, Polish landlords should be made assistants in local government, and the magistrates should be brought into close contact with the Polish inhabitants. Eventually, these measures would result in complete self-government by the local communities. Stosch held that his goal of making "our Poles real Prussians" could be realized only gradually. His aim, obviously, was to stimulate the initiative of the individual Polish peasant, win his confidence, and bind him more closely to the German nation.[91]

Like stress on individual independence and nationalism is evident in Stosch's attitude toward religious legislation. He disapproved of an abortive governmental bill in 1892 giving the Roman Catholic Church great powers over education,[92] because he felt it would weaken national feeling in the schools.[93] He even rebuked the Catholic priest at Oestrich for his opposition to governmental policy.[94] He also opposed a bill of 1894 which gave the General Synod of the Evangelical State Church the right to pass religious legislation, and he spoke against the measure in the Prussian Chamber of Peers on 15 March 1894. He deplored the increasing power of the church hierarchy and championed complete control by the local congregations; he suggested that pastors be elected for twelve years, like mayors, to curb their influence. Despite his arguments the bill passed the Chamber of Peers, but encountered strong opposition in the Chamber of Deputies. Rickert proclaimed that his faction of Left Liberals was in complete agreement with Stosch's stand; this declaration did nothing to counteract the legend

[91] [Albrecht von Stosch,] "Die preussische Polen," *Deutsche Revue*, XVI (1891), 309-18. Cf. *Memoirs*, I, 26, and Miquel's correspondence with Stosch in 1890 and 1891, Herzfeld, *Miquel*, II, 494-95.

[92] Eyck, *Wilhelm II*, pp. 56-60.

[93] To Freytag, Oestrich, 24 Feb. 1892, Memoirs, III, 267-68. Cf. *Memoirs*, I, 15.

[94] To Freytag, Oestrich, 23 June 1893, Memoirs, III, 293-94.

that they were close collaborators. However, the bill was approved
and sent to William II.[95] Stosch refused to accept defeat. He
published an anonymous article, "On the Evangelical Church," in
the 7 May issue of the National Liberal *Hamburgischer Korrespondent,* hoping that it would be laid before William II with other press
clippings and sway him to withhold his consent.[96] But the bill became law on 25 May 1894.[97]

Intense nationalism was likewise the keynote of Stosch's views
in foreign policy.[98] He favored German penetration into the
Transvaal even before the Krüger Dispatch (which he enthusiasti-
cally endorsed) focused attention on the Boers.[99] He believed it
the duty of German statesmen to consider the possibility of a war
with England and to realize that they could not count on the Triple
Alliance for support of *"German* interests." Germany's greatest
enemy was herself, and unity at home could best be preserved by
making German power felt abroad. He declared: "Only in battle
can Germany become great."[100] He traced English opposition to
Germany to competition in the world market. England would go
to war with her competitor as soon as she was allied with France
and Russia. This was the reason Stosch gave for occupying himself with the plans of an Anglo-German naval war. He concluded
his last letter to Roggenbach with the words: "If I were not such
an old fellow, I could be enthusiastic about war."[101]

4

Stosch thus took a lively interest in all that went on about him
during the thirteen years of his retirement. His philosophy was expressed in 1889: "One must create until he is lowered into his
grave." He delighted in meeting new people and observing their
characters. Although he had little love for music, he had a taste
for art and always went to the new exhibits when in Berlin. Books

[95] *Deutscher Geschichtskalender,* 1894, I, 239, 241-48; Batsch, "Stosch,"
Deutsche Revue, XXII, 362-65; Helmolt, *Freytag an Stosch,* p. 279.

[96] Batsch, "Stosch," *Deutsche Revue,* XXII, 362-64.

[97] *Deutscher Geschichtskalender,* 1894, I, 248.

[98] For his views of the Powers, see especially Memoirs, III, 253-54, 259-60,
310-11, 329-30. A favorable appraisal of his opinions is contained in Ulrich von
Hassell, *Im Wandel der Aussenpolitik* (4th ed.; Munich [1943]), pp. 222-23.

[99] To Roggenbach, Oestrich, 7 Jan. 1896, Memoirs, III, 338-39.

[100] To Roggenbach, Oestrich, 11 Jan. 1896, *ibid.,* III, 339-41.

[101] Oestrich, 14 Feb. 1896, *ibid.,* III, 342-44.

were his greatest recreation and he enjoyed most of all volumes of memoirs, history, and biography and treatises on practical subjects such as meteorology and wine growing. Poetry and philosophy held but little interest for him, although he did read some volumes of contemporary fiction.[102]

The preparation of his own memoirs took up much of his time. His view of historical writing is of interest in this connection. He wrote Normann in 1886 of the histories he was reading:

> I read hardly anything else, but the author vanishes for me in the observation of the subject . . . . The question of objectivity concerns me relatively little, because I think that is almost impossible. Therefore I read historians of all party colorings and seek to form my own opinion by comparisons from them.[103]

The idea of writing memoirs apparently occurred to him immediately after his retirement in 1883, and for the next ten years he collected material for them. He wrote his friends for the letters he had written to them, receiving the richest collection from Normann and Freytag, and he struck out all passages he did not desire to use. Most of his letters to Roggenbach were destroyed by the latter in 1888 and none appear in the memoirs before that date. Victoria returned his reports to her husband. These materials he supplemented by his memory, by letters and documents in his own possession, and by his diaries and journals for the wars of 1866 and 1870-1871.[104] The General's memoirs are, for the most part, a collection of letters with a minimum of connective passages. The only exceptions of any length are the narrative of his early life, the description of his conflict with Bismarck in 1866 and 1871, the exposition of his views of his constitutional position as Chief of the Admiralty, which open Volume Two, and his description of his relations with Rickert. The memoirs convey an impression of remarkable objectivity, and only when he defends himself from

---

[102] These statements are based upon references in his correspondence which are too numerous to warrant citing individually. Although repelled by naturalism in art, Stosch, like Bismarck (Sidney Whitman, *Personal Reminiscences of Prince Bismarck* [New York, 1903], p. 336), was fond of Zola's novels.

[103] Oestrich, 27 June 1886, Memoirs, III, 60.

[104] Freytag to Stosch, Wiesbaden, 20 Nov. 1883, in Helmolt, *Freytag an Stosch*, p. 146; same to same, Siebleben, 2 Sept. 1884, *ibid.*, p. 154; Stosch to Frau von Rosenstiel, Oestrich, 5 Dec. 1892, Memoirs, III, 282; *Memoirs*, I, 273-74.

Bismarck's charges concerning the incidents of 1866 and 1871 does his anger show.

While official honors ceased to be bestowed upon him after 1883, he was honored in other ways at various times. In the autumn of 1883 Stosch attended the ceremonies at the dedication of the Niederwald monument, which celebrated the victories of the Franco-German War. His figure appears among the other generals, princes, and statesmen on the bas-relief on the monument.[105]   A march was named in his honor,[106] and Stoschstrasse adjoined Gneisenaustrasse in his birthplace of Coblenz.[107]   On his seventieth birthday he received a flood of congratulatory telegrams and letters, as well as five addresses from German astronomers, geographers, meteorologists, naturalists, and the Naval Observatory that testify to the breadth of his interests. He commented: "All that has made me rejoice a great deal, as a free gift to a quiet man, who is without power."[108]

His military achievements were not forgotten and indeed received more recognition when Hönig's volumes on the Loire campaign[109] began to appear. Stosch wrote to Roggenbach on 5 December 1894:

> On the 3rd inst. I received a telegram from him [William II] at Kiel: "The old and young officers gathered together with me at a meal have given three thundering cheers to your health in memory of Orléans and to the organizer of our faithful Navy. William I. R."—You can imagine how surprised I was at this attention. The old Emperor was rich in that. It seems striking to me also that he mentions Orléans to me despite Prince Frederick Karl and Mecklenburg being my superiors in command. Years ago when the old Emperor once said something in praise of the Navy, Prince Karl [brother of William I and father of

[105] To Frau von Rosenstiel, Oestrich, 6 Oct. 1883, Memoirs, III, 3.

[106] Judging by the MS. copy in the possession of his grandson, Herr Ulrich von Stosch, it was probably written during his years as Chief of the Admiralty.

[107] His grandson possesses a plan of the city showing the new street. No date is shown upon it.

[108] To Normann, Oestrich, 24 April 1888, Memoirs, III, 158-59. William I sent a warm congratulatory letter on the fiftieth anniversary of Stosch's entrance into the Army. Priesdorff, Soldatisches Führertum, VIII, 318.

[109] On Hönig, see B. H. Liddell Hart, Thoughts on War (London, 1944), p. 144; Vagts, History of Militarism, pp. 24-25. Both in writing and by word of mouth, Stosch furnished Hönig with information for his work (Hönig, Volkskrieg, IV, 321 n.), and took an eager interest in his progress (see Memoirs, III, 256-57, 286, 300, 301, 305, 317, 346, 388).

Frederick Karl] remarked that I had only followed in the footsteps of Prince Adalbert, who had also directed me until his death.[110]

The Emperor sent him the goblet from which he had drunk the toast,[111] but Stosch's enthusiasm was somewhat dampened when he discovered that the Emperor suffered from "toast asthma."[112]   On 12 August 1895 he celebrated the sixtieth anniversary of his entrance as an officer into the Army.   Various deputations came to him, including a delegation of leading industrialists, who presented him with an address.[113]   He wrote Roggenbach: "It has greatly amused me that different newspapers take your presence [at the anniversary celebration] as documentation for my liberal convictions.   I learn there also that I was a candidate for Imperial Chancellor in 1892."[114]

The delights of winegrowing and the company of his family and friends enlivened his last years.   His domestic life was made happy by his love for his wife, Rosalie, and for his three children, Otto, Ulrich, and Luise, who had married Vice Admiral George, Baron von Hollen.   Two sons, Albrecht and Max, had died in infancy.   Stosch was often absorbed in his vineyards, and Freytag considered it a "lovable irony of fate that the Grand Admiral of the German Fleet had exchanged water for wine."[115]   When Stosch foregathered over a glass of wine with his old friend Freytag, conversation resulted which entranced the listeners.[116]   The deaths of his old friends, Holtzendorff, William I, Frederick III, and Normann made him feel very lonely.   He was deeply shaken by the death of his young granddaughter, Lilli Hollen, a few years later, and by the death of Freytag in May 1895.[117]   He admitted:

[110] Oestrich, *ibid.*, III, 319-20.

[111] This goblet, etched with the toast, is now in the possession of the Admiral's grandson, Herr Ulrich von Stosch.

[112] To Frau von Rosenstiel, Oestrich, 29 Dec. 1894, Memoirs, III, 321.

[113] To Roggenbach, Oestrich, 9 Aug. 1895, *ibid.*, III, 336.

[114] To Roggenbach, Oestrich, 23 Aug. 1895, *ibid.*, III, 337.

[115] To Frau von Stosch, Wiesbaden, 9 May 1890, in Helmolt, *Freytag an Stosch,* p. 231.   Cf. Stosch to Roggenbach, Oestrich, 29 Nov. 1889, Memoirs, III, 204.   There is *no* evidence to substantiate the picture of an embittered Stosch in Schröder, *Stosch,* p. 105; a view which is adopted by Morsey, *Die Oberste Reichsverwaltung,* p. 135 n. 50.

[116] Ulrich von Hassell, "Albrecht von Stosch," *Die Neue Rundschau,* CI (1940), 211.

[117] Memoirs, III, 346.

Freytag's death has hit me very hard. I have lived with him for 40 [*sic*] years in inner spiritual contact. No week passed without seeing or writing one another. Every one of his letters was a heartwarming and happy element, which is gone forever. His sickness began a few days before my birthday and I saw his life extinguished. He remained a dear fellow to the last moment. So one becomes more and more lonely. I am fortunate that I still have my old wife.[118]

He wrote Roggenbach: "I have experienced a loneliness in my intellectual life through this loss, which I can make up only by speaking my mind to you more often than before. Otherwise it would be quite still. Age makes one lonely and yet widens one's view of the world."[119] Stosch's friendship with Roggenbach was based on mutual esteem and confidence. In all their long friendship they had only one serious disagreement, when, in 1896, Roggenbach considered the Krüger Dispatch an error.[120]

Stosch's old leg wound began to trouble him in 1894,[121] and the celebrations attending the opening of the Kiel Canal and his golden wedding anniversary in Berlin on 18 October 1895 were a heavy strain on his physical powers.[122] Yet two observers still received an impression of great strength from his appearance on the latter occasion.[123] He wrote to his sister in October 1895:

The older man becomes the more he feels the faithfulness of love and the value of family ties. Old love is made more and more valuable not only by loneliness, which steadily increases with years, but also by the fact that the younger generation thinks differently and really loves differently. I often have the feeling that I am a sort of museum piece the historic importance of which is valued, but which must lie quiet in the showcase to be disposed of correctly.[124]

His death came suddenly on 29 February 1896; up to the end his mental powers were unimpaired. At his funeral the minister chose as the text the opening words of the one hundred and third Psalm:

[118] To Frau von Rosenstiel, 6 May 1895, *ibid.*, III, 328-29.
[119] Oestrich, 8 May 1895, *ibid.*, III, 329.
[120] Roggenbach to Stosch, Segenhaus, 10 Jan. 1896, in Heyderhoff, *Im Ring der Gegner*, p. 436.
[121] To Frau von Rosenstiel, 29 Dec. 1894, Memoirs, III, 321.
[122] *Ibid.*, III, 344.
[123] Hassell, *Tirpitz*, pp. 21-22; Hassell, "Stosch," *Neue Rundschau*, CI, 215; Ulrich von Hassell, *Erinnerungen aus meinem Leben, 1848-1918* (Stuttgart, 1919), pp. 153-55.
[124] To Therese Petersohn, Oestrich, 11 Oct. 1895, in Hassell, *Tirpitz*, p. 22.

"Praise the Lord, O my soul," presumably one of Stosch's favorites, and the words of William I: "You have always proved yourself, wherever I have placed you."[125] He was buried at Mittelheim at a funeral attended by the many officials and friends whom he had known in his long career as General, Admiral, and Minister of State.[126]

The final years of the life of Albrecht von Stosch are in direct contrast to those of his old opponent Bismarck. Both had left office, still feeling that a useful career had been cut short. Bismarck retired embittered and emptied the vials of his wrath and scorn on the heads of everyone who had, or who he thought had, opposed him. His memoirs are a testimony of his genius and his rage. Stosch retired disappointed, but found happiness and contentment. His memoirs are a penetrating and dispassionate self-portrait of an ambitious man of action and of common sense.

The concluding years of Albrecht von Stosch's life brought a more elaborate formulation of his political philosophy. His intense German nationalism showed no diminution. He wished to reverse Bismarck's maintenance of Prussian hegemony over Germany and defeat particularism by increasing imperial powers. He saw the union of the Imperial Chancellor and Prussian Minister-President in one person as protection of the Empire against Prussia, not Prussia against the Empire. He opposed the existing policy of Germanization of the Poles, because he felt it was self-defeating; the Poles should feel they were part of the German nation, whether they spoke the language or not. He took the short step from nationalism to imperialism well in advance of his contemporaries. The construction of a high-seas fleet, the acquisition of colonies and a world market, and the emergence of Germany as a world power were cardinal convictions. Unlike many German statesmen, he saw that the pursuance of these policies could only result in conflict with England, and he welcomed the prospect. Except his desire for some sort of national command of the Army, his nation-

[125] Memoirs, III, 345-47. The General's son, Ulrich von Stosch, added an account of his father's death and last days to the memoirs.

[126] Information furnished by the General's grandson, Herr Ulrich von Stosch; the present writer has visited Stosch's grave, which bears some marks of American gunfire. For William II's letter of condolence to Stosch's widow, see Priesdorff, *Soldatisches Führertum*, VIII, 318.

alism was placed within the bounds of the constitutional settlement of 1871.

This settlement determined the main lines of governmental organization and was generally accepted by Stosch as the basis for future German development. At the head stood the Emperor, who should make all final decisions, but should rely on independent advisers, particularly the Chancellor, for counsel. He should not thrust himself forward into the public eye and thus arouse the jealousy of his fellow princes. The Chancellor should be a soldier, so he could keep aloof from party divisions. Serving also as Prussian Minister-President and Chairman of the Bundesrat, he was the "keystone of German unity." He should control policy, which should be Bismarckian in inspiration. He was to curb the Emperor's impetuosity, but not dominate him. Stosch wished to maintain the Bundesrat as the seat of sovereignty and guardian of the rights of the reigning princes. The Reichstag, the focus of public opinion, should co-operate with the Government, but not control it. During the struggle over Caprivi's military legislation, Stosch believed that the Chancellor should yield to popular demands by introducing the two-year term of service and by reforming military justice, but he drew the line at an annual military budget. At the same time, he wanted the National Liberals, if not the Reichstag, to bridle the impulsive William II.

Within the Government itself, responsible ministers and officials were Stosch's ideal. Bismarck's ruthless crushing of initiative, which he himself had felt, provoked his opposition. Proceeding always on the practical basis of his own experience and knowledge, Stosch held that governmental business was most effectively and speedily performed by officials who acted independently with full responsibility. The affairs of the Navy might be divided among several high officers, as in the Army, but the Secretary of State should bear ultimate responsibility for all. While the Ministers and State Secretaries should be independent and able men, each stoutly defending his own opinions, they would be subordinated in Prussia to the Minister-President and in the Empire to the Chancellor. Ultimately and theoretically, the Ministers were responsible to the Emperor, but in practice Stosch's program would mean increasing accountability to the allied sovereigns, the imperial parliament, the Prussian Chambers, and the people. His fundamental emphasis on individual responsibility, which appears in his conception of ministerial responsibilities, lay at the core of his own religious belief.

Individual responsibility, initiative, and independence were the foundation of his attitude toward the organization of the Evangelical State Church, the Prussian Poles, the peasantry, and the urban workers. Believing strongly in the individual salvation of man through his own efforts and opposing the church hierarchy, he wished the Government to preserve and defend the supremacy and independence of the local congregations. Likewise in his solution of the Polish problem, he wished the Government to champion the equal rights of Polish subjects and to create an independent, loyal, and energetic peasantry. He also looked to a vigorous peasantry to settle German colonies. The German peasants were naturally faithful to the state and could be used as counterfoils to the urban worker. The worker could be weaned from dangerous agitation by encouraging his initiative and thus dividing him from his fellows. If uprisings came, Stosch favored the unbending use of force and, perhaps, would have suppressed the workers in anticipation of revolt.

The leisure of Stosch's last years gave him an opportunity to express in greater detail his political views, but they show no significant deviation from his earlier opinions. He remained a Bismarckian in general policy, differing from the fallen Chancellor, however, in greater emphasis on Reichstag participation in government, on nationalist and imperialistic measures, and on independent, but responsible, action by German officials.

IX

A GENERAL IN POLITICS

The persistence of the belief that Albrecht von Stosch was a confirmed liberal is almost a classic example of the misleading effect of historical evidence.[1] To the parliamentary debates, press reports, and official documents, each volume of hagiologic Bismarckiana added further confirmation of the legend. It was plausible enough. The General's most intimate friends, Karl von Normann, Franz von Roggenbach, Gustav Freytag, and Frederick III were, or were believed to be, men of the liberal persuasion. Stosch was apparently on cordial terms with Heinrich Geffcken and with the doctrinaire liberal Heinrich Rickert, with whom Stosch was publicly allied on a religious issue of the nineties. The legend even seemed to be documented by Stosch's published memoirs. He wrote rather enigmatically:

I was always interested in politics, but it has never been my nature to talk about them or my religious views. I was reared on the Rhine in liberal convictions and have remained true to them to this day [*ca.* 1892].

My successor, Minister von Caprivi, remarked to my son-in-law [Admiral Hollen]: "Your father-in-law is a liberal by inheritance from his father, who was inspired with that by Gneisenau." *That is true and false.* The liberalism of Gneisenau and my father consisted in wishing to put into force the constitution that King Frederick William III had promised for so long. There can be no blame attached to that today. However, my liberalism, like Gneisenau's, has always been consonant

---

[1] So, of course, is the legend of the "liberal" Crown Prince, until exploded by Dorpalen. The interesting circular argument was used that since the Crown Prince was liberal, his close adviser Stosch must be the same and, conversely, since Stosch was a liberal, his intimate friend Frederick William held like opinions. For a more striking case of the misleading nature of historical evidence, see Herbert Butterfield, *Man on His Past* (Cambridge, 1955), chap. v.

with the duties of a Prussian officer. I consider that a commendation, not a reproof.[2]

By "liberal convictions," he apparently meant that he merely adopted the liberalism of the Prussian military reformers and demanded a constitutional framework of government but no infringement of the sovereign's power. He was a "liberal," to be sure, in the importance he placed on the individual and on individual responsibility. He was also "liberal" in looking to an enlightened middle class for the future development of Germany. He wished its interests bound tightly to the state and its talents employed in government.[3] "Liberal," too, was his belief that the Ministers should co-operate with the Reichstag. But in every other aspect of his opinions, he was strongly conservative. Even his stress on the individual supported his conservative emphasis on a strong chancellor and sovereign.

Certainly Stosch did not adhere to the views of any liberal party. Indeed, none of the German parties gained his heartfelt allegiance. The Conservatives were Prussian particularists and too reactionary for him, the Liberal Imperials were Bismarck's sycophants, the Centrists were Roman Catholics and particularists, and the Social Democrats and Left Liberals were alike "revolutionaries." His supposed alliance with Rickert, the Left Liberals, and a "Gladstone Ministry" was a myth carefully fostered by Bismarck to discredit him. His closest friends among the deputies, Robert von Benda, Johannes von Miquel, and Rudolf von Bennigsen, were National Liberals, but Stosch distrusted their lack of common sense and energy. Guided by the pragmatic lessons of his own experience, he could not but be repelled by the abstract principles and class interests which characterized German parliamentary life. True, unlike Bismarck, he favored, in practice, greater Reichstag participation in government, but, like the Chancellor, he supported the ultimate power of the sovereign.

Nor did he seek any fundamental change in society. The Junker should keep his traditional position, buttressed by greater influence in local affairs. The middle class should remain strong

[2] Italics mine. *Memoirs*, I, 14.   [3] Cf. *ibid.*, I, 12.

and active.[4] There was little to distinguish Stosch's views of the peasants and workers from the opinions of the staunchest conservative. The peasants were the pillars of the state and the Army, but their conditions should be improved and their independence promoted. Faith in the peasantry and unfamiliarity with industrial conditions perhaps account for his persistent suspicion of the urban workers. He wanted to encourage the workers' initiative, so that self-interest would divide them. If they revolted, they were to be suppressed by military force.

National feeling, not liberal principles, permeated Stosch's every thought and action. Long before Bismarck, and in contrast to many of the liberals, Stosch demanded German unification by Prussian arms. His nationalism never faltered. The constitutional settlement of 1871 received his fervent support, but he feared the divisive goals of the particularists and advocated a greater accretion of power by the Empire than Bismarck contemplated. Not only did Stosch want greater centralization than the Chancellor, he opposed the Kulturkampf which divided the German people. At the same time, he combated the Crown Prince's aim of destroying the federal basis of the Empire. Intense nationalism, combined with interest in the Navy, led him to insist, long before most liberals, that Germany must build a high seas fleet and acquire colonies. Here too, he differed from Bismarck, whose adoption of imperialism was reluctant, half-hearted, and possibly delayed by aversion for the Chief of the Admiralty. Stosch thus passed from championing Prussia as the dominant German state, to supporting Germany, first, as the leading European nation and, finally, as a world power. Unlimited nationalism definitely made him a "modern" in contrast to Bismarck's Frederickian concept of limited objectives; Stosch's nationalism, like Moltke's, was more dangerous for European security and world peace than the Chancellor's reliance on state interest, more narrowly interpreted.[5]

Nationalism and loyalty to the Crown were the foundations of Stosch's political philosophy, if reflections made under the stimulation of momentary problems and events may be so designated.

[4] He believed the interests of the Army were tied to the middle class, not the Junker aristocracy; see, especially, *ibid.,* I, 12.

[5] This is suggested in the Foreword to Stadelmann's penetrating *Moltke.*

His monarchial devotion sprang from no romanticized notions of royal capabilities; he once observed that "princes are such a helpless bunch."[6] Rather he viewed princely qualities with a penetrating and objective eye. Yet no praise meant as much to him as the old Emperor's words: "You have been loyal to me and have proved yourself wherever I have placed you." William I seems, in fact, to have been to Stosch the embodiment of what a ruler should be. Practical, down-to-earth, filled with common sense, possessed of extraordinary perspicacity in picking able advisers and unusual skill in retaining their services, adopting counsel, even if unwelcome, and enduring personal conflicts, William I modestly and methodically performed his duties day-by-day. Only when William was in his eighties and his powers of decision weakened did Stosch criticize him for not curbing Bismarck sufficiently.

Frederick III's friendship with Stosch, cemented on the battlefield, was much more intimate. The General's willpower, common sense, nationalism, clearness of thought, and bluntness of expression endeared him to the weaker Frederick. Stosch endeavoured to educate Frederick to his future duties by persuading him to assume an active part in government and by teaching him to appreciate Bismarck's character and policies. Stosch's efforts stemmed from a legitimate personal ambition, a patriotic wish to serve his country, and traditional fidelity to the Hohenzollern Dynasty. Despite the good will with which his attempts were received, they were continually frustrated by Frederick's passivity, apathy, indifference, and lack of application. Only under the immediate influence of Stosch's personality or when Frederick's royal dignity and romantic nationalism were touched, did he show momentary interest. Yet Victoria, with paramount influence over her husband, had no better success. She came into serious conflict with Stosch for the first time when she attempted to ally her husband with the Left Liberals, and this estrangement continued into Frederick's brief reign. Stosch, faced with her opposition and Bismarck's, abandoned any ambition to play a part in the "Ninety-Nine Days." He had wished to bring Bismarck's supporters, the National Liberals, into contact with Frederick. Blocked by Vic-

[6] To Normann, Oestrich, 15 April 1886, Memoirs, III, 54.

toria, he turned toward Prince William and had the eventual satisfaction of seeing the National Liberal Miquel a force in government.

Stosch's relations with the young Emperor were purely formal. The General applauded his energy, but questioned his knowledge, intelligence, and firmness of will. William II, whose character perhaps owned more to Frederick III than has been generally recognized, acted erratically, egotistically, and noisily, much to Stosch's discomfiture. To control the Emperor, Stosch vainly called for an independent and strong-willed Chancellor and open criticism by the National Liberals.

No matter what the sovereigns' failings, Stosch never considered abandoning the monarchial system. He proposed rather to improve the rulers' characters through education, experience, and frank and unflattering advice. He always rejected any weakening of the Crown prerogative and its replacement by a Reichstag majority. The monarch held the ultimate authority, and it was to him that Stosch looked for personal redress of grievances. Backed by William I, he defied criticism and remained Chief of the Admiralty. When he felt his honor as a Prussian officer was insulted, he appealed not to public opinion but to the Emperor. Dragged unwillingly into the Geffcken affair, he asked William II to protect his son's career. Opposing religious legislation, he penned a newspaper article, so that the Emperor would read it and be persuaded. Stosch frequently criticized the decisions, personal characteristics, and beliefs of William I, Frederick III, and William II, but he never deviated from his steadfast devotion to the monarchy.

Monarchial devotion and nationalism were rooted more deeply in emotion than in reason. They, not abstract principles, played the determinative role in Stosch's political career. Bismarck's enhancement of monarchial powers and achievement of national aims stimulated Stosch's warm, but not uncritical, regard for the Chancellor. The antagonism between the two men proceeded from likeness of personality, not from difference of principle. Their iron-willed, ambitious, self-reliant, and pre-eminently practical natures violently collided. However much Stosch might succumb to the charm of the genius of Bismarck, he would never submit to his dictates. Throughout their long struggle the Chancellor had the advantage of a multitude of personal followers, dominance of public opinion, and control of the machinery of state. Perhaps more significantly, he pursued his end of dislodging Stosch with complete ruthlessness and an utter lack of scruple. That the General held office as long as he did speaks highly for his will-power, self-control, and technical ability. His dispassionate advocacy of Bismarck's policies, particularly with Frederick III, forms a grotesque contrast to the hatred, fear, anger, and brutality Stosch provoked in the Chancellor. Albrecht von Stosch was perhaps blinder than his great rival to the evil effects of intense nationalism and imperialism, but he had a much greater appreciation of the fearful results of the crushing of initiative, independence, and responsibility in the German people.

BIBLIOGRAPHY OF WORKS CITED

Bibliographical Note

The sources on the political career of Albrecht von Stosch are rich, but they have been inadequately exploited. Two previously published studies of his life (Koch, *Stosch* and Hassell, *Tirpitz*) are concerned primarily with his military and naval activity. The other accounts are either brief (Hassell's article in the *Neue Rundschau*), inaccurate (Petersdorff in the *Allgemeine Deutsche Biographie* and Priesdorff in *Soldatisches Führertum*) or highly colored (Schröder, *Stosch*), while all are insufficiently documented. Few studies of Bismarck's political activity fail to mention Stosch, usually in connection with the conflict of 1877. However, these accounts, whether liberal, conservative, or reasonably objective, usually accept Bismarck's version of Stosch's opinions. Many of these works have been consulted, but only a few have been used and cited. Their view of Stosch stems from Bismarck's speeches and memoirs and from articles in the inspired press, and it is to these that I have turned for the Stosch legend. Similarly, in appraising published correspondence, diaries, and memoirs, personal knowledge has been preferred to those retailing gossip and Bismarck's prejudices.

The division of the sources is of necessity somewhat arbitrary. Many of the secondary sources often contain a large amount of primary material. The unpublished second and third volumes of the memoirs of Albrecht von Stosch as well as two or three other scarce items were read at Herr Ulrich von Stosch's library.

Primary Sources

Albedyll-Alten, Julie v. *Aus Hannover und Preussen: Lebenserinnerungen aus einem halben Jahrhundert.* 2nd. ed. Potsdam, 1914.
Altmann, Wilhelm, ed. *Ausgewählte Urkunden zur deutschen Verfassungsgeschichte seit 1806.* Berlin, 1898. 2 vols.

Andreas, Willy, ed. *Briefe Heinrich von Treitschkes an Historiker und Politiker vom Oberrhein.* Berlin, 1934.

Anhang zu den Gedanken und Erinnerungen von Otto, Fürst von Bismarck. Stuttgart and Berlin, 1901. 2 vols.

Archives Diplomatiques. 1873.

Die auswärtige Politik Preussens 1858-1871: Diplomatische Aktenstücke. Berlin, 1933-1945. 12 vols.

Bamberger, Ludwig. *Gesammelte Schriften.* Berlin, 1894-1898. 5 vols.

Batsch, Vice Admiral. "Erinnerungen an Stosch," *Deutsche Revue,* XXI (1896), 31-42, 203-15, 321-30; XXII (1897), 352-66.

———. "General von Stosch über die Marine und die Kolonisation," *Deutsche Revue,* XXII (1897), 53-62.

Bernhardi, Theodor v. *Aus dem Leben Theodor von Bernhardis.* Leipzig, 1893-1906. 9 vols.

Bismarck, Otto, Prince von. *Die Gesammelten Werke.* Berlin, 1924-1932. 15 vols. in 19.

Blumenthal, Count Albrecht von, ed. *Journals of Field Marshal Count von Blumenthal for 1866 and 1870-1871.* London, 1903.

Bosse, Robert. "Erinnerungen," *Die Grenzboten,* LIII, vol. II (1904), 28-41, 157-65, 281-89, 399-409, 523-31, 642-48, 754-59.

Brandenburg, Erich, ed. *Briefe Kaiser Wilhelm des Ersten.* Leipzig, 1911.

Brandt, Major Heinrich v. *Aus dem Leben des Generals der Infanterie z. D. Dr. Heinrich von Brandt.* 2nd ed. Berlin, 1870-1882. 3 vols.

Brockhaus, H. E. *Stunden mit Bismarck 1871-1878.* Leipzig, 1929.

Bronsart von Schellendorf, Paul. *Geheimes Kriegstagebuch, 1870-1871.* Bonn, 1954.

Bülow, Prince von. *Memoirs of Prince von Bülow.* Boston, 1931-1932. 4 vols.

Busch, Moritz. *Bismarck: Some Secret Pages of His History.* London, 1898. 3 vols.

———. *Tagebuchblätter.* Leipzig, 1899. 3 vols.

Carol I, King of Rumania. *Aus dem Leben König Karls von Rumänien.* Stuttgart, 1894. 4 vols.

Chanzy, General. *Le deuxième Armée de la Loire.* 4th ed. Paris, 1871.

Cresson. "Les premiers Jours de l'Armistice en 1871: Trois voyages à Versailles," *Revue des Deux Mondes,* 1881, pt. 2, pp. 515-35.

Crowe, Sir Joseph. *Reminiscences of Thirty-Five Years of My Life.* 2nd ed. London, 1895.

Delbrück, Hans. *Erinnerungen, Aufsätze und Reden.* 3rd ed. Berlin, 1905.

Deutscher Geschichtskalender. 1888-1890. 1894.

Documents Diplomatiques Français (1871-1914). Paris, 1929 ff. 45 vols. to date.

Dove, Alfred, ed. *Gustav Freytag und Heinrich von Treitschke im Briefwechsel.* Leipzig, 1900.

Feder, Ernst, ed. *Bismarcks grosses Spiel: Die geheimen Tagebücher Ludwig Bambergers.* Frankfurt a. M., 1933.

Frederick Karl, Prince of Prussia. *Denkwürdigkeiten aus seinem Leben.* Leipzig, n. d. 2 vols.

Freytag, Gustav. *Briefe an seine Gattin.* Berlin, 1913.

———. *Gustav Freytag an Salomon Hirzel und die Seinen.* Leipzig, 1903.

———. *Karl Mathy/Erinnerungen aus meinem Leben.* Leipzig, n.d.

———. *Der Kronprinz und die deutscher Kaiserkrone: Erinnerungsblätter.* 6th ed. Leipzig, 1889.

"General von Stosch and the German Navy," *Journal of the Royal United Service Institution,* XXVIII (1884), 205-11.

Goldschmidt, Hans, ed. *Bismarck und die Friedensunterhändler 1871.* Berlin and Leipzig, 1929.

———. *Das Reich und Preussen im Kampf um die Führung: von Bismarck bis 1918.* Berlin, 1931.

Gontaut-Biron, Vicomte de. *Mon Ambassade en Allemagne (1872-1873).* 3rd ed. Paris, 1906.

Die grosse Politik der europäischer Kabinette, 1871-1914. Berlin, 1922-1927. 40 vols.

Hartmann, Julius von. *Lebenserinnerungen, Briefe und Aufsätze.* Berlin, 1882. 2 vols.

Hassell, Ulrich von (the Elder). *Erinnerungen aus meinem Leben, 1848-1918.* Stuttgart, 1919.

Helmolt, Hans F., ed. *Gustav Freytags Briefe an Albrecht von Stosch.* Stuttgart and Berlin, 1913.

Heyderhoff, Julius, ed. *Im Ring der Gegner Bismarcks: Denkschriften und Politischen Briefwechsel Franz v. Roggenbachs mit Kaiserin Augusta und Albrecht v. Stosch, 1865-1896.* 2nd ed. Leipzig, 1943.

——— and Paul Wentzcke, eds. *Deutscher Liberalismus in Zeitalter Bismarcks: Eine politische Briefsammlung.* Bonn and Leipzig, 1926. 2 vols.

Hinrichs, Carl. "Unveröffentliche Briefe Gustav Freytags an Heinrich Geffcken aus der Zeit der Reichsgründung," *Jahrbuch für die Geschichte Mittel- und Ostdeutschlands,* III (1954), 65-117.

Hohenlohe-Schillingsfürst, Prince Chlodwig zu. *Denkwürdigkeiten der Reichskanzlerzeit.* Stuttgart and Berlin, 1931.

———. *Memoirs.* New York, 1906. 2 vols.

Holborn, Hajo, ed. *Aufzeichnungen und Erinnerungen aus dem Leben des Botschafters Joseph Maria von Radowitz.* Berlin and Leipzig, 1922. 2 vols.

Janson, Sara von. *Erinnerungen aus dem Hause Holtzendorff.* Gotha, 1925.

Kessel, Eberhard, ed. *Moltke Gespräche.* 2nd ed. Hamburg, (1940).

Keudell, Robert v. *Fürst und Fürstin Bismarck: Erinnerungen aus den Jahren 1846 bis 1872.* Berlin, 1901.

Kohl, Horst, ed. *Bismarck-Jahrbuch.* Berlin and Leipzig, 1894-1899. 6 vols.

————. *Die politischen Reden des Fürsten Bismarcks.* Stuttgart, 1892-1905. 14 vols.

Lee, Arthur G., ed. *The Empress Frederick Writes to Sophie.* London, 1955.

Loë, Walter, Baron v. *Erinnerungen aus meinem Berufsleben 1849 bis 1867.* 2nd ed. Stuttgart, 1906.

Lucius von Ballhausen, Baron Robert. *Bismarck-Erinnerungen.* Stuttgart and Berlin, 1921.

Mackenzie, Sir Morell. *The Fatal Illness of Frederick the Noble.* London, 1888.

" 'Marineminister von Stosch und die Katastrophe bei Folkestone,' Fachmännisch beleuchtet, von einem vormaligen Seeoffizer," *Deutsche Revue,* III Jg., vol. II (1879), 67-75.

Meisner, H. O., ed. *Aus dem Briefwechsel des General-Feldmarschalls Alfred Grafen von Waldersee.* Berlin and Leipzig, 1928. Vol. I.

————. *Kaiser Friedrich III: Das Kriegstagebuch von 1870-1871.* Berlin and Leipzig, 1926.

————. *Kaiser Friedrich III: Tagebücher von 1848-1866.* Leipzig, 1929.

Mittnacht, Baron von. *Erinnerungen an Bismarck.* 4th ed. Stuttgart and Berlin, 1904.

————. *Erinnerungen an Bismarck. Neue Folge.* 4th ed. Stuttgart and Berlin, 1904.

Mohs, Hans, ed. *General-Feldmarschall Alfred Graf von Waldersee in seinem militärischen Wirken.* Berlin, 1929. 2 vols.

Moltke, Helmuth von. *Gesammelte Schriften und Denkwürdigkeiten.* Berlin, 1892. 7 vols.

————. *Moltkes Militärische Werke.* Berlin, 1892-1912. 4 vols. in 17.

Occupation et Libération du Territoire, 1871-1875. Paris, 1903. 2 vols.

Oncken, Hermann, ed. *Grossherzog Friedrich I von Baden und die Deutsche Politik von 1854-1871: Briefwechsel, Denkschriften, Tagebücher.* Berlin and Leipzig, 1927. 2 vols.

Pachnicke, Hermann. *Führende Männer im alten und im neuen Reich.* Berlin (1930).

Penzler, Johannes. *Fürst Bismarck nach seiner Entlassung.* Leipzig, 1897-1898. 7 vols.

Persius, L. *Menschen und Schiffe in der Kaiserliche Flotte.* Berlin, 1925.

Ponsonby, Sir Frederick. *Letters of the Empress Frederick.* London, 1929.

Poschinger, Heinrich von. *Fred Graf Frankenberg: Kriegstagebücher von 1866 und 1870/71.* Stuttgart, 1896.

————. *Fürst Bismarck und der Bundesrat.* Stuttgart und Leipzig, 1897-1901. 5 vols.

————. *Fürst Bismarck: Neue Tischgespräche und Interviews.* Stuttgart and Berlin, 1895-1899. 2 vols.

————. *Fürst Bismarck und die Parlamentarier.* Breslau, 1894-1896. 3 vols.

————. *Neues Bismarck-Jahrbuch.* Vienna, 1911. Vol. I.

Rich, Norman, and M. H. Fisher, eds. *The Holstein Papers.* New York, 1955 ff. 2 vols. to date.

Richter, Eugen. *Im alten Reichstag: Erinnerungen.* Berlin, 1894-1896. 2 vols. in 1.

Roon, Albrecht v. *Denkwürdigkeiten aus dem Leben des Generalfeldmarschalls Kriegsministers Grafen von Roon.* 5th ed. Berlin, 1905. 3 vols.

Scholz, Adolf v. *Erlebnisse und Gespräche mit Bismarck.* Stuttgart und Berlin, 1922.

Schuster, G., ed. *Briefe, Reden und Erlasse des Kaisers und Königs Friedrich III.* Berlin, 1907.

Stein, August. *Es war alles ganz anders. . . .* Frankfurt a. M., 1922.

[Stosch, Albrecht v.,] "Die Bedeutung der militärischer Lager, besonders für Preussen," *Die Grenzboten,* XXIV (1865), vol. III, 425-33.

————. "Deutsche Colonisation," *Kölnische Zeitung,* Sunday, 22 July 1883, zweite blatt.

————. "Der Deutsche Krieg im Jahr 1866," *Die Grenzboten,* XXV (1866), vol. IV, 201-10, 241-47, 295-303, 337-48, 385-92, 449-53.

————. "Der Krieg in Nordamerika von militärischen Standpunkt," *Die Grenzboten,* XXIII (1864), vol. IV, 281-90, 325-34, 389-95, 453-58; XXIV (1865), vol. I, 58-69, 227-38, 248-62, vol. II, 352-58.

————. " 'Das Leben des Feldmarschalls von Gneisenau,' von F. Pertz," *Die Grenzboten,* XXIV (1865), vol. I, 353-57.

————. "Die militärische Bedeutung der Herzogtümer Schleswig-Holstein," *Die Grenzboten,* XXIV (1865), vol. III, 192-99.

————. "Militärische Briefe über den Krieg im Schleswig," *Die Grenzboten,* XXIII (1864), vol. I, 513-17, vol. II, 28-36, 66-74, 115-19, 148-53, 191-93, 235-40, 270-76, 312-18, 355-60, 395-98, vol. III, 113-16, 277-80.

————. "Die preussische Polen," *Deutsche Revue,* XVI (1891), 309-18.

————. "Die Reise des Kronprinzen von Preussen," *Die Grenzboten,* XXIX (1870), vol. I, 81-88.

————. "Unsere Küsten in einem Kriege mit Frankreich," *Die Grenzboten,* XXVI (1867), vol. II, 246-48.

Stosch, Ulrich v., ed. *Denkwürdigkeiten des Generals und Admirals Albrecht von Stosch: Briefe und Tagebuchblätter.* 2nd ed. Stuttgart and Berlin, 1904. The manuscript copies of volumes two and three are in the possession of Herr Ulrich von Stosch.

Tempeltey, Eduard, ed. *Gustav Freytag und Herzog Ernst von Coburg im Briefwechsel: 1853 bis 1893.* Leipzig, 1904.

Tiedemann, Christoph von. *Aus sieben Jahrzehnten: Erinnerungen.* Leipzig, 1909. 2 vols.

Tirpitz, Alfred v. "Albrecht von Stosch: Zum 100. Geburtstag am 20. April," *Norddeutsche Allgemeine Zeitung,* Friday, 19 April 1918.

————. *My Memoirs.* London, n. d. 2 vols.

Verdy du Vernois, Julius v. *Im grossen Hauptquartier 1870-1871: Persönliche Erinnerungen.* Berlin, 1905.

————. "Im Hauptquartier der II. (schlesischen) Armee 1866," *Deutsche Rundschau,* CI (October-December 1899), 57-77, 232-62, 400-427; CII (January-March 1900), 43-72.

————. *With the Royal Headquarters in 1870-1871.* London, 1897.

Verhandlungen des Deutschen Reichstags. 1872-1885. 1889. 1892.

Waldersee, Alfred, Count v. *Denkwürdigkeiten des General-Feldmarschalls Grafen Alfred von Waldersee.* Stuttgart and Berlin, 1923-1925. 3 vols.

Werner, Anton v. *Erlebnisse und Eindrücke,* 1870-1890. Berlin, 1913.

Whitman, Sidney. *Personal Reminiscences of Prince Bismarck.* New York, 1903.

Wilke, Adalbert v. *Alt-Berlin Erinnerungen.* Berlin (1930).

Wilkinson, Henry Spenser. *Thirty-five Years 1874-1909.* London, 1933.

William I. *Militärische Schriften.* Berlin, 1897. 2 vols.

William II. *My Memoirs: 1878-1918.* London, 1922.

Wittisch, Lieutenant General. *Aus meinem Tagebuch 1870-1871.* Cassell, 1872.

Secondary Sources

Almanach de Gotha. 1870. 1882.

Anderson, Eugene N. *The Social and Political Conflict in Prussia, 1858-1864.* Lincoln, Nebraska, 1954.

Andreas, Willy. *Kämpfe um Volk und Reich.* Stuttgart, 1934.

"B." "Albrecht Theodor Emil v. Roon," *Allgemeine Deutsche Biographie,* XXIX, 138-43.

Barth, Theodor. *Politische Porträts.* Berlin (1923).

Batsch, Vice Admiral. *Admiral Prinz Adalbert von Preussen.* Berlin, 1890.

Becker, Otto. *Bismarcks Ringen um Deutschlands Gestaltung.* Heidelberg (1958).

Berdrow, Wilhelm. *Alfred Krupp.* 2nd ed. Berlin, 1928. 2 vols.

Bergsträsser, Ludwig. *Geschichte der politischen Parteien in Deutschland.* 5th ed. Mannheim, 1928.

Bethcke, Ernst. *Politische Generale! Kreise und Krisen um Bismarck.* Berlin, 1930.

Block, Hermann. *Die parlamentarische Krisis der national-liberalen Partei 1879-1880.* Münster i. W., 1930.

Brandenburg, Erich. *Die Reichsgründung.* Leipzig, n. d. 2 vols.

Bronsart, Friedrich v. "Das alte Kaiser und sein Kriegsminister von Bronsart," *Historische Vierteljahrschrift,* XXXI (1937-1939), 293-306.

Butterfield, Herbert. *Man on His Past.* Cambridge, 1955.

Carroll, E. Malcolm. *Germany and the Great Powers 1866-1914: A Study in Public Opinion and Policy.* New York, 1938.

Clapham, J. H. *The Economic Development of France and Germany, 1815-1914.* 4th ed. Cambridge, 1951.

Constabel, Adelheid. *Die Vorgeschichte des Kulturkampfes.* Berlin (1956).

Corti, Egon Caesar Conte. *Wenn . . . : Sendung und Schicksal einer Kaiserin.* Graz, Vienna, Cologne (1954).

Craig, Gordon. *The Politics of the Prussian Army, 1640-1945.* Oxford, 1955.

————. "Portrait of a Political General: Edwin von Manteuffel and the Constitutional Conflict in Prussia," *Political Science Quarterly,* LXVI (1951), 1-36.

Curtius, Julius. *Bismarcks Plan eines deutschen Volkswirtschaftsrat.* Heidelberg, 1919.

Dehio, Ludwig. "Eduard von Manteuffel und der Kaiser," *Deutsche Rundschau,* CCVI (January-March 1926), 40-48, 149-57.

Dickmann, Fritz Otto. "Bismarck und Sachsen zur Zeit des Norddeutschen Bundes," *Neue Archiv für Sächsische Geschichte und Altertumskunde,* XLIX (1929), 255-88.

————. *Militärpolitischen Beziehungen zwischen Preussen und Sachsen 1866-1870: Ein Beitrag zur Entstehungsgeschichte des norddeutschen Bundes.* Munich, 1929.

Dietrich, Richard. "Preussen als Besatzungsmacht im Königreich Sachsens 1866-1868," *Jahrbuch für die Geschichte Mittel- und Ostdeutschlands,* V (1956), 273-93.

————. "Der preussisch-sächsische Friedensschluss vom 21 Oktober 1866," *Jahrbuch für die Geschichte Mittel- und Ostdeutschlands,* IV (1955), 109-56.

Dorpalen, Andreas. "Emperor Frederick III and the German Liberal Movement," *American Historical Review,* LIV (1948-1949), 1-31.

Dove, Alfred. *Ausgewählte Schriften, vornehmlich historisches Inhalt.* Leipzig, 1898.

————. "Heinrich Wilhelm Dove," *Allgemeine Deutsche Biographie,* XLVIII, 51-69.

Eardley-Wilmot, S. *The Development of Navies during the Last Half Century.* London, 1892.

Earle, E. M., ed. *Makers of Modern Strategy: Military Thought from Machiavelli to Hitler.* Princeton, 1948.

Engelhardt, Wilhelm. "Rückblicke auf die Verpflegungsverhältnisse im Kriege," *Beihefte zum Militärwochenblatt,* 1901, pp. 483-552.

Eyck, Erich. *Bismarck: Leben und Werk.* Erlenbach-Zürich, 1941-1944. 3 vols.

————. "The Empress Frederick," *Quarterly Review,* no. 589 (July, 1951), pp. 355-66.

————. *Das persönliche Regiment Wilhelms II: Politische Geschichte des deutschen Kaiserreiches von 1890 bis 1914.* Erlenbach-Zürich (1948).

Ford, Guy Stanton. "Boyen's Military Law," *American Historical Review,* XX (1914-1915), 528-38.

Fuller, Joseph V. *Bismarck's Diplomacy at its Zenith.* Cambridge, Mass., 1922.

Gagliardi, Ernst. *Bismarcks Entlassung.* Tübingen, 1927-1941. 2 vols.

Geis, Robert. *Der Sturz der Reichskanzler Caprivi.* Berlin, 1930.

Görlitz, Walter. *Der Deutsche Generalstab: Geschichte und Gestalt 1657-1945.* Frankfurt a. M., n. d.

Gollwitzer, Heinz. *Die Standesherren.* Stuttgart (1957).

Gothein, Georg. *Reichskanzler Caprivi: Eine kritische Würdigung.* Munich (1918).

Goyau, Georges. *Bismarck et l'Église.* Paris, 1913-1922. 4 vols.

Gradenwitz, Otto. *Bismarcks letzter Kampf, 1888-1898.* Berlin (1924).

Grunwald, Constantin de. *Bismarck.* Paris (1949).

Häften, von. "Bismarck und Moltke," *Preussischer Jahrbücher,* CLXXVII (1919), 85-105.

Hallgarten, S. F. *Rhineland Wineland.* London (1952).

Hallmann, Hans. *Krügerdespesche und Flottenfrage.* Stuttgart, 1927.

―――. *Der Weg zum deutschen Schlachtflottenbau.* Stuttgart, 1933.

Ham, Heinrich von. "Erinnerungen an den preussischer Hof in Koblenz: Nach Aufzeichnungen der Frau v. Breuning (1850-1871)," *Deutsche Rundschau,* XXXII (1937), 97-105.

Hartung, Fritz. *Deutsche Verfassungsgeschichte.* 7th ed. Stuttgart (1954).

Hassell, Ulrich von (the Elder). *Tirpitz: Sein Leben und Wirken mit Berücksichtigung seiner Beziehungen zu Albrecht von Stosch.* Stuttgart, 1920.

―――. (The Younger). "Albrecht von Stosch: Ein staatsmännischer Soldat," *Neue Rundschau,* CI (1940), 209-15.

―――. *Im Wandel der Aussenpolitik.* 4th ed. Munich (1943).

Hazen, W. B. *The School and the Army in Germany and France: With a Diary of Siege Life at Versailles.* New York, 1872.

Herzfeld, Hans. *Deutschland und das geschlagene Frankreich 1871-1873.* Berlin, 1924.

―――. *Johannes von Miquel: Sein Anteil am Ausbau des Deutschen Reiches bis zur Jahrhundertswende.* Detmold (1938). 2 vols.

Hintze, Otto. "Das preussische Staatsministerium im 19. Jahrhundert," *Festschrift zu Gustav Schmollers 70. Geburtstag: Beiträge zur brandenburgischen und preussischen Geschichte.* Leipzig, 1908, pp. 403-93.

Hollyday, Frederic B. M. "Bismarck and the Legend of the 'Gladstone Ministry,'" Lillian P. Wallace and William C. Askew, eds., *Power, Public Opinion, and Diplomacy.* Durham, N. C., 1959, pp. 92-109.

Hönig, Fritz. *Loigny-Poupry.* Berlin, 1896.

―――. *Der Volkskrieg an der Loire.* Berlin, 1893-1897. 6 vols.

Howard, Burt E. *The German Empire.* New York, 1906.

Hubatsch, Walter. *Der Admiralstab und die obersten Marine behörden in Deutschland, 1848-1945.* Frankfurt a. M., 1958.

―――. *Die Ära Tirpitz.* Göttingen (1955).

―――. "Realität und Illusion in Tirpitz Flottenbau," *Schicksalwege Deutsche Vergangenheit.* Düsseldorf (1950), pp. 387-418.

Huber, Ernst Rudolf. *Heer und Staat in der deutschen Geschichte.* Hamburg (1938).

Jäck, Ernst. *Kiderlen-Wächter, der Staatsman und Mensch.* Berlin and Leipzig, 1925. 2 vols.

Jany, Curt. *Geschichte der Königlich Preussischen Armee.* Berlin, 1933. 4 vols.

Kardorff, Siegfried v. *Wilhelm von Kardorff.* Berlin, 1936.

Kessel, Eberhard. "Bismarck und die 'Halbgötter': zu dem Tagebuch Paul Bronsart von Schellendorf," *Historische Zeitschrift,* CLXXI (1956), 249-86.

———. *Moltke.* Stuttgart (1957).

———. "Die Tätigkeit des Grafen Waldersees als Generalquartiermeister und Chef des Generalstabs der Armee," *Die Welt als Geschichte,* XIV (1954), 181-211.

Kehr, Eckhardt. *Schlachtflottenbau und Parteipolitik, 1894-1901.* Berlin, 1930.

Klein-Hattingen, Oskar. *Bismarck und seine Welt.* Berlin, 1904. 2 vols. in 3.

———. *Geschichte der deutschen Liberalismus.* Berlin-Schöneburg, 1912. 2 vols.

Klein-Wuttig, Anneliese. *Politik und Kriegsführung in den deutschen Einigungskriegen 1864, 1866 und 1870/71.* Berlin-Grünewald, 1934.

Klocke, Helmut. "Die Sächsische Politik und der Norddeutsche Bund," *Neue Archiv für Sächsische Geschichte und Altertumskunde,* XLVIII (1928), 97-163.

Koch, Paul. *Albrecht v. Stosch als Chef der Admiralität.* Berlin, 1903.

———. *Beiträge zur Geschichte unserer Marine, Neue Folge.* Berlin, 1900.

Kratz, Werner. *Oestrich und Mittelheim im Rheingau.* Arnsberg, 1953.

Kremer, Willy. *Der soziale Aufbau der Parteien des deutschen Reichstages von 1874-1914.* Emsdetten, 1934.

Laband, Paul. *Le Droit Public de L'Empire Allemande.* Paris, 1906. 6 vols.

Langer, William L. *European Alliances and Alignments 1871-1890.* New York, 1931.

Lehment, Joachim. *Kriegsmarine und politische Führung.* Berlin, 1937.

Lettow-Vorbeck, Oscar von. *Geschichte des Krieges von 1866 in Deutschland.* Berlin, 1899. 2 vols.

Liddell Hart, B. H. *Thoughts on War.* London, 1944.

Lorenz, Ottokar. *Staatsmänner und Geschichtschreiber der neunzehnten Jahrhunderts.* Berlin, 1896.

Mantey, Vice Admiral von. *Histoire de la Marine allemande.* Paris, 1930.

Matter, Paul. *Bismarck et son Temps.* Paris, 1908. 3 vols.

Maurice, Sir J. F., ed. *The Franco-German War 1870-1871.* London, 1900.

Meisner, H. O. *Der Kriegsminister 1814-1914.* Berlin, 1940.

Meyer, Georg. *Lehrbuch des Deutschen Staatsrechtes.* 2nd ed. Leipzig, 1885.

Morsey, Rudolf. *Die Oberste Reichsverwaltung unter Bismarck, 1867-1890.* Münster i. W., 1957.

Müller-Bohn, Hermann. *Kaiser Friedrich der Gütige: Vaterlandisches Ehrenbuch.* Berlin, n. d.

Muncy, Lysbeth W. *The Junker in the Prussian Administration under William II, 1888-1914.* Providence, 1944.

Naumann, Friedrich. *Die politischen Parteien.* Berlin-Schöneburg, 1910.

Nelson, Richard J. "Notes on the Constitution and System of Education of the Prussian Army," *United Service Journal and Naval and Military Magazine,* 1839, Part III, pp. 14-18, 214-23, 498-522.

Nichols, J. Alden. *Germany After Bismarck.* Cambridge, Mass., 1958.

Nowak, Karl F. *Germany's Road to Ruin.* London, 1932.

Oncken, Hermann. *Historisch-politische Aufsätze und Reden.* Munich and Berlin, 1914. 2 vols.

———. *Rudolf von Bennigsen: Ein deutscher Liberaler Politiker.* Stuttgart and Leipzig, 1910. 2 vols.

———. "Zur 'Erinnerungen an Franz von Roggenbach' von Karl Samwer," *Historische Zeitschrift,* CVIII (1912), 624-33.

Ostwald, Paul. *Gustav Freytag als Politiker.* Berlin, 1927.

Petersdorff, Hermann v. "Albrecht v. Stosch," *Allgemeine Deutsche Biographie,* LIV, 576-607.

Pflügk-Hartung, J. v. "Die Auszeichnung des Generals Ferdinands v. Stosch über Gneisenau," *Beihefte zum Militärwochenblatt,* 1911, Heft 8.

———. *Krieg und Sieg 1870-1871: Ein Gedenkbuch.* Berlin, n.d.

Poschinger, Margaretha von. *Kaiser Friedrich: Im neuer quellenmässiger Darstellung.* Berlin, 1899-1900. 3 vols.

Pratt, Edwin A. *The Rise of Rail Power in War and Conquest 1833-1914.* Philadelphia, 1916.

Priesdorff, Kurt von. *Soldatisches Führertum.* Hamburg (1937-1942). 10 vols.

Rang- und Quartierliste der Königliche Preussischen Armee und Marine für das Jahr 1860. Berlin, n.d.

Ratzel, Friedrich. "Karl R. Ritter," *Allgemeine Deutsche Biographie,* XXVIII, 679-97.

Richter, Hubert. "Heinrich Geffcken und seine Veröffentlichung des Tagebuches Kaiser Friedrichs," *Festschrift Martin Bollert zur 60. Geburtstag.* Dresden, 1936, pp. 240-54.

Richter, J. W. Otto. *Kaiser Friedrich III.* Berlin, 1901.

Richter, Werner. *Kaiser Friedrich III.* Zürich, 1938.

Ritter, Gerhard. *Staatskunst und Kriegshandwerk: Das Problem des "Militarismus" in Deutschland.* Munich, 1954. Vol. I.

Robertson, Charles G. *Bismarck.* London, 1919.

[Robolsky, Dr.] *Unsere Minister seit 1862.* Berlin (1890).

Ropp, Theodore. "Continental Doctrines of Sea Power," in E. M. Earle, ed., *Makers of Modern Strategy,* pp. 446-56.

————. "The Development of a Modern Navy: French Naval Policy, 1871-1904." Unpublished Ph.D. dissertation, Harvard, 1937.

Rosinski, Herbert. *The German Army.* 2nd ed. (Washington, 1944).

Rubinstein, Adolf. *Die Deutsche-Freisinnige Partei bis zu ihren Ausein- anderbruch 1884-1893.* Berlin, 1935.

Samwer, Karl. *Zur Erinnerungen an Franz v. Roggenbach.* Wiesbaden, 1909.

Schmerfeld, von. *Graf Moltke: Die Deutschen Aufmarschpläne 1871- 1890.* Berlin, 1929.

Schmidt-Bückeberg, Rudolf. *Das Militärkabinett der preussischen Könige und deutscher Kaiser: Seine geschichtliche Entwicklung und staatsrechtliche Stellung 1787-1918.* Berlin, 1933.

Schnabel, Franz. *Deutsche Geschichte im 19. Jahrhundert.* Freiburg i. B., 1929-1937. 4 vols.

Schröder, Ernst. *Albrecht von Stosch, der General-Admiral Kaiser Wilhelms I: Eine Biographie.* Berlin, 1939.

Schüssler, Wilhelm. *Bismarcks Sturz.* Leipzig, 1921.

Schwarze, R. "Phillip von Stosch," *Allgemeine Deutsche Biographie,* XXXVI, 464-66.

Shanahan, William O. *Prussian Military Reforms 1786-1813.* New York, 1945.

Simon, Walter M. *The Failure of the Prussian Reform Movement, 1807-1819.* Ithaca, N. Y. (1955).

Stadelmann, Rudolf. *Moltke und der Staat.* Krefeld, 1950.

————. *Soziale und Politische Geschichte der Revolution von 1848.* (Munich) 1948.

Stern, Alfred. *Geschichte Europas seit den Verträgen von 1815 bis zum Frankfurter Frieden von 1871.* Stuttgart and Berlin, 1913- 1914. 10 vols.

Stevenson, R. Scott. *Morell Mackenzie.* London, 1946.

Sybel, Heinrich v. "Julius von Hartmann," *Allgemeine Deutsche Bio- graphie,* X, 691-96.

Taylor, A. J. P. *The Struggle for Mastery in Europe 1848-1918.* Oxford, 1954.

Trützschler von Falkenstein, Heinz. *Bismarck und die Kriegsgefahr des Jahres 1887.* Berlin, 1924.

Tschackert, P. "Eberhard Heinrich Daniel Stosch," *Allgemeine Deutsche Biographie,* XXXVI, 462.

————. "Ferdinand Stosch," *Allgemeine Deutsche Biographie,* XXVI, 462-63.

————. "Friedrich Wilhelm Stosch," *Allgemeine Deutsche Biographie,* XXXVI, 463.

Vagts, Alfred. *A History of Militarism: Romance and Realities of a Profession.* London (1938).

Valentin, Veit. *Geschichte der deutschen Revolution von 1848-1849.* Berlin (1931). 2 vols.

Vizetelly, Henry. *Berlin under the New Empire: Its Institutions, Inhabitants, Industry, Monuments, Museums, Social Life, Manners, and Amusements.* London, 1879. 2 vols.

Wahl, Adalbert. *Deutsche Geschichte 1871-1914.* Stuttgart, 1929. 4 vols.

Zedlitz-Neukirch, Baron L. v. *Neues Preussisches Adels-Lexicon.* Leipzig, 1836-1839. 5 vols.

Ziekursch, Johannes. *Politische Geschichte des neuen deutschen Kaiserreiches.* Frankfurt, 1927. 3 vols.

DECORATIONS AND HONORS AWARDED TO
ALBRECHT VON STOSCH

Anhalt: Order of Albert the Bear, Commander 1st Class (1865); Order of Albert the Bear, Great Cross (1868)

Austria: Order of Francis Joseph, Great Cross (1869)

Baden: Order of the Zähringen Lion, Commander's Cross, 1st Class (1868); Order of the Zähringen Lion, Great Cross (1871)

Bavaria: Royal Order of Military Merit, Great Cross (1870); Order of Merit of St. Michael, Great Cross (1868)

Greece: Order of the Redeemer, Great Cross (1869)

Hesse: Order of Louis, Commander's Cross, 1st Class (1868)

Italy: Order of the Crown of Italy, Great Cross (1870); Order of St. Maurice and St. Lazarus, Great Cross (1868)

Mecklenburg-Schwerin: Cross of the Military Order of Merit, 1st Class (1870); Great Cross of the Wendish Crown (1871)

Oldenburg: Order of the Oldenburg House, Grand Cross of Honor, with swords (1871)

Prussia: Iron Cross, 2nd Class (1870); Iron Cross, 1st Class (1870); *Pour le mérite* (1866); Royal Order of the House of Hohenzollern, Commander's Star (1871); Order of the Prussian Crown, 2nd Class (1865); Order of the Red Eagle, 4th Class (1858); Order of the Red Eagle, 3rd Class, with rosette (1863); Order of the Red Eagle, 2nd Class, with oakleaves (1873); Order of the Red Eagle, Great Cross, with oakleaves (1878); Knight of the High Order of the Black Eagle (1881)

Russia: Order of St. Stanislas, 1st Class (1869)

Saxe-Coburg-Gotha: Order of the Ernestine House, Commander's Cross, 1st Class (1865)

Saxony: Order of Albert, Great Cross (1867); Order of Merit, Great Cross (1871)

Sweden and Norway: Norwegian Order of St. Olaf (1875)

Turkey: Order of Medjidie, 1st Class (1869)

Württemberg: Order of Military Merit, Great Cross (1871)